The Antagonist Principle

Victorian Literature and Culture Series
Jerome J. McGann *and* Herbert F. Tucker, *Editors*

The Antagonist Principle

JOHN HENRY NEWMAN
AND THE PARADOX
OF PERSONALITY

Lawrence Poston

UNIVERSITY OF VIRGINIA PRESS
Charlottesville and London

University of Virginia Press
© 2014 by the Rector and Visitors of the University of Virginia
All rights reserved
Printed in the United States of America on acid-free paper

First published 2014

1 3 5 7 9 8 6 4 2

Library of Congress Cataloging-in-Publication Data
Poston, Lawrence, 1938–
The antagonist principle : John Henry Newman and the paradox
of personality / Lawrence Poston.
  pages   cm. — (Victorian literature and culture series)
Includes bibliographical references and index.
ISBN 978-0-8139-3633-8 (cloth : alk. paper) — ISBN 978-0-8139-3634-5 (e-book)
1. Newman, John Henry, 1801–1890—Psychology. 2. Personality—Religious aspects—
Christianity. 3. Polarity—Religious aspects—Christianity. 4. Personality in literature.
5. Polarity in literature. 6. Catholic converts—England—Biography. 7. Cardinals—England—
Biography. I. Title. II. Title: John Henry Newman and the paradox of personality.
BX4705.N5P645 2014
282.092—dc23

2014013662

For Carol
Cor ad cor loquitur

Contents

	Preface	ix
	Note on Citations	xiii
	Introduction	1
1.	Self and Others	15
2.	The Journey from Evangelicalism	39
3.	Polarities	63
4.	Notes of the Church	91
5.	Anglican Deathbeds	114
6.	"A Deliverance from the Nightmare"	137
7.	Building Community	158
8.	Reconstituting the Self	182
9.	Oppositions and Resolutions	209
	Afterword	235
	Notes	247
	Bibliography	261
	Index	273

Preface

Despite recent assertions that Newman is being edged out of the English literary canon, books and articles about him show no signs of slackening. But though the field of Newman studies is crowded, it has tended to be dominated by specialized theological studies and even, with his recent beatification, hagiography. Relatively few recent books attempt to treat him synoptically as a Victorian writer of multidisciplinary interest. This is one reason why, I think, such works as Henry Bremond's classic *Newman: Essai de biographie psychologique* (1906; translated in 1907 by H. C. Corrance under his own title, *The Mystery of Newman*) and Louis Bouyer's *Newman: Sa vie, sa spiritualité* (1952; translated by J. Lewis May in 1956) have had such a long shelf life. When in 1973 the Modern Language Association of America published *Victorian Prose: A Guide to the Research* under the general editorship of David J. DeLaura, only the chapter on Newman was parceled out between two writers, Martin Svaglic (on Newman as "Man and Humanist") and Charles Stephen Dessain (on Newman's philosophy and theology), implicitly suggesting that it takes more than one scholar to size up Newman's achievement, but that fortunately he can be readily divided up. Neither assumption is correct.

This book draws on a variety of disciplines to reevaluate Newman in terms of an overarching theme. As a single-author study, it stands somewhat aside from two generations of literary scholars who have productively reviewed Newman in connection with other Victorian figures: an earlier trio who moved beyond narrower rhetorical concerns (John Holloway, DeLaura himself, and George Levine), and a younger generation of theorists represented by Jonathan Loesberg, James Eli Adams, and Suzy Anger. My relationship to these works is best described as assimilative rather than competitive; they have made it possible to zero in again on Newman as a unique Victorian figure, the adjectives "unique" and "Victorian" being of equal importance. Essential to the work of all these scholars, and happily brought

Preface

to a conclusion while I was at work on this study, is the thirty-two-volume edition of Newman's *Letters and Diaries,* and the five volumes of heretofore unpublished sermons from Newman's Anglican period edited by Placid Murray et al. between 1991 and 2012. With these bibliographical resources and two informed modern biographies, by Ian Ker and Sheridan Gilley respectively, today's student of Newman is well equipped.

I began my own work on this project around 1998–99, and its thesis and general outline had started to come together by the time Frank M. Turner's controversial *John Henry Newman: The Challenge of Evangelical Religion* (2002) was published. Both our books provide ethical readings of Newman's published work and career, but structurally the two studies are very different. Turner writes as a historian and biographer and confines himself to Newman's Anglican career while drawing on a large range of archival sources and offering a dramatically revisionist theory of Newman's Anglican phase. On a much smaller scale than Turner, I write as a literary scholar working primarily with published sources and hoping to broaden the interest of those who may know Newman primarily through the *Apologia* or the lectures collected under the title *The Idea of a University.* Although I agree with some of Turner's criticisms of Newman's Anglican career, I am not always in accordance with his conclusions, and in extending the scope of my study to include the Catholic years, I find much to temper Turner's critique. My own work is centered on the idea of Personality in the Christian tradition, and its reverberations, beyond the more narrowly theological, to explain something of Newman's recurring efforts to organize his thoughts around that idea.

This study pursues Newman's life and work for the most part chronologically, but it is not a biography and it imparts no new biographical revelations. To the extent that certain events were of particular importance in spurring (or retarding) his development—his debate with Edward Hawkins over the Oriel tutorships; his publication, with John Keble, of Hurrell Froude's *Remains;* the Hampden controversy; the fracas over Tract 90; his later problems with F. W. Faber and the London Oratory; his clashes with the Vatican hierarchy—I have tried to say only as much as is necessary to sustain my own narrative and theme, since biographers and ecclesiastical historians have already had their day with these episodes. My principal concern is to re-situate Newman as one of the most combative of the Victorian seekers, whose spiritual quest, though it took place at the far right of the religious spectrum, nonetheless aligned him with a number of other pilgrims as disparate as Carlyle, Mill, Browning, and Pater. To be sure, mine is not a full-dress study of Newman's relationship to his contemporaries, like Edward Short's recent study of his more intimate friendships, but those contemporaries serve as reference points in my effort to stake out Newman's position, and are less likely to figure in accounts by theologians.

Finally, while this is a single-author study, it is not a study only for Newman specialists, although I hope they may find something of interest in it, but for a wider range of Victorian scholars who may be reacquainting themselves with him. I have tried not to deviate into special pleading, pro or con, but to see Newman steadily and whole.

This study was originally sidelined by several years in full-time academic administration, and I am grateful to the then dean of the College of Liberal Arts and Sciences at the University of Illinois at Chicago, Stanley Fish, for arranging a research leave that enabled me to reorient the study that I had begun several years before. As always in such studies as this, my debts to colleagues are numerous and the faults of the final product entirely my own. Valuable early interventions came from George Landow and Russell Wyland, both of whom suggested ways of thinking through some of what I had already begun to write, and I owe much to the encouragement of two University of Illinois colleagues who not only read the manuscript but have provided interdisciplinary stimulus over a number of years, Walter L. Arnstein (Urbana-Champaign) and James J. Sack (Chicago). Robert J. Klaus and Paul J. Griffiths have provided close readings of the manuscript from their perspectives in, respectively, British history and Catholic theology. The external readers for the University of Virginia Press provided much helpful and detailed commentary. I owe special thanks to the late Frank M. Turner, whose encouragement in the early stages and patient readings of and reactions to what emerged was decisive. Turner, his colleagues observed on the occasion of his untimely death in 2010, often said that all scholarship was "an exercise in friendship," and that was certainly the case for someone like me who never had the opportunity to meet him personally. Where I have not followed the advice of any of these readers on specific points, I have always been aware that it has been at my own peril, and they are responsible for none of the blemishes that remain. En passant, I also benefited from reactions at two conferences in which sections of the manuscript were first presented, the Midwest Victorian Studies Association at Wayne State University (2006) and the Northeast Victorian Studies Association at Princeton University (2010).

At the University of Virginia Press, I had many helping hands, particularly from the editors of the series in which this volume appears, Jerome J. McGann and Herbert F. Tucker, and from members of the Press staff including Cathie Brettschneider, Morgan Myers, and Raennah Mitchell. They proved calm and experienced in dealing with various authorial traumas and entanglements. I am also grateful to Colleen Romick Clark for the sort of careful copyediting that makes an author's life easier. Of this engaging crew, I have known Chip Tucker the longest, going back over three decades of friendly sparring, well before this study was even contemplated; he has certainly embodied Frank Turner's dictum in his own professional relationships.

Closer to home, I am indebted to the patience of my daughters, Rachel Feiler and Anne Poston; like many a technologically illiterate parent, I have been grateful for the latter's computer skills during this project. My longest-standing debt of all is to Carol Poston, who persistently lets the hot air out of my first drafts and ruthlessly edits what remains, taking no hostages. I have shamelessly appropriated the Cardinal's motto to describe what her personal influence has meant to me.

Sections in the first three chapters on Newman's Anglican preaching have been drawn from an article, "Newman's Tractarian Homiletics," first published in the *Anglican Theological Review* (37, no. 3 [Summer 2005]: 399–421). I am grateful to its managing editor, Jacqueline B. Winter, for permission to reprint those sections, now dispersed, which appear here.

Note on Citations

Citations of Newman's works are provided in the main text with the appropriate abbreviation and page reference. Where it has been available, the basis of those quotations has been the ongoing Birmingham Oratory Millennium edition, in progress from the University of Notre Dame Press. In other cases I have used the best (and in some cases, such as the *Parochial and Plain Sermons*, the most accessible) modern text, falling back on the heretofore standard turn-of-the-century edition of Newman's works (Longmans, Green, 1900–1904) as the default. In this text there is no collective title for all the volumes, and the volumes are not sequentially numbered throughout, so my bibliography simply cites the title and date of the volume in which the text appears.

Unless otherwise noted, quotations from Newman and his contemporaries reproduce emphases wherever they are present in the original. Where editors supply variant readings (for example, in the five-volume edition of the previously unpublished Anglican sermons [S] or in the *Letters and Diaries*), I have generally quoted Newman's final version only.

Quotations from Newman's poetry are taken from *The Dream of Gerontius and Other Poems* (Oxford, 1914).

A	*Apologia pro Vita Sua, Being a History of His Religious Opinions*
Arians	*The Arians of the Fourth Century*
AW	*Autobiographical Writings*
"Biglietto"	"John Henry Newman's *Biglietto* Speech"
C	*Callista: A Tale of the Third Century*
CD	*Certain Difficulties Felt by Anglicans in Catholic Teaching Considered* (2 vols.)
CNK	*The Correspondence of John Henry Newman with John Keble and Others*, edited at the Birmingham Oratory
D&A	*Discussions and Arguments on Various Subjects*

Note on Citations

DCD	*Essay on Development of Christian Doctrine*
DMC	*Discourses Addressed to Mixed Congregations*
ECH	*Essays Critical and Historical*
GA	*An Essay in Aid of a Grammar of Assent*
IU	*The Idea of a University*
L&D	*The Letters and Diaries of John Henry Newman*
LDN	*A Letter Addressed to His Grace the Duke of Norfolk on Occasion of Mr. Gladstone's Recent Expostulations*
LG	*Loss and Gain: The Story of a Convert*
LOJ	*Lectures on Justification*
O	*Newman the Oratorian: The Unpublished Oratory Papers*
OCF	*"On Consulting the Faithful in Matters of Doctrine"*
OUS	*Fifteen Sermons Preached before the University of Oxford between A.D. 1826 and 1843*
PN	*The Philosophical Notebook of John Henry Newman*
POC	*Lectures on the Prophetical Office of the Church*
PPS	*Parochial and Plain Sermons*
RPU	*The Rise and Progress of Universities* and *Benedictine Essays*
S	*Sermons, 1824–1843* (5 vols.)
SN	*Sermon Notes of John Henry Cardinal Newman, 1849–1878*
SSD	*Sermons Bearing on Subjects of the Day*
SVO	*Sermons Preached on Various Occasions*
TP	*The Theological Papers of John Henry Newman: On Faith and Certainty*

The Antagonist Principle

Introduction

JOHN HENRY NEWMAN was a divided and at times divisive personality. The self-effacing yet entrancingly powerful preacher at St. Mary's seems an altogether different person from the combative, zealous partisan of the Tractarian movement. To many former Anglicans, he was a turncoat; to some Roman Catholics, he was a potential double agent, lukewarm about bringing others over to his newfound communion and still harboring Anglican sympathies. Writing of Henri Bremond's classic "psychological biography," Martin J. Svaglic observed that Bremond's attempt to "steer a path between the apotheosizers and calumniators of Newman" foreshadowed an ongoing division of critical opinion. "Newman continues to attract or repel readers quite strongly, with the result that disinterested writing about him is relatively rare" (Svaglic 117).

More than a quarter of a century has passed since Svaglic wrote, but his words resonate to the present day. Animosities in Newman studies may slumber for a time, but they generally reawaken under provocation. Most recently, the beatification of Newman, at the hands of a most unlikely pope, has prompted an outpouring of literature that, if not outright hagiographic, might more politely be called devotional, and has generated a second round of assaults on Frank Turner's controversial 2002 biography, most notably an acrimonious exchange between Simon Skinner and Eamon Duffy in the normally staid pages of the *Journal of Ecclesiastical History*. The recent *Cambridge Companion to John Henry Newman* (Ker and Merrigan, 2009) handles the matter by ignoring Turner's work entirely.[1] Newman, and Newman studies, it appears, still have the capacity to enrage.

Whether this study successfully avoids the twin perils of hagiography

Introduction

and iconoclasm is for the reader to decide. My own attempt at a Via Media may be as problematic as Newman's attempt to articulate such a place for the Church of England, and my result may bear more resemblance to an oscillating pendulum than a steady forward march. My guiding principle throughout, however, is that Newman must be given credit for sincerity, despite the limitations of that term. In *Eminent Victorians*, Lytton Strachey put the case succinctly, if with characteristically sardonic shading, when he wrote that "in reality, no one, in one sense of the word, was more truthful than Newman. The idea of deceit would have been abhorrent to him, and indeed it was owing to his very desire to explain what he had in his mind exactly and completely, with all the refinements of which his subtle brain was capable, that persons such as [Charles] Kingsley were puzzled into thinking him dishonest. Unfortunately, however, the possibilities of truth and falsehood depend upon other things besides sincerity" (32–33).

While Newman's place in present-day Catholicism is secure, his status in Victorian studies seems less so today than a generation ago. What is the Victorian-ness of Newman? Most readers would agree that it lies preeminently in his religious quest. When religion was not an outright obsession, it was at the very least an urgent matter to the first Victorian generation. To this rule John Stuart Mill stands almost alone among the prominent figures of that generation when, in the second chapter of his *Autobiography*, he describes himself as "one of the very few examples, in this century, of one who has not thrown off religious belief, but never had it" (1:45). Some remained in the religion into which they were born, others adopted a new one, and still others drifted into neutrality or agnosticism. As important as what one believed was the process by which one got there. A searcher might by turns visit the terrains marked out by Newman's *Apologia pro Vita Sua*, Tennyson's *In Memoriam*, or, at a later date, Mary Arnold Ward's *Robert Elsmere*. Religion mattered politically as well because it was deeply embedded in English cultural and political history. Ever since the Elizabethan religious settlement, Roman Catholics, Jews, and Protestant Dissenters had been disadvantaged in civil and religious affairs by the presence of the established Church of England. The Church in its turn was enmeshed in the State. Bishops were appointed by the Crown on the recommendation of the government of the day; in Anthony Trollope's *Barchester Towers*, Archdeacon Grantly's hopes for preferment are dashed by an intervening change

INTRODUCTION

of ministry. The Regius Professorship of Divinity at Oxford was a Crown appointment, and Oxford politics (as Newman's own career illustrates) not infrequently spilled over onto the national stage.

Of all the major Victorian intellectuals, Newman most clearly and unequivocally sets out the argument for Christian orthodoxy in an age of secularization and religious liberalization—forces of which he was fully aware. Whatever the merits of historian J. C. D. Clark's argument that late Georgian England was still a confessional state, the terms of that confession were increasingly problematic in the wake of Catholic Emancipation (1829) and the First Reform Act of 1832. The young Newman hoisted his banner in protest against these threats to the hegemony of the Anglican Church and to the privileged role of its two historic universities. In his forecast of the likely consequences of these dismaying developments (as he saw them), he was almost certainly correct. He was first and foremost the great antagonist of a phenomenon he labeled "Liberalism," a complex term that remains to be disentangled later in this study but by which he meant most fundamentally an adherence, in all human but especially religious affairs, to the belief that as long as a person is sincere in his or her opinions, the truth of those opinions is a secondary consideration.[2] As the spokesman for a Christian orthodoxy historically passed down in the creeds, the writings of the Church Fathers, and the Apostolic Succession, Newman stands in opposition to almost every trend that post-Victorians find most interesting in the Victorian period—even in its religious perplexities. Today's secular readers are likely to find narratives of the loss of faith more compelling than those that describe how faith was won.

Newman indeed took his theology seriously, defending its legitimacy as an independent field of inquiry, and insisting on precision in the use of theological language and on the constitutive importance of the patristic tradition that struck many contemporaries, including not a few Churchmen, as largely historical irrelevancies or as antiquarian niceties that had become the badge of a religious party. Although an Anglican evangelical in his early formation, Newman opposed both the prevailing "religion of the heart" that had fed the Wesleyan revival, and the high-and-dry abstractions of the Establishment that had scorned Wesley, skirted deism, and provided the seeds for the Broad Church party. Often Newman's emphasis seems to lend credence to the contrarian view that the Spirit killeth and the Letter giveth life. Such considerations have led Robert Pattison, in his witty and iconoclastic study *The Great Dissent: John Henry Newman and the Liberal Heresy* (1991), to suggest that Newman no longer belongs among the Victorian sages but has become "a kind of parenthesis in Victorian studies" (v). Pattison implies that Newman instead deserves a place among other absolutists like Marx and Lenin—which some might argue amounts to a promotion in rank. But though Newman was a dogmatist, he was not an absolutist. He came to Rome in a state of exhaustion after failing to carry out his dreams for the Church of England, and his difficulties in accepting all aspects of Roman Catholic discipline and devotion were prolonged. The record taken as a whole suggests a more questioning and flexible mind, and one more attuned to contemporary dilemmas, than was true of more docile Catholic contemporaries as well as more militant agnostics. Newman may have been a voice in the wilderness (his own kind, not Carlyle's), but his wilderness was not a backwater, and by the end of the century he had gained a measure of acceptance, indeed reverence, among those who could not follow him to his religious conclusions.

Newman's entire career was fraught with paradoxes. As a conservative Romantic, more Southeyan than Shelleyan, who had originally hoped to maintain residence at his beloved Oxford for the rest of his life, he spent the second half of that very long life in a suburb of Birmingham without the genial privileges of a secure berth in the Establishment. Instead of tutoring England's future leaders, he was teaching working-class children. For years he endured many slights from the Roman hierarchy, some of them real and a few of them perhaps imagined, without regaining the influence he had wielded from the pulpits at the university church of St. Mary's and at St. Nicholas, Littlemore. Unlike some of his former co-religionists, Newman professed himself untroubled by Darwin, seeing *The Origin of Species* as a legitimate outcome of scientific inquiry that in no way undermined Revelation. This was not, as some scholars have made out, because he was indifferent to science. As an undergraduate, he had, of his own volition, attended William Buckland's lectures on geology, later regretting only that they had distracted him from the classical curriculum that was key to academic standing at that time and place. And this avatar of the liberal arts, whose lectures on the occasion of the new university in Dublin have passed into the same staple of inspirational commencement oratory as Tennyson's

INTRODUCTION

"Ulysses," took special pride in his role in establishing a medical school at that same university. To be sure, such paradoxes are not always signs of intellectual flexibility. Unusually learned among Anglican clergy in patristics and church history, Newman was provincial in an age of theological ferment. Unlike his coadjutant Edward Bouverie Pusey, who had studied in Germany, Newman knew no German (indeed, he seems to have been an indifferent linguist even in the Italian that might have served him well at Rome) and showed no curiosity about German thought, expressing only a disdain for the Lutheran divines whose writings he encountered when he was attempting to define a Via Media for the Church of England. Yet it is an open question whether in the intellectual terrain he had carved out for himself, he was any more provincial than his chief rival for the admiration of the young, Thomas Carlyle, despite the latter's superior German. To be sure, since their respective deaths, Newman has recently had the advantage of a concerted and powerful publicity machine in Rome, but if his mind seems in some ways narrower, it is often more subtle and nuanced than that of the Sage of Chelsea.

Among Newman's contemporaries, Matthew Arnold recognized him as the exponent of a liberal humanism not narrowly cabined by its own fideistic commitments. Victorian intellectuals could not shrug him off as an obscurantist. Late in Newman's life, Richard Holt Hutton twice invited him to join the Metaphysical Society, where Newman would have come in contact with men of science as well as other representative spirits of the age. Newman politely declined, perhaps out of a shyness more personal than ideological, perhaps because of advancing age, but the fact of the invitation suggests that he was already something of a Victorian icon. And the success of the *Apologia pro Vita Sua* in the 1860s may have contributed to the diminution of that British anti-Catholicism that had been a staple of much popular lore as well as ecclesiastical and political hostility ever since the sixteenth century. Doubtless that thawing of old animosities owed something to the liberalizing and secularizing currents of the age, and Newman knew as well as anyone that religious tolerance could be the offspring of religious indifference. Nonetheless, the Catholic whose personal struggles had been quite publicly broadcast played his own role in softening historical animosities. One of the most striking aspects of Newman's heritage is that—albeit within the terms of his own religious tradition—he is one of several Victorians, along with John Stuart Mill, who most dramatically illustrate what is at stake in the claims of individual conscience.

My title comes from a well-known passage in the *Apologia* in which Newman describes the early stirrings of the Oxford Movement after his return from Italy in 1833. In speaking of potential sympathizers among the old High Church party, such as William Palmer of Worcester and Dublin,[3] Newman wrote that "their *beau idéal* in ecclesiastical action was a board of safe, sound, sensible men. . . . I, on the other hand, had out of my own head begun the Tracts; and these, as representing the antagonist principle of personality, were looked upon by Mr. Palmer's friends with considerable alarm" (A 47–48). Newman relegates the term "antagonist principle" to a subordinate clause in this passage, referring only to his long-standing belief that while the reform of the Church of England required cooperation among like-minded individuals, those individuals would each give his personal stamp to a common effort. But the term "antagonist principle" has broader implications. Newman's career proceeded in large part through a series of antagonisms. His thinking, his imagination, and many of his public pronouncements were incited by the presence of an opponent and a polemical occasion.

The key to understanding Newman, I believe, lies in aligning the contradictions of his personality—his alternating self-effacement and aggression—with the progression of his intellectual development, from his boyhood conversion to an Evangelical position in the Church of England through his final years in the Roman Catholic communion. An organizing theme for that development is the double usage of "personality" as a psychological phenomenon (at least as it was understood in the pre-Freudian era) and "Personality" as it is defined in the Christian doctrines of the Trinity and the Incarnation. Newman seems to have embraced Trinitarian orthodoxy as a way of anchoring his strong self-will and sometimes wayward personality in the divine Other that is the Christian's object of faith. But when his idea of personality was severed from that fideistic confidence and took the form of dependence on others, the "personality principle" could become a straitjacket. It invited a return upon the self as the sole reality in the face of rejection by others. For Newman, all too often, there was no middle ground between unyielding loyalty, whether to principle or to himself personally, and outright rejection. Dangers lay at each end: at one, the cult of personality, which Newman claimed to abhor when he was its object; at the other, an unhealthy self-suppression.

In an important monograph, *Newman and the Gospel of Christ*, Roderick Strange argues that Newman's "stress on the harmonious union [of divine and human] in Christ amounts to a recognition that in Christ, man's potential for a share of the divine nature has been realized, has been resolved." The process of God assuming manhood promises a "lesson about human nature as well," disclosing a "capacity for an utterly harmonious union with the divine.... The harmony between God and man does not imply any devaluation of man, but rather the most exalted recognition of what it means to be human" (158–59). I have no doubt that this was Newman's hope, but here my path diverges from Strange's. Newman, I would argue, believed in the Incarnation, but he found it difficult to think and act incarnationally. His powerful sense of human self-delusion and frailty, which casts a shadow over many of his earlier sermons, tends to mute the liberating force of the doctrine Strange expounds. In practical affairs, Newman's hypersensitivity could obscure his perception of what was Christlike in another person. He had his share of human frailties, and his fragile sense of self, often cloaked in exceptional aggression, was projected onto others from whom he would have gladly welcomed the confidence that he did not feel. A present-day Anglican theologian writes, "To believe that God's word is spoken not just to us who believe, but to all those who live in the world and who share in God's world with us[,] is the essence of an incarnational theology. It means that we who hear God's Word in scripture and in the tradition of belief in the church must always be ready to hear the Word that God speaks to us in our neighbors, in those who may not yet know the God who speaks" (Griffiss 127). Given that Newman could not always hear this Word even in his fellow Anglicans, it is not surprising that his imagination had difficulty accommodating such an expanded idea of catholicity.

After his reception by Rome, Newman gradually became a more self-confident, relaxed, and generous opponent. His sermons after 1846 lack the edgy power of his Anglican sermons in part because they exhibit more (if sometimes overly luxuriant) poetry, more tranquility, and more confidence in the communion he had joined, if not in all its contemporary manifestations. In that communion he found it possible to be more liberal, not in the sense in which he decried Liberalism in his early years, but in the sense of imagining a greater freedom for the laity within an institution that set clear boundaries to belief. Why did this mellowing come about? Perhaps it was because as an Anglican he had to live with ambiguities not only theological but personal, and without an authority that would either certify or check the development of his views. Despite his disavowals, one side of him really did aspire to leadership, and this need for authentication was at war with another side of him that craved retreat and withdrawal from public view. The polity of the Roman Catholic Church demanded at least an initial act of formal submission to authority. It left Newman no room for dreaming about his future place in that communion, and held out no hope for immediate advancement. Unlike his most famous fellow-Anglican convert of a few years later, Henry Manning, Newman had no taste for ecclesiastical politics and no talent for choosing the winning side. Forced back on his inner resources by suspicion and misunderstandings, he became more charitable, more aware of his own frailties, and less quick to identify them in others.

Furthermore, and to an extent that is difficult for a present-day reader to grasp, Newman's decision to embrace Roman Catholicism in the climate of early Victorian England was an act of self-marginalization: renouncing the security of Oxford, risking the opprobrium that emanated from a hardy tradition of English anti-Catholicism and that was complicated by political disabilities only recently removed, in his own early adulthood, with the passing of Catholic Emancipation in 1829. To accept one's status as a member of a religious minority may encourage a self-defensive populism. In a reevaluation of Newman's politics, Gauri Viswanathan has argued, "What emerges as a fairly consistent rhetorical strategy in Newman's work is the advancement of an aggressive conservatism upholding both Catholicism and Englishness by recourse to an anti-elitist, populist agenda" (56). The "divide between parliamentary policy and popular will, and between secular participation and belief" that she describes (57) is redolent of Disraeli, whose own (at least initial) marginality as a Jew had not been fully erased by his baptism. Viswanathan's comments on *Loss and Gain* suggest that Newman's novel, belonging immediately to his post-reception years, has distinct affinities with Disraeli's Young England trilogy. His character Carlton portrays the medieval Church as "a vast extra-constitutional body," and although

Introduction

Carlton is not Newman's stand-in in the novel, he speaks recognizably for one aspect of his thought. Though Viswanathan appeals to the record of Newman's very earliest years in evaluating his anti-elitism, I would argue that his reception by Rome enabled him to appreciate the same popular ("superstitious") Catholicism of the Italian peasant that he had observed with distaste in his first venture on the Continent in his Anglican years.

Resolutely Catholic, resolutely English while capable, like Matthew Arnold, of mocking John Bullishness, Newman himself has provided the clue to the organization of this study. In his preface to the *Apologia*, he describes his discovery of how to defend himself. He would take literally Charles Kingsley's question "What, then, does Dr. Newman mean?" and interpret the words in a sense Kingsley almost certainly did not intend. Kingsley "asks what I *mean*, not about my words, not about my arguments, not about my actions, as his ultimate point, but about that living intelligence by which I write, and argue, and act.... I wish to be known as a living man, and not as a scarecrow which is dressed up in my clothes." The only way to do this, Newman saw, was not to confine himself to answering Kingsley's charges one by one, a method that would have complied with Kingsley's agenda, but rather to "draw out, as far as may be, the history of my mind" (*A* 12).

In these words, Newman conveys his long-standing belief that personality, whether individual or institutional, requires enactment in history. At the heart of the doctrine of the Incarnation is the assertion that God entered history in the Person of the Son, and that through history His will is understood. At the level of Newman's autobiographical apologetics, it means that one demonstrates developmentally the integrity of the self in the eyes of God. Writing in February 1865 to George William Cox, Newman complained about the vagueness of Henry Hart Milman's latitudinarian *History of Christianity to the Abolition of Paganism*, in which Milman seemed to have no very clear idea of Christianity as anything more than "the great conserving principle" of religious knowledge. "For myself, I think Christianity an historical fact, and to view it as disengaged from its historical characteristics, e.g. the principle of dogma and its actual dogmas, its sacramental ritualism, and its polity, is (in itself, not in those who do it) a dishonesty. Christianity is an individual phenomenon and can as little be split into parts as an individual man" (*L&D* 21:402). In the biography of the individual, he wrote in the *Apologia*, "it is the concrete being that reasons; pass a number of years,

Introduction

and I find my mind in a new place; how? the whole man moves; paper logic is but the record of it" (*A* 155).

Whatever Newman experienced in the way of self-doubt—and his relentless scrutiny of his own motives, that restless self-probing characteristic of an Evangelical conscience, suggests the depths of his self-doubt—he never wavered in his confidence that he had always witnessed as truly as he was able to the beliefs that he held. But to the observing world, he appeared inconsistent and sometimes duplicitous. The charge of "mysteriousness, shuffling, and underhand dealing," he wrote, "is a matter which I cannot properly meet, because I cannot duly realize it. I have never had any suspicion of my own honesty; and, when men say that I was dishonest, I cannot grasp the accusation as a distinct conception, such as it is possible to encounter." He could repel specific charges, such as a claim that he attempted to coax this or that person to Rome, "but my imagination is at a loss in the presence of those vague charges ... made up of impressions, and understandings, and inferences, and hearsay, and surmises." Hence in his response to Kingsley, not only does he resist any attempt to be drawn into a debate over a bill of particulars, but he ignores imputations that are both untrue and, in the manner in which they are couched, unanswerable. "I should be dealing blows in the air; what I shall attempt is to state what I know of myself and what I recollect, and leave to others its application" (*A* 152–53).

This study follows the development of Newman's mind as it is revealed textually, in print and in private correspondence.[4] One of Newman's own preoccupations was the sole reality of two and two only beings, himself and his Maker. Despite the very strong note of ethical injunction that runs through the St. Mary's sermons in particular, this feeling must have given many of his hearers the sense of sitting in on a private conversation. The tributes to his preaching and his reading of the liturgy suggest a total submission to an imperative outside himself, which for John Stuart Mill, writing in another context, distinguished poetry from eloquence.[5] Newman always spoke with the urgency of a convert, but not with what he deplored as the prolixity of much Evangelical preaching of his day. His boyhood conversion to an earlier, gentler Evangelicalism was far more fundamental than his nationally advertised change of communion. The first conversion, at fifteen, gave him the abiding belief that ultimately he stood alone, face to face, with his Maker. That is why it is more apposite to speak of Newman's *reception* by the Roman Catholic Church, or his *secession* from the Church of England, than his *conversion* to one from the other. Rome was receiving a full-blown Evangelical of a very English stamp. She was, of course, receiving a great deal more than that, but with the exception of a few beliefs he had by then discarded—for example, that the Pope was the Antichrist—the record of Newman's own development took the form of expansion outward, from his early Evangelicalism through his Tractarianism to his Roman Catholicism, in a process comparable to the growth of a tree whose trunk preserves the earliest rings of its life. He did not veer and tack between opposite poles. His journey, rather, to use a favorite metaphor of his own, was a journey into safe harbor, not a reversal of course on the open seas.

Hence the principal developments in Newman's career more nearly resemble adjustments, alterations of emphasis, than sudden shifts of course. One of the most important is his move during his Anglican career from an Evangelical emphasis on the Atonement to a High Church focus on the Incarnation, a move finally completed in his acceptance of the Mariology that he had rejected prior to his reception by Rome. His early history of the Arians, his saints' lives, his mid-century novel of an imaginary saint (*Callista*) are all attempts to read, either in history or in fictional dramatizations of history, examples of men and women who incarnated the ideal Christian personality, as well as of heretics whose very moral character betrayed their heterodoxy. His sermons set forth his doctrinal and ethical precepts, while his correspondence often exposes the gaps between belief and practice that were a source of dismay to anyone like Newman who read himself and his destiny in the way a believer does.

Though this study is for the most part chronological, chapter 1 and the afterword, by way of introduction and summary, constitute a series of soundings, or probes, into certain recurring problems in Newman studies. For some, the record reveals an essentially egotistical Newman who, it is claimed, saw God and himself as the only realities, and the result was a Newman who evinced little or no interest in the quotidian realities of injustice and human suffering. Such a believer, it has been argued, confronts a chasm of unbelief if the certainty of either himself or God is placed at risk. Newman was no hypocrite, but he himself realized that his intellect might have led him to a frightening relativism, even solipsism, in which he could be certain of no other reality than himself. Far from enjoying such a fantasy

Introduction

of uniqueness, he was terrified by it, partly because he was highly dependent on the support of others, partly because he distrusted any faith derived from the illusion of self-sufficiency, but mostly because he feared losing any verifiable standard of faith. Here the role played by the Tractarian concept of *ethos* and Newman's developing ecclesiology are both efforts to escape the trap of self and to articulate an objective faith verified by the similar, if not identical, experiences of a community of fellow believers.

Chapter 1 sets the stage by exploring more thoroughly what "personalism" means as a description of how Newman thought, and raises certain epistemological questions about the nature of religious belief which were entertained by Newman's contemporaries Carlyle and Pater as part of a larger cultural climate of religious questing. The afterword discusses how Newman himself has been seen, both in his times and in ours, as a skeptic, an egotist, or both. To respond to those particular lines of critique involves a reconsideration of Newman as a fundamentally solitary being, whose orthodoxy provided an anchor but who was always aware of what other lines of inquiry could lead to and resisted their pull.

The way to the afterword is suggested in chapter 6, which examines Newman's reputation in the weeks, months, and years following his secession to Rome, a very public Victorian event. *Loss and Gain* (1848), the novel to which we have already alluded, could only have offended his former co-religionists and confirmed, for individuals in both communions, the suspicion of waywardness and even theological instability that had already been implanted in some contemporaries by the publication of *An Essay on the Development of Christian Doctrine* (1846). Newman's reception by Rome caused a crisis for his closest friends in the Movement and evoked strong reactions from such former followers as James Anthony Froude and Mark Pattison, whose faith in Anglicanism had been undermined, at least in part, by Newman himself. It also triggered a quarrel with his insubordinate younger brother, Francis (Frank), with whom relations were already strained. The circumstances leading up to Newman's secession highlighted in some quarters the suspicion of an underlying tendency toward the very skepticism that he feared. It was a tendency identified by people as disparate as Samuel Wilberforce, James Martineau, and Leslie Stephen, and allegedly visible in two well-known "mirror" passages in the *Apologia* with which I begin chapter 1.

Introduction

Chapters 2 through 5 (on the Anglican Newman) and 7 through 8 (on the Roman Catholic Newman) are by contrast organized in terms of the development of Newman's ideas. I am not the first to see three of Newman's more extended works as constituting a kind of spiritual and intellectual trilogy: the *Essay on the Development of Christian Doctrine*, his last writing as an Anglican and his first publication as a Roman Catholic, his dramatization of his own development in the *Apologia*, and finally his examination, in *An Essay in Aid of a Grammar of Assent* (1870), of the processes by which one reaches belief. The first and third of these represent a significant departure from Newman's habit of writing oppositionally, in response to a particular person or situation, and in that sense, if we believe his own testimony, represent the kind of labor he would have liked to have undertaken more often. The *Apologia* is interwoven through much of my study to show how Newman in later life brooded over an event, a person, or topic and how the replaying of the past both relates to and differs from the original experiences that contemporaneous documents describe. In chapters 4 and 5, I review the critical first half of the 1840s, the period Newman described as his deathbed in the Anglican Communion, from two different vantage points: the public Newman as controversialist, and the private Newman of the letters and diaries who shared his dilemmas with only a few friends and not always fully or forthrightly with them. Chapters 7 through 9 describe the emergence of the Catholic Newman, at length finding a measure of peace both in Rome, with the award of the cardinalate, and in Oxford, at Trinity, his undergraduate college, with the award of an honorary degree. Throughout his career Newman betrayed no weakness for honors, but in these instances the honors were reparations that retroactively must have seemed to validate his journey.

In proceeding not biographically but through a series of focusing documents and relationships in Newman's life, I offer ways of thinking about him as a personality and understanding why he wrote the way he did *about* personality, both as a theological construct (when I capitalize the word) and as a term applicable to the ethos of oneself, others, and human institutions. The Newman that emerges from this study, I believe, is far from a saint, but he is neither dishonest nor insincere. He was not the imperturbable thinker of John Holloway's *The Victorian Sage*, but a more tense and tormented personality who was capable of great warmth but also stunning coldness.

Introduction

How he himself attempted to address those warring impulses through his conscious self-fashioning as an author, as well as through those works in which the self is rigidly repressed in the interests of his faith, is the challenge that he sets for every reader.

CHAPTER 1

Self and Others

ONE OF THE most memorable sections of Newman's *Apologia* is the passage opening with the strangely ominous words "The Long Vacation of 1839 began early" and culminating in his study of the Monophysite heresy.[1] Well before 1839, Newman, despite his own disavowals, was the acknowledged leader of the Tractarian movement in the Church of England, concerned to reinfuse the Establishment with the primitive Catholicity of which it had lost sight since the Elizabethan settlement. Thus when Newman claims his reading evoked his first doubts of the "tenableness of Anglicanism" and, by the end of August, had left him "seriously alarmed," it was not only Anglicanism but his own identity that was at stake. "My stronghold was Antiquity; now here, in the middle of the fifth century, I found, as it seemed to me, Christendom of the sixteenth and the nineteenth centuries reflected. I saw my face in the mirror, and I was a Monophysite" (*A* 108).

A second passage often juxtaposed with this first comes from the magnificent concluding section of the *Apologia*, in which the certainty of God's existence seems threatened by the visible evidences of the "world of men." Newman sees in that world "a sight which fills one with unspeakable distress. The world seems simply to give the lie to that great truth, of which my whole being is so full, and the effect upon me is, in consequence[,] . . . as confusing as if it denied that I am in existence myself. If I looked into a mirror, and did not see my face, I should have the sort of feeling which actually comes upon me, when I look into this living busy world, and see no reflexion of its Creator" (216). To see nothing in the mirror is to lack evidence not only for personal reality but for Divine Being. A world devoid of the divine imprint would be a world that offered no grounding for human personality. As Newman had written a few pages earlier, "I am a Catholic by virtue of my believing in a God; and if I am asked why I believe in a God, I answer that it is because I believe in myself, for I find it impossible to believe in my own existence (and of that fact I am quite sure) without believing also in the existence of Him, who lives as a Personal, All-seeing, All-judging Being in my conscience" (180).

In the first of the mirror passages, Newman imagines himself alienated from the true faith. In the second he fears that God has become alienated from him and indeed from His whole creation. At the heart of the recurring mirror metaphor in Newman are the Pauline texts "For now we see through a glass, darkly, but then face to face: now I know in part; but then shall I know even as also I am known" (1 Cor. 13:12) and "But we all, with open face beholding as in a glass the glory of the Lord, are changed from the same image from glory to glory, even as by the Spirit of the Lord" (2 Cor. 3:18). The mirror offers the promise of self-perception, but if it reflects God's image, it may also record His absence. Newman reads himself in the mirror held up to him by other people whose lives offer an alternative narrative of himself, whether as a pattern to be emulated or an alter ego to be feared. The coeditorship of Hurrell Froude's *Remains* (chapter 3) was an instance of the first possibility; the publication of Blanco White's *Memoirs* (chapter 5) was a striking example of the latter.

The first section of this chapter lays the foundation for a discussion of Newman's orthodoxy—Roman Catholic/Anglican, Trinitarian, creedal— and his difficulty in translating that orthodoxy into an ethic for dealing with other persons. He found guidance in the concept of *ethos*, derived from Aristotle but developed somewhat idiosyncratically by the Tractarians. The Monophysite in the mirror needed company. Newman, for all his powers of rejection, desired close friends, and perhaps the very strength of his social impulses accounts for the vehemence with which he sometimes rejected other people. In persons he might find an echo of the relationship with the Divine. In his relationship with the Divine, he might find a Person who cared for him more than any human being could. The primary site of this encounter was in the Eucharist. But as he himself realized, one direction of his thought could have led him to religious despair. The concept of ethos offered him a way to deal with that tendency in himself.

Self and Others

From the inner Newman we move outward in this chapter—his effect on his contemporaries at Oxford and thence his place on the larger Victorian stage. Here we discuss two other Victorians, Thomas Carlyle and Walter Pater, quite unlike Newman (and each other) in their respective religious orientations, but resembling him in some of their responses to the broader cultural scene. The possibilities and the limitations of the human personality were important in an age that Carlyle famously described as destitute of faith but terrified of skepticism. Does the self have any reality beyond itself, or does it exist as an isolate in a world emptied of traditional religious meaning? Believers and unbelievers alike confronted this question. Robert Browning, reared in an Evangelical household, expressed these puzzles of personhood in his dramatic monologues, and John Stuart Mill affirmed a value in the liberty of the individual as a necessary precondition to self-awareness as a citizen. Such contemporaries offer a reminder of what is *Victorian* about Newman, a point of view that too often escapes a narrowly theological or purely inspirational reading of his career. Nonetheless, it is important first of all to understand the nature of Newman's theology and its orthodox underpinnings.

Doctrine and the Difficulty of Knowing

The concept of personality and "persons" in this study operates on three levels: human, institutional, and doctrinal. Much of this study dwells on the oscillation between the first and third levels, while the second affords a locus for their engagement. The human level involves human beings themselves and their relationship to others. The third, capitalized, is a central term in Christian doctrine: the three Persons of the Trinity, the divine Personality as it is manifested in Father, Son, and Holy Spirit and as defined in the formularies of the Church (n. 1 above). For Newman there is a constant and mutually validating relationship between the human and divine levels in which personality can be understood. The "paradox" of which I speak in my subtitle alludes first of all to paradoxes of Newman's own personality as an individuating fact about him, his way of dealing with other people and with his own warring impulses. But doctrinal affirmations also involve a paradox, which in religion becomes a mystery: how can Jesus be both man and God without in any way compromising or diminishing either attribute?

In Christian doctrine, human beings participate in this divine nature but imperfectly and partially.

The second, or institutional, application of "personality," for Newman, is the Church itself, which not only is composed of human being but also bears traits of collective personality. For Newman, as for Carlyle, institutions may have their own life—or, in some cases, no life at all, or a stunted one. But it is such bodies—as spiritual and human entities, not as bureaucracies—that support the daily life *of* human beings *in* Christ. That is why Newman's ecclesiology is so central a part of his structure of faith, and it is perhaps what most decisively separates him from those Evangelicals who, depending on whether they stood inside the Establishment or outside it, tended either to downplay the role of the Visible Church in favor of personal experience or wholly to reject it in their commitment to an Invisible Church of all believers.

But it also needs to be said at the outset that the use of the term "personality," though convenient and indeed essential for our purposes here, is not reliably transparent. Tom Mozley, who married Newman's sister Harriett, registered his own reservations in later life, as Newman's secession to Rome was passing into history:

> A thousand times have I wished, and then resolved never again to let myself be plagued with the wish, that the word "Person" could be banished from our Symbols and Formularies.... If the object be to bring a stupendous mystery as much as possible within the reach of a mathematical intelligence, the word, for aught I know, may be as good as any other. But for any practical purpose, it must defeat its own object. We should set down any one as either a madman or a very vulgar jester who should address either Father, Son, or Spirit by the name of Person, or should so refer to him. (2:346–47)

And the contemporary theologian John Macquarrie cautions, "Everyone knows that the word 'person' at that time when these formulations were being made in the early Church did not bear the meaning that it has nowadays, of a conscious center of experience. It had in fact a much more shadowy meaning, and perhaps the wisest course is to leave the meaning shadowy.... Perhaps we would do better to think of 'movements' of Being, or 'modes' of Being (provided it is not in the sense of temporary modes), but these two would be symbols" (192–93). Nonetheless, he elsewhere concedes that "symbols and images drawn from personal life have the highest degree of adequacy accessible to us" (143). Newman would claim no more, but he would have disavowed Mozley's consigning of the use of such a metaphor to "mathematical intelligence." There was nothing mathematical about Newman's personalism; it belonged to a different world of discourse.

The term "personality" is thus a complex one, evoking different possibilities, and as an adjective, "personal" is equally evocative and hence perhaps equally unreliable.[2] Yet it is still the most readily available way to describe the divine in terms apprehensible by human understanding.[3]

In Trinitarian doctrine, "Personality" and "Persons" are metaphysical and ontological rather than psychological concepts. One of Newman's earliest Trinity sermons (May 1825), preached when he was curate of St. Clement's, explores the doctrine in its "practical and devotional" dimension (S 3:286). The practical consequence of adherence to the Trinity, Newman suggests, is not to understand the three Persons by each one's individual nature, but rather in their interactions. "The Father graciously consents to pardon—the Son to atone—the Spirit to purify.... They work a beautiful and wondrous work—and though each has taken a particular province, yet where one works, these work all" (3:284). They illustrate the variety of gifts existing in one spirit that Paul demonstrates in 1 Corinthians: one God but represented in three Persons. To the extent that Jesus is fully human, we may attempt to glimpse his "inner theater," as Newman does in his well-known sermon "Tears of Christ at the Grave of Lazarus." But to the extent that Christ as the Son is fully one and the same with the Divine Word, we can only draw inferences from the record of the biblical narratives showing His (human) ministry from the outside.

Newman returned to the question repeatedly. In August 1832 he asserted to Hugh James Rose that "we cannot form an idea of Personality except as viewed in action, passion, relation etc.—ideas inconsistent with the true notion of the Supreme Being—An infinite immutable Mind cannot be realized as a Person" (L&D 3:78). More than two decades later in late 1858, he wrote with some impatience to a restless Catholic convert, J. M. Capes, "I cannot understand the state of mind which can love our Lord really with the feeling upon it, 'After all, perhaps there is no such person.' It is loving a mere vision or picture, and is so unreal as to be degrading. I cannot fancy ... this existence of devotion without certainty. I could not throw myself upon any one here below, of whom I had the suspicion, 'Perhaps he is not trustworthy'" (*L&D* 18:472). And yet at times Newman seems to have been more at ease with these doctrinal formulations than with their translation into an ethical and interpersonal context.

When Newman opposed personality as the "antagonist principle" to the older High Church preference for boards and committees, or when, as in an Oxford University sermon preached in 1832, he spoke on "Personal Influence, the Means of Propagating the Truth" (*OUS* 62–77), he was not using the related terms in their full psychological and existential sense. Rather, he seems to have meant a partial disclosure of one person's character to another. Nor does Newman get much closer to the "insidedness" that we expect from the term "personality" when he responds to Kingsley's famous attack by referring to the "living intelligence" or "concrete being" that he proposes to exhibit. Personality on the human level, for Newman, is expressed in actions, agency, and fleeting unveilings of the inner self in face-to-face encounters; "personality" in this sense only approximates the idea of an inner theater of the mind, for in Newman's theater the curtains are only partially drawn. Even in human relationships, like those between priest and parishioner, or tutor and pupil, in which a pastoral or moral influence is exerted, personality cannot be fully disclosed, if by that we mean the private details that may account for a particular hue in that personality. From all this we may infer the need to understand the term both doctrinally and ethically. For Newman the latter usage is more emotionally fraught and less securely held. Theology can be tidy, even if the tidiness is sometimes itself a form of mystification. Human relationships are seldom tidy, though at their best, for the believer, they may be indices to a greater reality.

Newman's description of St. Peter is at the heart of these questions: "If Christ were not to be trusted, there was nothing in the world to be trusted" (*D&A* 250). From this flows our obligation not only to other human beings but also to the Church as the visible representative of Christ. "Faith is reliance on the word of another; the word of another is in itself a faint evidence compared with that of sight or reason. It is influential only when we cannot do without it ... when it is our informant about things which we cannot do without." Thus "love of God led St. Peter to follow Christ, and love of Christ leads men to love and follow the Church as his representative and voice" (252).

In its purely ethical sense, the core of Newman's personalism is expressed aphoristically in the letters to the *Times* first printed in February 1841 and later published as "The Tamworth Reading Room": "The heart is commonly reached," he wrote, "not through the reason, but through the imagination, by means of direct impressions, by the testimony of facts and events, by history, by description. Persons influence us, voices melt us, looks subdue us, deeds inflame us. Many a man will live and die upon a dogma: no man will be a martyr for a conclusion" (*D&A* 293). Man is not merely a reasoning animal, but one who sees, feels, contemplates, and acts. Newman caps this with the Carlylean assertion, "Life is for action. If we insist on proofs for everything, we shall never come to action: to act you must assume, and that assumption is faith" (295).

For Newman, Personalism in both human affairs and matters of faith has the capacity to move us to belief and action. Of the Divine Mystery we have the security, such as it is, of knowing that we do not know. In the fifteenth of his Oxford University Sermons, "The Theory of Development in Religious Doctrine" (1843), a preliminary sketch for his treatise, Newman stated, "As God is one, so the impression which He gives us of Himself is one; it is not a thing of parts; it is not a system; nor is it any thing imperfect, and needing a counterpart. It is the vision of an object. When we pray, we pray, not to an assemblage of notions, or to a creed, but to One Individual Being; and when we speak of Him we speak of a Person, not of a Law or a Manifestation" (*OUS* 222). But though that well-known passage just quoted from "The Tamworth Reading Room" leaves no doubt about the superiority of personal influence to dry logic, nonetheless personality in the context of human relationships is more problematic. Only God knows any of us fully, and if we ever do know others as we know ourselves, it will by His mercy be in the next world, not this one. For Newman, again, the epistemological paradox is generated by the demand of knowing others and our inability ever to know them. If others can be at least partially grasped, it is not, in Newman's view, through an intellectual apprehension but through a complicated sensory awareness of the ethos of another being.

Like other undergraduates of his day and place, Newman read Aristotle—one of his earliest published essays was "Poetry, with Reference to Aristotle's Poetics" in the *London Review* (1829)—and he would have understood the term *ethos* as Aristotle used it in the *Rhetoric* to denote how persuasion may be achieved through the orator's manifestation of his personal character as his claim to credibility.[4] But though this root meaning is certainly present in Tractarian use, it is more than a province of rhetoric, of the spoken or written word. It has to do with the entire conviction conveyed by a person's actions as well as language, indeed even by the quality of his or her reticence. The *Apologia* conveys its author's method through its very refusal at critical junctures to cross the line from reticence to revelation. The ethical appeal of that work lies as much in its silences as in its declarations.

Aristotle's *Nicomachean Ethics* is especially relevant to understanding Newman's engagement with these issues. In books 8 and 9, Aristotle discusses the offices of friendship and argues that sound friendship is a feature of our relationship with ourselves: "The good person should be a self-lover, since by doing what is fine, he will both be better off and benefit others" (9.8.235). Read in the context of Newman's contentious relationships, Aristotle's remark is striking. The power of ethos is problematized in the fracturing of Newman's relationships, whether caused by ideological disagreement or a change of personal circumstances like marriage or departure from the work of the Movement. Such severances suggest a lack of Aristotelian self-love on Newman's part. Given the underlying uncertainty at the heart of his own ethos, it is not surprising that the perception of another person had the potential to be either a steadying or a disturbingly evanescent phenomenon.[5]

James Pereiro's study of the Tractarian adoption of the term *ethos* suggests that it is expressed through the whole being of the person whose influence over others is promoted and quickened by it. If it is soundly based on moral premises, it becomes a potential healing force both for the person who possesses it and those whom he influences. When Matthew Arnold writes in "The Buried Life" of intimate moments of mutual disclosure, he is undoubtedly expressing not only a concept of romantic love but also the Oxford idea of friendship:

> Only—but this is rare—
> When a beloved hand is laid in ours,

> When, jaded with the rush and glare
> Of the interminable hours,
> Our eyes can in another's eyes read clear,
> When our world-deafened ear
> Is by the tones of a loved voice caressed—
> A bolt is shot back somewhere in our breast,
> And a lost pulse of feeling stirs again.
> The eye sinks inward, and the heart lies plain.
> And what we mean, we say, and what we would, we know.
> (lines 77–87)

The persistence of such an understanding of the twinned concepts of influence and ethos is evident in two sermons preached well into Newman's career as a Roman Catholic. Honoring Dr. Henry Weedall at Oscott, Newman described him as an English Catholic of the "old school," a person of "modest and unassuming simplicity" characterized by "solid piety" and "deep and calm devotion" (*SVO* 256–60). Fourteen years after that, in 1873, preaching at the funeral of his friend from Tractarian days, James Hope-Scott (*SVO* 263–80), Newman singled out Hope-Scott's entire absence of ambition and his liberality, so generous that he seemed not to have ever known how much he gave to charity. It was not just that these men were Roman Catholics. They represented the best of *England*, of the English ethos Newman had imbibed at Oxford.

A body of such men, within the framework of an institution, provided a leavening effect—in the case of these two men, one suspects, a leavening of the Italian Catholic loaf. Newman the Evangelical had begun with a strong sense of the centrality of personal holiness. As he moved in the direction of High Church sacramentalism, the institutional claims to personality came to supplement, though never supplant, that early individualism. Institutions, too, have personalities. Lacking them, they lack vital signs. The Church, when metaphorically conceptualized as a fully vibrant person, mediates between the individual believer and God through sacramental channels that provide a personal encounter with Christ as well as a sense of shared purpose among those participating in the ritual. John Coulson has written that "the language of ideas is intelligible only in terms of the community whose language it is and within which it has been formed and developed." If the Church is a living being, "it will be both as diverse as the human personality [and] as unified" (*Common Tradition* 61–62). But a church may also lack personhood; it may be a mere shell, or in the case of the Church of England, as Newman came to view it, no more than a department of the State. Looking back from the vantage point of the *Apologia* on his earlier effort to define the prophetical office of the Church, Newman wrote that "a *Via Media* was but a receding from extremes—therefore it needed to be drawn out into a definite shape and character; before it could have claims on our respect, it must first be shown to be one, intelligible, and consistent"; otherwise it was a mere "paper religion" (*A* 70). In other words, "I wanted to bring out in a substantive form . . . a living Church, made of flesh and blood, with voice, complexion, and motion and action, and a will of its own" (73). If a church could be neither visualized nor personified it was, to use one of Newman's favorite terms, "unreal."

The Oxford Stage

The Victorian interest in religion, coupled with the historic significance of its two oldest universities, meant that what might have been just another academic quarrel could take on national significance. Thus, in an atmosphere that now seems to us cloistered if not claustrophobic, a Newman, with a few highly publicized pronouncements, could quickly command wider attention in the climate of the Church into which he had been baptized and upon whose bishops he and his fellow Tractarians eagerly pressed the opportunity for the despoliation of their goods and martyrdom. The early Victorian Church was an indulgent mother, but she expected a certain measure of decorum in her children. The Tractarians were decidedly not decorous. Temperamentally, Newman stood somewhere between the older generation of Hugh James Rose and younger hotheads like William Ward and Frederick Oakeley. In combativeness, however, Newman was the equal of the latter, though it might have been better for him had he had more of Ward's mischievous sense of humor. Like his followers, Newman was impatient with the process of slow academic inquiry into the future shape of the Church because for him, salvation was at stake, a salvation dependent more on doctrinal purity than was common among Victorian Churchmen. Quarrels activated his imagination; the force of a contrary argument stimulated his thinking.[6] Sometimes extreme, often exhibitionist, he made for good press material. Henry Scott Holland, one-time Canon of St. Paul's, declared on the eve of World War I, when Newman's memory still lingered among the living, that all Newman's writings were situational, and that as a result his words "never quite acquire a simple, direct, objective value of their own. You have to know why this or that was written . . . and what was the motive at work which made Dr. Newman to write" (112–13). In our own time, David Goslee has written penetratingly on Newman's "agonistic" rhetoric: "Commitment, confrontation, and self-dramatization . . . form part of a complex heuristic through which he shapes not just his writing but his own identity" (156). This characteristic may explain why, when Newman could not find someone else to quarrel with, he quarreled with himself. Perhaps, as Francis Newman pointed out in his hostile memoir, the boyish home newspaper *The Spy*, which John founded and edited, represented the jealous surveillance of an elder sibling bent on manipulation and control of his juniors (F. Newman, *Contributions* 4–5), but it is only fair to note that John soon began yet another household newspaper, *The Anti-Spy*, whose sole purpose was to counter everything said in the first.

Newman's combative impulses exerted themselves at a cost. His correspondence is replete with laments at major projects left undone and energies diverted by polemical combat. To his younger admirer J. D. Dalgairns, Newman, alluding to his correspondent in the third person, lamented that though he could imagine that Dalgairns might be feeling dreary, "have not I vastly more [to] depress me when I look to the future than he can have? He has friends to make, and I have friends to lose—he has habits to form, and I have habits to break—I have come to that point in which life looks downwards, though I seem to myself hardly to have begun it, and each year seems to provide less of comfort and more of the wilderness" (*L&D* 8:421–22). Downwards-looking life or not, Newman was forty when he wrote this letter in January 1842, and it is only one of many occasions in which he seems to aspire to the relief of old age. With a self-pity perhaps bordering on paranoia, he wrote that same winter to Edward Bellasis, his longtime friend and legal advisor, describing his resignation to the fact that "hardly any thing is said to me or comes to me, even from friends, of a sympathetic character. . . . Eight years ago just the same suspicion, coldness, nay blackness of face was shown towards me as now, though of course now there are in some quarters much more acrimonious feelings. However, this has perhaps had the effect of making me more callous than I should be; I mean, that, as it seemed I could not please people, I have been very little solicitous to do so" (*L&D* 8:464–65). But to another friend, Dalgairns described Newman as the only person who could "for a moment hold things together. I attribute [this] less to his wonderful powers of mind, than to his wonderful love for all men. He thinks no human misery beneath him, and seems to love persons the better the wilder and younger they are. I am sure that my most intimate friends have snubbed and scolded me for certain perturbations, which he has taken as if they were his own, and does his very utmost to heal" (*L&D* 8:421, n. 2).

Others saw Newman as lacking in confidence. Isaac Williams, who had served as Newman's curate at St. Mary's for a decade (1832–42), described him as irresolute and conflicted, oddly incapable of hewing to a particular line and likely to modify it according to his audience and the occasion. Newman "was for some time accused by some of dishonesty and duplicity. But the fact really was, that he was wavering very much in his own mind; and the feelings and thoughts he would express for one person at one time, differed very much in consequence from what he might express to another or on another occasion. And I heard of his saying, 'My old friends are what I like, their ethos and character . . . but I like the opinions of my new friends, though not themselves'—meaning especially [William] Ward of Balliol" (112–13).

In the period Williams is describing (1840–41), Newman was in the process of abandoning his quarters at Oriel College, Oxford, and taking refuge a few miles away at Littlemore, where he had purchased some buildings that he hoped to turn into a monastic retreat. He was no longer the self-assured young firebrand of the 1830s but was riven with self-doubts that he had shared with only a few of his most intimate friends. Newman had always been a private man, and that sense of privacy antedated by more than a decade the anxious self-concealment, even from close friends, of his crisis in the early 1840s. In his preaching and pastoral styles, privacy took the form of rigorous self-repression.[7] How he dealt with this in the pulpit, a very public forum, has been the gist of many memories of those who knew him.

At the heart of almost every discussion of Newman's preaching stands this passage from Matthew Arnold's lecture on Emerson: "Who could resist the charms of that spiritual apparition, gliding in the dim afternoon light through the aisles of St. Mary's, rising into the pulpit and then, in the most entrancing of voices, breaking the silence with words and thoughts which were a religious music—subtle, sweet, mournful?" (*Complete Prose Works* 10:165). Given the inevitability with which this passage is cited as a canonical tribute, it may seem counterintuitive to argue, as I do, that its influence on the whole has been obfuscatory. David J. DeLaura has pointed out that Arnold's tribute is itself a pastiche of other people's memories, Arnold never having heard the particular sermon from which he proceeded to quote, and having divested himself of most of the tenets of Christian orthodoxy by the time he went up to Oxford in 1841 (*Hebrew and Hellene* 150–51). This aestheticized Newman is part of Arnold's own affectionately troubled view of Oxford as the home of lost causes, complicated by the fact that Newman and the poet's father, Thomas Arnold, had been antagonists. Not all Newman's hearers liked his sermons; some, such as the visiting American sectary John Alonzo Clark, found his pulpit manner "cold . . . as an icicle" (DeLaura, "'O Unforgotten Voice'" 25), and Thomas Arnold Jr., in contradistinction to his older brother, confessed himself disoriented by the long chains of scriptural references that too often freighted Newman's sermons (Cornwell 13). Still, Matthew Arnold's words do convey the greater part of surviving testimonies both from those who shared Newman's theology and from those who kept their distance from him. *Soft, sweet, thrilling, musical, strong, intense, piercing, melancholy* are among the adjectives that recur in testimonies of a variety of Victorians such as J. C. Shairp and William Ewart Gladstone. Newman's early admirer William Lockhart described the utter self-effacement of Newman the preacher: "Newman . . . had the power of so impressing the Soul as to efface himself; you thought only of the majestic soul that saw God" (*CNK* 391). Paradoxically, this sort of transparency seems actually to have lent weight to his personality. Newman the liturgist had much the same effect. "His delivery of Scripture," Frederick Oakeley remembered, "was a sermon in which you forgot the human preacher, a drama in which the vividness of the representation was marred by no effort and degraded by no art. He stood before the sacred volume as if penetrating its contents to their very centre, so that his manner alone, his pathetic changes of voice, or his thrilling pauses, seemed to convey the commentary in the simple enunciation of the text" (13).

Those who stress the penitential quality of Newman's sermons or the combative notes so frequently struck in the correspondence as well as in public controversy tend to overlook these more winning manifestations of his personality. *Pace* Matthew Arnold, Newman was no apparition. He was the storyteller, entertaining the children of married friends like Pusey. He was an enthusiastic amateur violinist who enjoyed playing Beethoven quartets and accompanying the children whom he taught to sing at Littlemore. Much of this may have been a reaction to the vicissitudes of his own early family life (the second of his father's two bankruptcies hastened Mr. Newman's death) and a longing for a substitute family for his own unsatisfactory brothers, whether it was with the young men at Littlemore or the Brothers of the Oratory. Whatever erotic overtones may be read into his relationship with Hurrell Froude or his younger admirers, whatever flight from eros may be implicit in his adoption of celibacy, his emotional drive was far too complicated to be conceived in erotic terms alone.

The enchantment of his voice and person did not always endure with some of Newman's admirers. One of them, Mark Pattison, wrote in later years that he "venerated Newman himself as having been so much to me in so many ways; and I had too little knowledge to see how limited his philosophical acquirements were. The force of his dialectic and the beauty of his rhetorical exposition were such that one's eye and ear were charmed, and one never thought of inquiring on how narrow a basis of philosophical culture his great gifts were expended." Pattison shrewdly judged Newman as intellectually insular, and that perception was part of his own movement toward Liberalism and finally skepticism (M. Pattison 210).

His memoir shows that Pattison had made up his mind where he stood with respect to Newman, and had shaken off his influence without much effort. James Anthony Froude's relationship with Newman was more conflicted. The future historian, arguably never a true disciple but at least for a time a camp follower, came to Newman's attention when he went up to Oxford because he was the beloved Hurrell Froude's younger brother. Like Pattison, Froude had warm memories of Newman. He was moved by his elder's "strange fascination.... For one thing he was kind, gentle, and utterly unaffected, with a most striking presence. His sermons, which I attended from the first, interested me more than any addresses which I had ever listened to, and I was never shy of him or afraid of him" (Dunn 1:47–48).

Nonetheless, Froude later acknowledged that his liking for Newman was "theoretical" in that he had not yet begun to piece together his own beliefs. That came later, when (as we will see in the next section) he found himself turning increasingly to Carlyle.

The Victorian Landscape

Today, as the introduction has indicated, we are not entirely certain that Newman belongs to the sages, or if indeed the term itself is still useful. Some object that he was hardly more than a narrow ecclesiastical partisan, an obscurantist trapped in a side eddy of anachronistic religious orthodoxy irrelevant to a changing intellectual scene. But this is, as it were, to deny that Newman was a real Victorian at all, and to neglect his intellectual connection even with those contemporaries who did not share his religious commitments. Carlyle and, more especially, Pater figure here because all three men were troubled with questions of religious belief, all tended to employ history as a tool for focusing issues of faith, and all were fascinated with the biographical method and with the possibilities of blurring the line between biography and fiction. The connections between Carlyle and Newman have been succinctly defined by George Levine in *The Boundaries of Fiction*, and those between Newman and Pater have been broadly developed by David DeLaura in a triad that also includes Matthew Arnold (*Hebrew and Hellene*). I want here, however, to trace a somewhat different intellectual genealogy by placing the theme of personality at the center.

James Anthony Froude's adoption of Carlyle as a mentor lay in his difficulties with Newman's belief that history could be subordinated to dogma. "Across these perplexities Carlyle's books passed like a flash of lightning." Froude was enraptured by Carlyle's view of the French Revolution as God's revenge on human wickedness, and Carlyle's belief that great men perceive and act on divine realities. "The question which Carlyle asked of every institution, secular or religious, was not, Is it true? but Is it alive? Life is not truth, but the embodiment in time and in mortality of a spiritual or animating principle" ("Reminiscences" 1:73). As Levine has pointed out, the publication of Carlyle's *The French Revolution* in 1837 made him "one of the forces directly opposed to Newman's influence at Oxford." One of Froude's fictional protagonists comes to embrace "the relativity of truth by discovering that Carlyle was equally as sincere and intelligent as Newman and yet was altogether opposed to what Newman stood for" (Levine 176–77). But as he himself seems to have perceived, and as the chronology outlined in Ciaran Brady's biography indicates, Froude's change of allegiance was perhaps less dramatic than he thought. For it was Newman, not Carlyle, who famously declared that "to live is to change, and to be perfect is to have changed often" (*DCD* 40).

Two and a half weeks after Carlyle's death in 1881, and about two months after George Eliot's death at the end of 1880, Newman wrote to Gerard Manley Hopkins, with shifting orthographies, "As to your implied question, I have read little of Carlile's [*sic*] and less of George Eliot, but I have ever greatly admired Carlisle's [again *sic*] *French Revolution* and, with you, think G. E., great as are her powers, nevertheless, over-rated. Perhaps, in number of pages, I have read much more of G. E. than of C. but one page of C. goes for many of G. E." (*L&D* 29:340). In fact, Newman had read Carlyle's *French Revolution* on its first publication, when he wrote to his sister Jemima describing it with somewhat qualified admiration as a "queer, tiresome, obscure, profound, and original work. The writer has not very *clear* principles and views, I fear, but they are very deep" (*L&D* 7:66). In April 1853 he was citing the final chapter of Carlyle's history for its portrayal of the folly of the revolution (*TP* 10).

Newman responded to Carlyle as a potential political soul mate, given Carlyle's own idiosyncratic version of anti-Liberalism, and he probably admired *The French Revolution* both for its dramatic power and for its apocalyptic view of history. But the resemblance of their minds was more temperamental than ideological. In his dislike of Evangelical soul-searching, Newman often sounds uncommonly like Carlyle inveighing against the disease of self-consciousness. Newman's remark in "The Tamworth Reading Room," that "the end of man is Action, not a Thought," echoes Carlyle's gospel of activism.[8] In his insistence on the limitations of theorizing and his declared preference for the concrete, Newman's mind had much in common with Carlyle's. Both men dwelt, as did Browning in poetry, on the limitations of human language, and both of them, in the sheer bulk of their published work, seem consistently to be pushing against linguistic barriers to communicate realities that defy logical exposition. And both men dramatize the difficulty of seeing into the depths of an individual person. After endless editorial fiddling with the scraps about and by the German professor that the English Editor of *Sartor Resartus* tries to decipher, it is only with an eyewitness account of Teufelsdröckh's laughter that Editor and Reader have a momentary glimpse of the Professor's inner life. Carlyle's heroes tend to be noble, inarticulate, imperturbable men of few words whose personality is manifest in their physiognomy. On the other hand, despite Newman's fascination with the lives of the saints, the "great man" theory of history has very little to do with his understanding of the past. Saints are important as holy exemplars of Catholicity and mediators between God and humankind; it is no necessary part of their makeup, however, that they move others to action, especially political action. Carlyle's definition of human potential is as divorced from institutional moorings as it can be—certainly when his hero is a man of the people coming to power or influence, like Cromwell or John Knox, by dismissing institutions like the Papacy as "old clothes." For all his temperamental resemblance to Newman, Carlyle provided a competing vision of personal influence rooted more in action than in ethos.

At the opposite end of the spectrum from Carlyle's muscular non-Christianity lies Walter Pater's aestheticizing of Christian rites and practices. Like many another of his generation, Pater imbibed the post-Tractarian atmosphere during his years at Oxford as undergraduate and tutor, where memories of Newman, forty years his senior, lingered and where, toward the end of his life, Newman made his peace with the university he had never ceased to love.

The influence of Newman undoubtedly shaped Pater's idea of personality as a kind of indeterminate but nonetheless real emanation from one human being to another. And it contains something very much like Newman's ideal of utter self-suppression, particularly the idea of gentlemanliness that does not loudly advertise itself. In 1864 the young Pater read his essay "Diaphaneitè" to the Old Mortality Club at Oxford. The essay was never published in his lifetime and was only somewhat reluctantly brought into print posthumously by his longtime friend and literary executor Charles Shadwell, of whom the essay (to Shadwell's embarrassment) was thought to be a portrait.[9] In this short paper, Pater describes a character type that he compares to Dante's Beatrice, one that does not "take the eye by breadth or colour; rather it is that fine edge of light, where the elements of our moral nature refine themselves to the burning point. It crosses rather than follows the main current of the world's life." Such a "colourless, unclassified purity of life" draws on the elements of the artistic, the speculative and the saintly, but has no value as coinage in the world's transactions" (*Miscellaneous Essays* 215–16). Pater aestheticizes the ideal of "simplicity in purpose and act" as the mark of "moral expressiveness" and "perfect intellectual culture" (217). At the heart of what he is attempting to convey is a high doctrine of ascetic fulfillment, "a colourless, unclassified purity of life" that he associates explicitly with the goal, "Sibi unitas et simplificatus esse, that is the long struggle of the Imitatio Christi" (216).

If "Diaphaneitè" is the imaginary portrait of an individual "diaphanous" spirit, the Pater of *Studies in the History of the Renaissance* (1873) much more strikingly echoes Newman's views of human relationships in the ordinary working of society. Newman's difficulty in knowing others was not merely personal; a philosophical assumption lay behind it. In an early (1828) letter to Blanco White, Newman wrote, "I agree with you . . . in feeling the incommensurability (so to speak) of the human mind. . . . Each mind pursues its own course and is actuated in that course by tenthousand [*sic*] indescribable incommunicable feelings and imaginings." Even when men converge in agreement on certain truths, they hold those truths in various ways (*L&D* 2:60). A more sweeping statement occurs in Newman's sermon "The Individuality of the Soul" (1836):

> Survey some populous town: crowds are pouring through the streets; some on foot, some in carriages; while the shops are full, and the houses too, could we see into them. Every part of it is full of life. Hence we gain a general idea of splendour, magnificence, opulence, and energy. But what is the truth? why, that every being in that great concourse is his own centre, and all things about him are but shades, but a "vain shadow," in which he "walketh and disquieteth himself in vain." He has his own hopes and fears, desires, judgments, and aims; he is everything to himself, and no one else is really any thing. No one outside of him can really touch him, can touch his soul, his immortality; he must live with himself for ever. (*PPS* 4.6.785)[10]

The only truth, then, would seem to be the truth of individual centers of consciousness; nothing outside the self exists. Such passages as these anticipate the radical subjectivism of the famous conclusion to Pater's *Renaissance* in which "the whole scope of observation is dwindled into the narrow chamber of the individual mind. Experience, already reduced to a group of impressions, is ringed round for each one of us by that thick wall of personality through which no real voice has ever pierced on its way to us or from us to that which we can only conjecture to be without. Every one of those impressions is the impression of the individual in his isolation, each mind keeping as a solitary prisoner its own dream of a world" (*Renaissance* 187–88).[11] Newman's theology provided a hedge against such implications. In sermons from the 1830s, his underlying claim was that such imperfect apprehension of others derived from the disconnection between man and his Maker. In his sermon "The Greatness and Littleness of Human Life" (1836), he argued that "the one desire which should move us should be, first of all, that of seeing Him face to face, who is now hid from us; and next of enjoying eternal and direct communion, in and through Him, with our friends around us, whom at present we know only through the mediation of sense, by precarious and partial channels, which give us little insight into their hearts" (*PPS* 4.14.874–75). Newman resumed the theme in "The Thought of God, the Stay of the Soul" (1839): "We know that even our nearest friends enter into us but partially, and hold intercourse with us only at times; whereas the consciousness of a perfect and enduring Presence, and it alone, keeps the heart open" (*PPS* 5.22.1160).

We have no way of knowing whether Pater read any of Newman's *Parochial and Plain Sermons*, which had become newly available in W. J. Copeland's republication, with Newman's permission, in 1868. My point here is not, however, to belabor inconclusively the possibility of a direct source, but to juxtapose two men who, despite their very different ideologies, tended to approach reality somewhat anxiously. Pater's "thick wall of personality" seems to foreclose any possibility of mutual understanding altogether. He begins with a Newman-like perception of the reality of human isolation but rejects the theological framework that, at least in Newman's view, alone can alleviate that sense of isolation and despair.

By the end of Pater's *Marius the Epicurean* (1885), the early skepticism of *The Renaissance* has been significantly modified.[12] Marius has been generally taken as both inspired by, and a reaction to, Newman's second novel, *Callista* (1856), in which Newman constructs the life of an imaginary saint.[13] *Callista* anticipates *Marius* in its virtual abandonment of plot for a focus on the unique individuality of a single character realized fully from the inside. As was to be the case with Marius, Callista exists without a clearly defined community, but unlike Marius she comes to have a clear idea of what sort of community she wants, and commits herself to the Christian revelation before she dies. In both novels Christianity is an institution still in formation, largely nascent and hardly visible except to those already on the inside. During her conversion process, we are told, Callista had long since abandoned any belief in the religion of her own country because "to worship a being who did not speak to us, recognize us, love us, was not religion." Her "instinctive notion of religion was the soul's response to a God who had taken notice of the soul." She seeks a "living intercourse" with "the intimate Divine Presence in the heart. It was the friendship or mutual love of person with person" (C 227–28). Even before her conversion, Callista is clear that she cannot sign an oath of loyalty to the old religion of Rome because it does not offer the same satisfaction of "the echo of a person speaking to me."

Callista has acquired a dawning conception of conscience against the grain of her culture. Like Marius after her, she is an inquirer who reenacts the inner turmoil of her author as he wandered through that "midway region of inquiry, which as surely takes time to pass over, except there be some almost miraculous interference" (C 246). Her extended martyrdom seems designed as a literal analogue to the metaphorical "deathbed" Newman was to describe as the site of his last days as an Anglican. The final step in Callista's conversion occurs when she reads the Acts of the Apostles, which opens "a new state and community of beings" to her eyes and awakens her to "the presence of One who was simply distinct and removed from any thing that she had, in her most imaginative moments, ever depicted to her mind as ideal perfection." Her intellect has sought this ideal but has been unable to originate it or purchase it, for what is required is grace, the grace of being granted the image of a Divine Person who is no dream but, as she now thinks, "the delineation of a real individual" (252–53). And so in her martyrdom and death she exudes an odor of sanctity.

Pater's novel has neither action nor even textual revelation, whereas

Newman's novel offers blood, torture, and madness. Textually, Callista's reading of the Acts of the Apostles recalls the words *Tolle, lege* ("Pick it up and read"), which, in his *Confessions*, Augustine records himself hearing. Newman also manages to create other characters who, at least in terms of the attitudes they embody, are real enough, while in Pater's novel, people other than Marius are seen only through Marius's own wistful and partial gaze. The clue to the difference lies in Pater's subtitle, *His Sensations and Ideas*, which promises a focus on inner stages of consciousness. Marius's stages are defined by his relationships with two other men, Flavian and Cornelius. Flavian, his schoolmate, dies early but, as a sort of projection of Marius's early Cyrenaicism, introduces him to a powerful impression of "perpetual flux" that eludes definition or fixity. His premature death clears the way for a new relationship with the centurion Cornelius, a kind but somewhat remote companion whose inner life is largely hidden from Marius. The "discretion of Cornelius, his energetic clearness and purity, more a charm, rather physical than moral; his exquisite correctness of spirit, at all events, accorded so perfectly with the regular beauty of his person, as to seem to depend upon it. And wholly different as was this later friendship, with its exigency, its warnings, its restraints, from the feverish attachment to Flavian, which had made him at times like an uneasy slave, still, like that, it was a reconciliation to the world of sense, the visible world" (1:233–34). Pater eroticizes what in Newman remains a metaphysical and spiritual search.

Pater's idea of saintly personality is a composite of Christian and Hellenist strains, filtered through Oxonian ethos. Cornelius as a character is opaque to Marius. His personality is foreshowed in Newman's sermon "Equanimity," probably preached in the late 1830s. The Christian possesses a "deep, silent, hidden peace, which the world sees not." He is "cheerful, easy, kind, gentle, courteous, candid, unassuming: has no pretence, no affectations, no ambitions, no singularity, because he has neither hope nor fear about this world" (*PPS* 5.5.1003).

The key to Cornelius lies in what he does, not what he professes; it also lies in the mysterious community to which he belongs, with its Christian rites of worship at the house of Cecilia. After witnessing his first Eucharist, Marius feels that "the natural soul of worship in him had at last been satisfied as never before" (2:140). In beginning to "read" Cornelius at the end of the novel, Marius "seem[s] to touch, to ally himself to, actually to become a possessor of the coming world" (2:209–10). As for Marius's own approach to this coming world by means of the aesthetic senses, there lingers here, with sexual overtones to be sure, the belief that divine Personality can be revealed through its incarnation in human beauty and the physicality of the sacramental action.

In dying into the Christian community, Marius remains, at least formally, unconverted, and that possession of the coming world, envisioned in the framing "seemed," remains highly provisional. Pater leaves his commitments indeterminate. The capacity of personal influence to direct others or to incite them to action is uncertain. Newman sought an answer to his spiritual needs in an orthodox faith that Carlyle rejected and Pater may have craved but seemed unable fully to embrace. Instead, Pater grasped the innate skepticism of wondering whether human beings can fully divulge themselves to each other, and he placed it at the thematic center of his novel.[14]

Newman's capacity to evoke responses of such varying sorts as those of the activist Carlyle and the aesthete Pater suggests the germinative powers of his imagination. As an uncompromising adherent to Christian orthodoxy, by century's end a minority position, he provided a clear standard against which unbelievers and secularists might equally measure themselves.

Styles of Engagement

What started with a small band at Oxford was the first act of a wider drama with some unexpected reverberations. Whereas it might be said that Carlyle, hurling his thunderbolts from Chelsea, hectored his society, and Pater (more inclined to rhetorical indirection than thunderbolts) kept his distance from it, Newman was far more engaged in that society than many of those more recently styled "sages." He was compelled to be a public figure in ways that he could not control. Those academics who today approach Newman with essentially secular premises tend to forget the maxim "Once a priest, always a priest." Everything Newman did was constrained by the fact that he was not only a priest but specifically also, in the second half of his career, a Roman Catholic priest who stood on the margins of British society but was compelled to represent his Church to it. To be a priest, at least one whose primary role lies outside the more cloistered world of a seminary, is to be enmeshed in daily obligations of which there was no shortage in Birmingham, with its shifting demographics. Coming to this new career from that of Anglican controversialist, Newman and everything he said were of public interest. He found himself constantly having to show loyalty to his new communion while being only slowly and imperfectly assimilated into it. He had more in common with the "Old Catholics" of England who had maintained their faith throughout the years following the Elizabethan settlement than with an Italianate hierarchy to which the chameleon-like Henry Manning so successfully adapted. Newman's position in the "papal aggression" controversy of 1850 with the resulting Ecclesiastical Titles Act,[15] and his discomfiture at the impending triumph of the Ultramontanes at the forthcoming Council of 1870 at which the doctrine of papal infallibility was promulgated, were not only evident to inquiring friends but also a matter of public concern among those on both sides of the issue.

Priestly duties occupy daily life: hearing confessions, visiting the sick, burying the dead, manifesting patience with boys in a parochial school setting, all were among Newman's quotidian duties. Doubtless the hierarchy much preferred him to be occupied with those duties rather than with his next publication, which was almost certain to cause trouble. A balanced assessment of his career requires at the outset the awareness that Newman's daily path lay along lines where sages seldom tread, and if he was a prophet, he was one who appealed to the past rather than the future.

Despite his sensitivities, such a life often gave Newman a hard-boiled realism when he needed it. David Anthony Downes has called our attention to an unpublished letter in the Yale Library in which recent visitors to Oxford reported on a meeting alleged to have taken place between Newman and Pater. Pater, it is said, greeted the distinguished visitor by saying that he hoped to hear him preach at the Jesuit parish of St. Aloysius, to which Newman replied that he hoped that Pater's attendance there was motivated by more than simple curiosity. If the account is to be trusted, Pater's attendance was indeed motivated by more than curiosity. In due course he appeared at St. Aloysius with a large missal decorated with the liturgical colors appropriate to the season (Downes 2, n. 3). To some of us, the incident may now appear merely risible, but it is difficult to imagine Newman, who distrusted show, being amused. Such shows, as well as quite public conversions to the Church of Rome, were in some quarters more suggestive of aesthetic tomfoolery, or worse, a badge of sexual deviance, than of unassuming faith. Nothing could be further from the truth to which Newman believed he had devoted his own life.

The Journey from Evangelicalism

NEWMAN'S LIFE AND theological development up to his embarkation on the fateful journey to Italy, undertaken in 1832 with Hurrell Froude and his father, Archdeacon Robert Hurrell Froude, represent a period of expansion in his outlook. His core Evangelicalism never left him, but in its contemporary manifestations it was insufficient to sustain him. His early journal entries, with their soul-searching and self-rebuke, would have been familiar to any Evangelical of his time, and those traits never deserted him. But at the time of his ordination nearly a decade before, the fuller development of his ecclesiology, his idea of the salvific power of a divinely instituted and visible, apostolic church working forgiveness through the sacraments and embodying the moral authority of tradition, was yet to come. Part of that development also involved a de-emphasis of the Atonement and a greater reliance on the Incarnation and on a Christology that was honed by his researches into the Arian heresy. The change in doctrinal emphasis does not, of course, mean that Newman ceased to believe in the Atonement. What he rejected was the Evangelical treatment of the Atonement, which, Newman felt, tended to rob it of its mystery and to reduce it to a transaction, a kind of legal bargain characteristic of covenant theology, rather than focusing on the *person* of Christ.

Evangelical Reading and Writing

Horton Davies has argued that the relationship of Tractarianism to Evangelicalism is as much supplementary as antagonistic. "Certainly, there might have been no Tractarian or Oxford Movement unless the Evangelicals had revived personal religion in the Church of England, and to this extent the latter movement is indebted to the earlier" (2:244).[1] Among the elements the two had in common were the idea of personal holiness and the living proof of faith by a life of sanctity. In this respect Thomas Arnold, despite his later liberalism in ecclesial matters, premised all that he did on the belief in Jesus as "a living Friend and Maker." It was only through Christ that one could know God at all.[2]

Newman demarcates his early stages of religious belief in the *Apologia*. When he was fifteen he came under the tutelage of the Evangelical Walter Mayers, who stressed the familiar Evangelical themes of personal conversion, a reverence for biblical authority, the Atonement, and the doctrine of election. Mayers's conversations and sermons contributed to the boy's adoption of "a definite Creed" and gave his mind "impressions of dogma, which, through God's mercy, have never been effaced or obscured" (*A* 17). From Isaac Watts, Newman derived an idea of "the Saints unknown in the world," angels in disguise who showed no outward signs distinguishing them from others. "Truth and authority," Watts wrote, "come, with particular force, from the mouth of one whom we trust and love" (250). But it was to the autobiography of Thomas Scott of Aston Sanford, *The Force of Truth*, that Newman ascribed special significance. He admired Scott's unworldliness, his candor, his opposition to the antinomian view (held by some extreme Evangelicals and Dissenters) that grace sets us free from moral law, and "the minutely practical character of his writings." Most particularly he remembered Scott's maxims, "Holiness rather than peace" and "Growth the only evidence of life" (*A* 18–19). Evangelicals seldom hesitated to rebuke the religiously wayward, as the sermons of one of the most prominent Evangelical preachers, Charles Simeon, show: better a rebuke than a false peace, or a mistaken charity that constituted mere passivity in the face of evil—and in this, the Tractarians followed the Evangelicals. For Scott, the integrity of the personality was dramatized in narrative, while the serenity of his conclusion testifies to the success of his journey. As Linda Peterson argues (15–18, 98–101), Scott's autobiography, with its narrative exposition and a concluding Augustinian meditation, was to figure implicitly in the structure of the *Apologia* many years later.

Newman was drawn to these men because of their piety and their lack of show, a virtue that he associated with an earlier Evangelical generation.

In John Scott's description of his father, Thomas, at family worship, Newman would have read, "It was not so much by preaching directly to them, as by living before them, making an edifying use of incidents and occasions, and being so consciously instructive, devout, and benevolent in family worship, that, under the blessing of God, he produced so striking an impression upon them" (*Life* 57). As we shall see, this ideal of the pastorate was to be upheld both publicly and privately.

Another and rather unexpected Evangelical source, this time for Newman's later interest in the patristic tradition, was Joseph Milner's *History of the Church of Christ*. Milner's stated purpose was to write history through personal portraits rather than through organizational or liturgical church history, focusing on holy men formed by the teachings of the New Testament. Evangelical though he was, Milner's appeal to antiquity and the patristic tradition, and his attack on mere pagan good manners, anticipated two of Newman's recurring themes. The book is a salutary reminder that Evangelicalism was never quite the simplistic affair that some Tractarian rhetoric made of it. In one of Newman's earliest sermons, the influence of Milner's way of thinking can be discerned in the argument that the best witnesses to the truth are "those whom we love best and reverence. . . . Have not the wisest and holiest of men been Christians? and have not unbelievers, on the contrary, been very generally signal instances of pride, discontent, and profligacy?"[3] Newman's history of the Arian controversy pursued this point with a vengeance. Heterodoxy and moral failings were directly correlative.

Newman's early journals, with their persistent and sometimes excruciating self-examinations, bear an undeniably Evangelical imprint. In 1821 he lamented, "I can read religious books, the most spiritual, with great pleasure, and, when so engaged feel myself warmed to prayer and thanksgiving; but let the appointed hour of devotion arrive, and I am cold and dead. My head is full of God during the day, and particularly of the salvation of others, and I can offer up heartfelt prayers in my solitary walk, but this dreadful listlessness comes upon me morning after morning, and evening after evening" (*AW* 165–66). During the summer of the same year, he reverted to the theme: "I speak of the process of conversion with great diffidence, being obliged to adopt the language of books. For my own feelings, as far as I remember, were so different from any account I have ever read, that I dare not go by what *may* be an individual case" (166). The Calvinist doctrine of final perseverance lends an edge to his fear that he has not undergone the redemptive process described in Evangelical conversion narratives, where a Pauline moment is a token of grace. Though feeling himself "less desirous of the things of the world," he accuses himself nonetheless of deficiency "in spirituality, in prayer, in brotherly love, meekness, humility, forgiveness of injuries, charity, benevolence, purity, truth and patience." To this he adds the vices of bad temper, vanity, and vehemence, to name a few (174).

The journals also contain a tone of self-reproach with respect to personal relationships, particularly familial: for example, his guilt-stricken reaction to his deceased father's prophetic caution that his son was liable to fall into extremes. Newman's early premonitions that he was destined to a celibate life were neither confident nor untroubled. "When I die, shall I be followed to the grave by my children? my Mother said the other day she hoped to live to see me married, but *I* think I shall either die within College walls, or a Missionary in a foreign land—no matter where, so that I die in Christ" (*AW* 203). In his 1826 birthday journal entry, he described his gradual abandonment of the mission goal and attributed it to his ambition and pride. "I fear thoughts of theological fame, desire of rising in the Church &c counteract my desire for missionary employment. What I want is a humble, simple, upright, sincere, straightforward mind. I am full of art and deceit, double dealing, display" (208). He was already imputing to himself the traits that many of his critics, including Charles Kingsley, were to see in him.

The Idea of Personal Influence

In his first meeting with John Keble in April 1822, Newman was won over by Keble's personality and its imprint on his theology. Like all Anglican ordinands, Newman had already read Bishop Joseph Butler's *Analogy of Religion* and taken into account Butler's theory of the role of probability in achieving assent to religious doctrines. Newman thought that Keble had avoided potential difficulties with Butler's argument by ascribing "firmness of assent" in religious matters "not to the probabilities which introduced it, but to the living power of faith and love which accepted it." Faith and love vivify religious assent by directing themselves toward an Object which, once "received in faith and love[,] ... renders it reasonable to take probability as sufficient for internal conviction. Thus the argument from Probability, in the matter of religion, becomes an argument from Personality, which in fact is one form of the argument from Authority" (*A* 30). Keble thereby spurred Newman's inclination toward personalism, as well as providing, with Butler, the materials for reasoning that led almost half a century later to Newman's *Grammar of Assent*. But Newman found Keble's explanation more "beautiful and religious" than logical, and he set about to supply a logical underpinning for what appealed to his emotions. As he developed it, his theory came to stipulate that "the constitution of the human mind" and the "will of the Maker" interact to produce a certitude equal to that derived from "the strictest scientific demonstration" (*A* 31).

The appearance of Keble's *The Christian Year* in 1826 cemented Newman's attachment to the older man. Newman was especially fond of quoting the opening stanza of Keble's poem for the Wednesday in Holy Week, inspired by Luke 22:42 ("Father, if thou be willing, remove this cup from me; nonetheless not my will, but thine, be done"):

> O Lord my God, do Thou thy holy will—
>   I will lie still—
> I will not stir, lest I forsake thine arm,
>   And break the charm,
> Which lulls me, clinging to my Father's breast,
>   In perfect rest.

Such a stanza met Newman's devotional needs perfectly, and his pre-Tractarian poetry tends to draw on Keble's self-effacing vein. In "Snapdragon" (1827), Newman describes himself as forever rooted in the cloister, a flower in mortar, not as one of the fairer flowers of Nature but as a humble dweller in monastic obscurity: "So for me alone remains / Lowly thought and cheerful pains" (lines 37–38). In "The Hidden Ones" (1829), he shifts from the personal and private to a discourse on the unobtrusiveness of true saintliness: "Hid are the saints of God; / Uncertified by high angelic sign" (lines 1–2); hence, "staid look, loud voice, and reason's might / Forcing its learned way" are of no avail in tracing the outlines of the "princely race" of Christ (lines 13–14). Such poetry is, on the whole, negligible, yet in its longing for the reclusive life of the scholar, it reveals much about Newman's state of mind. But the hopes it expressed were to be shattered first by a political and then by an academic quarrel.

Both conflicts were with Edward Hawkins, the provost of Oriel and one of Newman's earliest friends there. His debt to Hawkins was real enough. When he won the Oriel fellowship, Newman was still an exceedingly shy young man. Hawkins, who wanted the college to see the best of him, gave him over to Richard Whately to "bring the whelp out of his kennel." Hawkins also gave Newman a copy of his sermon on Tradition, and that undoubtedly contributed to the evolution in Newman's thinking begun by his exposure to Milner. Newman, in turn, had backed Hawkins over Keble when the Oriel provostship became vacant. The division between Hawkins and Newman dated to their disagreement over the Peel-Inglis parliamentary contest of 1829, which underwrote the emerging division between the younger High Church party (not yet distinguishable as "Tractarian") and the liberal "Noetics" who dominated the Oriel common room. Hawkins aligned himself with the moderate Peel, who felt the need to give way on the question of Catholic Emancipation; Newman, not at that time visibly harboring any Roman sympathies, opposed Peel because he felt that Peel had betrayed the independence of the university. The debate played out against the wider background of the repeal of the Test and Corporation Acts and talk of pending political reform that bade fair to put an end to Anglican hegemony in both politics and religion.[4]

Newman's next dispute with Hawkins in the summer and spring of 1830 was an important factor in sharpening his emerging theory of personal influence. Newman owed yet another debt to his Evangelical forebears for his thinking on the subject. In Watts's *The Improvement of the Mind*, he would have read that a good tutor exhibits "a natural candour and sweetness mixed with all the improvements of learning, as might convey knowledge into the minds of his disciples with a sort of gentle insinuation and sovereign delight, and may tempt them into the highest improvements of their reason by a resistless and insensible force" (75). Keble, for his part, had already anticipated the position that was to be staked out by his three juniors: more than a decade earlier, he had written to John Taylor Coleridge, "You consider Tuition as a species of pastoral care, do you not? otherwise it might seem questionable, whether a clergyman ought to leave a cure of souls for it. And yet there are some people at Oxford who seem to imagine that College Tutors have nothing to do with morals. If I thought so, I would never undertake the office" (J. Coleridge 73). Whether an appeal to the statutes could prove that the university formally adhered to this definition of a tutor's pastoral role was the arcane but by no means trivial question at hand. But it was only the presenting issue. Throughout their conflict, Newman and his younger fellow tutors, Robert Wilberforce and Hurrell Froude, stood on the side of *persons*, Hawkins on the side of *system*.

Under existing college practice, tutors, rather than having pupils assigned to them, chose classes from the common stock of pupils attending lectures. Students were arrayed in classes arbitrarily without regard to who their particular tutor was, the latter being obligated to discuss all lectures, whether his own or those of another man. Under the plan drawn up by the Newman-Froude-Wilberforce trio, each separate tutor would undertake the exclusive instruction of his own pupils in several subjects ranging from ethics and divinity to history. Thus many lectures would be private, confined to classes formed specifically for instruction by a particular tutor. The number of open lectures given to all would be reduced accordingly.

Hawkins had discussed the tutorships orally with Newman as early as November 1829. When he learned what the three tutors were putting into practice, he wrote the following May, with some show of reluctance but also chagrin, that the previous autumn "a system of Tuition was actually [already] in operation which was at variance, according to my judgment, with the system established and acted upon at Oriel for many years before" (*L&D* 2:229). Though he conceded that the tutor had a general duty to regard "the moral, religious, and intellectual proficiency" of his students, it could not be on this basis that they were assigned to him. He thought that Newman, in urging the claims of private tuition, had "carried a good principle . . . too far." There was plenty of room under the old system "for a most wholesome and valuable influence to be exerted by each Tutor over his own Pupils" (231). In another letter written the following month, Hawkins reminded the tutors that in the past he had always told parents that the college could not guarantee a particular tutor and that "their Sons would reap the benefit of instruction from all the Tutors indiscriminately" (240).

Newman explained that his objection to the existing order was that "the mere lecturing required of me would be incompatible with due attention to that more useful private instruction, which has imparted to the office of Tutor the importance of a clerical education." Newman cited, though he did not quote, the university statutes in support of his proposition that "each Pupil should on entrance be especially committed to the care of a particular Tutor" (233–34). The more combative Hurrell Froude put the whole case for change most succinctly. To comply with the established system, "I should be obliged to abandon all hope of knowing any pupils in the way in which I know them at present—and consequently of retaining that influence over them which I believe I now possess" (235).

Hawkins had the upper hand, and he had a short way with insubordination. When the three young rebels refused to give way, his response was to cease sending them pupils. His resentment over Newman's position on the Peel-Inglis election may have made him all the readier to pounce. But although Meriol Trevor has described Hawkins as a compulsive interferer (1:83–86), it is possible to see Hawkins's side of the case. No doubt an element of personal resentment and wounded *amour-propre* figured in his squelching the rebellion, but he was alert to the dangers of coteries and had principled reasons for concern over the reform's potential for disruption of the college's teaching program.[5]

Newman's motives were probably more complex than Hawkins's, and perhaps partly unclear to himself. He may have desired to test his strength while setting himself up for a defeat in which he might more easily assert a position of superior moral principle. Alternatively, his backing the winning side in the 1829 election may have encouraged him to think he could best Hawkins on the provost's own ground. In any case, his hypersensitivity to provocation, combined with his superior's peremptoriness, boded ill for cooperative work in the setting of an Oxford college.

If Newman had overplayed his hand and was really disappointed, he put the best face on the outcome that he could. Though in retrospect he often regretted his behavior to the provost, and though the result was both financially and personally injurious, he claimed in later years to have seen the hand of Providence in the entire episode. "I certainly was sorry I had helped in electing Hawkins [as provost]—but I cant [sic] say I ever wished the election undone," he told Pusey in 1882. "Without it, there would have been no movement, no Tracts, no Library of the Fathers" (*L&D* 30:107). The affair undoubtedly figured in shaping Newman's concept of personal influence, the subject of the fifth of his Oxford University sermons, "Personal Influence, the Means of Propagating the Truth," preached on January 22, 1832, on Hebrews 11:34 ("out of weakness made strong"). Newman began with the premise that lay behind his objections (by now in full play) to Evangelicalism and Liberalism alike. The purpose of the Written Word was "not to unfold a system for our intellectual contemplation, but to secure the formation of a certain character" (*OUS* 67). The Teacher of the Faith does not merely promulgate opinions that "may lodge on the surface of the mind," but participates in a divine work in "changing . . . the heart, and modelling all men after one exemplar; making them like himself, or rather like One above himself who is the beginning of a new creation" (69). Truth is upheld not as a system, not by written or oral argument or "temporal power," but rather "by the personal influence of such men as have already been described, who are at once the teachers and the patterns of it" (72). Thus a single individual who knows how to practice what he preaches excites a more powerful response than intellectual excellence. The "attraction, exerted by unconscious holiness, is of an urgent and irresistible nature; it persuades the weak, the timid, the wavering, and the inquiring; it draws forth the affection and loyalty of all who are in a measure like-minded; and over the thoughtless or perverse multitude it exercises a sovereign compulsory sway, bidding them fear and keep silence, on the ground of its own right divine to rule them" (74).

Newman here argues for a kind of influence based not on force but on mutual consent, the openness of one mind to another, the power of example rather than the wielding of authority. The point is clearer if we place his thoughts on the subject next to those of the most prominent Evangelical of his day, Charles Simeon of Cambridge. Though Simeon was a gifted extempore speaker, his best-known work was his *Horae Homileticae, or Discourses in the Form of Skeletons, upon the Whole Scripture*, a prompt book for young and inexperienced clergymen seeking guidance on preaching. First published in five volumes in 1819, it grew to twenty-one volumes; and according to Elisabeth Jay, who has edited selections, its popularity persisted "well into the second half of the century."[6] For Simeon the function of the sermons was to exercise authority as one whom God has set over others, to rebuke, exhort, and chastise those in his care. The effect is left not to the subtle aura of personal holiness, but to the exertion of a moral duty. The first of his seven sermon heads, "The use we should make of influence, influence of whatever kind it be, should be diligently improved;—1. To enforce the commands of God," and other clauses of a similar nature follow. The sermon outline for the subject "Abraham's Care of His Family" appeals to the patriarch of the Hebrew scriptures as a sort of role model not only for the clergyman in his parish but also for the father in his home.

Whereas Simeon based his model on the emerging nineteenth-century model of the paterfamilias, Newman did not have such a paternal model at hand in his own history, though he was no less averse to wielding authority from the pulpit. But in the celibate quiet of an Oxford college, his views on preaching were shaped by a more easygoing pattern of tutor-pupil relationships. This seemed threatened, however, by potential university reforms opening the doors to students from Dissenting backgrounds. Newman opined that the "intimacy bordering on friendship" between tutor and student would be compromised. He wrote to Hugh James Rose in 1834, "The tutor is often the means of forming his pupils' minds, of setting up a standard of thought and judgment in his society, and that, of course, in accordance with, or rather based upon, the doctrines of the church. Now consider what can be more different than the respective tempers, or *ethe*, of dissent and churchmanship,—the one founded on reverence; the other, on boldness and self-will.... How can a tutor do any thing for pupils whose first element of character differs from that of the church?" (*L&D* 4:209). The cost would also be borne by the tutor, whose freedom to inculcate his opinions without reserve or embarrassment would be checked by the presence of those over whom "he must mourn ... as aliens to the faith" (210). The Dissenting student who is the projection of Newman's somewhat overheated imagination "distrusts your religion and despises your coldness. There is one, the greatest secret of the heart, which you cannot discuss without dispute; and you cannot procure his confidence." Such a student will depart from the university "with the pride of a martyr, and the complacency of one who bears within him the ultimate standard of appeal" (211). This uncommonly deterministic point of view—that personal character is almost wholly the result of theological commitments or unexamined biases—represents a serious flaw not only in Newman's concept of individual tutoring but also in his charity. The possibility that a student, subject to the benign influence of a tutor, might actually change his religious course does not seem to have presented itself to Newman's imagination.

In his description of the one who persuades by example, through the exercise of "unconscious holiness," Newman expresses both his distrust of charismatic personalities and his idea of saintly self-effacement. But the encounter with Hawkins had also brought out his pugilistic side. His theory of personal influence had awakened him to the paradoxes of leadership. The self-effacing, reclusive scholar and poet, who tried to emulate saintly humility, was forced to confront the power of his own example and its sometimes unforeseen effects on others. To move men through the power of personal example was to awaken the exercise of that private judgment whose activity Newman feared, but on which he would have to call at the most decisive moment of his life.

From the Atonement to the Incarnation

On October 19, 1819, the young Newman had made notes for an essay on the doctrine of the Atonement, "the key stone of Christianity" especially crucial when, as now, "the days of a general apostasy are at hand" (*AW* 161). In the decade that followed, as Newman's early Calvinism receded, the Atonement gave way to the Incarnation as the central doctrine in his theology. Intrinsic to this development, as Placid Murray has put it, were Newman's "gradual acceptance of the doctrine of baptismal regeneration as a substitute for his earlier evangelical belief in conversion; the eventual supremacy of the mystery of the Eucharist in his own spiritual life, [and] his growing reserve about preaching on the Atonement" (*S* 1:xv).[7] In High Church theology, the pouring of water at baptism, the laying on of hands at confirmation and ordination, the reception of bread and wine in the Eucharist were all outward and visible signs of the transmission of grace, and thus an analogue to the Incarnation, for in their very materiality they confirmed the translation of sensory phenomena into vessels for the sacred. The doctrine of baptismal regeneration, which Newman first learned to value through the influence of Hawkins and the moderate Evangelical John Bird Sumner's *Apostolical Preaching*, spoke directly to Newman's own experience, for he felt he had never really fallen away from his own baptism. Baptismal regeneration affirmed that the Spirit had already been implanted in him through the materiality of the sacrament itself. Finally, the idea of membership, not in a spiritual church of individual believers, but in a visible community of common worship, fell into place with his adherence to the doctrine of the Apostolic Succession, in which grace was regarded as being transmitted through the laying on of hands from one generation to the next. Apostolicity was thus, in James Eli Adams's summary, both an honorific token of the sort that might characterize a secret society and a sacramental encounter between human beings (Adams 88–89).

In an early sermon (1824) on "the effect on the mind of the doctrine of the Cross," Newman's concentration on the humanity of Christ does not have the richness of his later writings on the Incarnation. He focuses almost entirely on Jesus's human connection with us, rather than on how the divine and human coexisted in him, arguing that "when God is revealed to us in the flesh, we have a perfect and yet an imitable example—one that warms and elevates the soul, without exposing it to the danger of an idolatrous and sinful attachment" (S 1:274–75). Newman does not yet explicitly state that the paradox might be bridged by the Incarnation.[8]

In another sermon preached the following year, Newman's subject was "the internal evidence of the evangelical doctrine." The emphasis remains on the Atonement rather than the Incarnation, but Newman suggests the necessity of imitating Christ, and to this end employs the analogy of human friendship to express the process by which the believer draws nearer to Him. Newman observes that "the gospel gives in the person of Jesus Christ a manifestation of the character of God. Let it be remembered that we cannot love any being till we in some degree know him." In this divine unveiling, example is more powerful than precept. For "we never think we know a person here below nor do we learn to love him, by being merely *told* of his goodness." Rather, we learn from his actions "instances of his virtue," as God has given us an instance in sending us Christ (S 2:383–84). In his Christmas sermon "Religious Joy" (1825) on Luke 2:10–11, in which the angel brings "good tidings of great joy," Newman is more overtly incarnational. Christ Himself, by taking on a lowly role, "altogether dishonoured what the world esteems," and hence the Incarnation brings us the highest good, the example of divine condescension that foreshadows heaven (PPS 8.17.1707–8).

Newman's fullest development of incarnational doctrine to date appears in the second of his Oxford University sermons, preached on Easter Tuesday 1830, "The Influence of Natural and Revealed Religion Respectively." This sermon marks a reaction against the high and dry school of theologizing that located the principle of assent in the head rather than the heart. It also crystallizes much of Newman's ongoing work on the fourth-century Arians, and hence can be taken as a kind of progress report. Newman describes the tradition of Natural Religion that instructs us in "the infinite power and majesty, the wisdom and goodness, the presence, the moral governance, and, in one sense, the unity of the Deity; but... gives little or no information respecting what may be called His *Personality*" (OUS 27–28). Natural Religion provides for some of our deepest and truest religious feelings, but what is missing is that tangible history of the Deity, the revelation of "His personal character" as an incentive to all right action. We see daily, says Newman, how even the most widely held and powerful cause requires "the definiteness of the practical impression which a personal presence produces" (28).

By 1830 Newman had recognized that the doctrine of the Incarnation offered a middle ground between the abstract God of philosophy and the degraded if intelligible God of paganism. Only revelation could "propose the Object in which they should both be reconciled" (OUS 29). Christ is "a second Creator of the world... as condescending to repeat... for our contemplation, in human form, that distinct personal work, which made 'the morning stars sing together, and all the sons of God shout for joy'" (30). Thus revelation presents us with "simple and distinct *facts* and *actions*, not with painful inductions from existing phenomena, not with generalized laws or metaphysical conjectures, but with *Jesus and the Resurrection*" (31). Newman knew, and many of his audience would also have known, Keble's poem for Quinquagesima Sunday in which Christ is the prism through which we see God, whose radiance is made bearable through "the rays that stream'd / From the mild Son of Man." In this sermon, Newman seems to have Keble's metaphor in mind when he says that Christ's life "brings together and concentrates" moral laws, truths that otherwise would "wander idle and forlorn over the surface of the moral world, and often appear to diverge from each other." The power of this phenomenon to collect scattered rays of light "into certain intelligible centres" is what is unique about Christian revelation. In place of the ancient philosophers' aspiration toward "a divine *principle*," the Christian substitutes a belief in "a divine *Agent*" (31). Not only do the scriptures refer moral excellence expressly to a supreme Being, but they also reveal the principle of Good that can be progressively enacted in our hearts and is embodied in a Person, "as if to mark strongly that it is not our own, and must lead us to no preposterous self adoration" (32). Nor is Christ the sole, though He is the supreme, embodiment of this belief. In Trinitarian doctrine, God and the Holy Spirit are also perceived as Persons. The forces of evil are similarly personified in Adam, who embodies the idea of original sin, and Satan, a very real and personal danger in Newman's sermons. The act of personation makes these evils intelligible.

Newman's acts of personation also apply to institutions and other collectivities. "The body of faithful men, or the Church, considered as the dwelling-place of the One Holy Spirit, is invested with a metaphorical personality, and is bound to act as one," to the practical purpose of "influencing and directing human conduct." The Episcopal system invests in its bishops "a personal type of Christ mystical, the new and spiritual man; a centre of action and a living witness against all heretical or disorderly proceedings" (*OUS* 32–33). This personification of the Church is an important step in the development of Newman's ecclesiology, as is its negative counterpart, the personality evinced by heretical movements. "It is the Incarnation of the Son of God rather than any doctrine drawn from a partial view of Scripture . . . which is the article of a standing or a falling Church. . . . And hence the Apostles' speeches in the book of Acts and the primitive Creeds insist almost exclusively upon the history, not the doctrines, of Christianity" (36).

Newman knew that this exposition of the idea of the Incarnation was inextricably caught in the web of human language with all its limitations. As he worked on his study of the fourth-century Arians, he told Hugh James Rose in a letter of August 1832 (excerpted in chapter 1) that "we cannot form an Idea of Personality except as viewed in action, passion, relation etc. . . . My conclusion is, that it is as difficult to conceive God one Person as Three, the difficulty being deeper than people suppose. The Personality of God, in our *notion* of personality, is a *mystery*" (*L&D* 3:78). The idea of God's Personhood can only be conveyed through actions a human being can understand.

The Arians

Newman's first book, *The Arians of the Fourth Century* (1833), was a shaping force in his development as a homilist and his future in the Tractarian Movement. Written originally in response to a request from Hugh James Rose for a history of the early Councils for Rose's Theological Library, it speedily took its own direction as the anatomy of a heresy, and because of both its theological implications and its failure to conform to the assignment, Rose rejected it and Newman found another publisher. The Arian history is very much a product of an academic imagination working in an academic environment. The casualness with which Newman threw off a number of contrarian statements, altogether alien to most non-Anglican Protestants and only somewhat less so to many Anglicans, suggests equally a conscious desire to shock and an unawareness of his audience.

Described by Stephen Thomas as "Newman's first novel" (*Newman and Heresy* 43), the history, in highly dramatic and personal terms, develops certain proto-Tractarian themes in historical context, such as the idea of Reserve, that is, the withholding of certain doctrinal truths from those not yet prepared to receive them, and the Economy, or the process by which such truths are partially unveiled, according to the readiness of the novice believer to receive them. In this respect the Arian history was strong meat for any Protestant: elitist in its tone, and all too redolent of "popish" concealment and mystery.

In its organization, the book traces the events leading up to and following the Council of Nicaea, which is placed at its physical center. The first half traces Jewish and Platonic backgrounds and the history of the Church's reluctance to commit itself to creedal statement. Alexandria and Antioch, Athanasius and Arius, orthodoxy and heresy are the defining poles of the combat. The good temper and candor of Athanasius is contrasted with the turbulence of Arius, the offender against order. The identification of character with belief is consistent throughout. Nowhere does Newman seem to recognize that a heretic might be quite sincere, and that what seems clear in the hindsight of later orthodoxy might not have seemed quite so self-evident in the earliest days of the Church.

In all heresy, Newman thought, lies the potential for a redefinition that would diminish the full Personality of Christ, human and divine, through inadvertence, theological haziness, indifference, or hostility. If that Personality sets the standard by which all of us judge and are judged as persons, then we, too, suffer a like diminution. Heresy, for Newman, always contains a partial truth, and is as dangerous for its incompleteness as for its explicit deviations from orthodoxy. For the Arians, the Son of God was a creature "made at God's good pleasure before the worlds, before time, after the pattern of the attribute Logos or Wisdom, as existing in the Divine Mind" (*Arians* 202). The "plain question" this view posed at Nicaea was whether the Son was good in as full a sense as the Father, or was only a creature whose substance had a "point of origin," that is, was secondary to the Father. Throughout the treatise, Newman discusses the apparent paradox that a Son and Spirit, in ministering to the Father, are thereby subordinate to Him, and yet equal to Him in nature. The mystery lies in our human inability to see the word *person* as "more than a mere character, yet less than an individual intelligent being" (*Arians* 155). Technical theological terms, Newman felt, tended to say either too much or too little.

In the Hebrew scriptures, Newman writes, the manifestations of divine presence and moral sovereignty were "singularly invested with the properties of personality" (*Arians* 153). In the New Testament, "the apparent Personality attributed to [the Word and Spirit] in the Old Testament, is changed for a real Personality, so clearly and explicitly marked as to resist all critical experiments upon the language, all attempts at allegorical interpretation." The Word is so personalized as the Son of God "as to be able voluntarily to descend from heaven, and assume our nature without ceasing to be identically what He was before; . . . though a man, as one and the same with the Divine Word who existed in the beginning" (153–54).

Scripture thus dramatizes the fact that "His Person could not be the same with that of the Father who sent Him, by any process of reasoning, which would not also prove any two individual men to have one literal personality" (*Arians* 126). But scripture by itself does not lay out principles of dogma. Trinitarian doctrine is "the shadow, projected for the contemplation of the intellect, of the Object of scripturally-informed piety." It is a doctrine "kept in the background in the infancy of Christianity, when faith and obedience were vigorous, and brought forward at a time when, reason being disproportionally developed, and aiming at sovereignty in the province of religion, its presence became necessary to expel an usurping idol from the house of God" (145). The uses of doctrine, however, are not merely defensive. The articulation of doctrine contributes actively to worship and thus to the tranquility of the mind, "the text of Scripture being addressed principally to the affections, and of a religious, not a philosophical character" (146).[9] Since scripture is unsystematic, "the faith which it propounds being scattered through its documents," the creeds concentrate the "general spirit" of scripture to provide security for the Church (147). A reluctance to impose a creed reflects the "highest state" of the early Christian community, but in the face of attack, the Church had no choice but to define its formularies, and thus risk the contemplation of its deepest truths by scoffers, heretics, and unbelievers. Newman seems to see the formulation of a creed as a Fall from the original innocence of the Church, which was compelled to resort to definitions and distinctions as a hedge against heterodoxy. Creeds, like Carlyle's "clothes" in *Sartor Resartus*, would appear to be a postlapsarian necessity.

Newman contrasts the reticence of the early Church with the promiscuous spoken and written theological disputation of a later era. He stresses the superiority of personal communication over books for the purposes of religious instruction, as he was to do more broadly in his writing on liberal education. Personality is better experienced by its physical presence than on the page. Herein lies the advantage of the first Apostles for whom Christ was physically present. And yet Christ, to bring Himself within the orbit of human understanding, had to practice that Economy which, under the circumstances, was a "gracious and considerate condescension to the weakness of His creatures" (*Arians* 77).

To the study of this period, Newman brought both a theory and a rhetorical method that were to be turned against him. The theory was the idea of the Economy and the closely related *disciplina arcana*, which his critics associated with shuffling and dishonest concealment. Newman's partisan zeal in defense of religious orthodoxy struck many contemporaries as akin to persecutorial animus. The doctrine of the Economy governs what the instructed can or cannot say, whether to novices or heretics, and the *disciplina arcana*, so to speak, controls the timing by which the beginner in religion is acquainted with successive and more complex truths. Newman writes combatively, as a partisan for orthodoxy, and the book is replete with cautions about the weaknesses of half-measures and the lukewarmness of mild-mannered people who are deficient in their practical judgment of heresy and fall into a false charity that leads them to hope for the best instead of opposing truth to falsehood. Heretical teachers must be stopped in their tracks before their false teachings damage others and endanger future generations. In this lies the difference between the treatment due to an individual in error, and to one who is confident enough to publish his reckless innovations. "The former claims from us the most affectionate sympathy and the most considerate attention. The latter should meet with no mercy; he assumes the office of the Tempter, and, so far forth as his error goes, must be dealt with by the competent authority, as if he were embodied Evil" (*Arians* 234–35). "Conciliatory measures" unaccompanied "by such a display of vigour as shows that concession is but condescension" are almost certain to backfire (281).

Newman was talking about the nineteenth century as well as the fourth, and readers recognized it. He tended to search the past for analogies to the present, and he found evidence in the Arian history for drawing parallels between Church parties then and now. Years later he came to identify the Anglicans with the semi-Arians of the fourth century (*A* 130). Inquisitorial language of the sort just cited was a rare phenomenon in the tempered and sometimes tepid exchanges of late eighteenth and early nineteenth-century Anglican apologetics. As we know from the *Apologia*, that passage in the Arian history elicited a letter of protest from "a Northern dignitary" accusing Newman of wanting to bring back the Inquisition. "I cannot deny that this is a very fierce passage," the older Newman wrote with mild amusement at his own youthful rhetoric, "but Arius was banished, not burned; and it is only fair to myself to say that neither at this, nor any other time of my life, not even when I was fiercest, could I have even cut off a Puritan's ears, and I think the sight of a Spanish *auto-da-fè* would have been the death of me" (*A* 53). But in highlighting certain dogmatic divides that seemed only likely to shatter the peace (or slumber) of the Church, Newman could have expected such remonstrances, especially had he paused to remember that issues that were life-and-death matters for him were not live questions for many fellow Anglicans. A balanced assessment of his achievement came from Richard Holt Hutton toward the end of the century, when earlier tempests had subsided. Though Hutton found the Arian history a "vigorous and strenuous work," he thought that an over-emphasis on dogma led to neglect of the core of revelation. "I think the book shows that to some extent Newman underrated this unfortunate effect of dogma on the most spiritual minds, and that he thought of dogma a little too much as the essence, instead of as the mere protective covering, of revelation" (Hutton 29–30).

Not only the tone, but the drift of the history troubled some contemporaries. The sixth of the Thirty-Nine Articles of Religion, a mainstay of Anglican doctrine and discipline since 1571, treats "Of the Sufficiency of Holy Scripture for Salvation." Was Newman not undercutting the authority of the Bible when he gave it a corollary, rather than predominating, authority as measured against the creeds? Bible Christians would have said yes, and this included many Anglicans. Newman could have pointed out to those Anglicans that the eighth of the Thirty-Nine Articles declared that the Creeds had their warrant in scripture and that the idea of the Trinity could be extrapolated from scriptural texts, read closely. Nonetheless, for Newman, scripture was not the whole standard of faith, the *sola scriptura* of the Evangelicals. The Bible was not intended to be probative of all points of doctrine or discipline. For many Victorians, the road from the Bible led in the direction of religious latitudinarian or agnosticism. Newman's road, by contrast, preserved scripture but did not subject it to a test of literalism which he predicted it would not survive. Tradition, the product of a body of believers including the Church Fathers, had its place as well.

Incarnational Preaching

Newman's study of the Arians contributed theologically to his homiletics, particularly in the Oxford University sermons, preached on what were as much academic as religious occasions and addressed to a sophisticated audience. By contrast, his *Parochial and Plain Sermons*, of which the first volume was published in 1834, were aimed (as the title suggests) at a broader audience, and belonged in a parish church rather than Christ Church Cathedral. In their totality these sermons, with their quiet biblical rootedness, amount to a blueprint for a realization of the Christian *ethos*. Newman's younger Anglican contemporary R. W. Church observed that it was the four o'clock sermons at St. Mary's, not the Tracts (and not, we would add, the University sermons) that were most influential in attracting support for the Movement (Church 129–30). The self-discipline taught by these sermons, Dean Church declared, "issued often in a steady and unconscious elevation of the religious character" (192).

Ferocity had no place in these sermons, but moral rigor did, and since Newman's time the austerity of the sermons has led such critics as Geoffrey Faber to declare that fear was "the driving-force of [Newman's] arguments." In Faber's view, they betrayed an Evangelical tendency to stress God's "condemnation and wrath" over His "love and mercy" (170–71). But there is little evidence in the contemporary descriptions of Newman's pulpit manner that he induced outright fear. Despondency was perhaps a more likely response, evoked by Newman's dramatization of the great gap between human aspiration and divine perfection. Certainly Baron Friedrich von Hügel thought so when he wrote to his niece in 1920, "I had thought of starting you on Newman's *Parochial and Plain Sermons*—certainly classics and well known to me. But then those sermons are rigorist—how they have depressed me! Just the opposite from Fénelon, who always braces me. And really, I cannot allow you to be depressed—at least I cannot organize depression for you" (von Hügel, *Letters to a Niece* 179).

Early Victorian contemporaries may sometimes have felt that way, and Newman himself was aware of the danger that he might predispose some of his younger hearers to despondency. In several variations of a lecture on confirmation that Newman gave between 1830 and 1841, he placed great emphasis on the danger of falling away from their confirmation vows. That danger, he thought, was especially acute in the case of younger persons who had not fully realized the seriousness of what they were undertaking. Christ's religion, he reminded his audience, is not gloomy, and some of the Prayer Book's most strenuous exhortations are really aimed at older witnesses who have fallen away from their own vows (S 3:68–71). But Oxford undergraduates of the 1830s and '40s, particularly those who had passed through the ministrations of a Dr. Arnold in their earlier years, were not today's undergraduates, and no doubt there were not a few, like James Anthony Froude, who remembered the sermons as both fascinating and fruitful in their ability to awaken aspirations to higher things, operating like "the springing of a fountain out of the rock" ("Oxford Counter-Reformation" 186). For Froude, the austerity posed a challenge rather than a depressant, perhaps the theological equivalent of a cold shower. It needs to be remembered also that Newman's sermons attracted a number of curiosity seekers, and this gave him the opportunity to address members of the "fast set" whose high living and low religious tone had appalled him in his undergraduate days at Trinity College.

Newman's Christmas sermon for 1834 on the Incarnation is an excellent specimen of his parochial manner. Next to the Oxford University sermon on the same topic, the style is simple and direct, though not always untechnical, and the treatment much more condensed. It involves a point made in his history of the Arian controversy: creedal expansion of the "reverent brevity" of such New Testament passages as his text for the day was a response to heretical derision. The creeds themselves "rouse in us those mingled feelings of fear and confidence, affection and devotion towards Him, which are implied in the belief of a personal advent of God in our nature, and which were originally derived to the Church from the very sight of Him" (*PPS* 2.3.246). The sermon translates into homiletic form the same balance struck in the treatise on Arianism: Jesus is not a vision or phantom, nor is he an ordinary man. His Divine Nature does not simply resemble God's; it partakes of God.

The same insistence on God as indwelling in us through Christ is evident in a sermon, "The Gospel Witnesses," that Newman preached two days later on 2 Corinthians 13:1: "In the mouth of two or three witnesses shall every word be established." St. Paul and the other Apostles do not exalt "a mere name or idea . . . but a Person, a really existing Master" (*PPS* 2.17.349). St. Paul's close agreement with the opening of John's Gospel is proof of the truth of a doctrine that could be agreed upon by such dissimilar men, not in "mere texts" but as "separate Witnesses" of the "Personality of the Divine Word." That witnessing certified the Christian character as grounded in love (its "essence"), and manifested in "resignation, and composure of mind, neither anxious for the morrow, nor hoping from this world—and its duties, almsgiving, self-denial, prayer, and praise" (356).

In Newman's developed view, as evidenced in "The Humiliation of the Eternal Son" (1835), the Incarnation is both a mystery and an aid to understanding. It bridges the divide between the believer and the ineffable mystery of the Trinity, which is beyond both our reason and our language, relating that mystery to subjects more accessible to that reason (*PPS* 3.12.583–93). Thus the phrase describing Jesus as "Son of God" is a mystery in its own terms, at best understood as meaning "more than a mere man," but it becomes accessible through analogy: We ourselves are described as sons of God (albeit only "adopted") and to that extent share in His Incarnation. Yet this real Son is indivisible from His Father. By becoming a servant and taking on a "lower nature," He embodies obedience and experiences humiliation. In echoing John's "the Word was made flesh," we must understand not that God selected a particular existing man to dwell in, but rather "that He became what He was not before, that He took into His own Infinite Essence man's nature itself in all its completeness" without "in any respect ceas[ing] to be what He was before" (588).

To Newman's way of thinking, such paradoxes—God as divine and human, all-powerful and a suffering servant, untemptable yet tempted—originate in mystery and can only partially be brought within the limits of the human mind. In the ensuing section of the same sermon, Newman lays out what is, in fact, a problem both of belief and of homiletics. "In truth, until we contemplate our Lord and Saviour, God and man, as a really existing being, external to our minds, as complete and entire in His personality *as we show ourselves to be to each other*, as one and the same in all His various and contrary attributes ... we are using words which profit not" (591, emphasis added). The theology of this latter day, "under the pretence of guarding against presumption, denies us what is revealed" (591). We must avoid dividing the earthly Jesus from the Christ, the anointed Son of God. For when such a bifurcation occurs, the learned are in danger of falling into unbelief, while the sentimentalists who preach "the so-called religion of the heart, without orthodoxy of doctrine" are unable to defend that doctrine (592).

In another (already mentioned) sermon of his early Tractarian period, "Tears of Christ at the Grave of Lazarus," Newman speculated (uncharacteristically) on why, aware as he was of the ultimate powerlessness of death, Christ should have wept at all before summoning Lazarus from the tomb. Newman would have deplored an Evangelical sermon on the subject as an indecorous probe into Jesus's mysterious inner life. His own sermon, however, an attempt to invest Christ with humanity, seems designed to perform an incarnative act through narrative. "Christ, the Son of God Made Man" (1836) likewise attributes humanly understandable motives to the Christ (*PPS* 6.5.1220–29). Drawing on Hebrews 9:11, "Christ being come, an High

Priest of good things to come, by a greater and more perfect tabernacle, not made with hands, that is to say, not of this building," Newman compresses the entire purport of the earlier Lazarus sermon in a discussion of God's mercy in taking on our nature. When Jesus prayed, it was not as a man supplicating God, but the Son addressing the Father under new circumstances. His tears at the grave of Lazarus, his regret at the Jews' hardness of heart, his anger and his compassion, all manifested the attributes of God "as if indirectly through the outlets of that manhood with which He had clothed Himself." When he spat on the ground to make clay and anoint the eyes of the blind man, "He exerted the virtue of His Divine Essence through the properties and circumstances of the flesh. When He breathed on His disciples and said, 'Receive ye the Holy Ghost,' He vouchsafed to give His Holy Spirit through the breath of His human nature" (1226). In all such actions His manhood was not a mere instrument or garment, nor was it merely entered into as a tabernacle from which He could depart at will. Rather "it was really taken into the closest and most ineffable union with Him" (1227).

Newman's incarnational theology, essentially in place by the early 1830s, spoke not only to eternal truths as he saw them but also to his own divided self. Torn between the largely unacknowledged desire for leadership and yearnings for a peaceful and unostentatious, uncontentious retreat, between self-assertion and self-abnegation, an oscillation physically reflected through the decade in his journeys between his rooms at Oxford and his retreat house at Littlemore, he found in the figure of Christ a resolution of competing impulses: the desire for mastery and the aspiration to servanthood.

If an insistence on personal holiness was at the core of both Evangelical and Tractarian theology, what distinguished them? For Newman, Tradition enriched worship and kept the believer from becoming focused solely on himself. The patristic idea of Personhood was different from those Evangelical ideas of individuality that, from a High Church perspective, often assumed an atomistic self-sufficiency. The revelation of Jesus for Newman was transmitted through Jesus himself but sealed with the achievements possible only in relationship, beginning with the Trinity and continuing through the early years of the Church. In the patristic tradition, "a 'person' is by definition a being in communion, a relational being who cannot be saved by himself alone" (Lossky 79). In consequence, a visible Church is a requisite, both as guardian of the faith and as a community of persons themselves incarnating a corporate body of Christ, not an invisible church of all true believers.

Looking at the Tractarian phenomenon in this way, today's scholar can see Tractarianism as another alternative Victorian vision of community, one which, Carlyle to the contrary, was no adherence to dead forms but to living doctrine, capable of bringing an atomized society together. But in the Tractarian program that remained to be named and was to be developed after Newman's return from Sicily, it seemed to many of the Evangelicals that the authority putatively granted to Tradition amounted to a disparagement of Holy Writ.[10] And Newman's abrasive tone, too often redolent of the peevish self-obsessed academic, did not help matters. Underneath the surface, and perhaps not so far beneath, the lines were being drawn, and academic disputation was bound to spill over into the larger culture, with consequences for a public still substantially made up of worshipping communities.

Polarities

Newman had concluded *The Arians of the Fourth Century* on a note of intermingled hope and anxiety. "And so of the present perils, with which our branch of the Church is beset, as they bear a marked resemblance to those of the fourth century, so are the lessons, which we gain from that ancient time, especially cheering and edifying to Christians of the present day." Heresy exists now as it did then, but "though the present tyranny [over the Church] has more of insult, it has hitherto had less of scandal, than attended the scandal of Arianism." Rejoicing in the "piety, prudence, and varied graces of our Spiritual Rulers," we may be confident that a present-day Athanasius and Basil will release the Church from its Erastian subjugation to the State (*Arians* 393–94).

The references to Athanasius and Basil suggest why Newman frequently turned to the writing of the lives of saints both as a relief from contemporary controversy and as a way of explaining it. Ever since his early reading in Milner, Newman had felt, in Carlyle's words, that history was "the essence of innumerable Biographies." The outcome of that view during the 1830s was reflected in a set of papers published in the *British Magazine* and subsequently gathered for *The Church of the Fathers*. It might better have been called *The Fathers of the Church*, because it is a series of portraits, not an institutional history. The friendship between Saints Basil and Gregory is a central topic, for the two together seem to represent the conflicting sides of Newman's own nature, the activist and the solitary. But these two in turn are distinguished from practical, bold, and worldly Fathers like Ambrose, Hildebrand, and Athanasius.

For Newman, biography was self-clarification. In his own life he had to confront a series of conflicts into which his mixture of passivity and aggressiveness led him. The Hampden controversy and the publication of Hurrell Froude's *Remains* were to be harbingers of the crises of the 1840s. The pugnacity Newman exhibited in these episodes was quite at odds with the ideal of the pastoral office he and fellow Tractarians attempted to popularize. His growing hostility toward contemporary Evangelicals within his own Church confirmed the view of many Churchmen of whatever stripe that he was the leader of just another party himself. In the 1830s, Newman was beginning an all-too-familiar pattern of burning as many bridges as he built.

The Movement's Beginnings

Despite the hopeful note struck at the end of the Arian history, Newman was already in a state of depletion when he began his journey to the Continent with the Froudes. Lying on board the Hermes off Corfu, he wrote to his sister Harriett that he could wish he were back in his rooms at Oriel stretched out on his sofa and "sporting the oak" on his door to warn away visitors. "After all, every kind of external exertion is to me an effort.... I shrink involuntarily from the contact of the world—and ... deliberately as I have set about my present wanderings, yet I heartily wish they were over, and only endure them; and had much rather *have* seen them than *see* them, tho' the while I am extremely astonished and almost enchanted at seeing them" (*L&D* 3:177–78). The double consciousness of enjoying what he sees even as he wishes the act of seeing to be behind him, to move immediately to the memory of an event without prolonging the event itself, is characteristic of the relentlessly autobiographical movement of Newman's mind. But he did not know, or disclaimed knowing, exactly how he might want to remember himself. Describing his seasickness in a letter to Isaac Williams, he declared, "I certainly am not cut out for a great politician, or as any instrument of change little or great in the Church, for it makes me wretched to be in motion—yet I suppose in these times we must all of us more or less expect to find our duty lie [sic] in agitation and tumult[.] I seemed to realize somewhat of the cross of that blessed Apostle who was in watchfulness and weariness so often, as I lay tossed in my luxurious berth in the steam packet" (*L&D* 3:193). The "agitation and tumult" that Newman sometimes craved is far from his mind; in the letter to Harriett, he evinces a strong revulsion against it.

Most readers know Newman's Mediterranean journey through the later testimony of the *Apologia* rather than through the journals, notes, and letters of the time. Those letters and the revisitation of his illness in Sicily in several manuscripts written after his return to England help to flesh out the inner uncertainties, the highly conflicted emotions that the *Apologia*, with its dramatic and purposive sense of forward movement, effectively reinscribes. The surviving evidence from the 1830s suggests that Newman's sense of alienation was caused more by the circumstances surrounding his departure from Oxford than by anticipations of the future. Writing shortly after his return to England on August 4, 1833, in the manuscript on the Sicilian journey, he associated his illness with a deep sense of guilt and anguish over what was finished, not what might be beginning. He feared that in his behavior toward Hawkins he had exhibited "the willfulness of my character generally" despite his sermon against willfulness preached the day before leaving Oxford. He found comfort only in the fact that "in bringing myself into my present situation, I had not . . . run counter to any advice given me, and I said, 'I have not sinned against light,' and repeated this often" (*AW* 118). The illness, if a verdict, carried a suspended sentence because, mysteriously, he had not "sinned against light." Newman's obsession with these words may merely mean that he worked by the best light he could find at the time. But considered more closely, the words also insulate his admittedly presumptuous behavior to Hawkins from the charge of a serious deviation from the light; he had been self-willed, but in the right cause.

While in Italy, Newman had conceived the idea of forming an "Apostolical Brotherhood," and when he returned to England five days before Keble's Assize Sermon, he found that "several zealous and able men had united their counsels, and were in correspondence with each other" (*A* 44). By August he was writing to J. W. Bowden with a newfound sense of energy and purpose: "We are just setting up here Societies for the Defence of the Church. We do not like our names known but we hope the plan will succeed. We have already got assistance in five or six counties." The Newman of the early days of the Movement is no longer the exhausted, self-doubting recluse of 1832, but the combative partisan reminding Bowden in the same letter that even the Apostles "did not sit still; and agitation is the order of the day" (*L&D* 4:34).

Central to Newman's own early conception of the Movement was that it was the work of individuals rather than committees, of spirit rather than organization. The reference to "several zealous men" already at work is one of his many later efforts to downplay the importance of his own agency. He told R. F. Wilson that societies ("the seeds of revolution") had been planted in various counties with the object of maintaining the doctrine of the Apostolic Succession and preserving the Liturgy from "illegal alterations" (*L&D* 4:44). The tone of the prospectus that he prepared on the subject put some of his correspondents on the alert. R. L. Cotton complained that "it sets the Association in such a light as rather to frighten men from it than attract them to it. . . . I should recommend that your Letter . . . not be circulated, and that in its place a simple statement of the *two [?] great objects of the Association* should be propounded with a calm but solemn and urgent appeal to the Clergy to support them."[1] Closer friends than Cotton took alarm for different reasons. Two years into the Movement, in November 1835, Pusey wrote anxiously about the new "Theological Society" to his wife: "It promises well, but I almost fear I see elements of disunion, in that John will scare people" (Liddon 1:336).[2]

Those of Newman's contemporaries who had read his study of the Arians might be forgiven for finding his disavowal of party intention somewhat disingenuous. After all, Newman had written there that "strictly speaking, the Christian Church, as being a visible society, is necessarily a political power or party. It may be a party triumphant, or a party under persecution; but a party it always must be, prior in existence to the civil institutions with which it is surrounded, and from its latent divinity formidable and influential, even to the end of time" (*Arians* 257–58). Newman now tacitly qualified this by describing the Movement as an "Association" built upon Gospel doctrines, and the word "Association" implies connection of a loose and shifting kind. The book is really about parties *within* the Church, which of course more accurately foreshadowed the direction of Newman's own activities. But if the party represented by the Oxford Movement purported to speak for a true church whose outlines had to be recovered from the debris of history and rescued from the Erastian heritage of the English Reformation, it was no longer a party in the narrow sense. Tractarians would make all men of their party, and their party would thereby *become* the Church.

Newman's views on boards and committees are akin to what Carlyle and Matthew Arnold respectively called "Mechanism" and "Machinery." In the *Apologia*, Newman was to claim he had never wavered from a preference for spontaneity over organization. He wrote that there was no obvious leader other than William Palmer, but that Palmer was a problematic leader because he had never "really grown into an Oxford man" (presumably the Dublin imprint was too strong) and could not see the importance of "the force of personal influence and congeniality of thought in carrying out a religious theory" (*A* 47). By contrast, "living movements," as Newman saw them, did not "come of committees, nor are great ideas worked out through the post, even though it had been the penny post" (46). The "far more essential unity" lay in common antecedents, memories, and continuing contact of mind with mind.

Newman tried to persuade Palmer of the necessity of reconciling the principle of individual personality with the demands of a common cause: "Individuals, who are seen and heard, who act and suffer, are the instruments of Providence in all great successes." Tracts coming from a society suggested an assumption of formal teaching, a common authority behind them, thus making them "cold and formal and impersonal," while greater weight would be given to a statement emanating from an individual mind. The formation of an Association assumed a very concrete and specific object that generalized references to the doctrine and discipline of the Church could not provide. "Thus gradually certain centres, in correspondence with each other, and of a proselytizing nature in their respective neighbourhoods, are formed" (*L&D* 4:68–69). Yet as with the earlier reference to the implantation of the new societies in various locales, the passive voice here suggests a disavowal of personal agency. To Arthur Philip Perceval, Newman wrote in July 1834 with respect to the Tracts that "every one has his own taste. You object to some things, another to others—If we altered to please everyone, the effect would be spoiled. They were not intended as symbols è Cathedra,—but as the expression of *individual* minds—and individuals, feeling strong, while ... incidentally faulty in mode or language, are still peculiarly effective. No great work was done by a system—whereas systems arise out of individual exertions" (*L&D* 4:308). Under this procedure, Newman thought, individuals took risks for themselves without implicating others in their opinions.

Writing a decade later in his retrospective *Narrative of Events Connected with the Publication of the "Tracts for the Times"* (1843), William Palmer analyzed the flaw in Newman's reasoning. Like Newman, Palmer felt that the dangers that faced the Church in 1833 required a concerted effort to combat, and he remained loyal to Newman even through the controversy over Tract 90 (chapter 4 below). But while recalling that the "general tendency" of the Tracts had "seemed good," Palmer also remembered being taken aback by "the rapidity with which they were composed and published, without any previous revision or consultation" and the presence of "language calculated to give needless offence" (120). At the time, he had tried to persuade Newman to exert his influence either to cease or to suspend publication until a "Committee of revision" could be appointed to review all the Tracts prior to publication. Newman's decentralist line of thinking, Palmer believed, was somewhat disingenuous, for "although it was true, that the Tracts were really only the production of individuals . . . yet still the mere circumstance of their being published *anonymously, in the same place,* and in a *series . . .* did, and would continue to impress the public with a belief, that they were *not* the writings of individuals—that they represented the doctrines held by our Association—and that we should be held responsible for all the statements contained in the Tracts" (121–22). To his mortification, his plea for pre-publication review fell on deaf ears.

Palmer admitted that he and those of his opinion did not interfere because they feared that such a breaking of the ranks would give an opening to their common foes. But he also saw that behind the anonymity and unchecked freedom of the individual writers of the Tracts, there was an incipient cult of personality, leading to just the party spirit the Tractarians claimed to avoid. A zealous desire to defend embattled leaders reflected a tendency to rely on human rather than divine guidance. For Palmer, a lack of charity and a suspension of loving intercourse with those whom the Tractarians stigmatized as "uncatholic" were true signs of a party spirit, as was the belief that "piety and goodness are restricted to one set of men in the Church" (139–40). But when Newman responded to Samuel Rickards's view that the Tracts were written in an "irritated and irritating spirit," that response, urging that the Tracts be read as part of a whole, undermined Newman's own defense of them as the products of individual minds (*L&D* 4:117).

Newman's account in the *Apologia* of the early days of the Movement, where he portrays himself as a largely passive leader, is either forgetful or self-deceived. Did he ever really understand the contrast between the public persona he thought he had adopted and the person others saw? A principle of antagonism had already begun to undermine his program, foreshadowing the later and finally decisive split between the Tractarians and the older High Church generation that might have remained allies.

Pugilist

In the early months of the Movement, it was Newman's friends who first felt the sting of his combativeness. But they could have reasonably expected it from the Arian history or from poems in which very little kindly light is manifest. In one such poem, "Zeal and Love," Newman declared that a scholar should resign his "easy dreams" and "learn . . . how to hate" if he is to achieve perfect love: "Hatred of sin, and Zeal, and Fear, / Lead up the Holy Hill; / Track them till Charity appear / A self-denial still" (lines 5–8). Such poems as "The Sign of the Cross," "The Patient Church," and "Jeremiah," all written before the end of that year, similarly commingle penitential thoughts with militant hopes. In "Jeremiah," the Hebrew prophet's temptation to leave behind the pains of prophecy for solace in "some silent vale" seems a projection of Newman's conflicts:

> If his meek spirit err'd, opresst
>   That God denied repose,
> What sin is ours, to whom Heaven's rest
>   Is pledged, to heal earth's woes? (lines 9–12)

The sonnet "Abraham" praises the imperviousness of those who commune "with God and not with each other," and in "The Greek Fathers" Newman portrays Clement, Dionysius, Origen, Basil, and Gregory Nazianzen as "tongues and weapons of His power" (line 5). "Flowers without Fruits" (1833) suggests that "he who lets his feelings run / In soft luxurious flow" will be incapable of undertaking hard service and will faint, unsoldierlike, "at every woe" (lines 5–8). And in another poem of the same month, "Zeal and Meekness," Newman strives to explain the paradox by which one must be peaceful and zealous at the same time. Though Christ "bade his followers take the sword," He also chided Peter for cutting off the servant's ear, for "meek hands alone may rear" the "sword of strife" (lines 5–6).

The term "zeal" recurs in Newman's sermons, reflecting an underlying theology of combat. In 1834 he preached sermons on "Jewish Zeal a Pattern to the Christian" and "Christian Zeal." The first of these is on the words of Deborah in Judges 5:31: "So let all thine enemies perish, O Lord, but let them that love Him, be as the sun when he goeth forth in his might." Newman defines zeal as "a strict attention to [God's] commands—a scrupulousness, vigilance, heartiness, and punctuality, which bears with no reasoning or questioning about them—an intense thirst for the advancement of His glory—a shrinking from the pollution of sin and sinners—an indignation, nay impatience, at witnessing His honour insulted—a quickness of feeling when His name is mentioned, and a jealousy how it is mentioned." Service to God must be rendered "at whatever sacrifice of personal feeling—an energetic resolve to push through all difficulties ... when His eye or hand but gives the sign." Even friends and relatives may take second place to this holy combat (*PPS* 3.13.595). A similar note is present in "Christian Zeal," on the text from John 2:17, "The zeal of Thine house hath eaten Me up," the words of Jesus driving the moneylenders from the temple. Here more briefly Newman describes zeal as "a love for the Truth and the Church so strong as not to allow that man should divide what God hath joined together" (*PPS* 2.31.468). This curious appropriation of a phrase from the marriage service to describe a highly divisive activity is followed by a simpler definition: "the earnest desire for God's honour, leading to strenuous and bold deeds in His behalf, and that in spite of all obstacles." In this Tractarian precursor of muscular Christianity, chivalric religious honor requires readiness to come to the defense of Christ, with zeal tempered only by the reverence a sinner owes to his Maker. Simon Peter himself, who came from the Zealot sect, turned his zeal to the Lord's service in just this way, thus escaping the judgment of Revelation against those who are "neither cold nor hot" (Rev. 3:15). Positive unbelief, indeed, was to be preferred to religious indifference, because of its power to aid a righteous cause.

For Newman, zeal is a healthy contrast to the religious sloth of his own day. In "Jewish Zeal," he argues that the more pacific passages of the New Testament do not lessen the need for an active temper of mind, even though the line should be drawn at physical violence. The mixture of "goodness and severity" in the character of Jesus seems for Newman to reflect the interdependence, not the contrariety, of the Old and New dispensations: "Meekness and charity are compatible with this austere and valiant temper of the Christian soldier" (601). In both sermons, such figures from the Hebrew scriptures as Deborah, Ezra, David, or Elijah are evoked as patterns for Christian action. In "Christian Zeal," he asserts, "It is the present fashion to call Zeal by the name of intolerance, and to account intolerance the chief of sins; that is, any earnestness for one opinion above another, concerning God's nature, will, and dealings with men" (471). By today's standards, the Apostles were among "the most intolerant of men," and St. Paul can be reckoned among their number for that particular virtue.

Newman's condemnation of lukewarmness strikes a familiar note in Christian apologetics. Dante had reserved a place in hell for the "neutrals" who lent themselves to no cause, and the theme appears in other sermons of the 1830s. In one from 1835, "Contest between Truth and Falsehood in the Church" (*PPS* 3.15), Newman goes so far as to argue that misplaced religious zeal, even if it were to lead to the destruction of the Church, is better than tepidity in the cause of right (618–19). In "Obedience without Love, as Instanced in the Character of Balaam" (1837), Balaam is a forerunner of a particularly modern type: "uprightness and conscientiousness" without a genuine desire to love and fear God. "Beware of trifling with your conscience," Newman warns his hearers. "It is often said that second thoughts are commonly best; so they are in matters of judgment, but not in matters of conscience. In matters of duty, first thoughts are commonly best—they have more in them of the voice of God" (*PPS* 4.2.755). Newman's tendency to make matters of conscience out of what others saw as questions of permissible individual judgment caused him many personal difficulties. Here he also suggests that once one's own conscience was clear, one might speak out without consulting anyone else's judgment. A more Protestant principle could hardly be imagined.

A complement to Newman's sermon on Balaam is "Tolerance of Religious Error," preached at the end of 1834. We live, according to Newman, in an age in which good taste, tolerance, even beneficence, advance at the expense of truth or at the risk of minimizing the very real exigencies of living the Gospel. In a rare lapse into the first person singular, Newman confesses, "I wish I saw any prospect of this element of zeal and holy sternness springing up among us, to temper and give character to the languid, unmeaning benevolence which we misname Christian love. I have no hope of my country till I see it" (PPS 2.23.409). To regard God's goodness only, and not His severity, is to disregard the fact that fear, as much as hope, is a component of true faith. In a frequently quoted passage in "The Religion of the Day" (1832), Newman declares, "I will not shrink from uttering my firm conviction, that it would be a gain to this country, were it vastly more superstitious, more bigoted, more gloomy, more fierce in its religion, than at present it shows itself to be" (PPS 1.24.205).[3] Newman sprinkles this line of argument with cautionary admonitions: one must never resort to violence, and zeal should be tempered in dealing with truly distressed souls. Nonetheless, "the more zealous a Christian is, therefore is he the more charitable" ("Jewish Zeal" 602). In "Christian Zeal," he reminds us that zeal is an imperfect virtue, "very apt to be self-willed; it takes it upon itself to serve God in its own way" (473). But "it is no faulty zeal to labour to preserve it in the form in which Christ gave it" (475). The occasional softening of tone does not really mitigate its overall severity.

Newman's line of argument has not only Dantean but biblical and patristic roots. In their introduction to Froude's *Remains*, Newman and Keble referred to Psalm 139:21, "Do I not hate them, O Lord, who hate thee? I hate them with a perfect hate," to justify their friend's combativeness. In Luke 14:26, Christ admonishes his hearers, "If any man come to me, and hate not his father, and mother, and wife, and children, and brothers, and sisters, yea, and his own life also, he cannot be my disciple." And in book 1, chapters 9 and 10, of *The City of God*, Augustine had written of sinful men of "detestable wickedness and impiety" and our guilt in evading our responsibility "to instruct and admonish them, sometimes even with sharp reproof and censure" (15). If "the good and the wicked are equally afflicted," it is because the love of temporal things makes even the good less eager to reprove others or to be "unsparing in their condemnation of sin" (17).

Newman may have felt that he successfully separated the personal respect he felt for a worthy opponent from the outrage with which he reacted to a violation of principles, but not all those whom he affronted felt that he had done so.[4] In "The Duty of Self-Denial" (1830), he distinguishes hatred from anger and explains why the latter is to be avoided. Anger is not always a sin—Jesus himself became angry—but it is a danger for fallen man to indulge in it; it brings on other sins and poisons the soul. Hatred, by contrast, is "that perfect distaste for an object, that you wish it put away and got rid of; it is to turn away from it, and to blot out the thought of it from your mind" (*PPS* 7.7.1475). Attachments that may be good in themselves must be sternly put away in order to respond to a higher call, if it comes. In this context, hatred is simply a form of deliberately avoiding certain persons (1476). He put this into practice even within his own family. After a spat with his brother Frank, he wrote to his sister Jemima in 1837, "What a very uncharitable thing it is, his saying I want to make a sect. I say nothing of *him*, I judge him in no way. I only say that God tells me to avoid persons who make divisions—and he makes a division" (*L&D* 6:24). His anger only hardened over time. In the *Apologia*, he wrote more unsparingly of the same event, "I would have no dealings with my brother, and I put my conduct upon a syllogism. I said, 'St. Paul bade us avoid those who cause divisions; you cause divisions: therefore I must avoid you'" (53). Frank had every reason to be more than annoyed at this family matter being aired so publicly.

Newman's attack on the orthodoxy of Renn Dickson Hampden's Bampton lectures offers an example of how he acted on his own precepts. His pamphlet *Elucidations of Dr. Hampden's Theological Statements* (1836) was designed to derail Hampden's pending appointment as Regius Professor of Divinity at Oxford. Newman's pamphlet was regarded by many then, and not a few now, as the product of personal jealousy, for Hampden had replaced Newman as one of the dismissed tutors at Oriel in the wake of the debacle with Hawkins. The first and most influential of Newman's critics into the fray was Thomas Arnold, whose article in the *Edinburgh Review*, "The Oxford Malignants and Dr. Hampden," was, as was customary in periodicals of the day, given its running title by Francis Jeffrey, the editor. It was a raw title for a raw polemic, but no evidence exists that Arnold ever objected to it. Arnold's attack evinced an entire absence of interest in the very real theological questions at issue between Hampden and Newman, regarding the status of tradition and the patristic writings in the light of the Gospel dispensation, and (to the embarrassment of some of Arnold's allies) showed him to be thoroughly capable of descending to the same ad hominem methods that he imputed to his Tractarian opponents (Stanley 2:7–10).

Arnold had a score of his own to settle. Several years before, the rumor had reached him that Newman had questioned "whether Dr. Arnold was a Christian."⁵ Arnold's indignant response on that occasion to his representative, Anthony Grant, had set the stage for the later battle with the "Malignants":

> I confess that my feeling in this matter is nothing personal to N. but refers to that party to which he has attached itself [sic]. When they talk and write as if they alone were humble and devout followers of Christ, imputing unscrupulously to those who differ from them all sorts of unworthy motives[,] ... they should at least be required to explain what they mean: that so their charges may have the weight that belongs to the intellectual character of their authors, and may not acquire an adventitious force by being understood according to the plain meaning of the words, and so believed the more readily for their very heinousness,—in as much as no good man could be supposed to utter them lightly. (L&D 4:108)

Arnold defends Hampden by arguing that the real nature of a man's religious views is to be collected from his general pastoral preaching to his own congregations, not from lectures on a particular subject "of an abstract and unimpassioned character." Hence the "elucidator" had given "an utterly inadequate and unjust view of Dr. Hampden's character" by concentrating on the different views of "the influence of the scholastic philosophy on Christianity" ("Oxford Malignants" 231). Though these conspirators had been baffled for the time being by the firmness of the proctors, Arnold felt there was no doubt they would return to the attack. "Meanwhile, we may be thought to have given undue importance to these Oxford squabbles, and to have unwisely gratified the vanity of a few obscure fanatics by noticing them in this Journal. The *individuals*, indeed, are sufficiently insignificant;—nor shall we, by naming them, confer on them that notoriety for which nature has not designed them. But the *party*, unworthy as it is, is yet strong enough to be mischievous" (233). In describing the group as a party, Arnold signaled his belief that the action of the Malignants was part of a larger reaction against progress and reform. He attacked their motives, their fanaticism, their obsession with ecclesiastical trappings and superstitious adherence to "the form of Episcopal government, without the substance." They constituted a "Judaizing" party resembling the "zealots of circumcision and the ceremonies of the law" in St. Paul's day (233–34). They substituted slander and vilification for proper intellectual debate, hiding under the cloak of anonymity and finding their strength in the "fanatical persecution" of a good man.

No tears need be shed on behalf of Hampden, who proved perfectly capable of attending to his own best interests.[6] Nor were the Tractarians alone in their judgment of him; Evangelicals took umbrage at Hampden's "anti-dogmatic use of scripture," and some moderates had questioned the rationalistic tone of the lectures (Nockles, "'Lost Causes'" 230). Arnold's bitterness persisted into his last year of life, and it had much deeper roots than the Hampden controversy. To an old pupil, probably Arthur Stanley himself, he wrote in October 1841 that "my feelings towards [a Roman Catholic] are quite different from my feelings towards [a "Newmanite"], because I think the one a fair enemy, the other a treacherous one. The one is the Frenchman in his own uniform, and within his own praesidia; the other is the Frenchman disguised in a red coat, and holding a post within our praesidia, for the purpose of betraying it. I should honour the first, and hang the second" (Stanley 2:289). Thus early were rumors circulating that Newman had already gone over to the enemy.

Newman's zest for fray was whetted rather than set back by such episodes. There is no evidence that he ever regretted his reaction to Arnold's or Hampden's liberalizing tendencies, and when it came to the Evangelicals (whom he now stigmatized as the "Peculiars"), he looked forward to the publication of his book on the prophetical office of the Church in early 1837 with almost gleeful anticipation at the blows it would deal to the latter party. "It seems to me like hitting the Peculiars etc. a most uncommon blow in the face," he told his sister Jemima. "Pusey however compared it to a blow that takes the breath out of one. He says they will be so out of breath as not to be able to answer—and that before they recover, one or other of us must give them another" (*L&D* 6:6). Newman seems to have had a particular dislike for Anglican Evangelicals because he thought they should know better. It was easier to dismiss Dissenters uncharitably, as in a sermon of 1835, as "full of self-importance, irreverence, censoriousness, display, and tumult" ("Religious Worship a Remedy for Excitements," *PPS* 3.23.700).

In his later years Newman was more temperate, but an underlying premise remained unchanged. In 1868 a correspondent had invoked the text "Beati pacifici" to ask Newman whether it was right to "strive" within the Church. Newman agreed that "it is desirable not 'to strive—' in the sense in which the Apostle so speaks—but it must be recollected that the very first and principle [sic] of the Tract movement was 'Truth before peace—'... If the first Tractarians had taken this divine beatitude as their only rule, perhaps Ritualism now would not exist, and if you carry it out yourself you will give up the prospect of converting the Wesleyans or Dissenters" (*L&D* 24:172). That Wesleyans or Dissenters would have been favorably impressed with Newman's methods, however, seems at best a highly dubious proposition, even though one of Newman's earlier mottos, "Holiness rather than Peace," had come from the unimpeachably evangelical Thomas Scott.

In the Oxford boxing ring, the posthumous publication of Hurrell Froude's *Remains* led to a battle that could never have ended well, and in the event, it effectively put an end to the uneasy Evangelical-Tractarian alliance that from time to time had functioned in response to events of common concern, as in the Hampden affair (Nockles, "'Lost Causes'" 234–35). Writing to John Bowden in October 1837 before publication of the *Remains*, Newman exulted that "a fresh instrument of influence is being opened by these Papers. They do certainly portray a saint. They bring out, in the most natural way, an *ethos* as different from what is now set up as perfection as the East from the West. All persons of unhacknied [sic] feelings and youthful minds must be taken by them—others will think them romantic, scrupulous, over refined etc. etc." (*L&D* 6:145). Newman did anticipate some criticism, telling S. L. Pope that "unless I was pretty well used to it by this time, I would have enough to annoy me" (6:178). Both Newman and Keble, the joint editors of the project, either underestimated the almost complete disjunction between their assessment of Froude's personality and the portrait that emerged in the *Remains*, or were motivated by a sense of mischief perhaps more characteristic of Newman than Keble. Their biggest mistake lay in thinking that the full personality of their friend would emerge in all its remembered charm and persuasiveness.

It doesn't. What Newman labeled "romantic" or even saintly in Froude is likely to strike readers now as, at best, humorless and egocentric scrupulosity. Froude's papers reveal a man almost entirely engrossed in himself, for whom other people seem hardly more than stage props. In their preface, Newman and Keble rather defensively argued that it was right to publish the thoughts of a person unable to realize the full potential of his influence in his own lifetime, but the result is more of an outing of Froude than a monument to him.[7] Having defended their right, indeed obligation, to publish, they stated that "if there be any who are startled at the strong expressions of self-condemnation . . . he will please to consider that the better any one knows the more severely will he judge himself, and since this writer sometimes thought it his duty to be very plain-spoken in his censure of others, in fairness to him it seemed right to show that he did not fail to look at home."[8] Froude's sole modern biographer, Piers Brendon, in echoing the hopes of Newman and Keble, has revisited this line of defense by suggesting that any opinion that Froude was priggish and high-handed needs to be anticipated by his "self-abasing awareness of his own unworthiness" (Brendon 12). Perhaps so, but this line of argument is a two-way street. As the case of Newman himself shows, harshness toward oneself does not guarantee a compensating tenderness toward others. Hurrell's angularities, as Brendon aptly calls them, do not comport easily with the claim that he was a remarkably "zealous, chivalric, self-sacrificing nature" (196), though we can allow the word "zealous" to stand.

Resolved to make an icon of his friend, Newman little knew that his and Keble's textual memorial would evoke a counter-memorial, the actual monument to the martyrs of the English Reformation (Latimer, Ridley, and Cranmer) that stands to this day in the form of George Gilbert Scott's sculpture (1843) at the south end of St. Giles. Newman's one-time friend and now opponent C. P. Golightly undertook to embarrass the Tractarians by initiating a very public subscription for the memorial in 1839, thus taking the battle out of the library and into the streets. Had they seen the nervous letters exchanged by Newman, Pusey, and Keble as to whether they should subscribe or risk being branded as Romanists, the anti-Tractarians would have been even more gleeful at their counterpunch. Two could play at Newman's game, and, in a harbinger of what was to occur over the next six years, his opponents were newly emboldened.

Pastor

The pugnacity of the Tractarians in ecclesiastical controversy seems quite at odds with their stated ideal of the pastoral office. In the exercise of that office, personal influence is exercised precisely through the suppression rather than expression of a particular ethos. We should "think of Christ's ministers," Newman wrote in a sermon delivered several times in the 1830s, "not their *personal* characters, but in their *office*, to consider them, just as the baptismal water itself and the bread and cup in the Lord's supper, as mere instruments—as part of one great divine institution, the Church" (*S* 4:106).⁹ Tract 29, *Christian Liberty; or, Why Should We Belong to the Church of England?*, illustrates the point. It was written by John Bowden, Newman's earliest friend at Oxford, who narrates here the imaginary history of John Evans, a layman tempted to abandon the parish church for the Dissenting meeting house. Well-intentioned but clearly in need of a Tractarian talking-to, Evans is impressed by the preacher's energetic and vehement preaching, together with his appearance of earnestness in the holy cause of God. "Compared with the fervor of this man, the quiet but sound discourses of his Rector seemed spiritless and tame, and John came out of the meeting under the influence of such enthusiastic feelings, as led him to resolve to visit it again the first opportunity" (Tract 29:2). But the kindly rector, Dr. Spencer, persuades him of his error and the need for a visible Church community, rather than a reliance on the ministrations of forceful individuals.

Newman certainly did not discountenance the practice of private, even impromptu prayer. As a Roman Catholic he also took increasingly to preaching from notes rather than a prepared text. But his Tractarian views are couched in the context of the Visible Church in which preaching, prayer, and sacraments represent a communal ideal rather than the reign of vehemence and idiosyncrasy that the Tractarians laid at the door of Evangelical preaching. Bowden's portrait of the unassuming rector embodies Newman's views on the exemplary functions of the pastoral office. Even in private confessions, forms offered a protection to both priest and parishioner. When in June 1834 Newman wrote to R. F. Wilson on the difficulties of the parochial charge, he gave especially characteristic advice on the tending of the sick. Wilson, Newman said, should not reproach himself for feeling distant from a sick person at the time of a first visit. Not words but *"the sight of your earnestness"* will impress the sick person "with the *reality* of what makes you earnest." Daily attendance at the bedside, the sacrifice of one's own "ease," mildness of manner, will all demonstrate to a dying man "the next world *as a fact* before he gains perhaps any definite knowledge of the way of salvation.... Doubtless you will be all the while teaching him more or less of the matter of revelation—but I lay a stress upon this to show that you need not fear you are doing no good, on the mere ground you know not what to say" (*L&D* 4:281–82). Three years later, Newman wrote to Lord Lifford in response to Lifford's objection to Newman's sermon "Self-Contemplation." Imagine a situation, Newman said, in which a clergyman of the "modern school" visits a dying parishioner. He probes her conscience with leading questions about the state of her mind, rather than drawing on the service for the Visitation of the Sick, which begins with the articles of the Creed and continues with an exhortation to repentance, forgiveness, and the making of amends. In Newman's view, recourse to ritual and set words of prayer provided privacy more charitable than a personal appeal to arouse the sufferer to weigh her own state. The well-known words of the Book of Common Prayer, he thought, carried their own sufficient earnestness and reflected a shared, communal tradition in which others have preceded us. Recourse to such aids is far more consoling, and more Christian, than demands that the dying person fall back on her own resources for self-examination and preparation for death (*L&D* 6:131–32).

Newman's idea of self-effacement, illustrated by Bowden's quiet rector, Dr. Spencer, is not only a function of personal modesty in keeping with familiar and consoling ritual, but also a practical consequence of the Tractarian doctrine of Reserve.[10] Newman's early development of the idea in his Arian history was connected to the need of the primitive Church for self-protection against the prying of the unfaithful. But the vestiges of the idea may have survived in the old High Church party's views of decorum, brevity, and logic. In the previous century, William Paley (hardly a member of the Tractarian brotherhood) had written on the "morality of the Gospel," in the course of which he pointed out that "our Lord's discourses in their *negative* character are significant for what they do not tell us, whether of the invisible world or of the next life." Though Jesus affirms rewards and punishments as an attribute of the latter, "as to the rest, a solemn reserve is maintained." For Paley, reserve (in its more general sense) is an antidote to the "enthusiasm" of much Dissenting worship, and though like Newman himself he admired genuine manifestation of piety of the sort practiced among Methodists, Paley found their rhetoric out of keeping with the method of that gentlemanly High Churchman Jesus, whose "calmness," "sobriety," and "good sense" lent authority to his discourses (Paley 2:60–64). Reserve as restraint is rather less forceful than the Tractarian idea of Reserve as a badge of holiness and a guardian of religious mysteries, but Newman would not have discountenanced Paley's use of the term.

In the Arian history, Newman had associated Reserve with the idea of the Economy, the process by which certain forms of religious knowledge are only gradually unveiled as the Christian catechumen progresses. Isaac Williams's Tracts 80 and 87, *On Reserve in Communicating Religious Knowledge* (1838 and 1840) are sometimes taken as the locus classicus for the doctrine, arguing as they do that the manner by which God reveals Himself is based on the receptivity of the human heart and intellectual capacity of the individual, but Williams was merely drawing out in more popular (and, as a consequence, more controversial) form the nexus of ideas that Newman had developed a decade earlier. Newman felt that the function of the sermon was to witness to hearers rather than to convert them. To witness was not to unveil the self, but to stand in as the spokesman for revealed truth, exhibiting in one's own rhetorical demeanor the self-sufficiency of the Gospels as patterns for action, just as a set liturgy was sufficient for communal prayer. In the thirteenth of the *Lectures on Justification* (1838), "On Preaching the Gospel," Newman was in many respects merely restating what he had learned from his youthful perusal of John Bird Sumner's *Apostolical Preaching*, in which Sumner (who represented an older generation of Evangelicals) subordinated eloquence to "piety, earnestness, and diligence." For Sumner, eloquence could be a positive hindrance to the preacher's usefulness. If he is to be faithful to scripture, "he must put off all sense of personal importance, and assume the character of his office; he must forget himself and remember only his situation as the messenger of Christ" (Sumner 10). Newman echoed Sumner when he declared that "the true preaching of the Gospel is to preach Christ" (*LOJ* 325), not to rely on words and vehement eloquence to bring the hearer *to* Christ. He went on to declare:

> True faith is what may be called colourless, like air or water; it is but the medium through which the soul sees Christ; and the soul as little really rests upon it and contemplates it, as the eye can see the air. When, then, men are bent on holding it ... in their hands, curiously inspecting, analyzing, and so aiming at it, they are obliged to colour and thicken it, that it may be seen and touched. That is, they substitute for it something or other, a feeling, notion, sentiment, conviction, or act of reason, which they may hang over and doat upon. (336)

One infers from this that true preaching must also be very nearly "colourless," as opposed to Evangelical preaching generally, which Newman rather unfairly described to James Stephen in March 1835 as "rudeness, irreverence, and almost profaneness ... making a most sacred doctrine a subject of vehement exclamation, an instrument of exciting the feelings" (*L&D* 5:45). Newman conceded to Samuel Wilberforce that "my Sermons are not adapted to *influence*; first I have selected them on purpose on a different principle, next the Christian preacher using his own words cannot dare hope to be more than a Baptist preparing the way for the Gospel" (5:21). A somewhat more considered statement of the same view appears in a letter to the Marquise de Salvo written not long after Newman's reception by the Roman Catholic Church. "To argue and preach out of place is just the way to disgust Englishmen with religion. I feel more and more as regards myself ... that the *fact* that I have become what I am is a preaching—that my presence is an exhortation. The sight of a convert is the most cogent and withal the most silent and subduing of arguments.... It was said that our Saviour should not strive, nor cry, nor lift up His voice—He *drew* hearts where they were to be drawn" (11:224). Newman is now addressing a Roman Catholic, not an Anglican, correspondent, but his point is the same. This time, however, it was directed at the suspicion of his new co-religionists that he was not serious about bringing about other conversions.

As early as November 1829, Newman was citing Hooker to the effect that "the sermon is far inferior in dignity to the prayers," and arguing that while preaching had been necessary in an earlier day to "rouse a world slumbering in sin," it was not as urgent a matter now that the Church was formed, for "His Spirit speaks neither by miracle nor preaching, but quietly and without observation" (*ECH* 2:111).[11] Preaching carried with it the temptation to curry favor and enhance one's reputation; it was at best an adjunct, not a substitute for direct ministrations, which can be tailored to the individual temper of the recipient, and for the sacraments of the Church. A parish priest lives out his role in service, "waiting on God in a daily perusal of the Bible which is in fact absolutely necessary for our arrival at any sound knowledge of divine truth" (*S* 1:21).

The very title of Sumner's treatise, *Apostolical Preaching*, is an index to Tractarian principle, though Sumner was no High Churchman. According to Hurrell Froude in "The Duty of Following the Guidance of the Church" (1831), the claims of the apostolically ordained are based on their authority or commission, not their personality. In fact, as Froude puts it, the danger lies the other way, in allowing the power of persuasion to decide whether a clergyman says the things the church member would like to hear. Froude grounds this claim on 2 Timothy 3:14, in which Paul claims credit not for his excellent rhetoric or human wisdom, but on the concrete evidence of God's power through miracles. It is thus not relevant by Froude's lights whether the congregation is pleased or even convinced by "mere evidence" (*Remains* 1.2.230–43). On September 21, 1833, in his tract *Adherence to the Apostolical Succession the Safest Course*, Keble chimed in with a similar admonition: the clergy is commissioned by God through Episcopal agency, not just expediently appointed as by a presbytery. As Newman so often did, Keble employs the analogy of a parent or "dear friend in another hemisphere" who, upon returning home, would not want to find that his delegation of trust had been abused in his absence. Adherence to the Apostolical church should be based "not merely on civil or ecclesiastical grounds, but from real personal love and reverence, affectionate reverence to our LORD and only SAVIOUR" (Tract 4:6). Thereby the faithful are strengthened in daily acts, but above all by the reception of the Sacraments.

In Tractarian thought, then, the studied avoidance of "effects" in sermons is complemented by reliance on set forms of prayer rather than extempore addresses to God. In several sermons from 1831 and 1832, such as "Profession without Hypocrisy," "Profession without Ostentation," and "Knowledge of

God's Will without Obedience," Newman defended set forms of prayer as protection against self-display on the one hand and discontent or despondence about one's ability to pray on the other. Extemporaneous prayer was by no means a measure of a true Christian; indulgence in it might signal an abandonment of fixed forms of prayer in a search for something more personally meaningful, and might be merely a first step toward abandoning prayer altogether. According to Newman, God requires only faithful obedience in those who come to Him, bringing nothing but their confession of sin to the altar. Common prayer in which all participate builds up the body of the faithful; it does not leave individual believers at sea or in perplexity as to how to exercise their own religious imagination. In "Knowledge of God's Will without Obedience," Newman attributes some worshippers' preference for the sermon to the fact that they find prayer too difficult. A sermon conveys knowledge; prayer is not passive receptivity to another's words (though it may involve waiting receptively on God), but it requires an act of obedience as well as a reaching-out (*PPS* 1.3.26).

Christians who receive the Gospel "literally on their knees" manifest a spirit very different from "that critical and argumentative spirit which sitting and listening engender," Newman wrote to James Stephen in the letter previously cited (*L&D* 5:46). A humble act of devotion is an entire submission to God's will, characteristic of the saint who strives to please and obey God and imitate Christ in every act. In "The Visible Church for the Sake of the Elect" (1836), Newman describes the saint as "unconscious of what his endowments are, and what they make him in God's sight" (*PPS* 4.10.833). It is not self-assertion, but self-effacement, approaching transparency, that Newman held up as the most potent form of personal influence. In a Christmas Day sermon ("Christ Hidden from the World," 1837) on the verse from the opening chapter of St. John, "The light shineth in darkness; and the darkness comprehended it not," Newman pressed the difference between worldly persons who maintained a decent and sober exterior and those who could not be distinguished from them on the surface but nonetheless were unworldly. "Though we have no right to judge others, but must leave this to God, it is very certain that a really holy man, a true saint, though he looks like other men, still has a sort of secret power in him to attract others to him who are like-minded, and to influence all who have any thing in them like him" (*PPS* 4.16.889).

While loyal adherence to the rites of the Church provided a check to what might otherwise become individual self-indulgence, preaching, dependent as it was on the individual personality of the preacher, could easily violate the communal spirit built up through prayer. This is why, though Newman regarded preaching as subordinate to catechesis, prayer, pastoral care, and the administration of the Sacraments, he seems to have prepared his own sermons with exceptional care. At the heart of his beliefs on how homilies could best fulfill their appropriate function was his idea of the Christian temper. In "The Gospel Witnesses" (1834), he describes how various witnesses to the faith, as apparently disparate as St. Paul and St. James, are really unified in their testimony on such questions as Eternity or "the Personality of the Divine Word." By understanding this underlying unity, we are enabled "more clearly to ascertain the main outlines of the Christian character; for instance, that love is its essence,—its chief characteristics, resignation, and composure of mind, neither anxious for the morrow, nor hoping from this world—and its duties, almsgiving, self-denial, prayer and praise" (*PPS* 2.17.356). Newman was enjoining a common duty on clergy and laity. "Guilelessness" (1831) is based on Jesus's words at his first sight of Nathaniel: "Behold, an Israelite indeed in whom there is no guile" (John 1:47). In its defense of simplicity and unworldliness, the sermon faintly anticipates the later sermon "Wisdom and Innocence," which incurred Kingsley's wrath for its apparent justification of duplicity, but in "Guilelessness," Kingsley's serpent is missing from the picture. For Newman, to be without guile is "to love without dissimulation, to think no evil, to bear no grudge, to be free from selfishness, to be innocent and straightforward" (*PPS* 2.27.442). Guileless men lack no security in a wicked world, for they are free from "the tyranny of . . . base thoughts" and are without recollections of former sin. Hence they are free from the bondage and fear of the irreligious. Possibly such men "have not received a learned education, and cannot talk fluently; yet they are ever a match for those who try to shake their faith in Christ by profane argument or ridicule, for the weakness of God is stronger than men" (443). Innocence must, to be sure, be supported by "prudence, discretion, self-command, gravity, patience, perseverance in well doing," but innocence is the first requirement for possessing the rest.

For Newman, priestly influence was most centrally exercised in Eucharist celebration, when the priest reenacted Christ's self-sacrifice in the Last

Supper. In the previously cited letter to James Stephen, which remains a crucial document in our understanding of how the Tractarians viewed the pastorate, he wrote, "I would persuade and win over by the tenderness and mysteriousness of our ordinances, while I prepared for them and guarded them by the severity of preaching" (*L&D* 5:47). Austerity and rigor (both in doctrine and in self-suppression) were always to be balanced by the common devotional temper that the rites and ordinances of the Church were designed to subserve.

The Slippery Slope: From Evangelicalism to Liberalism

A more serious issue was at the heart of Newman's dislike of the self-probing that he ascribed to the Evangelical temper. That larger issue was his growing conviction that the present-day Evangelical system tended ultimately toward skepticism, whether rationalist, Socinian, or latitudinarian. In this respect he followed a well-known line of argumentation that has been traced back to the eighteenth-century writer John Bowles, who argued in reference to the Unitarian movement of the 1770s and 1780s that the advocacy of private judgment and scripture as the sole and sufficient guide to faith (*sola scriptura*) had been "more injurious to the interests of Christianity, than even the arrogant pretensions and daring usurpations of the Church of Rome" (Nockles, *Oxford Movement* 107). In the *Apologia*, Newman was to write that "the Evangelical party itself, with their late successes, seemed to have lost that simplicity and unworldliness which I admired so much in Milner and Scott. It was not that I did not venerate such men as Ryder, the then Bishop of Lichfield, and others of similar sentiments ... but I thought little of the Evangelicals as a class. I thought they played into the hands of the Liberals" (40). Newman's employment of the term "Liberals," here as in most of his work, refers not to a political party but to a particularly irreligious, because undogmatic, freedom of inquiry.[12] Just as Evangelicalism, in Newman's view, pried intrusively into the believer's heart, requiring an unhealthy self-searching to ascertain the extent of one's own redemption, so did Liberalism as a form of theological inquiry pry indecorously into the meaning of terms. For Newman, Liberalism was the halfway house between Evangelicalism and unbelief. To Walter Farquahar Hook, the High Church vicar of Leeds who had mentioned the writings of Frederick Denison Maurice, Newman, though he correctly identified Maurice as a Coleridgean rather than an Evangelical, wrote that Maurice was "of the Cambridge School—and from the little I have seen of those men, they seem to me never satisfied to take things as they find them, but to be always meddling and (as they think) improving truths which have been from the beginning—and to believe sacred doctrines, not because they have received them, but because they can prove them from philosophy." Though he understood Maurice himself to be a man of high character, he wished that all such men might have more of "childlike faith" (*L&D* 5:180). In "Apostolical Tradition," an essay written the following July, Newman asked rhetorically, "Does not, then[,] . . . the theory that Scripture only is to be made the guide of Protestants, lead them to a certainty, when it is mastered, to become liberals?" In such an instance, it is likely "that the definition of a Christian will be made to turn not on faith in the doctrine, but on faith in the document, and Unitarianism will come to be thought, not indeed true, but not unreasonable, not unchristian, not perilous."[13] For Newman, the Evangelical appeal to the heart is really an appeal to human, not divine, standards.

In a powerful revisionist reading of these years of Newman's life, Frank Turner has argued that in the *Apologia* and thereafter, "Newman assiduously recast the Tractarian attack on evangelical religion into a struggle against liberals and liberalism whose victim at Oxford he claimed to have been." In this argument, "Newman transformed the liberalism of the 1830s into something to be deplored in 1864 by both Roman Catholic and Protestant audiences" (Turner 9). Whereas in *Certain Difficulties Felt by Anglicans in Catholic Teaching Considered* (1850) Newman had placed the blame for his defeat more directly on evangelical Anglicanism, this did not give him cover of the sort that the *Apologia*, with its shift of the blame to liberalism, promoted. "In almost no serious instance," avers Turner, "did he associate liberalism during the Tractarian era with secular rationalism or secular critical thought which was the chief connotation of liberalism in Victorian intellectual life during the second half of the century" (10–11).

No doubt Newman did not anticipate the full range of implication that the term "liberalism" would take on after 1850. But whether he was engaged in a conscious renaming of Evangelicalism as a foe, the dangers of a frame of mind that could indeed lead to apostasy (as he saw it) and to an essentially secular mind-set are so closely associated with liberalizing tendencies in Newman's mind that in the *Apologia* he may simply have conflated two terms to describe a common product of what he felt was the restless, probing human intellect, unaware of its own proper boundaries.[14]

This view of the matter has support in two sermons Newman preached on consecutive days in Easter Week 1835 that were essential to his critique of forces in the Establishment contrary to his own: "Saving Knowledge" and "Self-Contemplation." It is notable that in neither of them does Newman use the terms "Evangelicalism" or "Liberalism." Rather, in "Self-Contemplation," the phenomenon he describes is generally referred to as this "modern system" (*PPS* 2.15.333) or, on one occasion, "the mixed multitude of religionists" of the day (331). The closest he comes to the two terms is to single out the "modern system" rather pointedly as "utterly unevangelical" (335).

"Saving Knowledge" is drawn from the text in 1 John 2:3: "Hereby do we know that we know Him, if we keep his commandment." In arguing from the text that "Obedience is the test of Faith," Newman adopts a quite Carlylean tactic of promoting action over "a certain frame of mind" based merely on "certain notions, affections, feelings, and tempers." These latter, to be sure, may indeed be "a necessary condition of a saving state," but to give them priority over obedient action is to invert the Apostle's order of values (*PPS* 2.14.325). Newman does not rule out self-examination but insists that too close a preoccupation with the state of one's own soul (again like Carlyle's disease of self-consciousness) is only half the picture. Our duty lies in acts.

In "Self-Contemplation," based on Hebrews 12:2 ("Looking unto Jesus, the Author and Finisher of our faith"), Newman attacks the substitution of self-examination for a more "scriptural" contemplation of Jesus himself. To brood on "the heinousness of sin," the necessity of Christ as our personal Savior, and our inability to save ourselves—chastening and holy as these thoughts may be—still, "our hearty reception" of them, Newman believes, "is scarcely ascertainable by a direct inspection of our feelings" (331). When Justification by Faith is taken as the one cardinal principle of the Gospel and made a precondition of good works, then we shall never leave off brooding rather than acting, or if self-convinced of our merits, we will assume that good works will take care of themselves. The correct view of the matter, according to Newman, is that faith and works are interdependent; good works are both the cause and consequence of faith.

This "modern system" of self-contemplation, Newman believes, disparages both the Gospel and the Creeds because of its emphasis on "a certain state of heart" as its main object. Though its practitioners may argue that "the existence of right religious affections" is a security for adherence to sound doctrine, the conviction of one's righteousness before God will lead to a disparagement of orthodox standards, an ignoring of the "strict and technical niceties of doctrine" that cannot be said to induce any change in the heart and that therefore become unnecessary, or at best secondary, to faith. The result is an emphasis on the "work of Christ" rather than on His person, and the Incarnation loses its centrality in the Gospel while the doctrines of Justification and the Atonement assume its place. The result of such "false wisdom" is "to deny that in matters of doctrine there is any one sense of Scripture such, that it is true and all others false" (333). In short, to argue that "inspiration speaks merely of divine operations, not of Persons" is to relocate the center of truth to the mind of the individual believer. The result is an obliteration of "the great Objects brought to light in the Gospel . . . and thus to frustrate the design of Christ's Incarnation, so far as it is a manifestation of the Unseen Creator" (334). Newman believes that "in labouring after a certain frame of mind, there is an habitual reflex action of the mind upon itself" (336).

In Newman's thinking, such a system risks a highly selective approach to scripture itself. It has not been sufficiently noted that one of the complaints Newman lodged against the Evangelicals was that they concentrated on the Pauline epistles at the expense of the Gospels. In later years, writing to the Scottish Free Church clergyman David Brown, he recalled with some amusement that "certainly it used to seem to me thirty years ago to be one of the faults of the English Evangelical School, that they depreciated the Gospels, and seemed to know nothing of the New Testament beyond one or two texts of St. Paul. A friend told me about the year 1826 that he was walking and talking with a dissenting acquaintance and happened to quote in defence of what he had said some words of our Lord. On which his companion stopped short and said to him, 'Where do those words occur?' and on his answering 'In the Gospels,' the other replied, 'My dear friend, don't you know you have quoted a most unevangelical part of scripture?'" (*L&D* 26:187). To a mind like Newman's, Evangelicals had hurt the cause of unity by their dependence on the Epistles, which (read incautiously) invite too much fretting over such terms as *faith* and *works*. In "Saving Knowledge," Newman had insisted on the priority of the Gospel and the Creeds as dramatizing and expounding the Person of Christ Himself; the Gospels, he said on that occasion, "may be called the text of the Revelation; and the Epistles, especially St. Paul's, are as commentaries upon it ... raising history into doctrine, ordinances into sacraments, detached words or actions into principles, and thus everywhere dutifully preaching His Person, work, and will" (326). Newman, of course, frequently preached from the Epistles; but here he is arguing less for their actual subordination to the Gospels than for the unity of fabric that the two parts (broadly defined) of the New Testament exhibit. To tear them asunder was to court distortion, to elevate Pauline argument over Gospel fact. "We are apt," Newman said in his sermon on Balaam, "to act towards God and the things of God as towards a mere system, a Law, a name, a religion, a principle, not as against a Person, a living, watchful, present, prompt and powerful Eye and Arm" (*PPS* 4.2.752).

In "Saving Knowledge" and "Self-Contemplation," Newman disclaims any intention of saying that those who hold such views necessarily follow their own logic to such evil results. In such a case, it is the result of saving grace that we do not always adhere to our own worst principles. But the fact that the "modern system" exists *as* a system makes it singularly destructive and anti-Christian in tendency. Such a way of thinking, Newman declares in "Self-Contemplation," has already taken a toll on the Church of England since the Reformation and may betoken a still "more fearful triumph" (337). The situation calls, then, for watchfulness and a recollection of Christ's words, "Blessed is he that watcheth, and keepeth his garments, lest he walk naked, and they see his shame" (Rev. 16:15).

Thus did Newman stake out his critique of the "modern system." It boils down to what, in "Reverence a Belief in God's Presence" (1828), he saw as two frames of mind that, though opposite from each other, derive from a common source: a failure to recognize a continuous Divine Presence. A lack of reverence is a failure to act as if God were present. One group thinks that it was never under God's displeasure; the other, that it once was under His displeasure but is now justified. The one group feels that awe is inconsistent with reason, the other, that it is inconsistent with the Gospel freedom (*PPS* 5.2.967–76). From the early 1830s onward, Newman's reaction against this "modern system" that led to such strange bedfellows affected practically every significant religious choice he made. No longer motivated by the staying apprehension of the Divine Person as a standard of our conduct, the proponents of this modern system reached, by different paths, the anarchy of private judgment. It was, he felt, destructive not only to belief, substituting a system for a Person, but also to community. Yet despite his own advice, Newman found it difficult to practice what he called in "Jereboam" (1830) "the part of true faith": the waiting patiently on God's revelation of his purpose (*PPS* 3.5.526).

Debates of the kind rehearsed in this chapter—over homiletics, liturgical forms, and the nature of the clerical character—may seem at first too technical to have any broader cultural ramifications. It is certainly true that dealing with Newman requires attention to treatises like Sumner's pamphlets, and indeed the Tracts themselves, which tended to have mostly clerical circulation—quite aside from private correspondence. Much of this material seems salient mainly to the church historian. But the practical consequences of these debates, for the churchgoing Victorian, might play out in many congregational settings.

The novelists knew this well, and they assumed a literacy among the broader public about the issues that were the source of hope, discomfort, and anxiety in the pews. In Charles Kingsley's *Alton Locke* (1850), the eponymous tailor-hero asks a farmer about the quality of the local clergy. The answer: "There's two or three nice young gentlemen come'd around here but they're all what's-em-a-call-it?—some sort o' papishes—leastways, they has prayers in the church every day, and doesn't preach the Gospel" (121–22). Thus did the great debates at Oxford and London penetrate even the rural, and still mostly Anglican, churchgoers whom George Eliot analyzed in *Scenes from Clerical Life* and *Adam Bede* at the end of the same decade. By the turn of the century, the Anglo-Catholic Pryor (alternately comic and sinister) in Samuel Butler's *The Way of All Flesh* was as familiar to churchgoers as the inept and stuffy Low Churchman Theobald Pontifex, tyrannical at home and incompetent in his parish duties. But increasingly, such figures, and the divisions they represented, were relics of a departing era.

Notes of the Church

NEWMAN HAD COMMITTED himself to the creation of a new spirit in the Church of England. The question was whether the Church was capable of sustaining the burden he put on it. Was it ready to renounce its connection with the State, should circumstances warrant, or to right what Newman saw as the excesses of the Reformation and restore the Catholicity of its doctrine and discipline? For him, the answers to such questions were subject to the test of Personality: what kind of collective personality the Establishment of his day exhibited and what justified its assumption of teaching authority.

Newman's essays in the *British Magazine* and the *British Critic* (the second of which he edited from 1838 to 1841), and to some degree his *Prophetical Office of the Church* (1834–37) and *Lectures on Justification* (1838) seemed to some of his fellow communicants to transmit a mixed message. Whatever Newman's public pronouncements during this period, private uncertainties were never very far below the surface. His need to establish the apostolic and dogmatic credentials of the Victorian Church was the manifestation of an internal struggle on the outcome of which, he felt, the safety of his soul depended. Like Carlyle, Newman sought refuge from doubt in action. In the concluding sections of his lectures at Adam de Brome's chapel on the Bible and the Catholic creed,[1] Newman told his hearers, "It surely cannot be meant that we should be undecided all our days. We were made for action, and for right action,—for thought, and for true thought. Let us live while we live; let us be alive and doing; let us act on what we have, since we have not what we wish. Let us believe what we do not see and know.... We do all things in this world by faith in the word of others.... Why should

Religion be an exception?" (*D&A* 214). This anti-theoretical bent is an important component of Newman's mind. Though he was no mean logician, the idea of personality, whether of persons or of institutions, had a reality for him that abstractions did not. It was by the power of personality that he hoped to gain the attention of a slumbering Church and the practical infidels who came on Sundays out of habit, in short to revive the Church as the nation's spiritual center.

Polemics

In his essay "Home Thoughts from Abroad," published in the *British Magazine* in 1834,[2] Newman set forth what in the *Apologia* he recalled as "the argument in behalf of Rome ... with [a] considerable perspicuity and force" that alarmed his more conservative friends. But Newman had not intended to stake out an imprudent claim. He hoped to bring forward the fullest and fairest arguments he could for an audience whose anti-Romanism seemed to him shallow and uninformed, but uppermost in his mind was the fact that "a number of persons were unsettled far more than I was as to the Catholicity of the Anglican Church. It was quite plain that, unless I was perfectly candid in stating what could be said against it [the Catholicity of the Anglican Church], there was no chance that any representations, which I felt to be in its favour, or at least to be adverse to Rome, would have had any success with the persons in question" (*A* 104). Like John Stuart Mill, he thought that an argument should be exposed to as full and fair a counterargument as possible. But some of his friends thought he was giving away the Anglican store. Despite his rhetorical powers, Newman was often something of a naïf when the issues, however technical, ultimately resonated across denominational boundaries. He often failed to remember that the kinds of argument he deployed for one imagined audience might not suit another. He failed in 1836, as he was to fail with Tract 90 in 1841, to realize that adverse reaction was predictable in the overheated theological atmosphere of the day.

Newman's development during this period took a new direction when he reviewed William Palmer's *Treatise on the Church of Christ* in the *British Critic* in 1838. Newman saw the treatise as a welcome sign of the new interest in articulating Anglican principles. He attributed the dearth of systematic theology in Anglicanism to the fact that writers in that tradition had often been heavily burdened by clerical duties and obliged to respond to special events and "particular assailants" in the course of which a pamphlet might grow into a folio without the writer's ever developing a set of first principles. As a result, Anglican divinity (of which Newman saw himself as a representative) had gained in vitality but lost in coherence. But Palmer's work seemed to open up a theological terrain much disparaged by the ultra-Protestant party. Newman thought that Palmer, though learned, was not original, but that he had been successful in working out a "few great principles, which sometimes come to the surface, but are generally hidden" (*ECH* 1:189).

What struck Newman chiefly was Palmer's concept of "Notes of the Church." These were indices by which one might gauge the degree to which an ecclesiastical body upheld traditional Catholic teachings. Palmer argued that the four "Notes" of the English Church in "its obvious and popular character" lay in its being One, Holy, Catholic, and Apostolic. Newman, however, detected in the history of that Church an obscuring of those Notes. He described the Establishment metaphorically as a woman shut up within walls, clothed in "tawdry or homely attire," forced to mingle with sectaries, stopping short only of outright indignity, "so they gave her golden chains, and fed her, not with bread and water of affliction, but in king's palaces and at kings' tables" (*ECH* 1:194). Newman thought it would have been better for her to suffer affliction than to become, by implication, the kept woman of the State. "Political and civil catchwords" had been substituted for Palmer's four Notes. Palmer had presented Newman with an unfinished program.

Newman's uncertainty about the Notes of the Established Church persisted in such essays as "The State of Religious Parties" (later retitled "Prospects of the Anglican Church") in the *British Critic* (1839) and "The Catholicity of the English Church" in the same journal the following year. Liberalism in theology had no power to stir emotional allegiance, while Puritanism and continental Protestantism offered no principle of "union, permanence, and consistency" and hence "no principle of life" (*ECH* 1:295). The Via Media that Newman sought seemed to have been dislodged by a vacuous Protestantism from the space between Catholic faith and rationalism. In these essays, Newman seems to view Anglicanism as a road traveling toward Rome but forking off before reaching it. The question was now whether that was a viable alternative: whether Anglicanism could pursue its own road to a Catholic destination without succumbing to Roman error.

At the outset of the Movement, we will recall, Newman had tried to distinguish between the work of a party and that of a loosely knit association in which supporters might contribute their own views without binding others to their expression of them. In "The State of Religious Parties," even as he sought to personalize the Church, he depersonalized the Movement, which had now become a sort of numen, an upwelling of spirit independent of external circumstances. He located in Tractarianism a spirit "within us, rising up in the heart where it was least expected, and working its way, though not in secret, yet so subtly and impalpably, as hardly to admit of precaution or encounter, or any ordinary human rules of opposition" (*ECH* 1:272). Through this rhetorical strategy, which he employed also in private letters of the period, Newman suggested an inevitable force of history while downplaying personal agency, implying that individuals were no more than the various "organs of One Sentiment" rising up spontaneously in many different places (274).[3] The "Movement" in question was no longer even a human effort; rather, human beings had been acted upon by the Spirit. Newman's strategy, however, had a more limited purpose as well. If he could make this view prevail, it would explain why the "principal advocates" of Tractarianism could not restrain their younger followers, persons whose characters and views were still in formation, and who latched on to the Movement in varying degrees of enthusiasm or extravagance (277).

While realizing that the Movement could be blamed for the zeal of its less-disciplined camp followers, Newman defended the probity of its soberer leaders and their tolerance for those who were in a transitional state. But those who adhered to error did not deserve the Church's protection. In a note appended in later years, he insisted that he was speaking only of "the duty of *cross-examining*, pressing hard *in argument*, and forcing into *consequences*, the originator of an heretical opinion" (*ECH* 1:279n). This in itself was an act of charity that might open the heretic's eyes. Quoting from the original language of the Tracts' editors, Newman reminded his readers that they had disavowed the support of "loud and voluble advocates" who did not really feel the truths they propounded, and that the editors had hoped for the support of those who, "in the silent humility of their lives, and in their unaffected reverence for holy things," had demonstrated their acceptance of the Movement's principles as "real and substantial" (280).

To those who would call for moderation and judiciousness, the Newman of 1839 responded that they should be "plainly asked, whether by moderate and judicious opinions they do not mean just those very opinions, neither more or less, which do not shock themselves." Such people confuse "*strong* opinions" for what are really "*clear* and *distinct* opinions" (*ECH* 1:301). But, he continued, "In the present day mistiness is the mother of wisdom" (302). In language anticipating the *Apologia*, Newman criticizes those who feel the Church needs "sensible, temperate, sober, well-judging persons, to guide it through the channel of No—meaning between the Scylla and Charybdis of Aye and No." For "premises imply conclusions; germs lead to developments; principles have issues; doctrines lead to action" (302–3). The Anglican Newman hopes for a metamorphosis of doctrine, a system "rising up superior to the age," in which the primitive system comes to be accepted naturally rather than resisted as it is by the present-day Church of England (292). But he believes that there has really existed, ever since the Caroline divines pointed to it, a "true and intelligible mean between extremes" (306). It was better to direct this current of the age into the exploration of the Anglican past than to propel it toward either Rome or Geneva.

"The State of Parties" is a somewhat paradoxical essay. It dehistoricizes the Movement while appealing to history as the object that the Movement sought to reclaim for the Church in the present (Victorian) day. In the longer works of the period, Newman returned once again to refiguring the collective personality of the Anglican Church. But in his disavowal of the role of personal agency in the Movement and his consequent refusal to take direct responsibility for the excesses of its followers, Newman was sowing the seeds of failure for his Anglican project. What the next six years were to show was that even to withdraw from responsibility was to be responsible, and that to urge restraint on one's most devoted adherents was to resist the convergence of Zeitgeist and the individual conscience, a convergence propelling his younger followers toward Rome even before he was ready to go there himself. Much of the essay, despite its stated purpose of defending the Movement, betrays a nervous self-criticism. He could not remain in this position long.

The Prophetical Office of the Church and the *Lectures on Justification*

If in the accepted language of faith the Church is the body of Christ, then by Newman's logic individual churches display varying attributes of the corporate personality of the Church Catholic. In a recuperative moment in the chapter on the history of Newman's religious opinions from 1839 to 1844, the *Apologia* looks back to the end of 1835 or beginning of 1836 as a period when he tried to distinguish between the decrees and traditions of both Romanism and Anglicanism, condemning excesses on both sides. In "Home Thoughts from Abroad," after decrying the Church of England's insularity, Erastianism, "historical rancour," and reliance on private judgment as "Protestantism" or "ultra-Protestantism," Newman, in a passage he later quoted in the *Apologia* (105), trained his sights on Rome. Rome, too, had departed from primitive Christianity because of its "practical idolatry, the virtual worship of Virgin and Saints ... and the degradation of moral truth and duty, which follows from these" (*D&A* 17). He wanted Roman Catholics to admit that "Popery," as constituted by its "popular system of beliefs and images," was deficient in its own right. But the *Apologia*, in its phrasing of the difference between the two communions, was to tilt the balance: "I saw that the controversy lay between the book theology of Anglicanism on the one side, and the living system of what I called Roman corruption on the other." A book theology cannot compete, in Newman's mind, with a living system, however corrupted. Canterbury appeals to historicity, Rome to Catholicity. In an essay on Nicholas Wiseman that he did not reprint, Newman wrote, "The Romanist gives to the existing *Church* the ultimate infallible decision on matters of saving faith, the Ultra-Protestant to the *individual*; and the Anglican to *antiquity*, giving authority to the Church, as being the witness and voice or rather the very presence of Antiquity among us."[4] But a witness and voice are considerably less potent figurations than an arbiter and a judge. The theory of the Via Media was to be ultimately abandoned because Newman came to feel that he had imposed it *on* history rather than deriving it *from* history. It had no living personality; it could not be reflected in a mirror.

The Prophetical Office of the Church hews to an anti-Roman position more reflective of Newman's state of mind in 1834 when he began work on it than was the case by 1837, when it was finished. It veers between a Rome who is "a pitiless and unnatural relative, who will but triumph in the arts which have inveigled us within her reach" and a "friend who is not himself" (*POC* 128). Still, Newman has no way of personating an Anglican alternative. In Lecture 5, "On the Use of Private Judgment," he writes that the Via Media represented by the Church is a mean and as such partakes of the peculiar "indeterminateness" of English theology. As a result, "it has never been realized in visible fulness in any religious community, and thereby brought home to the mind through the senses" (166).

In the *Prophetical Office*, Newman continues to invoke a Church Catholic that neither Rome nor England fully represents. He personifies it as a gentle, loving mother who waits patiently for the time to speak, who is persuasive when the opportunity for persuasion arises, and who accommodates her communications to the understanding of her children, keeping silence when the utterance of truth is not timely. No more than an earthly mother does this idealized Church "assume infallibility . . . yet it would argue a very unpleasant temper in the child to doubt her word, to require proof of it before acting on it, to go needlessly to other sources of information" (*POC* 274). This mother may be mistaken in "lesser matters" and even corrected by her child, yet neither her teaching prerogative nor her expectation of dutiful obedience is thereby diminished.

Newman confirmed the importance of the *Prophetical Office* to his development by reprinting it in 1877 under the title, *The Via Media of the Anglican Church*. In his introduction to the modern edition, H. G. Weidner argues that the work marks a decisive step in Newman's transference of earlier High Church claims away from their Erastian basis and in the direction of a Christology that would give these claims ecclesial independence (*POC* lviii). Throughout, the Incarnation figures in the Church's extension as Christ's body, sacred and yet subject to human weaknesses, whether on the Anglican or the Roman side. By teaching Christ in his threefold office as Prophet, King, and Priest, the Church ministers to the world. Newman's 1877 preface clarified the point that the Church is like one person fulfilling different and sometimes apparently incommensurable functions. It is in the slippage between any two of these three offices, for example between the prophetical and the devotional, that abuses or excesses may appear. The Church is always limited by her own human material.

Newman was aware that the Church's voice might falter, and that in its leaving an ambiguous record through its history, the voice he thought he heard from the past might merely be an echo of his own. In January 1838, while at work on *Lectures on Justification*, he told John Bowden that he was "a good deal fussed" about the project. "It is the first voyage I have yet made *proprio marte*, with sun, stars, compass, and a sounding line, but with very insufficient charts. It is a terra incognita in our Church, and I am so afraid, not of saying things wrong so much, as queer and crotchety—and of misunderstanding other writers" (*L&D* 6:188–89). The absence of precedents in Anglican practice for Catholic discipline was a continuing concern as well. Two years later he was to write apprehensively to Bowden about Pusey's desire to set up an order of Sisters of Mercy: "I feel sure that such institutions are the only means of saving some of our best members [from] turning Roman Catholics, and yet I despair of such societies being *made* externally. They must be the expansion of an inward principle" (*L&D* 7:240–41). He was doubtful that Anglican soil could produce naturally the sort of institution necessary to preserve and advance Anglican Catholicity.

The *Lectures on Justification* have been described as "perhaps the key theological document of the Oxford Movement" (Brilioth 282). They criticize both Evangelical homiletics and Evangelical theology, particularly on the disputed subject of baptismal regeneration. The work draws a line between justification by faith and justification by obedience. By focusing on the indwelling of Christ in the Christian, justifying faith "takes the mind off self and buries itself in the absorbing vision of a present, indwelling God" (Turner 273). In *Lectures on Justification*, justifying faith is not an abstraction but a substantive reality working on the individual soul. Newman's sacramentalism, particularly as set out in the twelfth of the lectures, avoids both the Protestant emphasis on outward atonement and the Roman tendency toward a doctrine of merit, in which (he felt) one bargains with God as if with an equal to gain an advantage. Baptism, then, has virtue in itself, external to the believer, but the virtue is implanted in the newly baptized in a sacramental rite and sustained by faith and the Eucharist, whereas for the Protestant the faith of the recipient is the conserving principle of the righteousness imputed to the believer (Toon 141–70).

Newman's treatment of baptism is itself a Via Media between two different Anglican schools: the subjectivism of the Evangelical party and the formalist view of the old High Church wing, which (Newman felt) had retained the doctrine but emptied it of its spiritual significance.[5] For Newman, the Evangelical test of the experience of redemption had never been borne out empirically in his own life; he felt that grace had come to him at baptism, well before his conversion experience at the age of fifteen (Sheridan 173). While many Evangelicals believed that a conversion fixed forever the destiny of the individual in the Invisible Church, for Newman "the body of Christ" denoted an organic body of individuals united by the Visible Church. Thus the doctrines of Baptism and Justification were connected by the epistemological question "How do I know that I am saved?" Evangelicals felt, on the whole, that the conversion experience was effective proof of the finality of the believer's justification; Tractarian and High Church doctrine answered the question in spiritual terms, by denying that, once procured, salvation was always assured. In adopting the latter view, Newman both committed himself, and gave additional theological sanction, to his dynamic conception of personality. The Christian is always a work in progress.[6]

Newman never renounced his early Evangelical belief in personal holiness, but as we have seen, he came to understand it as membership in a visible community of believers, situating the ideal not in the person singly but in the person as part of a community. The community, that is, the Visible Church, was a safeguard against the excesses of private judgment. Newman had made this move by 1828, but well into the 1830s he still occasionally seems to have glimpsed the possibility that Evangelicals might be allies against Liberalism. Personal holiness was still the great theme of his preaching, a holiness that repelled the advances of sin by cooperation with an indwelling Spirit. Newman's understanding of the Spirit's work of regeneration did not consist merely in moral betterment but in a communication of the divine nature to man through the "indwelling presence" (Sheridan 242). Lived faith, manifested in works and infused with love, was the fruit of justification. The assurance of salvation was not based on the certainty of a private conversion experience but on the Christian's belonging to the body of believers.

Newman's views on preaching in the *Lectures on Justification* reiterate his familiar distrust of verbal formulas, words divorced from living facts. What was at the outset an attack on Evangelical homiletics is now broadened into a critique of post-Reformation Christianity. In the eleventh lecture, "The

Nature of Justifying Faith," he lays the groundwork for his view by pointing out, in a variant of his idea of the ultimate privacy of the individual personality: "One man is said to be the same as another man, when the mind contemplates them *as* men; yet after all the mind can but contemplate, it cannot create or alter what is external to it. In spite of our arbitrary abstractions, each existing man exists to himself, as an individual, complete in himself, independent of all others, differing from all others, in that he is he, and not they nor one with them, except in name" (*LOJ* 255). Approaching the familiar and false dichotomy of faith and works from another angle, he criticizes post-Reformation theological distinctions by arguing that people may use the same terms to describe faith while not at all meaning the same thing or acting the same way. It is not definition, but being-in-action, that convinces Newman: "I wish to deal with things, not with words. I do not look to be put off with a name or a shadow. I would treat of faith as it is actually found in the soul; and I say it is as little an isolated grace, as a man is a picture. It has a depth, a breadth, and a thickness; it has an inward life which is something over and above itself; it has a heart, and blood, and pulses, and nerves, though not upon the surface" (265). "This then," he concludes, "is what is meant by the doctrine that faith is not justifying unless informed or animated by love" (266). Newman here anticipates his later admiration of the serene indifference of Roman Catholicism to forms of faith outside its own, its quiet confidence in its own judgment. His language is itself incarnative: it appeals to the physical as a source of metaphor for understanding the invisible workings of faith.

The *Lectures* negotiate a space between private and public utterance, expounding a theme Newman had long pressed in his sermons: the difference between true faith and self-contemplation, the latter leading to a tendency to elevate preaching over prayer and praise. In the Primitive Church, Newman felt, the sense of worship was embodied in the objective presence of Christ not only in Word but in Sacrament, Altar, and Cross, not only on Sundays but as part of the fabric of everyday life. Newman now places holiness above justification as he had earlier placed holiness above peace. It has been argued that suffering and joy in Newman, once removed from Luther's interplay of Law and Gospel, become interiorized in a depleted conception of good works and a pietistic approach to pain and transformation, and that the result is an "impassioned self-idealization" and a "narcissistic vision of perfection" (O'Leary 177–78). The charge of egoism, as we have noted, is a recurring one in Newman scholarship, but it seems a rather heavy burden to lay upon the *Lectures,* where Newman preaches an active Gospel of Incarnation.

Newman's attempts to look for authentic Catholicity in the Notes of the Anglican Church was a consequence of his belief in the reality of a Visible Church as a community of souls in various stages of remaking. But the events of his last decade as an Anglican were to propel him in a direction ironically more characteristic of Evangelical ways of thinking about the Church.

Turning Points

Newman did not remain content with the formulations he had reached in the *Lectures.* His metaphors for the Anglican idea of Catholicity were curiously at odds with each other. In looking to the Primitive Church, he saw a combination of mutual independence amid a union of charity, and he felt that that union, as set forth in the Anglican system, involved seeing the various dioceses as a dispersed family, deriving from the first founders and bishops. But a dispersed body does not have a single identity. The crisis of 1839, the recognition of the Monophysite in the mirror, was followed shortly by Wiseman's comparison of Anglicans to Donatists in his article "Anglican Claims" in the *Dublin Review.*[7] In the same letter to Bowden in which he described his anxiety about his work on the *Lectures on Justification,* Newman wrote anxiously, "As for Dr. Wiseman's article I do not think you have hit the point of it.... He maintains first that the present *look* of Christendom is such, that St Austin [Augustine] or St Basil coming among us would say at once 'That is the Catholic Church—and *these* are the heretics'—meaning Rome and us respectively—and next that the said Fathers and all the Fathers teach that that 'look' of things was ever meant to be a providential note, in order to *save* argument;—without going into the question who excommunicates whom etc etc. I frankly confess I cannot deny either of his positions" (*L&D* 7:241). In his article "Private Judgment," published in the *British Critic* in July 1841, he retained this emphasis on looks and faces. One may judge persons more rapidly and expertly than doctrines or books. "Every one, even a child, has an impression about new faces; few persons have any real view about new propositions." The vivid reality of persons or "bodies of men" calls for approval or disapproval "with distinctness to which pen and ink are unequal" (ECH 2:353). With respect to bodies of men, "the simple question ... is, Has the English Church *sufficiently* upon herself the signs of an Apostle? is she the divinely appointed teacher to *us?*" (362). The actions of that body's representatives are the clues to its authenticity and authority.

As Newman recalled the period 1840–41 in the *Apologia*, he wrote that "it was not at all certain ... even that we [the Church of England] had not the Note of Catholicity, but if not this, we had others" (A 121). In "Catholicity of the English Church," first published in the *British Critic* in 1840, Newman wrote that "there can be no greater proof of a particular communion being part of the Church than the appearance in it of a continued and abiding energy, not a more melancholy symptom of its being a corpse than torpidity" (ECH 2:53). After all, one had to make allowances for what Anglicanism had endured: "It has been practiced upon by theorists, browbeaten by sophists, intimidated by princes, betrayed by false sons, laid waste by tyranny, corrupted by wealth, torn by schism, and persecuted by fanaticism. Revolutions have come upon it sharply and suddenly, to and fro, hot and cold, as if to try what it was made of. It has been a sort of battle-field on which opposite principles have been tried." Yet in spite of all this, it has "grown towards a more perfect Catholicism than that with which it started at the time of estrangement; every act, every crisis, which marks its course, has been upward" (55). And he presses ahead hopefully to the conclusion that the Anglican Church has providentially survived. She has the note of "vigorous" life along with "ancient descent, unbroken continuance, agreement in doctrine with the ancient Church" (59).

It does not seem to have occurred to Newman that his portrayal of the Church of England as a suffering victim had deprived it of a compelling personality. And a battlefield is simply a site of contest, a space, not a person. Perhaps recognizing a certain metaphorical difficulty, Newman was less confident in private, writing to his sister Jemima a few months before this article, in November 1839, that "our Church is not one with itself—there is no denying it. We have an heretical spirit in us. Whether it can be cast out, without 'tearing' and destroying the Church itself is quite beyond me" (L&D 7:183). Yet he hesitated to put it to that test; a recurring metaphor of his correspondence is that such a test will be like proving a cannon to see if it will survive its own first blast or merely blow up in the face of the gunners. That test came with Tract 90, *Remarks on Certain Passages in the Thirty-Nine Articles*, which attempted to prove that despite the highly Protestant tone of the Thirty-Nine Articles, they were nonetheless capable of bearing a Catholic interpretation. The point was profoundly political, not merely theological, since every one of the Church's ordinands, indeed everyone who wished to matriculate at Oxford or graduate from Cambridge, was required to subscribe to the Articles.

One source of Newman's problems in Tract 90 was that there was so little of his own personality in it. Dry, technical, and (like his attack on Hampden) highly selective in its use of evidence, it invited and still invites charges of shuffling, logic-chopping, and inconsistency.[8] Newman appears to have felt that a dry tone, and a close parsing of what the Articles did not say as well as what they did, would deflect criticism, and perhaps allow the Tract to pass under the radar while keeping some of his younger followers in check. No doubt a complex mixture of prudence, timorousness, and calculation figured in his strategy, but on Newman's side it must be said that, arguably, he "shuffled" no more than do the Articles themselves. His miscalculation was that he was so focused on that younger audience, the generation of William Ward and Frederick Oakeley, that he forgot he had other audiences. In the long term, he neither kept the young in check nor persuaded the old of his loyalty.

One of the most nuanced approaches to Tract 90 came from James Anthony Froude, writing at a time when the controversy was still a living memory. Froude saw that Newman, in setting himself to minimize what the Articles said, was on reasonable ground. Froude treated the Thirty-Nine Articles as a kind of committee report, and such reports are generally compromises. The Elizabethan settlement was framed to enable Protestants and Catholics to shelter under the Articles in a form of civil rather than religious adhesion, and it was papal allegiance, not Catholic doctrine, that was the real issue of the day. But Froude also thought that the more specifically anti-Roman wing of the Church, especially after 1688, had changed the landscape; the dominant Protestant interpretation of the Articles had become the coin of the realm. For this reason, Froude concluded, Newman's strategy was right as a narrative of origins, but wrong in its assessment of the religious climate of the 1840s ("Counter-Reformation" 200–202).

Froude's analysis says something very interesting about Newman. As with his earlier interpretation of the Oxford statutes on the tutorship question, Newman had tried to determine the original intent of the Articles' framers. In neither case did he go badly wrong, but he swept aside years of subsequent development and proceeded in a kind of vacuum to assert that, strictly read, the statutes in the first instance, or the Articles in the second, justified his position. Had he challenged the adequacy of the Articles to speak to the contemporary religious scene, or (alternatively) had he undertaken a patient historical analysis to show why that original intent could be put to the service of toleration, he would at least have acknowledged the complexity of what he was trying to make simple. He might have openly declared that the Articles did not fully encompass the range of Anglican beliefs and practice, and thus defended their teaching authority while seeing them as subordinate to Councils, Creed, and Church Fathers. But paradoxically he was both too impatient to take a coolly analytical view and too timid to remove the Articles from their position of authority, probably because in all their imperfections he saw them as the Church's last breakwater against Dissent and rationalism. Never, or at least not yet, a thoroughgoing anti-Erastian, he may have feared that to dethrone the Articles would be construed as the first step toward dissolution of the Establishment. As it was, he led all but his closest friends to believe that he was Romanizing and that his party had to be put down. In the heat of controversy, Newman's obsessively close parsing of the Articles triumphed over political common sense.

Newman had to explain himself to his own diocesan, Bishop Richard Bagot of Oxford, and their correspondence on this as on other issues saw Newman trying in vain to persuade the bishop to exert his episcopal authority in the exacting sense that Newman, almost alone for his time, defined that authority. Since Tract 90 had attracted a storm of condemnations from the Episcopal bench, and since Bagot was among the few who were willing to affirm the good intentions of the Tractarians (though they clearly made him uncomfortable), his support was especially desirable. When Newman responded in March 1841 to the bishop's statement that Tract 90 was itself "objectionable, and [might] tend to disturb the peace and tranquility of the Church," he tried simultaneously both to convey his dutiful assent to the bishop's concerns and to defend himself. He assured the bishop (perhaps disingenuously) that he had not anticipated that the Tract would cause any upset, and that had he not written at all the position of the Establishment would have been no stronger. "It is easy for those who do not enter into these difficulties to say, 'He ought to say this and not say that'; but things are so wonderfully linked together, and I cannot or rather I would not, be dishonest. When persons too interrogate me, I am obliged in many cases to give an opinion, or I seem to be underhand. Keeping silence looks like artifice.... All these things make my situation very difficult" (*L&D* 8:100–101).

Newman's self-pity over a situation that he had largely created for himself drew rather different responses from two of his friends. The first was Isaac Williams, Newman's former curate, still an admiring friend but one increasingly unable to follow in Newman's steps. Williams professed himself puzzled at Newman's reaction to the fracas over Tract 90: "I used to be surprised he had not more learned to look on persecution as a matter of course, what a good man must expect to meet with, and which should be to him a satisfaction, as indicating him to be in the way of truth" (110). Williams recalled that "most intimately as I was united with him, I cannot remember when my prayer for him was not rather that he might be preserved from error and the dangers to which he was exposed from his peculiar temperament, than for his perfection" (103).

William Palmer was less patient, and he did not share Williams's disadvantage of being Newman's junior. He identified Newman's reaction to Episcopal censure after Tract 90 as the beginning of his own doubts about Newman's ultimate intentions. In Newman's appearance of submission to the bishop, coupled with his sense of being insufficiently supported, Palmer read a strong self-will that countenanced no alternative to his ideas on how the Church should be rebuilt. In 1883 Palmer returned to Tract 90 in a supplementary section added to the original *Narrative:* "Had [Newman] been patient, could he have submitted to control—could he have entertained the notion that the fault of this collapse lay in some degree at his own door, his immovable obstinacy, and his rashness—could he have entertained the notion that his system was not wholly faultless, and that he might have some mistakes to acknowledge—he might have endured, as Pusey did, the censure of his works, submitted to the storm, and in time resumed all his influence" (Palmer 236).[9] In Palmer's eyes, Newman deserved criticism for a hostile spirit deficient in "Christian charity and humility." Perhaps this was too severe. Palmer, though himself a man of strong views, was not the person to make allowance for Newman's internal conflicts over questions to which he himself attached less decisive importance. But since Palmer had initially supported Tract 90, he had reason to feel that he had taken on himself a not inconsiderable risk, and that Newman's subsequent attitude was ungrateful as well as unhelpful.

The Safety of Continuance

At the end of 1841, Newman preached a series of four sermons that became part of a larger collection, *Sermons Bearing on Subjects of the Day* (1843), examining "the safety of continuance in our communion." They are the most curious, and certainly the most atypical, of his Anglican sermons, for they do not present settled doctrine but rather experiment with an approach to the problem of "continuance" with which Newman himself is obviously uncomfortable. Far from engaging contemporary secular issues in a Christian light, as their title would suggest to most readers today, they take up a series of narrowly defined issues having to do with ecclesial loyalties.

Although some of the sermons date back to the previous decade, the collection as a whole serves two closely interrelated purposes. The first is to reexamine the "Notes of the Church," the second to put forward a highly idiosyncratic view of Newman's relationship to it. On the first point, Newman by now had totally retreated from the position that the Anglican Communion had any distinct notes of life. Such notes, rather, were to be found in the lives of individual believers—rather as if one could continue to be an Anglican at heart without the Anglican Church. This in turn enabled his second purpose, to project himself as a latter-day Elijah mustering the believers outside the Temple but sustaining a legitimate role within his dispensation. He and others of the like-minded must do without "the outward signs of God's presence" and rejoice that they could be found within a grouping of individual believers. Ironically, for the purpose of this argument, Newman takes cover in something very much like the Invisible Church of the Evangelicals.

If the sermons give the impression that Newman was arguing with himself in public, it is because they betoken a pastoral strategy in caring for the perplexed and uncertain, among whom he numbered himself. Do we have signs that Christ has left us, and if not, are we not obligated to remain where we are? Each of us should ask himself "whether he may not have more tokens, real and intimate, that Christ is with himself and his brethren in our ordinances, than he has evidence ... that Christ is not with him" ("Invisible Presence of Christ," *SSD* 321). Newman appeals to his hearers' experience of moments of peace, of illumination through their experience of the sacraments or of exemplary Anglican deathbeds, for evidence that a "Divine Presence" lingers among Anglicans still.

The theme is reiterated in "Outward and Inward Notes of the Church," on 2 Timothy 1:12: "I know when I have believed, and am persuaded that He is able to keep that which I have committed unto Him against that day." Newman first examines the distinction between religion as "a personal, private, and individual matter," consisting in a "communion between God and the soul" (325), and the Gospel as a social religion, bolstered by the prophetic vision of a city on a hill. Isaiah's prophecies speak of outward and visible tokens, but with St. Paul the emphasis shifts to the inward, for in Paul, "the general had become particular; the external had flowed into his secret soul ... and thus, just as we need not read a friend's writing when we hear his voice, so ... the blessed Apostle needed not [to] seek Him abroad, who had graciously condescended to 'come under his roof,' and manifest Himself unto him" (*SSD* 327–28).

What, then, was the relationship between outward and inward Notes in a day when the Divine Friend was no longer physically present? Newman argues that the public Notes of the Church are aimed more at the unbelieving world than at the faithful body of Christian followers, more at those Christians partly outside the Apostolic body than at those who, once within, experience the external Notes as "practically superseded" (*SSD* 328). They are still a support and a comfort to those within the pale, but nonetheless the Church's special promise to them is of a different kind, for "they first see her glory from without: next they taste her good gifts from within" (330). It is also true, however, that even those still seeking may benefit from "personal and private intimations" (331) and not merely the external tokens of the kingdom. Thus, public Notes attract the seeker, "but when he once has tasted the good word, and in proportion as he is partaker of it, that word itself in its inward power, in its power upon himself, will keep him firm in his allegiance to her" (334–35). Newman now wishes to assure his audience that "the public Notes of the Church are not her only tokens, and a failure or deficiency in them here or there, is no argument that the Presence of Christ is away" (338). Though this misfortune diminishes her influence, stunts her growth, and hampers her purveying of the truth, yet her fruits may remain. For what actually draws anyone to the Church is not outward display but the experience of her benefits upon the believer. This argument *de minimis* marks a retreat from Newman's earlier confidence in the possibility of discerning the (true) Notes of the Church in Anglicanism. The assurance from which he attempts to derive a now sadly dwindled comfort is that many different people, not knowing each other, have been tempted to find the true Church elsewhere and yet, when approaching the boundary that separates England from Rome, have "felt ... a nameless feeling within them, forbidding and stopping them" (339). Newman does not allow for the possibility that such a feeling might be merely the last vestige of a cultural revulsion, a long-seated prejudice against all things Roman. Rather, he prefers to identify this coincidence of feeling among many independent and fearless minds as having in it something perhaps of divine origin. But even if the individual tempted to secede is without experience of that restraining feeling, "yet the mere fact that others around us bear witness to it, should weigh with himself, and he should guide himself, at least for a while, by the direction thus given to his brethren" (341).

In "Grounds for Steadfastness in Our Religious Profession," Newman distinguishes between genuinely religious persons who are taunted with not understanding the grounds of their inherited religion, and others adept at rehearsing their faith without believing in it. The latter are often well-educated persons of ability who show to advantage in the world but argue from rote. The only satisfactory test of religion is within the believer and the effects it produces in that believer, not the arguments with which it is proved. Here Newman is on familiar ground: "But still it holds good, that a man's real reason for attachment to his own religious communion ... is not any series of historical or philosophical arguments, nor anything merely beautiful in its system, or supernatural, but what it has done for him and others; his confidence in it as a means by which men may be brought nearer to God, and may become better and happier" (*SSD* 347). Newman appeals to this test of experience in his letters to wavering correspondents. In 1844 he told Mrs. William Froude that after reading Wiseman's comparison of Anglicans to Donatists, he had affirmed that God wanted us to resist doubts about where we are placed. If He intends for us to change, "He will call us again as He called Samuel.... Fancies, excitements, feelings go and never return—truth comes again and is importunate" (L&D 10:201). In the sermon, he continues by asserting, "Surely that is a Church visited by the influence of Divine grace, which contains in her pale men so saintly in their lives, so heavenly in their hearts and minds, so self-denying, so obedient, as are vouchsafed to her even in this degenerate time. Is it not safe to trust our souls in their company? is it not dangerous to part company with them in our journey across the trackless wilderness?" (355–56).

In an unacknowledged but significant shift of emphasis away from the external Notes of an authentic church, Newman now suggests tests by which waverers may estimate the validity of their doubts. Is the impulse to change communions a temporary frame of mind only? We must look calmly over the years for proof of improvement, "not mere comfort or transport" (SSD 358). Religious bodies should be tested and judged by their fruits. "And if the outward Notes of the Church are thus matter [sic] for our judgment, surely its inward power may be religiously inquired into also" (360). There are only two instances in which it may be a duty to leave one's communion: "first, some clear indisputable command of God to leave it, and secondly, some plain experience that God does not acknowledge it" (361). Thus, despite his description of objective and empirically verifiable criteria ("some clear indisputable command," "some plain experience"), Newman is reduced to what looks inevitably like subjective criteria for secession.

Newman's defense of the Established Church had now come to rest on the persistence of "piety and earnestness" among individuals who remained in it, even when the Anglican hierarchy, as in the Jerusalem Bishopric affair, seemed intent on undercutting the Church's claim to ancient truth.[10] In an anguished letter to A. P. Perceval in December 1841, he asked, "If a number of persons have for years been preaching the existence of the Holy Catholic Church, what is the inevitable and immediate effect of the Church of England by its rulers declaring she is *not* that Holy Catholic Church, but to send people to Rome by *exhaustion*, because there is no other Church?" The occasion required a strong protest against the Jerusalem Bishopric of the sort that he had just made publicly, "especially if that Jerusalem matter passes sub silentio, which I assure you is weakening the faith of men in our Catholicity in the most awful manner" (*L&D* 8:394–95).

In sum, to defend Anglicanism under these evolving circumstances, Newman shifted increasingly from reliance on Notes of the Church corporately to notes of individual men and women as members of that Church. It was at bottom an Evangelical move because of its stress on individual holiness and an invisible Church over the gathered faithful, but it also reflected his longing for a return to a primitive, pre-creedal Church of the sort he had envisioned in his Arian history. It had been prefigured at the beginning of the concluding lecture in the *Prophetical Office*: "After all, the Church is ever invisible in its day, and faith only apprehends it" (*POC* 338). Newman's late Anglican writings focus increasingly on holy personalities by whom a church is measured, and on a Christianity above party. "When Providence would make a Revelation, He does not begin anew, but uses the existing system," Newman wrote in his review of Henry Hart Milman's *History of Christianity* in the *British Critic* (January 1841). "He does not visibly send an Angel, but He commissions or inspires one of our own fellows.... When He would consecrate or quicken us, He takes the elements of this world as the means of real but unseen spiritual influences" (*ECH* 2:194). In sermons of the years immediately preceding Tract 90, Newman contrasted the character of Paul with the tepidity of a self-proclaimed Christian of his own day. Christ disclosed His love in deed, not word, and Paul's preaching depended not on strong evidence but on "the novelty, and what may be called originality, of the claim, its strangeness and improbability considered as a mere invention, and the personal bearing of the Apostle."[11] Christians of the early Church in their simplicity saw God as the Good Shepherd and were identified by their hearts, hands, and cheerful features.[12] The true primitive Christian of today "has no aim of this world ... no wish to be other in this world than he is; whose thoughts and aims have relation to the unseen, the future world" ("The Apostolical Christian," *SSD* 279). Again, Newman's line of argument recalls the appeal some ultra-Protestant sects made to the stark simplicity of the primitive Church as a witness against the corruptions of Rome.

Having introduced the theme of the Notes of the Church, Newman's second theme in the *Sermons Bearing on Subjects of the Day* is a scattered, homeless church. In "Elijah the Prophet of the Latter Days," Newman suggests an Old Testament analogue to what he has now come to see as the anomalous position of the Church of England. Elijah "was not in communion with the Church of Moses in his lifetime, [and] did not worship at the Temple," a fact "not without an element of encouragement even for us" (SSD 370–71). Despite his separation from the main body of believers, Elijah carried out a divine purpose as one of the Prophets delegated "to do a half work; not to heal the division of the kingdoms, but to destroy idolatry; not to restore outward unity, but to repress inward unbelief; not to retrace the steps of the wanderers, but to keep them from wandering still farther" (373). In Newman's highly idiosyncratic rendering of his own state of mind, Elijah symbolizes the power of holy personality among the estranged. Like Newman, he "fled to Antiquity, and would not stop short of it, and so he heard the words of comfort which reconciled him to his work and to its issue" (376). In "The Christian Church a Continuation of the Jewish," Newman revisits this theme by seeing in the dispersed Christendom of his day a replica of the Judaic diaspora that still retained its own sense of catholicity. By this analogy, the saving remnant in the Church is the "token of identity of the Church, in the mind of her Divine Creator, before and after the coming of Christ." The Church is a pilgrim on earth with no secure dwelling place (SSD 195).

Newman thus attempts to explain the provisionality of the English church by linking it to the grand Hebraic narratives of estrangement and redemption. Images of loss, exile, and the harsh unremitting perils of pilgrimage are pressed into service to show that the present state of Anglicanism is not unlike that of the larger Church and the Jews before it. It was met with bafflement by many of his friends, and by 1843 Newman was dwelling more on the perils of disunity, blurring the distinction between collective exile and personal alienation in another sermon, "Connection between Personal and Public Improvement": "We cannot hope for the recovery of dissenting bodies, while we are ourselves alienated from the great body of Christendom. We cannot hope for unity of faith, if we at our own private will make a faith for ourselves in this our small corner of the earth" (SSD 133). The small corner of the earth on which Newman now perched was not even the Church of England. It was a small Church of his own making, about the size of Littlemore.

When he first read Wiseman's article, Newman had sought to bolster Anglican claims by imputing a negative personality to Rome. But by the end of 1844, that attitude had been almost completely reversed by his failure to establish a collective personality for the Church of England. He now felt, in one recent formulation, that "the Church of England above all lack[ed] that basic condition of intelligent life, self-consciousness." For Newman, "the true analogy of the Church [was] not a grain of mustard seed, nor yet a vine, but a sentient human being" (Prickett, *Modernity* 183). In revisiting his essay "The Catholicity of the English Church" after he became a Roman Catholic, his shift of position was almost total. The Church was no longer authenticated by the local Church as type and symbol of a larger but dispersed reality, but by the spirit of the Church as a whole, and only secondarily by individuals. "It is the great Note of an ever-enduring *coetus fidelium*, with a fixed organization, a unity of jurisdiction, a political greatness, a continuity of existence in all places and times, a suitableness to all classes, ranks, and callings, an ever-energizing life, an untiring, ever-evolving history, which is her evidence that she is the creation of God, and the representative and home of Christianity" (*ECH* 2:88). The body of Christ, in which dwells one spirit, is antecedent to Episcopacy; "in it, and not in Episcopacy, lie the transmission and warrant of the Divine privilege" (96). In the *Letter Addressed to His Grace the Duke of Norfolk* (1874), the elderly Newman was to defend the "doctrine of the Church's individuality and, as it were, personality" as reflected in the Papacy and in a reading of the Gospel as "no mere philosophy thrown upon the world at large, no mere quality of mind and thought, no mere beautiful and deep sentiment or subjective opinion, but a substantive message from above, guarded and preserved in a visible polity" (*LDN* 119–20).

A new note suffuses the concluding sermon in *Sermons Bearing on Subjects of the Day*, "The Parting of Friends," which is both the best known and the least typical of the volume. The sermon has jarred some because it seems to elevate its preacher to the level of the suffering Christ, but a more charitable approach would acknowledge that those greater samples of friendship—Jesus, St. Paul, St. Ignatius—are Newman's source of comfort. In imitating Christ, one does not become Him. With the words "We indeed to-day have no need of so high a lesson and so august a comfort" (*SSD* 396), Newman certifies his intention of avoiding self-exaltation. The autumnal date of the sermon (September 25, 1843) lends additional weight to the metaphor of a spiritual as well as temporal harvest stored up for the winter Newman surely knew lay ahead.

"It was a glad time when we first met here," Newman reminded his audience, alluding to the fact that the day of the sermon was the anniversary of the Littlemore Chapel's opening. He urged his hearers to keep this latter feast, albeit "in haste, and with bitter herbs, and with loins girded, and with a staff in one hand, as they who have 'no continuing city, but seek one to come'" (*SSD* 399). The phrase from Hebrews 13 shifts the sermon to the exilic key of its predecessors. To part is to give up home, like Jacob to leave father and mother, like Naomi to accept the ministrations of Ruth even as she feels the pain of Orpah's desertion, like David and Jonathan swearing to maintain their "true love unfeigned" (402). Such examples console, for they are ultimately rewarded acts of self-sacrifice.

What Newman had sought in the collective personality and practice of the Church of England did not furnish what his own personality required. The sometimes warring and almost always inconclusive metaphors with which he had sought to describe it, whether as battlefield, as abused woman kept by the State, or as a dispersed family linked by Apostolical descent and a broad agreement on principle, were inadequate to give it life. And the failure of Bishop Begot to come to his defense as strongly as he had hoped contributed to Newman's doubt that the English Church could assert any claim to true apostolicity. The *Sermons Bearing on Subjects of the Day* were as far as he could go in public. Beneath these public displays of uncertainty, another more private drama was taking place.

CHAPTER 5

Anglican Deathbeds

NEWMAN'S UNCERTAINTY AS to how to deal with his friends is manifest in the correspondence leading up to his reception by Rome. He was not certain how much he could reveal to Keble and Pusey about his true state of mind, or how long he could keep his younger followers in check. His hand was forced by external events during the period 1843–45: the knowledge that William Palmer was about to publish a critical narrative of the Movement, the publication of the memoirs of Joseph Blanco White, and the pending translation of Bishop Bagot from Oxford to the see of Bath and Wells, almost certain to be replaced by an anti-Tractarian. (In the event, the Oxford see went to the hostile Samuel Wilberforce.) As we have seen in the *Sermons Bearing on Subjects of the Day*, Newman's inner uncertainties were already spilling out into the public arena. His last significant writing as an Anglican, *An Essay on the Development of Christian Doctrine*, similarly occupies a terrain somewhere between public and private realms in which internal debates are brought out, if not into full public view, at least in veiled form for what the public could make of them.

In the *Apologia*, Newman was to claim that he had given up his "place in the Movement" in 1839, and that rather than energetically seeking new converts for Anglicanism, his "utmost endeavour was to tranquilize such persons, especially those who belonged to the new school, as were unsettled in their religious views, and, as I judged, hasty in their conclusions." He also claimed that once he had turned his face Romeward, he gave up any thought of influencing others: "How could I in any sense direct others, who had to be guided in so momentous a matter myself?" (*A* 196–97). Newman had to weigh the danger of being entirely open about his Romeward movement against the obloquy that would attach to him should this drift prove to be temporary. He feared misleading others who turned to him for guidance and inciting them prematurely to paths in which he could not yet follow them. But disclaimers to the contrary, he remained a spiritual counselor to some, and a threat to many. His very withdrawal to Littlemore, the suburb of Oxford in which he had purchased several cottages as a basis for a retreat center, could be interpreted, not as a withdrawal, but as evidence of an intention to *reculer pour mieux sauter*.

Craft or Candor

Between the desire for frankness and the need for reticence, Newman left himself very little room. Candor in controversy made him vulnerable to imputations of zealotry; reticence opened up suspicions about his candor. The sermon of 1843 that Charles Kingsley seized on twenty years later, "Wisdom and Innocence," attempted to reconcile the two warring sides of his own personality, to turn his private dilemmas into homiletic form, but it misfired, and not just with Kingsley.

In the sermon, Newman argues that the wisdom of Christians has been called craft; their profession of innocence has been called hypocrisy. Yet to be as innocent as the dove "is the truest wisdom; and this conduct accordingly has preeminently the appearance of craft" (*SSD* 299). This is because sobriety and self-restraint seem artificial, because the feelings of religious persons cannot be known to "the gross, carnal unbelieving world" (300). The early Christians gave outward obedience without interior assent to heathen authority and hence were accused of double-dealing, yet there were many instances in which "it is our duty to obey those who nevertheless have no power over our belief or conviction" (301). Cheerfulness and an apparent acceptance of the world's triumph inevitably have about them "an appearance of craft and deceit" (302), and when Christians, in resignation, are silent, their silence is itself suspicious, for the world expects them to speak out and show a natural and honest indignation. For the world, submitting to calumny proves that the calumny is all too true.

Though Kingsley's indictment of "Wisdom and Innocence" for its defense of duplicity is plausible, the sermon equally reflects Newman's desperate and sometimes fearful attempt to hide his growing concerns even from himself. Later in the century, the generally sympathetic Richard Holt Hutton thought the sermon lacked frankness (a charge short of outright duplicity), and that Newman should have made more allowance for the fact that "Churchmen, in obeying their Lord's command, have been apt to mingle a good deal too much of the wisdom of the serpent with a good deal too little of the harmlessness of the dove," and as a result "have evolved a type of character inferior instead of superior to the worldly, which devotes itself to the same order of affairs" (Hutton 123). Newman undoubtedly erred on the side of "craft," but he did not consciously play a duplicitous game. Still, to make a sermon a disguised plea for privacy is incompatible with its normal teaching function. The importunities of newspapers and strangers in trying to penetrate a silence that looked more like secrecy than self-protection, the anxiety of those really close to him who wanted to follow him could they but find out his intentions, contributed to his pain. Guided by the precept "Physician, heal thyself," he wrote in a famous passage, "I wished to go to my Lord by myself, and in my own way, or rather His way. I had neither wish, nor, I may say, thought of taking a number with me" (*A* 198).

By the summer of 1843, Newman's simmering anxiety about retaining his post at St. Mary's had reached new levels. He was as insistent in deploring his deficiency in really knowing his parishioners as in fearing his own influence over those (especially undergraduates) whom he did know and to whom he was particularly drawn. As early as 1840 he had confided to J. R. Bloxam, "Every thing is so cold at St. Mary's—I have felt it for years. I know no one. I have no sympathy. I have many critics and carpers—If it were not for these poor undergraduates, who are after all *not* my charge, and the Sunday Communions, I should be sorely tempted to pitch my tent here [at Littlemore]" (*L&D* 7:261). Writing to Samuel Rickards in March 1843, he was preoccupied with the twin dangers of being either overpraised or accused of double-dealing in his verbal professions. "I assure you, nothing has haunted me more continually for years than the idea that Undergraduates are trusting me more than they should—and I have done many things by way of preventing it. I should not wonder if the feeling ended in separating me from St. Mary's, about which I have thought many times" (*L&D* 9:270). Newman's inward drama bordered on paralysis; it was as Matthew Arnold had described it in his 1853 preface to his poems, an Empedoclean state of mind in which suffering found no vent in action.

In part because he had not fully confided in them, Pusey and Keble were slow to take the measure of Newman's difficulties. Keble, though reluctantly conceding that it might be necessary to resign St. Mary's, was doubtful that Newman was seeing as plainly as he ought that despite his uncertainties, he might go on with his parochial duties. In July 1841 Keble suggested that "unreserved confidence in some *really worthy* Confessor might be a great help to you at times: I mean the sort of submission which would make you put by a subject if he bid you, without his assigning any reason." He added, in words that could not have been helpful under the circumstances, that "it may be well for one to watch and pray, especially against the temptation of always being on the move, which I suppose is the portion of some minds" (*L&D* 9:449). Newman responded that he had begun a journal for the possible purpose of seeking a confessor but that the only person he could have chosen was Keble himself, and he was reluctant to increase Keble's anxiety. Given Newman's apparent reluctance to seek spiritual direction from anyone, the letter is a melancholy reminder that sincerity and self-perception do not necessarily travel hand in hand (*L&D* 9:463–65).

Keble, however unworldly he may have been in politics, was wiser in matters of the heart. His common sense was evident in the spring of 1843, when Newman was facing a barrage of criticism for Tract 90 in the Charges issued by the bishops to their diocesan clergy. Neither Keble nor Pusey lent much weight to such episcopal judgments. Keble wrote, "I do not think so much of the Bishops' words in their Charges now as you do, and as I did myself, now that I have found out how they might act on them and do not, thereby proving themselves not in earnest." Since the bishops had not yet openly condemned Tract 90, Keble asked, why force them to the point (*CNK* 216)? Pusey, remembering hearing Newman's lament at Littlemore, "Oh, Pusey, we have leant on the Bishops and they have broken down under us!," recalled his mental reaction: "At least I never leant on the Bishops, I leant on the Church of England!" (Liddon 2:227). Newman felt that his friends were missing the point. The bishops' Charges were a source of distress to him because they were, first, "in some sense protests and witnesses to my conscience against my secret unfaithfulness to the English Church" and, second, "average samples of her teaching and tokens how very far she is from even aspiring to Catholicity" (*L&D* 9:327–28). But Newman was unable to bring himself to the sticking point by fully stating his feelings. In this he was not only more than a little unfair to his friends, but exhibiting the same resistance to authority that had undermined his relationship to Bishop Bagot and prevented him from seeing a confessor.

The summer of 1843 brought a blow of another sort. Proceedings were instituted against Pusey for preaching a sermon at Christ Church on May 14, 1843, on "The Holy Eucharist a Comfort for the Penitent," which anti-Tractarians interpreted as expounding a dangerously Romanizing argument on the remission of sins and as verging on an argument for transubstantiation. If the sacramental system of which the Eucharist was the climax was a sinner's true refuge, then implicitly Pusey seemed, to the Evangelical party at least, to be denying the Protestant idea of justification and "the unique instrumentality of faith."[1] The sermon was essentially a defense of the doctrine of the Real Presence, for which there was adequate precedent in the Caroline divines and which Newman himself had upheld, without apparently raising any hackles, five years before.[2] In a mockery of due process, Pusey was denied the opportunity to respond to any charges against him, and the Hebdomadal Board, which showed no signs of reading the sermon any more closely than the Tractarians had read Hampden, inhibited Pusey from preaching for two years from June 1843. The suspension casts a somewhat unflattering light on Newman's preoccupation with his own agonies. Pusey's unswerving belief in the ability of the Church to reform itself, coupled with his proven capacity to survive such personal catastrophes as the death of his wife, enabled him to bear this inhibition with equanimity, though he vigorously and publicly dissented. The deprivation of access to the pulpit was arguably a burden far greater than Newman had ever had to bear, but with characteristic humility Pusey took it as a punishment for "secret faults" (Liddon 3:95). For Newman, however, the episode seems to have served principally as further proof that the Establishment had become a persecutor of orthodoxy. Thus he wrote to the Rev. William Dodsworth on the necessity of offering Pusey visible support: "If one thing after another is done against the holder of Catholic doctrines, without protest from any quarter, the imaginations of certain persons will be gradually affected with the notion that the Church of England does not hold them, and is not their place. And they will look for a place elsewhere" (*L&D* 9:370).

Secessions

Newman's growing concern about the possibility of others seceding to Rome was fueled both by his annoyance that the Anglican hierarchy seemed to be driving people in that direction, and by his need to feel that he still exercised sufficient personal influence to prevent such secessions. When called upon to give advice to others in the subject, he sometimes tried to project a confidence that he did not feel personally. Thus he urged his friend the Rev. S. F. Wood to remain at Margaret Street in London in terms that he did not apply to himself: "I think you can be of great use to other men in directing their thoughts to interior religion as a sufficient occupation, to say the least, for the present" (*L&D* 8:416). To laity, he generally urged extreme caution before taking the step he himself had not decided upon. In this he was following the line he said he had taken in 1839: "I determined to be guided, not by my imagination, but by my reason ... Had it not been for this severe resolve, I should have been a Catholic sooner than I was. Moreover, I felt on consideration a positive doubt ... whether the suggestion did not come from below. Then I said to myself, Time alone can solve that question.... If it came from above, it would come again,—so I trusted,—and with more definite outlines and greater cogency and consistency of proof" (*A* 112). Newman took pains to emphasize his own consistency of conduct: "Since I have been a Catholic, people have sometimes accused me of backwardness in making converts; and Protestants have argued from it that I have no great eagerness to do so. It would be against my nature to act otherwise than I do; but besides, it would be to forget the lessons which I gained in the experience of my own history in the past" (119). His advice to others both derived from and reinforced the attitude he took in the third of his four 1841 sermons on the obligations of remaining in the Anglican Communion.

The secession of his admirer William Lockhart came home to Newman as a personal failure. Lockhart had promised that he would not make such a move for three years, but his growing convictions on the matter led him to make a retreat under the priest Luigi Gentili of Loughborough, as a result of which his reception became certain.[3] Newman's feelings were exacerbated by the fact that, as he wrote to Keble, Gentili "did not make any overtures whatever to [Lockhart] and only admitted him, when (as he thought) his duty obliged him."[4] When Newman personalized an action in this way, and then proceeded, with somewhat dubious logic, to use it as the grounds for resigning St. Mary's, Henry Wilberforce minced no words: "If you are resolved, nothing that I can say is likely to change your purpose—but I cannot but think that you are acting *very wrong,* and doing what will tend more to injure the cause than can be conceived—It is just what the enemy will triumph over, and you will concede the principle which they are contending for, viz., that no voice of several Bishops, uttered in the way that ours have spoken, is decisive. This appears to me to be a surrender of every Church Principle—What would be the effect of all the Bishops acting *in accord* and therefore with authority, is another question" (*L&D* 9:482, n. 3). Wilberforce's argument had considerable merit, but it came too late. The occasion of Lockhart's secession, Newman argued, gave him cover for a resignation on the grounds that although the scandal had fallen on him unfairly, he must still bear some degree of responsibility. This is hard to understand, since Lockhart's special pledge to Newman, though known to a few friends, was far from a matter of public record. And by asserting a degree of responsibility Newman ran the danger of being perceived as inflating an influence in the Movement that he had previously disavowed.

On September 7, 1843, Newman wrote to Bishop Bagot resigning St. Mary's. He cited the condemnations of the episcopal bench and the failure of anyone (including, as he thought, his own diocesan) to support him in his own interpretation of the Articles. To Archdeacon Henry Manning the next month, Newman dramatized himself as having been effectively disowned by his own communion. Somewhat self-pityingly, he told Manning, "If ever there was a case in which an individual has been put aside, and virtually put away, by a community, mine is one. No decency has been observed in the attacks upon me from authority, no protests have appeared against them" (*L&D* 9:573). In reply, Manning urged, as Keble had urged, that Newman take a longer view. "Surely you cannot feel that the Church of England regards you as a foreign ingredient. With whose writings has it so strongly and widely sympathized? For years, who has been more loved and revered?" Not only this, Manning implied, but his colleague was somewhat unrealistic in expecting to change the views of the Church "in a few years, and at one bidding" (584).

Had Newman been guided by his own emerging theory of doctrinal development, he might have been able to see Manning's argument as a constructive application of his own principles. He had already departed from arguments he himself had made to others in the matter, writing to R. W. Church at the end of 1841 that "I should think lightly of that man who for some act of the Bishops should all at once leave the Church. Now considering how the Clergy really are improving considering that this row is even making them read the Tracts—is it not possible we may all be in a better state of mind seven years hence to consider these matters? and may we not leave them meanwhile to the will of Providence?" (*L&D* 8:384). By 1843, seven years had, to Newman, become an eternity. Patience with the long course of history was a theoretical, not a personal matter.

In rejecting the cautions of friends like Keble, Manning, and Henry Wilberforce, Newman had arrived at a halfway house of his own choosing. Indeed, he had made a very Evangelical move, a decision of private judgment, in which it is difficult to distinguish personal pique from principled objection. The best reader of his motives in 1843–44 seems to have been John Keble. Although Newman was the more aggressive political infighter, Keble had a practicality honed by his parochial duties at Hursley. Unlike Pusey, whose mind could not take in why Newman might seek an alternative to the Church of England, Keble, once faced with the facts, probed Newman's state of mind with no small insight: "Such tendencies [of being enticed or driven out of the Church] one can imagine in your case; among the rest a certain restlessness, a longing after something more, something analogous to a very exquisite ear in music, which would keep you . . . intellectually and morally dissatisfied wherever you were. . . . May it not perhaps be your duty, according to your own line of argument [in *Sermons Bearing on Subjects of the Day*] to suppress your misgivings, nay what seem your intellectual convictions, as you would any other bad thoughts, making up your mind that the conclusion is undutiful, and therefore this [*sic*] must be some delusion in the premises?" (*L&D* 10:100). Keble was phrasing the possibility as a polite hypothesis, but the letter comes as close to an accusation as it could. It was also a remarkably perceptive reading of Newman's incurable restlessness, and may explain why Newman had resisted submitting to Keble's spiritual direction some months before.

Ignoring Keble's implication that he had failed to follow his own advice, Newman replied the same day (January 23) that he had already received letters from others indicating an unsettlement of mind analogous to, but not deriving from, his own. "If my thoughts had been led through the early church to Rome[,] why should not others?" (*L&D* 10:102). Why assume, he asked, that all such persons were under his influence in so acting? Perhaps only someone so firmly committed to personal influence could so ardently protest his own innocence of any attempt to exercise it.

Behind the Scenes

In private, Newman was quite capable of diagnosing his motives—self-corrosively so. They were occasioned notably by the periodic retreats at Littlemore, within a long walk of his rooms at Oriel, and we know something of his state of mind there and elsewhere by the notes from 1838 to 1847 labeled "personal and most private." In Lent 1843 he harbored deep anxieties over his proper use of his gifts, his tendencies toward self-will and disobedience, his deficiencies in the cure of souls at St. Mary's. The acute and relentless self-probing, characteristic of his Evangelical years, had never left him. A more alarmed note, however, is apparent in an entry on December 20, 1843, three and a half months after his resignation at St. Mary's. This was written in the course of an abbreviated (five-day) Ignatian retreat at Littlemore with four other companions, where he recorded an anxious mental image that had come to him during his meditation on sin:

> I kept thinking intellectually on the sin of the Angels. I found it difficult ... to argue from their sin to my sin. One thought impressed me, that "I have been all but damned"—just as when you saw a man fall from a horse, you might say that he had been all but killed, & had a very narrow escape indeed. And then this image came on me, but I could not help beginning to think how it would dress for a composition of some kind. Suppose their footing giving way, when persons were on some high ground, & they rolled down with the swiftness of lightning down, down, a steep descent round a chasm; let them fall on it, & let one be caught by a projecting rock. That was I, but this was not all. I clamber up a little, but the sides are slippery, whether with snow or some other cause—& the footing scarcely possible, & the

greatest care is necessary to hinder destruction after all—that is I now. (*L&D* 10:65–66)

Untrained as they were in Ignatian spirituality, and without an experienced director, Newman and his four friends were engaged in a very dangerous pursuit.[5] Its effects on Newman confirmed his sense of spiritual dryness, imbued here with an almost Calvinistic sense of reprobation. Even in private notes, his self-consciousness persists (in thinking how his imaginings would "dress" for a composition), while he is possessed by a sense of precipitate descent and narrow escape. This waking dream came on the heels of a day in which he had rebuked himself for "greediness, self-conceit, and wandering in prayer," a list to which a few days later he added "impatience, impetuosity, rudeness, inaccuracy in speech sometimes approaching to lying, which I have not as yet mentioned" (67). The ambiguity of the mental image lies in the uncertainty of its cause: accident? judgment from without? the self-will that so often brought Newman to this pass? Was it Anglican ground giving way, or was he climbing back to the "safety of continuance" in the Anglican communion? Was his confidence in his own motives eroding or was he clambering toward the rock of Peter?

The downward slope of Newman's mental "wanderings" is no bad metaphor for the state of his mind at the end of 1843. What is particularly noteworthy is his recitation of sins as "sometimes approaching to lying, which I have not as yet mentioned." In all likelihood, it was not as yet mentioned because it was painful to put his suspicion of himself on the table even if these were only the private notes from a retreat. Only a man like Newman, sometimes self-deluded but scrupulously honest, could be so disturbed by doubts of his own veracity.

Two days later, the retreatants devoted time to a contemplation of death and judgment. Newman's meditation focused on "the horrors of a lost soul being stripped of the graces which were (only) lent it, not made its own— e.g. becoming cruel, desperate, &c &c parallel to the countenance becoming deformed. What seems to throw light on this, is my apparently great *inconsistency* of character, so that persons who know me well would be puzzled, saying I was reverent yet profane, considerate yet cruel, gentle yet violent &c all showing that I have *gifts* contrary to my real nature" (*L&D* 10:67). At moments like this, Newman seems torn between a desire to maintain his privacy and a half-articulated hope that someone might violate it so that, without assuming the burden of confession, he would be better understood.

This anxiety of double-dealing persisted for many months. Newman wrote to his aunt Elizabeth Newman in July 1844 after revisiting his grandmother's house in Fulham. Remembering fondly his visits to his grandmother and her quiet biblical faith, he burst out, "Alas, my dear Aunt, I am but a sorry bargain, and perhaps if you knew all about me, you would hardly think me now worth claiming; still I cannot help—I am what I am—and I have grown into what I am from that time at Fulham" (*L&D* 10:303). His dream, or waking nightmare, was being realized. The ground was indeed giving way, but (to alter the metaphor), Newman had yet another year on his own Anglican "deathbed." He had already unveiled his innermost feelings to Pusey in February 1844 in the hope of dispelling his friend's illusions about where he stood: "I fear that I must say that for four years and a half I have had a conviction, weaker or stronger, but on the whole constantly growing, and at present very strong, that we are not part of the Church." Though he did not as yet feel any call to take action, if he arrived at a full belief in this proposition he would be "anxious and much perplexed" (126). He referred Pusey to a note on the subject in *Sermons Bearing on Subjects of the Day* that declared the necessity of being fully convinced of Roman claims before leaving the Church of England. There he had written that "mere impressions, impulses, fancies, frames of mind, logical deductions, or the blindness which follows on religious carelessness" must be seen as something short of conviction (126, n. 1). But Newman was not sure at what point conviction would lead to action.

The year 1845 brought unwelcome memories of another Anglican deathbed with the posthumous publication of the memoirs of Joseph Blanco White, whom Newman had known at Oxford nearly twenty years before and with whom he had ended relations when White became a Unitarian. White's *Life*, as his Unitarian editor John Hamilton Thom called it, combines autobiographical narrative, extracts from White's journals, and a portion of his correspondence. Of Irish extraction, White was born in Spain and grew up with Spanish as his first language. As a Roman Catholic, he had early developed an abiding hatred of priestly hypocrisy, auricular confession, Ignatian exercises, the tedium of the Breviary, Aristotelian logic, scholastic theology, and the Inquisition, a fairly exhaustive catalogue. As a mostly non-practicing Anglican clergyman enjoying a second career as a Fellow of Oriel, he came to believe that the liturgical practices and clerical discipline of the Church of England amounted to a watered-down popery. He resigned his Anglican orders, embraced Unitarianism, and took up residence in Liverpool, where he became a correspondent of John Stuart Mill and a contributor to the newly merged *London and Westminster Review*, as well as an admirer of the sermons of the young James Martineau and a transatlantic correspondent of William Ellery Channing. Having rejected the doctrines of Christian orthodoxy, White had in his own words taken refuge in "the great Truths of Religion, namely, the paternal character of God, by none so clearly exhibited to mankind as by our greatest benefactor under God—Jesus of Nazareth; the call to immortality; the readiness of God to forgive on repentance; the certainty of that forgiveness without either payment, or a strict claim on our part; the reasonableness of submitting to what is evil *to us*, committing the final result to our heavenly Father" (White 2:125).

There is not a little spiritual pride in all this, as Newman realized, but that does not account for the alarmed outpouring in his letter to Henry Wilberforce on April 27, 1845, shortly after the *Life* appeared. He called it "the most dismal horrible work I ever saw," the work of a man dying as a virtual pantheist. "Yet his Biographer actually calls him in last moments a *Confessor*—confessor to what? not to any opinion, any belief whatever—but to the *Search* after truth; ever wandering about and changing, and therefore great. Is this the *end* of Life?.... But what a view does it give one of those Unitarians and id genus omne! They really do think it is no harm whatever being an Atheist, so that you are sincerely so, and do not cut people's throats and pick their pockets" (*L&D* 10:639–40). As Newman proceeds, his attention turns from White to himself:

> Here is Blanco White, sincere and honest. He gives up his country and then his second home—Spain, Oxford, Whately's family, all for an idea of truth, or rather for liberty of thought.[6] True, I think a great deal of morbid restlessness was mixed with his sincerity, an inability to keep still in one place, a readiness to take offence and be disgusted, an inward irritability and a fear of not

> being independent, and other bad feelings. But then the thought forcibly comes upon one, why may not the case be the same with me? I see Blanco White going wrong, yet sincere, Arnold going wrong, yet sincere; they are no puzzle to *me*. I can put my finger on this or that point in their character, and say, *Here* was the fault. But *they* did not know the fault—and so it comes upon me, How do I know that I too have not my weak points which occasion me to think as I think? how can I be sure that I have not committed sins which bring this unsettled state of mind on me as a judgment? (*L&D* 10:640–41)

Such scrupulosity borders on paralysis. The panic that underlies his letter to Wilberforce clearly indicates that he saw White as a kind of alter ego, a Unitarian in his own mirror.

This ghost from the past spoke to Newman directly across the years. "B. W.'s book has tried me in another very different way," he told Wilberforce. "I am nearly the only person he speaks of with affection in it among his English friends. At least, he says more about me than any one else.... It seems as if people were just now beginning to praise me when I was going away" (*L&D* 10:641). But White's references to Newman were not uniformly flattering. Preoccupied by the bigotry of these "High Church Pietists," especially in the Hampden affair, White did, to be sure, make allowance for Newman. In a letter of 1834 to his patron Lord Holland, he had written that he loved both Pusey and Newman "for their talents and good nature," Newman in particular being "one of the most liberal, well-informed, and kind-hearted men I knew" (White 2:213). But he was less dithyrambic in a journal entry of 1836: "Newman, who has raised himself into a Protestant Pope, and who, as sure as he lives, would persecute to the death if he had the direction of the civil power for a dozen years—Newman expresses the utmost tenderness for those who holding any opinion whatever, will only whisper them tremblingly into his ear" (213). He added a few days later that "Newman's deceiving pride is more deeply seated [than Pusey's] and more difficult to be suspected by himself.... When will it please Heaven to put an end to all priesthoods?" (223). These once-private words were now laid bare to public gaze.

Newman had learned of White's defection the month before these journal entries, and although he had not preserved a copy of his own letter to White, he could read in White's journal entry of March 23, 1836: "I have this morning received a most melancholy letter from my excellent friend Newman, of Oriel. The letter is nothing but a groan, a sigh, from beginning to end" (White 2:117). He acknowledged to Newman with every appearance of affection that their states of mind were very different, that "I must follow the light that is in me. If that light be darkness, it is so without my being aware of it, without the slightest ground for suspecting that it is willfully so" (118). For Newman, however, the point of White's letter lay in another sentence: "As long as the notion, that opinions can decide the fate of immortal souls, shall exist, the most excruciating sufferings await the best minds." Nothing could be more alien to Newman, for whom life and death, the securing of immortality, hung on those decisions that were a matter of religious profession, not a mere opinion or bias of the mind. He could not make excuses for White, and he could not make excuses for himself either.

When Gladstone wrote for information pertinent to a biographical sketch of White that he was preparing for a forthcoming number of the *Quarterly Review*, Newman's rhetoric betrayed his feelings. In a letter of 12 June 1845, he told Gladstone: "I do not understand why, though it is thirteen years since I saw him, and I only had one letter from him since, his image haunts me more than the dearest friends whom I have lost, and I can fancy him before me, and have a vivid impression of his voice countenance and manner." Like most hauntings, this one ended in a shudder. White's hatred of Rome, Newman told Gladstone, was "a deep, awful, personal feeling. . . . It is a curious question whether one can feel sinful resentment towards an abstract body" (*L&D* 10:700–01). In his anti-Roman phase, Newman had harbored similar feelings. He resorted next to a direct comparison. Just as White had seen no resting place between Christianity and unbelief, "I am not an unbiased judge on the point, as approximating to the doctrine which his career seems to exemplify, 'There is no medium between the Church of Rome and Infidelity.' But he added quickly, "I cannot deny, as I have said above, that he was a fanciful reasoner—and went off upon sudden notions" (703).

In his earlier letter about White to Henry Wilberforce, Newman had lamented, "Now my prime of life is past, and I am nothing. . . . How dreadful it is, to have to act on great matters so much in the dark! Yet I, who have preached so much on the duty of following in the night whenever God may call, am the last person who has a right to complain. It struck me as curious, that in my verses to my brother Frank which I have with others, I say, 'O may we follow undismayed / Where'er our God should call'" (*L&D* 10:642).[7] Blanco White and Francis Newman had taken one direction; though in a contrary direction, John would follow their example.

Given the pressure of familial as well as Oxford memories and the parallels that presented themselves so forcibly to Newman, his brother was almost the last person he needed to hear from. But he did. A letter from Frank dated August 6, 1845, urged him not to take the step virtually everyone who knew him now knew he was contemplating. Frank wanted to know whether his brother was choosing Rome as the least evil or as a good in itself. Should he not adhere to some independent Episcopal system as existed in the United States or Scotland?[8] If he were younger he might "find a valuable career" in the Roman Catholic Church, "but now, your attainments and your acquired influence do not fit you for that. . . . Your name would lose at once all influence with nine tenths of those who were used to respect you, and among Romanists you would be received with condescending pity as a novice who had yet much to learn and unlearn" (*L&D* 10:744). Frank was no bad prophet here, but he was an inept diplomat urging an untimely case. Newman saw his brother's intrusion as nothing more than an argument from expediency. On the margin of the letter he wrote, "That I could be contemplating questions of Truth and Falsehood never entered into his imagination!" To his brother he wrote sharply on August 7 a letter of which the following seems to be a précis:

> It is from no idea of the Roman system being the most bearable of the existing forms of religion that I contemplate accepting it.
>
> I have always resisted, and do heartily resist, the notion of choosing a religion according to my fancy.
>
> I have no desire at all to leave the English Church. I feel the utmost disgust at the thought of forming a new sect. I have no temptation that way at all.
>
> My reason for going to Rome is this—I think the English Church in schism. I think the faith of the Roman Church the

only true religion. I do not think there is salvation out of the Church of Rome. (*L&D* 10:745)

If indeed some such letter was sent to Frank, it would have been clear to the younger brother that John would not be a happy convert.

Development and the Individual

Newman's vehement feelings toward his brother reflected unresolved issues of his own. Secessions from the Anglican communion in Newman's day took at least three directions: toward Rome, toward existing Dissenting sects, or toward Liberalism, believing or unbelieving. The erratic and impulsive migration of Frank to Liberalism via John Nelson Darby and the Plymouth Brethren was one such instance of an alteration of views which has occupied less historical attention than the Tractarian drama.

With his own early Evangelicalism as well as his natural acuteness of observation, John could not but be aware that leftward secessions bore a striking resemblance to the driving forces behind the Tractarian movement itself: the nostalgia for a purified Apostolic church (Turner 424). The divisions on the left were numerous; Grayson Carter (255–56) distinguishes no fewer than four major groupings of Evangelicals at Oxford by the 1830s. Ultra-Calvinism (both inside and outside the Establishment) and Quaker-like affirmations of the inner light were both manifestations, in Newman's view, of the workings of unchecked private judgment. Though Anglican Evangelicals like Charles Simeon at Cambridge preached "Church regularity" and remained suspicious of anything that looked like Wesleyan disorder, forceful personalities were numbered among them. Henry Bulteel's fiery sermons at St. Ebbe's in Oxford were the Evangelical counterpart of Newman's sermons at St. Mary's, and outside the Anglican fold, Francis Newman's admiration of Darby's combination of tenderness and certainty suggests that Darby had become a surrogate for an autocratic older sibling. The Plymouth Brethren mission to Baghdad that Francis joined was for Newman yet one more piece of evidence of the intellectual untidiness, theological disarray, and quixotic spirit evident in newer and more deviant forms of Protestantism, the same spirit that some opponents saw in the Tractarians themselves.

Viewed in this context, *An Essay on the Development of Christian Doctrine* is first of all a rejection of hasty choices and an attempt (in veiled, quasi-autobiographical form) to emphasize the deliberateness of Newman's spiritual journey away from what he saw as the formlessness of Evangelical peregrinations. Discussions of this work have rightly focused on its status as a theological treatise, especially ways in which it anticipates the later *Essay in Aid of a Grammar of Assent*. But Newman repeatedly linked the progress of the work to the process of his own decision making. Thus he wrote to his sister Jemima on August 17, 1845, at the time he was fending off Frank's clumsy interventions, "The probability is that the appearance of my book will be the signal of my going—and people must take it as such" (*L&D* 10:748). Wanderings in prayer were one thing; wanderings in pilgrimage were another and more serious fault. As in a labyrinth, there might be an occasional cul de sac, but the goal was always the same, and to establish retrospectively a trajectory of development would show consistency between past and present beliefs and behaviors. Newman had always worried about his own consistency and the processes by which he found himself being led. In what is probably, according to Francis McGrath, the draft of a letter written to Keble on October 30, 1844, he had said, "I do not know how to do justice to my own reasonings and impressions. . . . The process of argument is like a scaffolding taken down when the building is completed. I could not recollect all the items which went to make up my convictions, nor can I represent it to another with that force [with] which it came to my mind" (*L&D* 10:376). Both history and the preoccupation with understanding one's own mental processes are at issue in this uneasy letter, in which Newman is uncertain as to whether the products of his journey are "impressions" (as McGrath's text makes clear, he had originally written "conclusions") or "convictions." The *Development* charts a path leading to both the *Apologia* and the *Grammar of Assent*. It argues from continuities to place the argument from history on a new footing. The *Apologia* dramatizes the self as a case history; the *Grammar*, the internal processes that lead to personal conviction. In the *Development* and the *Grammar*, Newman is an implied actor; in the *Apologia*, he is his own case history. But the *Development* clears Newman's way to Rome. He did not need to go back to the Primitive Church if he could show that Christian doctrine had a traceable genealogy.

The idea of development, personal or historical, had been germinating in Newman's mind for a long time. In *The Prophetical Office of the Church*, he had stated that everything Jesus did and said was "characterized by mingled simplicity and mystery," his miracles and parables testifying to "a legislature in germ, afterwards to be developed" (305). There he had gone so far as to accept the Roman response to Protestants who would accuse Catholics of falling away from the original simplicity of the Gospels. The Romanist answer, which Newman endorsed, was that the function of the Church was to serve as Christ's successor, unveiling the consequences of His legislative "germ." The Church had maintained its corporate identity through change. As he wrote in "The Catholicity of the English Church," "The full-grown fulfillment, to superficial observers, necessarily seems different from what it was in its rudiments, just as a friend, not seen for many years, is strange to us at first sight, till, by degrees, we catch the old looks, or the well-remembered tones, or the smile or the remark, which assure us that, with whatever changes of age or circumstance, he is the same man" (*ECH* 2:43).

The autobiographical matrix of the *Development* is rhetorically suppressed; the letter to Jemima confirms that. Its context is the events immediately prior to Newman's secession, including the publication of the Oxford University sermons, issued in 1843 under the title *Sermons, Chiefly on the Theory of Religious Belief*, which, its modern editors observe, "have all the immediacy of a journal" to which "Newman often turned . . . when writing the *Apologia*" (Earnest and Tracey, *OUS* xiii). Sermon 15 on development provides a bridge to both the *Development* and the *Grammar* by describing the psychological process by which we come to apprehend religious truth and by which its implications are unfolded in our minds. The analogue of individual and collective process, reminiscent of Newman's earlier analogue of private and corporate personality, is now applied to the study of doctrine.[9]

Hugh MacDougall has argued, and I would concur, that in reading Newman, we are not to equate development with nineteenth-century Whig ideas of progress but with a movement "toward a deeper understanding of old truths. There was a constant reaching-back demanded to ensure that a development retained true to its origins. . . . For Newman the object of development, paradoxically, was preservation more than progression" (157–58). Nor, it should be added, does the *Development* really anticipate Darwin's *Origin of Species* (1859), to which it has sometimes rather hastily been compared, though, as the recent work of Suzy Anger shows, it is certainly related to a larger cultural mood reflected in such writers as Charles Lyell and Robert Chambers.[10] Though Newman thought historically, "development" has for him a very idiosyncratic meaning. It does not characterize an organic process. Rather, it involves the bringing to light of phenomena (in this case in theological history) that were always already there, implicit in germ in the earliest development of the Christian faith.[11] If read in personal terms, the *Development* is also a justification for Newman's deliberation and delay. Given the constitution of the human mind, he argues, the maturation of an idea requires time to work its result. Truth may not be immediately understood by all its potential recipients. It is not just a matter of individual consciousness but of the collision of ideas that truth, like a stream, is not greatest nearest its source but requires a bed that is "deep, and broad, and full" for its growth (*DCD* 40). It needs to be disengaged from what is transitory, and its identity needs to be articulated "not in isolation, but in continuity and sovereignty" (39). Truth, amid the errancies of the individual human mind,

> remains perhaps for a time quiescent; it tries, as it were, its limbs, and proves the ground under it, and feels its way. From time to time it makes essays which fail, and are in consequence abandoned. It seems in suspense which way to go; it wavers, and at length strikes out in one definite direction. In time it enters upon strange territory; points of controversy alter their bearing; parties rise and fall around it; dangers and hopes appear in new relations; and old principles reappear under new forms. It changes with them in order to remain the same. In a higher world it is otherwise, but here below to live is to change, and to be perfect is to have changed often. (40)

Like the waking dream that Newman had recorded in his Littlemore retreat notes, the strikingly kinetic quality of this passage reflects his internalization of the same process. In the half-groping and sometimes flailing method by which he had made his own "essays" at religious belief, he recognized that parties had risen and fallen around him during his journey toward the discovery of "old principles" under "new forms." Newman's suspicion of committees and boards persists in his remark that "coalitions in politics and comprehensions in religion" may for a time connect discordant elements, but that coalitions are not communities and therefore offer no true principle of union. Newman's appeal, paradoxically, is both to the stability of the Church's authoritative teaching and to the subjective working of the individual mind, and it is not surprising that this sometimes generates an internal tension.

Newman's concern with how others perceived him is evident in the same kind of forensic technique he was to display in the *Apologia*. A foreshadowing instance is his point that the true character of an individual may be assayed in law so as either to fully acquit a defendant or to undermine his reputation with a merely technical acquittal (*DCD* 114–15). As with theological propositions, so with individuals, and this constant oscillation between the individual mind and the history of doctrine is a constant in the *Development*: "An idea under one or other of its aspects grows in the mind by remaining there; it becomes familiar and distinct, and is viewed in its relations; it leads to other aspects, and these again to others, subtle, recondite, original, according to the character, intellectual and moral, of the recipient; and thus a body of thought is gradually formed without his recognizing what is going on within him." External circumstance elicits these thoughts and shapes them into formal statements, themselves requiring analysis, formal defense, and a scrutiny of their interdependence. The result is a transmutation of moral principles into their logical consequences and principles for which the mind has a natural sympathy, and hence "logic is brought in to arrange and inculcate what no science was employed in gaining" (190). In short, Newman could tell both friends and foes that he had not been fully conscious of the processes going on in his mind; logic followed where sympathy led him, but that took time. Only belatedly does an individual recognize whither his mind and prospects have been tending.

The *Development* foreshadows the concluding chapter of the *Apologia* in which Newman dramatizes the collision of ideas within the Church. Newman writes, "When an idea, whether real or not, is of a nature to arrest and possess the mind, it may be said to have life, that is, to live in the mind which is its recipient" (*DCD* 36). Once it begins to circulate and become an "active principle" in other minds, it is transmuted into doctrine, a perceived definition or justification for a certain intellectual system. After time it is brought into collision or adjustment with other ideas or doctrines; it may be modified or assimilated by them, or itself take on an assimilative power. A dual process of defense and interrogation of the doctrine ensues, coupled with whatever it already has of "native vigour and subtlety." It may grow "into an ethical code, or into a system of government, or into a theology, or into a ritual, according to its capabilities." The idea will still be true to its origins, but its "complete image" is a result of the suggestions and corrections of many minds, and the illustration of many experiences" (37–38). Development is therefore the "germination and maturation of some truth or apparent truth on a large mental field," in which all its diversified aspects in their totality attest to the stability of the truth. Development may be rapid or repeatedly interrupted, but—and here Newman perhaps draws closer to the later Darwinian system—its survivability is at least a partial index to its truth. Bad doctrines may cling tenaciously to life or even be brought back to life, but bad doctrines carry the seeds of their own destruction.

The treatise describes seven "Notes," Notes this time of true doctrine rather than a church, by which we distinguish authentic development from its aberrations: "preservation of type," "continuity of principles," "power of assimilation," "logical sequence," "anticipation of its own future," "conservative action upon the past," and "chronic vigour." These are not only features that Newman has come to find in Roman Catholic doctrine, but aspects of his own development. We will return in chapter 8 to the relevance of these to the structure of the *Apologia*, but pause here on the sixth of them, "conservative action upon the past," a standard for evaluating the truth of a development by its continuity with, or minimal disturbance of, the past. Newman again is speaking as surely about the phenomenon in the life of the individual as about the corporate development of doctrine through ecclesial history. "It is an addition which illustrates, not obscures, corroborates, not corrects, the body of thought from which it proceeds; and this is its characteristic as contrasted with a corruption." Thus "a gradual conversion from a false to a true religion, plainly, has much of the character of a continuous process, or a development, in the mind itself, even when the two religions, which are the limits of its course, are antagonistic" (*DCD* 200). Quoting from his own Tract 85, *Holy Scripture in Relation to the Catholic Creed*, as if to demonstrate the continuity between the Anglican Newman and the Roman-Catholic-about-to-be, he writes that the process is one of addition and increase rather than subtraction and decrease (201).

Anglican Deathbeds

In Newman's case, aside from the one or two corruptions to which he had earlier adhered and which he had long since renounced (for example, the belief that the Pope was the Antichrist), continuity lay in gathering up the strands of the past. A sincerely religious mind drawn out of heathenism or heresy into religious truth would not sacrifice what was usable from the past, but gain what it had not had earlier (*DCD* 200–201). The process is not governed by what elsewhere he called "paper logic," but by "slow, spontaneous, ethical growth, not the scientific and compulsory results, of existing opinions" (336). The continuing process of exchange between internal and external development reappears when Newman draws a parallel between the operations of the conscience in the life of the individual mind and the operations of the dogmatic principle in the history of Christianity. Dogmatic truth, unlike heresy, has that assimilating power that is the mark of a truly catholic comprehensiveness. Newman detects in Tertullian at least a partial resolution of "the two antagonist principles of dogmatism and assimilation." And as the treatise moves toward its conclusion, the principle of the Church comes into play as the middle term between the individual conscience and the universal progress of corporate truth. "The theology of the Church is no random combination of various opinions, but a diligent, patient working out of one doctrine from many materials. The conduct of Popes, Councils, and Fathers betokens the slow, painful, anxious taking up of new truths into an existing body of belief" (366).

Newman makes it clear that in Rome he has now found an identity, a personality that the Church of England lacks. Like those who fall asleep, exhausted from their exertions, and awake refreshed by the temporary cessation of their labors, so it has been with a once-slumbering Church. "Doctrine is where it was, and usage, and precedence, and principle, and policy; there may be changes, but they are consolidations or adaptations; all is unequivocal and determinate, with an identity which there is no disputing" (*DCD* 444). The asterisks with which the essay breaks off imply a divide between institutional experience and the personal address to the reader that concludes the work. Here Newman as narrator retreats into the third person, as if to stress that he is now one with his own conclusions: "Such were the thoughts concerning the 'Blessed Vision of Peace,' of one whose long-continued petition had been that the Most Merciful would not despise the work of His own Hands, nor leave him to himself," and this omniscient Narrator—for such the gesture seems to imply—cautions the Reader that "time is short, eternity is long." The Reader should not put aside what he has discovered, nor consign it to the arena of current controversy; and he should not be seduced by the mistaken belief that the treatise "comes of disappointment, or disgust, or restlessness, or wounded feeling, or undue sensibility, or other weakness" (445). But the effect of this is to put precisely those possibilities in the reader's mind. Is Newman addressing the reader or himself? It is he, after all, who is most clearly in need of the reminder that he should not seek refuge in "the associations of years past"; those very associations—Trinity, Oriel, St. Mary's, Littlemore—were part of himself, and he could no more deny them than the truths he believed he had reached. The quotation of the Nunc Dimittis at the end suggests a work accomplished, but the caution against making "an idol of cherished anticipations" seems to augur the disappointments that awaited him in the not-so-distant future.

If the writing of the treatise offered Newman the solace and determination he needed, then it accomplished its task by giving a shape to his own journey—covertly here, as he was to do openly in the *Apologia*. In any case, like Newman himself, we pass over the details of the night of October 8, 1845, when he was visited by the Passionist priest Father Dominic. The publication of the *Essay on Development of Christian Doctrine* was the first public statement of the Roman Catholic Newman, and for his contemporaries it was for all practical purposes inseparable from the circumstances that led to his reception by Rome. Contemporary responses were not long in coming.

CHAPTER 6

"A Deliverance from the Nightmare"

WHEN TONY BLAIR announced his decision to join the Roman Catholic Church, the news made scarcely a ripple. Rowan Williams, whose appointment to the see of Canterbury had been effected under Prime Minister Blair, wished him happiness in his new spiritual home; others commented on the joy of seeing husband and wife in the same communion. The slight whiff of an earlier tradition was evident only in Blair's delaying his decision until after stepping down as head of the government.

By contrast, Newman's secession, whether scandalous or welcome news to his contemporaries, was a very much publicized matter. Of course, Tony Blair was an actor on the political stage, not much given to public introspection, while Newman's spiritual tergiversations had become the focus of public debate; nonetheless, religion to the Victorians was a much more serious business than it has been for their descendants. The ripple effect of Newman's action, well beyond the scope of this study, could be pursued not only through the press but in a variety of literary texts such as Browning's *Christmas-Eve and Easter-Day* and "Bishop Blougram's Apology," and countless journals and much private correspondence.[1]

This chapter confines itself to the effects of that secession upon Newman's coworkers in the Movement, Keble and Pusey and (to a lesser degree) William Palmer, as well as his younger brother Francis Newman, all of whose views on Newman's behavior leading up to and immediately following his reception by Rome were based on close knowledge, if not always strong sympathy. After considering the effects of the publication of the *Development of Christian Doctrine* on these inner circles shortly after his reception, we look at his single major production, the satirical and certainly by no means irenic novel *Loss and Gain*. Published in 1848, the novel immediately precedes two other works that it may have provoked, Francis Newman's *The Soul* (1849) and *Phases of Faith* (1850). James Martineau's critique is perhaps the first major sally of a non-Anglican Protestant, assessing Newman's standing and influence as a mid-Victorian thinker.

Those Left Behind

The question that Newman's *Development of Christian Doctrine* raised among some of his friends was whether Rome had gained an adherent or a skeptic, a question also being asked by some of his new fellow communicants. An anxious Gladstone breathed a sigh of relief on completing the treatise, believing that it did not, after all, offer any clear justification for moving to Rome, but he also noted more ominously that it might constitute a threat to objective revelation. "Newman's book interests me deeply, shakes me not at all," he wrote to Henry Manning at the end of 1845. "I think he places Christianity on the edge of a precipice; from whence a bold and strong hand would throw it over" (P. Butler 196). William Palmer's delayed reaction, like Gladstone's, grew out of a traditional High Church distinction between Anglicanism and Roman Catholicism. Palmer faulted Newman for not distinguishing adequately between developments that were "*inferences* from Revelation" and those that were "mere *expressions* of Revelation" (*Narrative* 169). Newman's theory, Palmer believed, did not erect a sufficient barrier against plausible but secondary beliefs that might amount to corruptions:

> It is not possible to see what may be the termination of such theories. Romanism may not be the only eventual gainer from that theory of Christianity, which supposes it to have existed originally *in germ* only. There is a subtle Rationalism in such a notion; nay, something still worse, if possible. If the Gospel is to be developed by reason; if its lineaments are to be filled up by the human mind; if it was originally *imperfect*; is there not some danger of supposing that, after all, it is only a philosophy, a science, a creation of the intellect? And again, if its processes are

analogous to those which we see in nature, may not the inference be drawn that, like them, it has its period of decay as well as perfection, of extinction as well as of germination? (171–72)

Palmer partly misstates Newman's case, but Newman's fifteenth Oxford University sermon, "The Theory of Development in Religious Doctrine," with its emphasis on the place of reason in religious inquiry, would have provided fodder for his critique. In that sermon, Newman, having thrown the natural sciences under the same suspicion of subjectivity that unbelievers imputed to theological development, seems to have recognized such dangers himself, reassuring those who might fear that his theory would lead "to a dreary and hopeless scepticism," and counseling them to trust in God's Providence: "All is dreary till we believe, what our hearts tell us, that we are subjects of His Governance; nothing is dreary, all inspires hope and trust, directly we understand that we are under His hand.... What is it to us whether the knowledge He gives us be greater or less, if it be He who gives it?" To secure this fideism from a wholly atomized Evangelicalism or ultimate solipsism, Newman presses the case to humanity at large. "If our senses supply the media by which we are put on trial, by which we are all brought together ... and are disciplined and are taught, and enabled to benefit others, it is enough." The role of instinct is effectively that of the conscience: external necessity forces us "to trust our senses, and we may leave the question of their substantial truth for another world" (OUS 233–34). To believers of the time, this might be less than reassuring; for the determined skeptic, it might amount merely to a papering over of an ideological chasm. God will inevitably seem, from the rationalist point of view, as if brought in to fill the void resulting from the application of an empirical test. Newman did not apply the same standard to doctrinal development that, in a sermon of 1836, "Moral Consequence of Single Sins," he had applied to the individual soul: "We know that two lines starting at a small angle, diverge to greater and greater distances, the further they are produced, and surely in like manner a soul living on into eternity may be infinitely changed for the better or the worse by very slight influences exerted on it in the beginning of its course" (PPS 4.3.757). That an institution might similarly exhibit such a trajectory seems not to have figured in his thinking.

In the *Apologia*, Newman drops a veil over both his reception and his parting with his friends, mentioned by name only: Manuel Johnson, W. J. Copeland, R. W. Church, Henry Buckle, Mark Pattison, and Edward Pusey. In his farewell to his first tutor, James Ogle of Trinity, "I took leave of my first College, Trinity, which was so dear to me. . . . Trinity had never been unkind to me. There used to be much snap-dragon growing on the walls opposite my freshman's rooms there, and I had for years taken it as the emblem of my own perpetual residence even unto death in my University." From the time of his departure in February 1846 to the writing of the *Apologia* eighteen years later, Newman never saw the place, "excepting its spires, as they are seen from the railway" (*A* 213). That most pervasive of Victorian industrial symbols, the railway, cuts a swath between the Oxford of Newman's past and his new life in Birmingham, between the gleeful young controversialist plunging into the early work of the Movement and the sobered older man who wrote to Ambrose St. John in January 1846, one month before his departure from Littlemore, "You may think how lonely I am. Obliviscere populum tuum et domum patris tui has been in my ears for the last 12 hours. I realize more that we are leaving Littlemore, and it is like going on the open sea" (*L&D* 11:95).

When he quoted this letter in the *Apologia* (212), Newman juxtaposed it with the seagoing metaphor in the opening paragraph of the concluding chapter: "I was not conscious to myself, on my conversion, of any change, intellectual or moral. . . . I was not conscious of firmer faith in the fundamental truths of Revelation, or of more self-command; I had not more fervour, but it was like coming into port after a rough sea; and my happiness on that score remains today without interruption" (*A* 214). Two days after the letter to Ambrose, he told Maria Giberne, one of his most faithful woman correspondents, that he felt "nothing at leaving Oxford, or St. Mary's—I feel a good deal leaving Littlemore" (*L&D* 11:96). The treatment of both events in the *Apologia* suggests that he had not yet taken the full measure of his departure from the University, increasingly out of place though he had come to feel there, and the depth of his attachment to the university is evident, beneath the satire, in *Loss and Gain*.

Newman's own narrative of his path to Rome has so dominated subsequent discourse with its aura of inevitability that only recently have scholars come to interrogate the *Apologia* more closely. Certainly Newman's reception seemed far from inevitable to some of those who knew him best. In a letter which Isaac Williams's biographer O. W. Jones assigns to 1843, Williams had written to Keble:

> As for Newman's case, it stands alone and is quite peculiar. I have never doubted but that it is entirely constitutional and that whatever position he had been born under, that he would in his mind and thoughts occupy a position foreign to and beyond it, from something in his family and constitution.... As both his brothers are quite external to our Church, and always will be so, so there is in himself a tendency to be so under the very greatest difference of circumstances imaginable. This I feel certain is at the bottom of it, although of course it operates through channels exceedingly different, and he will come to his conclusions through the Fathers and his extraordinary intellect, and the train of his thoughts mixed through the whole in him with everything that one must love and honour exceedingly. (Jones 58)

While Williams's reference to the Church Fathers does indeed hint at a Romeward drift, his allusion to Charles and Francis Newman describes a morbid restlessness that could equally lead to a left-wing secession or, in Charles's case, apparently entire unbelief. Williams implies that Newman's choices were limited by his natural inclinations, that they were not choices in anything like what we would now call the existential sense. Such a perception, obscured by the passing of Newman's generation and the testimony of the *Apologia* itself, has been rearticulated in our own day by Frank Turner, who has argued that "to reconceptualize Newman as a potential secessionist clergyman who did not secede [to the left] emphasizes that his life and career emerged from a series of choices made and not from a web of inevitabilities in which he stood entangled" (Turner 617). For Turner, Newman's departure from the Establishment resulted primarily from a failure of personal relationships; he "became a Roman Catholic so that he could continue to remain a monk, and, if possible, a monk surrounded by his Littlemore male friends" (629). Turner overstates the case, but he does identify Newman's failure to realize that he could not carry old relationships with him wholesale to Rome.

Admittedly, a number of personal slights and adventitious external cir-

"A Deliverance from the Nightmare"

cumstances helped to push Newman over the edge earlier rather than later, but that case can be pressed too far. A close perusal of the original letters of Newman's Anglican period does not suggest any conscious misrepresentation of his intellectual and religious development in the *Apologia*. But the *Apologia* does portray a man hunted out of the Church of England, while the letters reveal a man motivated by strong self-will whose journey was fueled by both support and antagonism. Newman's bias against Roman discipline, of which he had the scantiest knowledge, and his suspicion of Roman clergy, of whom he had had hardly any personal acquaintance, had kept him stationary for a number of years. Perhaps the sheer will to believe was all that was left in Newman by 1846. If what propelled him to change communions was indeed a series of proximate and secondary causes, one might ask if such contingencies necessarily call Newman's final decision into question.

As the classic contrast of St. Paul and St. Augustine shows, people are converted in very different ways. Newman moved toward Rome in large part by reading and writing—in the latter case, as has been argued, by objectifying personal experience in the form of a treatise on doctrinal development. It is striking that his reception, the second most important religious turn of his life (for his youthful Evangelical conversion always took pride of place) was neither driven nor shaped by personal influence. Father Dominic was known to him only by reputation, and was hardly more than a convenient instrument at hand. Newman's mistreatment (as he saw it) by Anglican authorities fed his decision but can hardly be said to have been its primary motive. Even so, the authenticity of a conversion, or reception into a new communion, need not be seen as tainted merely by the fact of mixed motives. Human beings are, finally, converted as human beings with all their limitations and contradictions. Conversion, or the experience of a final step toward one's own truth that fundamentally alters one's commitments, does not magically eradicate the frailties brought with it.

Keble had already taken a view of Newman's case when Williams wrote. In 1841, he had preached a University sermon, "Endurance of Church Imperfections," in which he declared that a particular mind and temperament required the acceptance of affliction, and that times of trial demanded "the plain straightforward keeping of the Commandments of God" through a pure and humble life lived in the fear of God and devotion to daily obligations. Keble argued that "to serve God loyally in doubt and anguish and perplexity concerning the faith ... is as great a trial of disinterestedness, as to serve Him in the midst of outward and bodily discontent" (*Sermons Academical and Occasional* 296–97). The disunity of Christendom was exacerbated by the temptation among some "ardent and devout minds ... to long and reach after such helps as they imagine may be found in other Communions" (305). It required a commitment to the way of the cross, a familiar theme in Keble's sermons as it was in Pusey's. The desire for comfort and full clarity of revelation symptomizes human delusion if indeed it is not a snare of Satan himself. Those who forsake good works, patience, self-denial, and humility, and "pass from one section of the Catholic Church to another," give up "the guide of their youth" and thus in a manner "excommunicate and unchurch" the Church of their youth (313–14).

Keble's reference to passing "from one section of the Catholic Church to another" reflects the belief, increasingly held by the Anglo-Catholic party, that Roman, Anglican, and Orthodox churches all had equal claims to apostolicity and the true deposit of the Catholic faith. This reduces a change of communions to a mere quibble on the one hand, but a betrayal of trust in one's parent church on the other. In the preface to the volume in which the university sermon was published he wrote that a Greek or Englishman throwing in his lot with Rome was "deciding on his own authority what are the limits of the Kingdom of Christ, what the evangelical terms of salvation ... [and] consigning millions, who had no other thought than to live and die true subjects of the visible Catholic church, to the comparatively forlorn hope of incurable ignorance and uncovenanted mercy" (xxvi–xxvii). Keble's warnings against this form of self-indulgence as he saw it were sharpened by Newman's secession in 1846[2] and persisted as late as 1857, in a treatise *On Eucharistical Adoration*. At first blush, this would appear to have been triggered by an unrelated matter, a defense of the Anglican entitlement to the doctrine of the Real Presence resulting from a recent court case in which the Church had challenged that doctrine, threatening further secessions. Harking back to the earlier Gorham Judgment,[3] Keble argued that such declarations by those in temporal authority should have no weight in an individual believer's decision to join another body. "This has something in it so very unreal, and so like ill-temper, that it gives but a bad omen for peace" (*On Eucharistic Adoration* 174–75). Certainly Keble had not made peace with Newman's decision, even after the lapse of a decade.

Pusey's response to Newman's secession was quite different. More than forgiving, it showed active sympathy for Newman's position, one that Pusey could not embrace himself but that he could see through Newman's eyes. At the heart of Pusey's capacity for sympathy was his fundamentally optimistic view of the long-range prospects of the English church. He was less inclined than Keble to what the latter's first biographer, John Taylor Coleridge, called "querulous forebodings" (340), or what a present generation has learned to dismiss as cries of "The Church in danger."

When Newman was received by Rome, Pusey did not wait for the dust to settle but wrote a letter to an unidentified (and possibly imaginary) friend published in the *English Churchman* of October 16, 1845, less than two weeks after Newman's letter to him announcing his decision. Pusey sought to soften the blow by appealing to a broader providential schema. Beginning with an expression of sorrow over the loss of a co-worker, he asked his fellow Anglicans whether they had been deficient in the prayer, love, and support that might have kept Newman with them. But God, Pusey declared, was still with the Church. "Engaged in great works, especially with that bulwark against heresy and misbelief, St. Athanasius, [Newman] was yet scarcely doing more for us than he would if he were not with us. Our Church has not known how to employ him." For Pusey, Newman was still doing his work obediently and patiently, albeit in another part of the vineyard, perhaps finding fuller employment than his fellow Anglicans could have given him. "And who knows what in the mysterious purposes of God's good Providence may be the effect of such a person among them?" It might well be a prelude to greater understanding, and finally fuller union, between the two communions (Liddon 2:461). God is always with, but greater than, his Church, and the future of the Church of England had never rested only in Newman's hands.

Loss and Gain

Despite his categorical rejection of the claims of the Church of England that he had sought so long to uphold, and despite his confidence in his

"A Deliverance from the Nightmare"

rationale, Newman was far from easy in his immediate circumstances. He had established to his own satisfaction that the Established Church was without a defining personality of its own, but he was not certain of the personality that he was embracing in Rome.

However Newman reconstructed his experience in the *Apologia* as a coming into port, memoranda and other evidence from the weeks following his reception suggest that he was still on the open sea. The notes he made in Latin (translated by Dessain) of his retreat at St. Eusebius, Rome, in April 1847, before his ordination to the Roman Catholic priesthood, are, like his Littlemore notes, acutely self-critical. "I creep along the ground, or even run—well enough for one who creeps or runs, but I cannot fly. I have not in me the elements required for rising or advancing" (*AW* 245). And shortly thereafter: "I am querulous, timid, lazy, suspicious; I crawl along the ground; feeble, downcast and despondent" (246). The persistence of the metaphor suggests a subconscious merging of two references in Genesis, to "everything that creeps on the earth" which is of God (1:20) and the serpent condemned to go on its belly all the days of its life (3:14). Newman rebukes himself not only for a lack of ambition but (as at Littlemore) for a want of something more than mere dutifulness. He is attracted to the Oratorian order but is unready to accept the rule; he wants security and tranquility among friends and books. He fails to seek out God's will in lesser things. His new liturgical regimen is unfamiliar; he feels self-centered and wed to habit. A wounded pride is interwoven with a sense of loss and a feeling of abasement in having to go to school again. He sees his spiritlessness as a kind of spiritual illness, in fact a despair of God's grace. His reception has not brought him inner peace or that reconciliation with painful memories that inhibit his attaining that peace:

> In a variety of ways I have fallen away from hope. In the Church of England I had many detractors; a mass of calumny was hurled at me; my services towards the Church were misrepresented by almost everyone in authority in it. I became an exile in a solitude, where I spent some years with certain of my friends, but not even in that retreat was I safe from those who pursued me with their curiosity.... And now the cheerfulness I used to have has almost vanished. And I feel acutely that I am no longer young,

> but that my best years are spent, and I am sad at the thought of the years that have gone by; and I see myself to be fit for nothing, a useless log. (*AW* 247–48)

Newman's way of dealing with the burdens of the past and his spiritual aridity now found an outlet, for the first time, in fictional form.

Throughout his life Newman, like Macaulay, was a reader of novels. But the novel form was not natural to him as a writer. *Loss and Gain*, the first of his two novels, depends on the exchange of ideas rather than on the dramatic unfolding of character. Its outcome is never in doubt, but its method of argumentation—for it is essentially fictionalized argument—was such as to make Samuel Wilberforce's reaction understandable. It was, Wilberforce wrote to his brother Robert, "about the most mischievous book I ever read, so suggestive of skepticism. Newman all over" (Newsome, *Parting of Friends* 313). From the point of view of his own friends, such as Keble and Pusey, the very appearance of the novel, with its satiric and sometimes scathing Oxford portraits, must have seemed not only untimely but ungracious. But Newman's pleasure in writing it was the consequence of his uncertainties. Read in the context of some of his own letters and notebooks of the period, it seems a way of shoring up his resolve.

The novel's execution was rendered easier by the fact that Newman stayed close to his own experience even as he distanced it by assigning his protagonist, Charles Reding, to the younger Oxford generation. Alan G. Hill has pointed out that Reding begins his intellectual and spiritual journey in 1840. "The chronology of the novel, from Michaelmas 1840 to autumn 1846, is carefully worked out to correspond with the period from Newman's abandonment of the Anglican Via Media to the aftermath of his conversion, and Reding's development has to be simplified and speeded up to fit into this six-year period" (*LG* xiv–xv). In the 1848 Advertisement that prefaced the novel, Newman was careful to say that it was not "the history of any individual mind among the recent converts to the Catholic Church," and that—within limits—is true. Newman relocated his own experience in the mind of a member of the second generation, simplifying the narrative and short-circuiting his own anxieties over Tract 90. Charles finds the Articles unclear as soon as he begins to study them, and is thus spared the complication of taking Anglican orders. Newman also constructed an intellectual and fideistic trajectory simpler than his own. In this less encumbered version of his experience, Charles becomes one of those younger disciples at Oxford for whom the path to Rome was relatively straightforward. At the same time, by portraying Charles as gentle and thoughtful, given more to private concerns than public fireworks, Newman eliminates the headlong extravagances of Oakeley and Ward and effectively re-fathers himself. In this sense, at least, he had some justification for his claim in the Advertisement.

Another reason for accepting Newman's avowed intent of authorial distance lies in the fact that rather than using Charles Reding merely as his stand-in, Newman splits himself between Reding and Reding's friend Willis, who precedes him into the Roman Catholic communion. The Reding-Willis relationship is the central one in the novel, and in the figure of Willis Newman creates someone whose passion and early determination to seek his home in Rome contrasts with Reding's deliberation, which more nearly mirrors Newman's agonized hesitations in real life. Willis is first described as a kind of Newman: "a nice, modest-looking youth, who, like a mouse, had keen darting eyes, and ate his bread and butter in absolute silence" (*LG* 27). The words that introduce him distinguish him from other bustling, assertive personalities who attempt to claim Charles's allegiance. Willis's simple transparency associates him with a personality type that Newman had singled out in "The World's Benefactors" (1830). It is in private life that we see "the true signs of God's presence, the grace of personal holiness manifested in His elect" (*PPS* 2.1.231). Yet such unworldliness masks a steely resolution, as Charles learns when he attempts to exact a promise from Willis that he will not repeat his visit to a Catholic Chapel, and Willis, gently saying, "That is too much," disengages himself from Charles's grasp (67). Newman does not in any way discountenance the relative deliberateness with which Charles reaches Willis's conclusions, his refusal to be moved early, but in Willis's almost total lack of personal ambition and the fervor of his faith, Newman projects an alternative that he clearly admires and may have wished he had lived out.

Charles invites other comparisons to his author. He plays the violin and is attracted early by the idea of celibacy. His special relationship to his sister Mary is drawn from Newman's to his own deceased sister of the same name, and thus looks back to the 1820s. Charles early embraces the dogmatic principle, but he is less susceptible than Newman to the shock of unexpected recognitions; as far as we can tell, Charles never saw a Monophysite in his own mirror. "A new idea was not lost on him, but it did not distress him, if it was obscure, or conflicted with his habitual view of things. He let it work in its way and find its place and shape itself within him, by the slow spontaneous action of the mind" (*LG* 48). When the liberal Brownside (modeled on Hampden) argues in a sermon that "the most celebrated questions in religion were but verbal ones" (51), Charles rejects the message because it does not pass the dogmatic test: "first, that there are a great many opinions in the world on the most momentous subjects; secondly, that all are not equally true; thirdly, that it is a duty to hold true opinions; and fourthly, that it is uncommonly difficult to get hold of them" (48).

Charles's name, with its Old English root (to *rede* in the sense of "interpret") suggests that life for a sensitive young man in Oxford is, if not hermitic, nonetheless hermeneutical: one must learn to read character as a way of "reding" ideas. In making Charles the son of a country parson of modest pretensions and simple faith, Newman revisits with gentle criticism the pastor of Wordsworth's *Excursion* while projecting his own long-thwarted desire for a perfect home, one untouched by the urbanizing commercial society in which his own home was shattered by his father's financial failures.[4] Though devoted to his parochial duties, Mr. Reding recognizes his own limits, and he justifies his decision to send his son to Eton by the fact that devoted though Charles is to him, his father cannot read his inmost being. "Seclusion . . . is no security for virtue. . . . The heart is a secret with its Maker; no one on earth can hope to get at it or to touch it. I have a cure of souls; what do I really know of my parishioners? Nothing: their hearts are sealed books to me" (*LG* 5). Mr. Reding's words echo Newman's complaint to Keble about his lack of knowledge of his own parishioners. But if Mr. Reding shares Newman's own sense of the impossibility of knowing the souls in his care, he lacks that commitment to the dogmatic principle that would provide a partial solution. Though a self-effacing and devoted pastor as well as a kind and anxious parent, Mr. Reding represents the vulnerability of the Anglican position when exposed to the light of historical and theological examination. His death at the end of part 1 inspires Charles to lay aside for a time the doubts he has started to harbor about that position and to plan to devote himself to the same unremitting round of parish duties that his father shouldered. "The Church of England as it was, its Articles, bishops, preachers, professors, had sufficed for much better persons than he was; they were good enough for him. He could not do better than imitate the life and death of his beloved father" (112).

As a gesture of reconciliation that he was never able to extend to his own father in the latter's lifetime, Newman plays out one aspect of Charles's relationship to a previous generation in the Church. More difficult for Charles to deal with is his father's friend Mr. Malcolm, the elderly fellow of an unnamed college who represents that vanishing generation and a more relaxed churchmanship which can be fanned into zeal only by vigorous antipapalism, Malcolm is "a shrewd, easy-tempered, free-spoken man, of small desires and no ambition; of no very keen sensibilities or romantic delicacies, and very little religious pretension; that is, though unexceptionable in his deportment, he hated the show of religion, and was impatient at those who affected it" (*LG* 24). Having taken an avuncular interest in Charles and his sisters from an early time, Malcolm is now reduced to idle Oxford chitchat interspersed with cautions against celibacy, despite his singular lack of qualification to speak to the alternative. His most significant intervention comes when, on the eve of Charles's conversion to Rome, he appears at the tail end of a series of inconsequential and absurd religionists of various sects to cluck over Charles's apostasy. He tells Charles accusingly that he used to be a "frank, open boy" before the Jesuits got hold of him, but now he is a youngster like all too many who think they know more than their elders. Charles blushes and feels guilty, not because of his course of action, but because his early childhood associations with Malcolm no longer provide any "opening of heart towards him, nor respect for his judgment" (286). Stung by the accusation of concealment, however, he responds in the accents of his author: "Now, do think, had I known this or that priest, you would have said at once, 'Ah, he came over you.' If I had been familiar with Catholic chapels, 'I was allured by the singing or the incense.' What can I have done better than keep myself to myself, go by my best reason, consult the friends whom I happened to find around me, as I have done, and wait in patience till I was sure of my convictions?" (288). Malcolm's parting prediction that Charles will return to the Church he is leaving, his tail between his legs after he has sampled Romanism at its most superstitious, offers no common ground for further discussion. Malcolm's complacency with his fixed ideas renders him incapable of understanding that Charles's decision might, after all, have come after reasoned judgment and with full integrity.

Carlton is the single figure in the novel capable of bridging Charles's Anglican and Roman Catholic lives, though since the novel itself ends a few hours after Charles's reception, we do not see this possibility played out. Often identified with Keble, and thus closer to Charles's own generation than that of his father, Carlton certainly resembles the Keble of the 1840s correspondence in his counsel of patience if not his sometimes facile optimism: "Our business is to make the best of things, not the worst. Do keep this in mind; be on your guard against a strained and morbid view of things. Be cheerful, be natural, and all will be easy" (*LG* 159). But there is a still more important difference between Carlton and Keble. Carlton, though respectful of the learning of the Tractarians and their defender against unfair attacks, remains clearly apart from them: "I cannot deny that some things they have done have an unpleasant appearance, and give plausibility to the charge [of "aiming at influence and power"]. I wish they had, at certain times, acted otherwise" (129). The remark is more reminiscent of Palmer than Keble.

Carlton accurately diagnoses why the Anglican Church is so conducive to party spirit. "Whatever and wherever a church does not decide religious points, so far does it leave the decision to individuals," and private judgment, so far as it is exercised, "necessarily involves parties" (*LG* 123–24). Yet when Charles says that "a party man must be very much above par or below it," Carlton suggests that he look at the question differently, for Charles seems to be thinking that a party leader is "conscious of what he is doing.... Surely there is such a thing as unconscious influence?" (127). Charles responds that the existence of parties is no fault of the Movement. Its members "are but claiming their birthright as Protestants. When the Church does not speak, others will speak instead, and learned men have the best right to speak. Again, when learned men speak, others will attend to them, and thus the formation of a party is rather the act of those who follow than those who lead" (129). Here Reding voices Newman's belief in the centrality of personal influence while shifting responsibility for its results to those who come under its sway.

The minor characters of Newman's college generation—Brownside,

"A Deliverance from the Nightmare"

Vincent, Bateman, Freeborn—all speak, in various ways, for particular religious or intellectual positions. They are foils rather than characters. Little by little they fall away from any genuinely active role they might have had, as the novel comes increasingly to center on the relationship between Charles and Willis. Willis's impetuosity is a strong contrast to Charles's deliberateness, and there is no doubt that however much Newman divides himself between the two characters, his sympathies on this point are with Charles. The compression of a movement of mind, not unlike Newman's, into a span of about six years, however, does not conceal the fact that from beginning to end Charles feels his way through instinct much more quickly than Newman did through intellection. Increasingly estranged at Oxford, he tells his sister Mary, "My dear Mary, when people bear witness against one, one can't help fearing that there is, perhaps, something to bear witness against.... When a number of people tell me that Oxford is not my place, not my position ... perhaps it isn't" (*LG* 177). Charles reflects that "all the paper arguments in the world are unequal to giving one a view in a moment. There must be a process, they may shorten it, as medicine shortens physical processes, but they can't supersede its necessity.... Conviction is the eyesight of the mind, not a conclusion from premises" (203–4). But where intellection flags, personal encounters—with Willis, and finally with the Roman Catholic priest with whom he falls into conversation on the train—do the work. Willis's obvious happiness—more than that, his sense of stability—comes to the fore in a conversation with Charles two years after his last appeal. "What you want is faith. I suspect you have quite proof enough; enough to be converted on. But faith is a gift; pray for that great gift" (228). Before disappearing into the night, Willis plants a kiss on Charles's cheek. The kiss, more benedictory than erotic, is a sacramental encounter that pledges the reunion of two halves of a divided personality. It seems to Charles "as if the kiss of his friend had conveyed into his own soul the enthusiasm which his words had betokened. He felt himself possessed, he knew not how, by a high superhuman power.... He perceived that he had found, what indeed he had never sought, because he had never known what it was, but what he had ever wanted,—a soul sympathetic with his own" (229).

Charles's train journey to London, during which he encounters the priest, rewrites Newman's farewell journey from Oxford to Birmingham, with the difference that Charles is not yet formally converted and is even at this late stage still hesitant to take the step that has been so easy for Willis. Like the fateful journey of 1846, this one is from pastoral retreat to urban setting, from a sense of rootedness in vicarage and college to the threat of displacement and anomie that threatens a Catholic convert in an unbelieving and urbanizing age. This exilic movement persists until the Eucharistic climax at the end of the novel. The priest on the train, an escort between the two worlds, assures Charles, "A man's moral self . . . is concentrated in each moment of his life; it lives in the tips of his fingers, and the spring of his insteps. A very little thing tries what a man is made of" (*LG* 260). It takes an act of the will in cooperation with reason and prudence to "embrace the truth, when nature, like a coward, shrinks" (265).

As he was to do in the *Apologia* some sixteen years later, Newman conceals the moment of Charles's reception into the Church. But he does employ the metaphor that pervaded his thinking about such matters: Charles has been reborn into a new community and feels something like the "stillness which almost sensibly affects the ears when a bell that has long been tolling stops, or when a vessel, after much tossing at sea, finds itself in harbour" (*LG* 296). In his last encounter with Willis, now Father Aloysius, Charles understands that home is not a physical place but the assurance of a world not yet seen.

Fraternal Discord, Liberal Critique

As Newman was closing his Anglican accounts in *Loss and Gain*, his brother Francis Newman was about to raise dust in another quarter. Both Newman's secession and the irritating air of certainty that pervaded his novel had much to do with Frank's timing of his two works, *The Soul, Her Sorrows and Her Aspirations* (1849) and the autobiographical *Phases of Faith* (1850). Frank had some unsettled business of his own. His brother's career had held center stage in the public eye; it was time to put distance between them on his terms, not John's.

These apparently unlike brothers were not, in reality, dissimilar. John's personalism was a means of appealing beyond solipsism to a concrete Object of Faith, a Person not oneself even as the meaning of one's own self is validated by that Other. The community of belief apprehended that Person as the center of divine fact. Francis Newman, too, asserted, that "God is a

"A Deliverance from the Nightmare"

Person; and the love of Him is of all affections by far the most energetic in exciting us to realize our highest ideal of moral excellence, and in clearing the moral sight, so that that ideal may keep rising" (*The Soul* 123–24). Consistent with this principle, he rejected pantheism as a purely deistic rationalism, saying that the Deist reliance on pure intellection "halted at the very frontier of [religion's] inward life" (215). But he also saw personal contact with God as unmediated. Nothing stands between the Soul (whose properties are never very distinctly explained) and God. For Francis, religion without dogma is a joyous religion. Anyone who knows that he is loved by God in a personal relationship lives in an expanding universe of joy. Furthermore, the soul's "inward movements towards God proceed exactly as if there were no other creature beside itself in the universe" (102). No dogma, no *ecclesia*. Person-to-person human contacts have nothing to do with either. In this day and age, Francis Newman says, Jesus can no more be a personal example any more than St. Paul. Even the New Testament, great though it is, cannot substitute for "God himself, as our source of inspiration" (200). If the New Testament fails to provide what the present age requires, much less can the philosophy of the apostolic age be brought back to life, despite its appeal to "thousands of women and . . . men of feminine understandings" (211). These feminine voices proclaim that "*we shall not have God in our Souls, except by the sacrifice of our understandings*" (212). Religion must therefore become "purely Spiritual," appealing only to the Soul (215). The idea of an Incarnation has no place in it.

Phases of Faith, a more extended autobiographical treatment of these questions, was published the next year. U. C. Knoepflmacher, its modern editor, points out that the work deserves to be read in the light of Tract 73, *On the Introduction of Rationalistic Principles into Religion*, as illustrating what the older brother abhorred, namely treating the Word of God as the word of man, and hence undoing the very testimony of the Gospels (8). Knoepflmacher also accurately identifies the intense inwardness of *Phases of Faith*. Figures external to the author, some of whom are unnamed, are expedients for the argument rather than personalities (14–15). The focus is solely on the internal reasoning by which the author has moved through his various "phases."[5] Francis Newman approvingly paraphrases the well-known twenty-fifth "moral and religious aphorism" from Samuel Taylor Coleridge's *Aids to Reflection:* "He who begins by loving Christianity more than Truth, will proceed by loving his sect or church better than Christianity, and in loving himself better than all" (*Phases* 71). Frank was pointing the aphorism at John, but the latter would have been likely to respond that he who loved truth in the abstract better than Christianity would end by holding to no firm truth at all.

By 1860 *Phases of Faith* had gone through six editions. Its shelf life extended well beyond the Newman-Kingsley debate, and it is reasonable to speculate that if Kingsley is the explicit target of the *Apologia*, Francis Newman's book is also within its sights. The highly articulated form of the *Apologia* reads like a direct rebuke to the formlessness of *Phases of Faith*. Francis Newman's embrace of intellectually restless and probing demythologization reduces all theology to a simple assertion of trust in a pure unmediated God. In the opening pages of his autobiography, he describes an oppressive elder brother who "never showed any strong attraction towards those whom I regarded as spiritual persons; on the contrary, I thought him stiff and cold towards them." The gulf was both personal and doctrinal; among his targets, Frank reckoned baptismal regeneration and the sacred obligations of the episcopate. "I demanded reality and could not digest legal fictions" (7). His unflattering portrayal of growing religious estrangement occupies several paragraphs. Frank names few of his mentors or friends, but he names his brother.

While Frank distrusted his brother's theory of personal influence because that influence in practice had lain so heavily on himself, he assigned it in its positive sense to his encounters with John Nelson Darby, the founder of the Plymouth Brethren under whose spell he came at Oxford. He wrote, "I have learnt, that if it be dangerous to a young man . . . to have no superior mind to which he may look up with confiding reverence, it may be even more dangerous to think that he has found such a mind; for he who is most logically consistent, though to a one-sided theory, and most ready to sacrifice self to that theory, seems to ardent youth the most assuredly trustworthy guide. Such was Ignatius Loyola in his day" (*Phases* 21). The chapter in which this passage occurs is entitled "Strivings after a More Primitive Christianity," implying that an ultra-Protestant sect can aspire to the ante-Nicene church of Newman's Arian history. But for Francis Newman, a primitive church is one stripped of all tradition and all authority. The sudden outbreak of raw emotion in a studiedly calm account is striking. "In my brother's conduct, there was not a shade of unkindness, and I have not a thought of complaining of it. My distress was naturally great, until I had fully ascertained from him that I had given no personal offence. But the mischief of it went deeper. It practically cut me off from other members of my family, who were living in his house, and whose state of feeling towards me, through separation and my own agitations of mind, I for some time totally mistook" (34). In Frank's account, John neither showed him those traits of excellence that would have commanded fraternal love, nor recognized the excellences of his younger sibling.

Phases of Faith asserts a position that John Henry Newman had endorsed: that there was no halfway house between Rome and unbelief. But the trajectories of the two brothers could not have been more different. Whereas John made a definitive choice, Francis Newman stopped just short of that unbelief to which he might reasonably have been led, resting with a minimalist creed in which Jesus seems to have neither historical reality nor spiritual significance. Like his brother, Francis finished his journey a vigorous critic of Evangelicalism, albeit from the Left rather than the Right. With those Evangelicals committed to the lodestar of Truth, he had no quarrel. They were potential Liberal allies, as he and his brother both understood.

Others on the religious Left, free of such fraternal complications, wielded their scalpels more deftly than the hapless Francis. In 1856, a decade after Newman's move to Rome, James Martineau published an article in the *National Review*, "Personal Influence in Present Theology," which purported to trace the chief schools of religious thought at the Victorian midcentury. Martineau identified the major figures on this landscape as Newman, Coleridge (along with F. D. Maurice and the Cambridge school), and Carlyle. Acknowledging Newman's "unrivalled power of personal influence which few sensitive minds can resist" (1:231), Martineau attempts to analyze the reasons for this peculiar power and raises his central question: why is Newman both admired and distrusted? "The secret, perhaps, is this,—that his own faith is an escape from an alternative skepticism which receives the *veto* not of his reason but of his will. He has, after all, the critical, not the prophetic mind. He wants [lacks] *immediateness* of religious vision" (1:233). For Martineau, Charles Reding's conversion in *Loss and Gain* is evidence of this turn of mind. Of the scene in which Willis encourages Charles to seek a confessor immediately, Martineau observes that Charles "does not in the moment yield to the advice," but subsequently acts upon it "without any great advance in his mental preparation, and before ever witnessing a service in a Catholic Church." Martineau sees this as evidence that faith only involves "trying the experiment of an unknown religion, and denying it at hazard, and has no further reference to *conscience*, which stands quite neutral towards a church not yet appreciated.... The word thus becomes an engine that will work in advance or in reverse; whether you believe your conscience or disbelieve it, it keeps you on the pious track"—a more than typical specimen of "Oxford casuistry" (1:241–42).

By classifying Newman with the Coleridgeans and Carlyle, Martineau argues that Newman is fundamentally a force for good in discerning "the perennial indwelling of God in Man and in the Universe" (1:280). The leader is salvaged, but not his party. Of the Tractarians as a whole, Martineau writes:

> The one grand sin which we must set off against their merits, is a certain want of unconditional and ultimate trust in their own principles. Their system has too often the appearance of being constructed on purpose as a refuge from doubts they dare not face. Their intellectual men have been fond of playing with fire and flinging about brilliant skepticisms, eating into the very heart of life, for the chance of inducing fright into their protecting fold. It is hard for a proselyte of terror to become a child of trust, and the brand of fear deforms the forehead of their party. (1:249)

With a stroke, Martineau re-creates the atmosphere of gloomy superstition that pervades J. A. Froude's *Nemesis of Faith* and accounts for why Newman induced a kind of religious despair and skepticism by turns in some of his own followers. Martineau's diagnosis accounts for a particular frame of mind among those whom Newman had alienated. One can do no better than cite the retrospective judgment of his former follower Mark Pattison, who in his *Memoirs* recorded his belief that Newman's secession "was a deliverance from the nightmare which had oppressed Oxford for fifteen years" (236). For Pattison, Newman's departure had removed the last remaining obstacle to Oxford's entering the modern era. By his reading, the morning after was truly a dawn, the promise of Oxford's relief from the fogs of clericalism and its evolution into a modern university. Newman's dawn came more slowly.

CHAPTER 7

Building Community

THE SEARCH FOR community—how to define it, how to live in it—was a major preoccupation of Newman's years between his reception by Rome and the publication of the *Apologia*. Newman's attraction to the Oratorian order and its sixteenth-century founder, St. Philip of Neri, was challenged by the rift between him and his fellow Anglican convert (and also Oratorian) Frederick William Faber. But Newman's preoccupations were not wholly dictated by questions of internal order. In three collections of addresses he gave between 1849 and 1852—*Discourses Addressed to Mixed Congregations, Certain Difficulties Felt by Anglicans in Catholic Teaching Considered*, and *Lectures on the Present Position of Catholics in England*—the question of community is raised more obliquely, often in the satirical vein that Newman had mined in *Loss and Gain*. He takes the measure of the communion he has left and the one he has joined, sometimes as an intermediary, sometimes as a critic of Anglicanism.[1] In the process, he raises larger questions of faith and national loyalty from his own unique vantage point.

Just as Newman sought for community within his new religious communion, so did he seek it in the opportunity to assist at the founding of the new Catholic University in Dublin. His interest in the history of educational institutions was doubtless prompted both by his appointment as rector of the new university and by his self-willed exile from Oxford.

Building Community

Oratorian Ideals and Realities

At the heart of Newman's interest in the Oratorians is his desire to relive his Oxford experience while reimagining it in unequivocally monastic terms. He wrote (rather absurdly) in the fifth of his Oratorian papers from January/February 1848, "Take ... an [Oxford] College, destroy the Head's house, annihilate wife and children and restore him to the body of Fellows, change the religion from Protestant to Catholic, and give the Head and Fellows missionary and pastoral work, and you have a Congregation of St [sic] Philip before your eyes" (O 191–92). Perhaps Newman thought that in organizing such a house he might continue in the freewheeling ways that had characterized his life at Oriel. Continuity and minimal dislocation were what he hoped for.

Newman had never been able to do quite what he wanted to do at Littlemore, and this may account for the satisfaction he expressed to James Hope after his first meeting in November 1845 with Wiseman, who "distinctly stated that 'he wished Old Oscott [Newman's new place of residence near Birmingham] to be Littlemore continued'"—a provisional refuge for laity or clergy with various mission duties (L&D 11:47). As an Anglican, he had craved episcopal support; as a Roman Catholic, he was to prove suspicious of it. The Oratorians commended themselves to him because, as he wrote Dalgairns late in 1846, their quarters reminded him of a college, "their whole line ... has been a sort of domestic one—easy, familiar, and not rigid" (L&D 11:305). Oratorian duties took up only part of the fathers' day, and allowed for learning and study as well as preaching and teaching. Such obligations, he told the widow of his friend John Bowden, "has great recommendations for me personally—It gives me what I want, active work, yet as much or as little as I wish—time for reading and writing—and a rule without being a severe one" (L&D 12:45). In dwelling fondly on the names of Oxford friends joining him, he does not seem to have anticipated that his love of continuity might not be entirely compatible with the larger demands of the Roman Catholic Church. He also overestimated the extent to which he would wield some authority over that community. Whereas the Anglican Newman longed for the show of episcopal authority that he had never procured, the Roman Catholic Newman sought a latitude in the Oratorians that he did not find in the Jesuits or Dominicans. Though he greatly admired certain individual Jesuits, Newman did not crave a life in which he would come or go at the orders of a superior. He wanted the nest (*nido*) promised by the order of St. Philip. But he also wanted to be Father General.

It was the old story in a new setting: Newman's desire to lead conflicted with his love of retreat and self-effacement. "It is plain indeed," he wrote in the third of his Oratory papers, "that nothing can possibly be a principle of harmony in conduct, in word and work, between man and man, but either a vow or personal attachment," and the latter, which he clearly preferred, depended for its efficacy on a relatively small circle of men (*O* 168–69). He also associated St. Philip with Keble: the two men, he told his sister Jemima early in 1847, were "formed on the same type of extreme hatred of humbug, playfulness, nay oddity, tender love for others, and severity" (*L&D* 12:25).

Compared to the Jesuit warriors, whom Newman admired from a distance, the Oratorians were gentlemen, purged of those traits of "fastidiousness, self-importance, and loftiness" which marked gentlemen of the purely secular variety. Newman's portrait of these saintly, well-bred men is, in germ, a depiction of the true gentlemanliness he sought between the lines of what is the most famous, and gently satiric, passage in the *Idea of a University*. Two passages from the *Discourses Addressed to Mixed Congregations*, written about this time, indicate the persistence of a theme that a younger Newman had stressed in his sermons at St. Mary's. Fashionable young men are all too often lacking in "the largeness of mind, the candour, the romantic sense of honour, the correctness of taste, the consideration for others, and the gentleness which the world puts forth as its highest type of excellence," and when such a person expresses contempt for any religion, he has only "a smattering of knowledge" and secondhand opinions. He is "a bad imitation of polished ungodliness" ("God's Will the End of Life," *DMC* 114–15). Benevolence, kindheartedness, generosity are no proof of any particularly Christian "meekness, purity, or devotion" ("Nature and Grace," *DMC* 154). These well-known admonitions distinguish the worldly from the Oratorian gentleman. Gentlemanliness, he thought, "may set off and recommend an interior holiness, just as the gift of eloquence sets off logical argument." Good nature, good society, good classical education assist in the "unimpeded development" of a saintly character (*O* 189–90). A community of such men is bound by love, not vows. In an evocation of the Oxford ideal, Newman praises the mixture of old and young, conversing freely in the Oratory. Such a community is governed from within, rather than by external laws.

Although Newman may have hoped that his work in his new order would ease his transition, his own personality threw up obstacles. His new diocesan, W. H. Ullathorne, had something of a struggle to absorb the new sheep into the fold. After a number of disappointments on both sides, he had written to Newman, "I am pained to witness the acute sensitiveness with which several little matters have been viewed of late. Believe me, my dear Mr. Newman, that this cannot be without a hidden ingredient of self love[,] a most subtle spirit, and the object of the fears and combats of the humble saints of God" (*L&D* 12:352). Even such a gentle reproof rankled. Newman wrote a few days later (December 3, 1848) to Wiseman complaining that though, as his bishop, Ullathorne had the right to call him to account, "he spoke about me *without knowing me*." Having no experience of others similarly circumstanced, "he spoke of me on a *theory*" (*L&D* 12:363–64). Being viewed theoretically rather than as a person was tantamount to not being seen at all. A body of like-minded men could provide the assurance that unknowing superiors could not. But Newman lacked the assurance of authority. "I wish . . . I had more confidence in myself," he had written to Mrs. Bowden early in 1847. "I may be of use by past recollections of me and by personal influence, to bring and keep others together—but that I shall be able to *do* any thing by myself, beyond being the bond of union, I do not feel" (*L&D* 12:45). This querulousness and despondency persisted into his Oratorian involvements and foreshadowed future difficulties.

Despite his need to hold onto old personal attachments, Newman also took comfort in the impersonal strength of his new church and the spiritual comfort of the community of saints, that company to which he had turned so often as an Anglican when living people disappointed him. After his reception, Newman's idea of friendship was increasingly penetrated by an active hunger for saintly exemplars. In Milan in September 1846, he thought back on his first sight of the relics of St. Ambrose, that saint for whom he had begun to acquire a special veneration in his earliest readings in Milner. When Frederick William Faber announced a project of lives of Italian saints, Newman responded supportively, "The exhibition of a person, his thoughts, his words, his acts, his trials . . . have a charm for every one; and where he is a Saint they have a divine influence and persuasion, a power of exercising and eliciting the latent elements of divine grace in individual readers, as no other reading can have." Such lives were instruments of conversion.[2] For him, the life of St. Philip provided just such a steadying influence.

Even as Newman was revisiting his Oxford years in *Loss and Gain*, the Oratorian ideal was being subjected to the strains of a personality quite unlike his own. It is not necessary here to dwell in detail on the histrionic, emotionally unstable, self-indulgent and self-centered F. W. Faber. The origins of the tension between them dated back to the very early years of the Oxford Movement, when Faber's attitude toward Newman was already ambivalent (Bowden 22). Humility was not Faber's strong point. He renounced his Anglican orders publicly and quite theatrically at an evening service at his parish in Eldon without advance notice, leaving his bereft parishioners weeping and confused. Faber's correspondence often breathes a quite exaggerated sense of self. "God has given to me a peculiar, to my mind a very peculiar talent, at first sight alien to my character, of attaching people to myself." When a convert quoted the words of a fellow schoolboy at Harrow from years before ("I cannot tell why it is, but that Faber fascinates everybody"), Faber continued, "This sunk deep into my mind, and I could not but feel that I should hasten to lay this talent at the foot of my Redeemer" (Bowden 33). Newman had his egotistical side, but nothing in the record quite compares to this piece of preening self-congratulation.

The first symptom of difficulty came in January 1848, when Faber urged that the Oratorians form one body in Brompton, a suburb of London, rather than Birmingham. Newman was afraid that the resulting body would be too large, and he pressed his case for small, compact, self-sufficient bodies, geographically distributed for wider effect, as opposed to the large one he feared would emerge from the amalgamation. He also feared a diminution of his own influence, reminding Faber that upon joining the Oratorians, he had been assured by Wiseman that the Oratory would consist of several distinct bodies under himself as "Father General."

Newman's view of personal influence, as it had differed from J. A. Froude's, was also quite different from Faber's idea of personal attachment. Faber's dramatic and florid preaching attracted converts and various adorers, and Newman, with some justice, took somewhat the same view of Faber that Hawkins had taken of Newman himself. He could have only had Faber in mind when he told R. A. Coffin that "persons form lasting attachments far more by their *views* of things than their *feelings*" (*L&D* 13:64). He had just demonstrated this in the protagonist of *Loss and Gain*, Charles Reding, whose shift of personal allegiances corresponded to his change of religious profession. Newman also knew that personal contact carried risks of its own. Friendships and mutual influence of minds could no longer exist in the same way when fundamental commitments had changed. Love among those of like minds was another matter. Newman always referred that human love to its divine analogy of love between a human being and God. In the eleventh of the *Discourses Addressed to Mixed Congregations*, "Faith and Doubt," preached about this time, he told his hearers, "Give me for my friend one who will unite heart and hand with me, who will throw himself into my cause and interest, who will take my part when I am attacked . . . and, if he is critical . . . will be so from very love and loyalty" (*DMC* 219).

Newman's belief that the Oratory should be a self-regulating corporation was interpreted by some as an abdication of authority, a curious and perhaps suspicious passivity in forwarding the aims of the body. When, in a second challenge to the peace of the two houses, J. D. Dalgairns preached a farewell sermon in the spring of 1849 on the occasion of his transferring to the London house, Newman rebuked him for putting himself above the Congregation (*L&D* 13:131). Like Faber, Dalgairns had in Newman's view substituted the cult of personality for the quiet discipline of personal influence. And like Lockhart a few years earlier, he had also abandoned a former mentor—Newman himself. Neither Dalgairns nor Faber seem to have understood that moral authority might be best exercised by a refusal to crack the whip, an acceptance of self-abnegation. In a sermon of 1850, Newman invoked the self-effacing St. Philip against Savonarola, whose pulpit vehemence "converted many, but frightened or irritated more." Philip shied away from the pulpit, winning souls by conversation and discourse, drawing souls "as the magnet draws iron" (*SVO* 237). Fully aware that Brompton gossip portrayed him as lacking in zeal, Newman told his own house that "if we *have* reason to suspect, that we are thus inferior to our vocation and our mission, then nothing is to be said for us," but if "all the complaint means is that we do not puff and advertise it to the four quarters of the earth, then I do rejoice in it, as a mark, special and singular, of our being the children of St. Philip" (*L&D* 17:48–49).

Building Community

John Coulson has written that the Newman-Faber dispute reflects a larger division in the Church then and now. "Newman is for growth, Faber for autocratic rule. Here, in a nutshell, is that collision between conscience and authoritarianism which marks the unresolved dilemma of Catholicism." Faber and the Ultramontanes thought of the authority of the magisterium as "a divine ordinance to be strictly imposed upon unregenerate nature," whereas Newman placed ecclesial authority on the foundation of a Church conceived as the "whole people of God" (*Common Tradition* 99–100). The rift foreshadows Newman's later conflicts in the Roman Catholic Church, particularly with Archbishop Cullen in Ireland and with Manning in England and Rome. Those attracted to power could not credit Newman's self-effacement, which led him to throw up his hands at the thought of becoming a bishop, and they tended to attribute his shyness to diplomatic maneuvering.[3] "What [Cullen] means by 'diplomacy' in me, I say it in the face of God, I do not understand, nor am at all conscious," he told one correspondent. "I suppose the word means either having some secret end, or using some underhand means. I am quite conscious *always* of not liking to tell people how keenly I feel things, both from tenderness to them, and again from a consciousness that, when I once begin, I am apt to let out and blow them out of the water" (*L&D* 14:143). Newman's self-analysis is cogent.

In 1855 another chain of events initiated by the Oratory in London widened (and effectively finalized) the rift between these two strong personalities. The Fathers at Brompton sought an exception to their Rule at Rome which would allow them certain freedoms not normally attached to their order. Though the dispute may now seem trivial, it went to the very heart of the Oratorian definition of community, to draw souls toward it rather than to go in search of them; external commitments distracted one from one's place in the community. Dalgairns (again) wanted to undertake the spiritual direction of nuns, an activity expressly forbidden in the Rule. Under Faber's urging, the London house applied to the Congregation for the Propagation of the Faith (Propaganda) in Rome for an exemption. Newman became concerned when his own bishop, Ullathorne, referred to a rescript on its way from Rome that the bishop assumed would apply to both houses. Newman's alarm at the unilateralism of the move suggested to some in London that he was trying to keep Brompton on a tight leash. This may have been true, but Newman's deeper fears centered on the danger of Roman interference that would weaken confidence in the Oratorian vocation and the standing of the order in Birmingham, where he had labored hard to see it assimilated into English life.

In the spring of 1856, a letter of apology came from Fr. Richard Stanton on behalf of the London house. Newman thought it no apology at all, since it evinced no understanding of the heart of his objections, but merely expressed regret that he had been hurt. Angrily he told Stanton that he had had nothing more from London than "a unanimous, deliberate refusal in official notes, compositions, with balanced periods, and nothing besides them" (L&D 17:249). In summarizing the affair in a letter to the Birmingham Fathers, written from Dublin on June 14, 1856, Newman left no doubt that the breach was irreparable. "Certainly, I must in some way or other have misused my influence with them, that they should have treated me in a manner, to me so mysterious. . . . It is a fact . . . arising, alas! out of our experience of their insensibility to so urgent a request, that our confidence in them is gone." The sad moral Newman drew from all this was that St. Philip, as the founder of the Order, must have meant for the Oratorian congregations to "see little of each other." Their friendship would best be maintained at a distance, with each house relying on its own center: friends, associates, traditions (L&D 17:270). Newman may have been making an English virtue of Italian necessity, for at the time of the founding of the order travel between various Italian centers was difficult. But the railway and the telegraph had brought two houses and their leaders into unwelcome proximity.

Newman never trusted Faber again, and he was less than charitable even when Faber was on his deathbed a few years later. This was a depressing consequence of Newman's hypersensitivity. His standard of loyalty was at times impossibly high, and he apparently did not entertain the possibility that Faber might simply have been unable to grasp what had gone wrong.[4] Years later, when Brompton made conciliatory gestures after he was awarded the cardinalate, Newman refused to make peace. A decade of experience, tinged with disillusionment, pervaded the letter Newman wrote in response to a recommendation of a candidate for the Order: "An Oratorian House is a trying one. . . . We have not a rule, strong enough to support and carry on every one. And again, our Superiors are bound to use little else but gentleness and persuasion in their treatment of their subjects. Then again there are no vows. It is plain then that a specific vocation is necessary for the Oratory and one not often found in devout but uneducated minds" (*L&D* 31: Suppl. 76*).[5] Newman now grasped the frustrations of living in a community dependent on the elusive knowledge of when to stand fast and when to give way.

Division or Reconciliation?

The publication of *Discourses Addressed to Mixed Congregations*, originally a set of lectures delivered in Birmingham from February 2 to October 27, 1849, and *Certain Difficulties Felt by Anglicans in Catholic Teaching Considered* the following year, must have only deepened the rift between Newman and his former Oxford colleagues. As is the case with *Loss and Gain*, the effect of these works is hardly irenic. They are products of the satiric Newman, and the satiric Newman is not particularly attractive. The "mixed congregations" (that is, hearers of more than one denomination) must, to be sure, have posed something of a difficulty to a lecturer trying to ingratiate his hearers into accepting the presence of a Catholic house in Birmingham. The second group of essays is addressed to Anglicans who might be considered ripe for conversion. In his defense of the good faith of lay and clerical Catholics, Newman was unknowingly rehearsing for the *Apologia*.

In the first twelve of the *Discourses*, Newman is, once more, burning bridges, not building them. There is nothing conciliatory in his tone toward his former co-religionists. This may have resulted from a conviction that he had been treated unfairly, or reflected a desire to ingratiate himself with his new communion. Perhaps such shock tactics would make Anglicans realize the errors of their ways. And perhaps, as is often the case with Newman, the answer is "All of the above." By contrast, in the remaining discourses, he takes stock of how he has broken down the earlier prejudices he had entertained against Rome, particularly in terms of his newfound veneration of the Virgin Mary.[6] The discourses on Mary form an interesting coda but seem rather at odds (in their conception of audience) with the first twelve discourses.

A return to a more polemical stance is evident in *Certain Difficulties Felt by Anglicans in Catholic Teaching Considered*. Here Newman again addresses himself to those of his colleagues in the Oxford Movement who had not followed him to Rome. Though designed to "help forward members of the Established Church towards the Catholic Religion" (CD 1:1), the tone, now less bitter but more satiric, hardly seems designed to make converts. In the introduction to *Certain Difficulties*, Newman states his need to "fortify" those waverers whose "timidity, scrupulousness, inexperience, intellectual fastidiousness, love of the world, or self-dependence of individuals" blocked their taking the step he had taken (1:x). This amounted to a serious, if undocumented, charge. Indeed, as had been in the case in the *Discourses*, Newman now seems more sympathetic to the marginalized Dissenters whose lack of worldly advantage placed them on a par with Catholic clergy than he is to his former Anglican colleagues. Would Anglicans, he inquired, extend the same indulgence to the Methodists that they demanded from Rome? Would they concede that personal excellence, signs of grace and sanctity, might be evident among non-Anglican Protestants?[7] One might have responded to Newman that some Anglicans had no trouble ascribing these graces to those outside the Establishment, and that he argued as if the Church of England was defined by the Tractarianism to which he had once been dedicated. Newman's overriding problem was with the idea of comprehensiveness itself, and his questionable assumption that he might win over the intellectually fastidious by satirizing them.

Whereas the first seven chapters of *Certain Difficulties* decry Anglicanism's lack of corporate personality and hence its inability to provide an adequate spiritual community, the last five lectures attempt to remove those difficulties that prevent sympathetic Anglicans from joining the Roman Catholic Church. Newman dismantles his own earlier Anglocentric notions about Mediterranean Catholic devotion. He identifies Anglicanism with the world itself in its "cold, cruel, selfish system, which this supreme worship of comfort, decency, and social order necessarily introduces," a world in which "the many are sacrificed to the few, the poor to the wealthy," and "an oligarchical monopoly of enjoyment is established far and wide, and the claims of want, and pain, and sorrow, and affliction, and guilt, and misery, are practically forgotten" (1:252). Only a brief time in Birmingham seems to have opened the former Oriel tutor's eyes to a world very different from Oxford. His sense of joining a persecuted minority had quickened, perhaps liberated, a nascent social conscience.

The change is not irrelevant to our larger theme. One of Newman's intentions in such passages as this is to rebuke the sober, decent Establishment for failing to look beyond the demarcation of class privileges. Rome was concerned with "realities," England with "decencies." "Faith is illuminative, not operative; it does not force obedience, though it increases responsibility; it heightens guilt, it does not prevent sin; the will is the source of action, not an influence, though divine, which Baptism has implanted." The feeble old woman who steals a neighbor's prayer book or handkerchief "worships and she sins; she kneels because she believes, she steals because she does not love; she may be out of God's grace, she is not altogether out of His sight" (1:286).

By being swept up into a larger sphere of human activity, Newman tells his Anglican listeners, the Catholic believer is released from the prison of self and buoyed by a common object of adoration in a common atmosphere of faith. In Newman's view this proves that the Catholic Church is merciful where Protestantism offers no comfort. The rituals which the young Newman had observed with distaste and incomprehension on his first trip to the Continent turn out on close examination to be a stay and support, rather than mere superstitious outcroppings or the product of designing minds. The believer already knows who and where he or she is, and what he or she must do to receive forgiveness, whereas "the poor Protestant adds sin to sin, and his best aspirations come to nothing" because he has nothing objective to fall back on (*CD* 1:291–92). Newman's former argument against Evangelicalism is now turned against Protestantism as a whole. In his revised view, individual holiness is supported by the collective personality of the Roman Catholic Church even as, reciprocally, individual holiness contributes to that corporate personality. While the Protestant is thrown back on lonely soul-searching, the Catholic is offered a secure and visible hope. Thus does Newman close the door on his earlier self.

Universities, Real and Ideal

The lectures originally published as *Discourses on the Scope and Nature of University Education Addressed to the Catholics of Dublin*, and now routinely collected under the title *The Idea of a University*, are perhaps more often quoted than read. For those who quote from them as a timeless defense of liberal education, Newman's Catholicism may often seem an annoying excrescence to be set aside, and the famous passage beginning "Hence it is that it is almost a definition to say that [a gentleman] is one who never inflicts pain" is taken out of context as a normative view, alien to the main drift of the lecture in which it appears. The lectures are about liberal education, to be sure, but liberal educations grounded in faith, and are designed in large measure to defend the autonomy of theology as a legitimate branch of research with its own rights and its own scope of inquiry, a perimeter that cannot be breached by other disciplines with different aims and methods. The lectures are also marked throughout by Newman's personalism, his insistence that "God is an Individual, Self-dependent, All-perfect, Unchangeable Being, intelligent, living, personal, and present." Because of the mystery of His presence in the world and His centrality in its creation and sustenance, he is "the subject-matter of a science, far wider and more noble than any of those which are included in the circle of secular Education" (*IU* 27).

Newman distinguishes this individual all-seeing, all-judging God from a mere "principle, or a centre of action, or a quality, or a generalization of phenomena" to which He is sometimes reduced. As Newman drily remarks, God as a sort of constitutional monarch is difficult neither to "conceive" nor to "endure." But if thereby He is the sum total of natural laws rather than a Being in His own right, He has no claim to be an object of study (*IU* 28–29). Newman does not exalt Theology above all other disciplines, but claims a place for it among them. He was not wed to a bibliocentric view of the creation, and he was untroubled by scientific advances. In justifying theology as a discipline alongside the sciences, though not encroaching on them, he is arguing that faith requires the assent of the intellect, not a submersion in subjective feelings and appetites. Like any form of knowledge, faith sees more than is conveyed by the senses, and it reasons upon what it sees. Newman withholds the full arsenal of Catholic apologetics, being content to ground his argument on the idea of God as a Personal Being. In his argument for divine Personality, he is also signaling that the expression of human personality in teaching is critical for the communitarian ideal of the university. He is preoccupied by the university as a teaching institution, depending on face-to-face relationships, not as a center of research, which in Newman's humanistic orientation remained for the most part a solitary, not a joint, activity.

This orientation helps to explain the enthusiasm with which Newman embarked on the university project. To be present at the creation of a new institution provided the opportunity to escape the dead weight of tradition while drawing on the best of it (Harrold 91–117). Personal relationships were especially important to his organizational task because he recognized his vulnerability to the charge that he knew little of Ireland, and he needed coadjutors to keep him straight. But just as important was the relationship among the persons themselves. What he must do at Dublin, he wrote to Wiseman in the summer of 1854, was not to begin with the appointment of professors, whose functions lay primarily in the lecture hall, but "to have an external *manifestation* and the beginning of an inward and real *formation*" requiring "a few persons who thoroughly understand each other and whom I entirely know, who can quietly and without show be bringing into shape the students who come to us" (*L&D* 16:27). To D. B. Dunne he stressed teaching, advancing the Oxford tradition of small colleges, face-to-face communities in which a dean, who would be an ordained priest, would head the governing body of each house and its teaching staff. The latter would be composed of "young, unmarried men [who] would have nothing whatever to do with discipline directly. They would give lectures for (say) three hours a day. The rest of their time would be their own. I should wish these to be intermediate between the Dean who would be a Priest and the young men—to gain the confidence and intimacy of the young man—and, in this way, to smooth the Dean's work" (*L&D* 16:207–8).

The disillusionment Newman experienced with the project, recorded in a retrospective memorandum of November 25, 1870, and recopied in January 1873 (*AW* 277–333), has been the subject of much biographical discussion. Suffice it to say that his situation involved a number of disagreements with his hosts, many of whom tended to favor something more like an advanced theological school than a comprehensive university. Archbishop Cullen failed for long periods of time to answer his letters, and the hierarchy seemed suspicious of any lay role in the institution's governance. The tendency of Newman scholars to take his view of the case for granted has in recent years been modified by Colin Barr's history, which probably offers the best case for Cullen's behavior. Newman was alternately an absentee Rector at the University and an absentee Father General at the Oratory, and when he complained in either locale of being unsupported, he failed, characteristically, to understand the effect of his absences on either side of the Irish Sea.[8] Much of *The Idea of a University* implicitly reflects his divergence from the hierarchy, particularly on the subject of academic freedom. In a brief of March 20, 1854, Pope Pius IX, as Newman paraphrased him, declared that all disciplines were "to go forward in the most *strict league* with religion, that is, with the assumption of Catholic doctrine in their *intrinsic* treatment; and the Professors are directly to mould... 'the youth to piety and virtue, and to ground them in literature and science in conformity with the Church's teaching'" (*AW* 322–23). The Catholic faith should be safeguarded, Newman agreed, but this did not mean that it should be patrolling areas of knowledge that did not fall within its purview.

In contrast to the seminary model that the ecclesiastical sponsors of the Irish university had in mind, Newman's idea of the university as a self-regulating body, like his idea of the Oratory, depended on a delicate balance between personal influence and the judgment of the entire community. "Compromise," he wrote, "... is the first principle of combination"—and, he might have added, confidence (*IU* 16–17). The disciplines required both interconnectedness and separability, and the members of the community themselves had to move between these two poles. "An assemblage of learned men, zealous for their own sciences, and rivals of each other, are brought, by familiar intercourse and for the sake of intellectual peace, to adjust together the claims and relations of their respective subjects of investigation. They learn to respect, to consult, to aid each other. Thus is created a pure and clear atmosphere of thought, which the student also breathes." That atmosphere itself guarantees the development of a "habit of mind" in the student characterized by "freedom, equitableness, calmness, moderation, and wisdom"—in short, the outlines of a "philosophical habit" (*IU* 76).

Dwight Culler has suggested that in his enthusiasm for the English models, Newman forgot he was speaking to Irish Roman Catholics, and that words with one meaning in Protestant Oxford meant something very different in Catholic Dublin (Culler 258). Newman's idea of a self-regulating body is posed in a much more famous passage of the lectures when he envisions an imaginary university with no professors or examinations, in which the young teach each other. He compares that model to a university with examinations and degrees but without residential requirements or tutorial superintendence. The first will at least be a lively community with a doctrine and code of conduct, giving birth to "a living teaching, which in course of time will take the shape of a self-perpetuating tradition, or a *genius loci*" (*IU* 111), while the second is no more than a bureaucracy. Implicitly Newman is criticizing those proponents of a tightly controlled preprofessional school emphasizing lectures and formal examinations. Its apparently anarchic alternative, however, while it disposes of professors, does not eliminate the tutor.

Newman's belief in the capacity of young minds to awaken each other, while seriously urged, is also lightly ironic.[9] What prefaces that famous passage is the reminder that institutions bringing together boys in the public schools, then young men in the universities, also bring together all their moral deformations, a "hollow profession of Christianity," and heathen ethics, yet even here such young persons make heroes of many different men "conspicuous for great natural virtues, for habits of business, for knowledge of life, for practical judgment, for cultivated tastes, for accomplishments, who have made England what it is,—able to subdue the earth, able to domineer over Catholics" (*IU* 110). Likewise, the irony of the remark that a gentleman is one who never inflicts pain is best seen in the context of the *Parochial and Plain Sermons*, in which the gentlemanly character is frequently faulted for its indifference to religion. Even the philosophical habit that Newman praises is capable of being realized in entirely pagan terms. Under a false dispensation, trained aesthetic judgment may react to evil with distaste, but that is not the same thing as a moral judgment. In the reported dying words of Julian the Apostate contemplating his own virtues, Newman reads a sermon for the nineteenth century. Philosophical habit, a virtue in learning, is no guarantor of sanctity; Julian becomes the mere philosopher ignorant, in his passionless self-contemplation, of the very idea of sin.

Yet Newman was aware that though gentlemanliness did not make the saint, this did not mean that a saint might not be a gentleman—like St. Philip of Neri (Culler 238–43). Some years later he wrote to a correspondent, "I should say that the Apostles *were* gentlemen—not that they could make a good bow, wore kid gloves, or spoke Attic Greek, but their minds and their hearts were refined. I have always maintained that St. Paul, as seen in his Epistles, was the first of gentlemen—and that, if you would look for precepts of that courtesy and grace, which the world so much admires, you must go to him for them" (*L&D* 26:331). Courtesy is, then a desirable attribute, but not at the expense of Christian zeal; St. Paul exemplifies both. Yet such moments in Newman may reflect an ambivalent self-recognition. In an 1865 entry in his *Philosophical Notebook*, he asked himself whether "a man who acts from principle is *morally better* than one who acts from nature? yet the man amiable from nature is far more beautiful than one who, acting from self-control, is angular and partial in his good temper and has outbursts of passion or bitterness" (*PN* 2:163, 165). In the privacy of a notebook entry, the question "Which am I?" can be confronted.

If today we read the lectures through an Arnoldian humanist lens, which indeed they invite (Newman's contrast strongly resembles Arnold's opposition of Hebraism and Hellenism), some Roman Catholics in Newman's audience might have wondered why he was not more explicit in giving orthodoxy its due. While putting forward an apparently modest role for theology as one of a number of disciplines entitled to its own methodology and curriculum, Newman manages at the same time to imply, through ironic shadings and admiring tributes to the gentlemanly ideal, the priority of faith in all learning. Take, for example, his discussion of the perfection of the intellect that results from this ideal: "It is almost prophetic from its knowledge of history ... almost heart-searching from its knowledge of human nature; it has almost supernatural charity from its freedom from littleness and prejudice; ... almost the repose of faith, because nothing can startle it; ... almost the beauty and harmony of heavenly contemplation, so intimate is it with the eternal order of things and the music of the spheres" (*IU* 105). The gently persistent "almost" serves as a reminder of the gap that separates secular gentleman from saint (Vargish 137). Gentle irony also pervades the comparison of the man of a "scientific formation of mind" who is not a believer with that of the scientist who is. If we understand the terms "scientific" and "scientist" in the broad sense of intellectual inquiry, we can conclude that the former has a grasp of realities, a sense of how to proceed in his understanding, the power to discriminate truth from falsehood and things of greater worth from those of lesser, "an acquired faculty of judgment, of clear-sightedness, of sagacity, of wisdom, of philosophical reach of mind, and of intellectual self-possession and repose" (*IU* 115). It is entirely laudable to desire these qualities as the goal of one's education, but in the words of the Gospel according to Luke, *porro unum est necessarium*. Liberal education, viewed as knowledge only, "exerts a subtle influence in throwing us back on ourselves, and making us our own centre, and our minds the measure of all things." It circumscribes revealed religion with the idea that the human intellect is superior to revealed truth. "A sense of propriety, order, consistency, and completeness gives birth to a rebellious stirring against miracle and mystery, against the severe and the terrible" (165). Religion brings its own enlargement of mind, and, unlike the speculation of unbelievers, "an enlargement, not of tumult, but of peace." Newcomers to the faith are changed by it; for them, "the world, no longer dull, monotonous, unprofitable, and hopeless, is a various and complicated drama, with parts and an object, and an awful moral" (100–101).

The seldom-read conclusion to *The Idea of a University*, a disquisition on St. Philip of Neri, is the summation of Newman's attempt to redefine gentlemanliness in the true Christian character, as well as a reminder to the reader that St. Philip's ideal of liberal education takes account of its role within the circle of revealed truth. It is not a fully independent agency of development; St. Philip was not called to be a martyr or a zealous reformer, but "to yield to the stream, and direct the current, which he could not stop, of science, literature, art, and fashion, and to sweeten and to sanctify what God had made very good and man had spoilt.... All he did was to be done by the light, and fervour, and convincing eloquence of his personal character and his easy conversation" (179). In his accessibility to all comers and his humility, he was "great simply in the attraction with which a Divine Power had gifted him" (181). Newman's concluding note brings the lectures full circle to the Oratorian ideal that he wanted to see embodied in the life and work of the university he helped to establish.

The lectures in *The Idea of a University* treat the role of personality and personal agency in the atmosphere created by the contact of mind with mind as well as with Mind. In delimiting the properties of the gentleman, they also stress the danger of separating personal and social graces from religious faith. A more thorough elucidation of the idea of personal influence occurs in a series of papers Newman originally published in the *Dublin Catholic University Gazette* from June 1 to October 19, 1854, under the title of *Office and Work of Universities* and now known as *The Rise and Progress of Universities*. In these Newman speaks of the superiority of oral instruction to books, "the personal influence of a master" far exceeding the effectiveness of a text. "The general principles of any study you may learn by books at home, but the detail, the colour, the tone, the air, the life which makes it live in us, you must catch all these from those in whom it lives already" (*RPU* 9). As in the pursuit of knowledge, so in religion itself, what is required is "the personal presence of a teacher, or, in theological language, Oral Tradition. It is the living voice, the breathing form, the expressive countenance, which preaches, which catechises. Truth, a subtle, invisible, manifold spirit, is poured into the mind of the scholar by his eyes and ears, through his affections, imagination, and reason" (14).

The *Rise and Progress* is more relaxed, more genial, more historical, and less abstract than the lectures, and more imaginative in its development of certain dramatic situations and characters. Something about his move to Rome had activated Newman's fictionalizing imagination; *Callista*, after all, belongs to the same period. Mary Katherine Tillman has reminded us that "the portraits and actions of individual persons were Newman's best and most frequently used media of communication" (*RPU* xxiv). In the new series, Newman provides an imaginary portrait of a young foreign student casting anchor at Piraeus to take up a life of study in Athens, a kind of mini-novel within the larger expository discourse. Newman's sense of the dramatic is equally activated by historical portraiture in which the idea of a university attains a number of concrete realizations in time. Yet, as Tillman adds, the idea of personality is kept in check by the counterweight of discipline. Abelard represents the dangers of unchecked individualism. On its side, discipline can also be repressive. What is new about the *Rise and Progress* is how Newman plays out this dichotomy in complementary and sometimes competing structural terms, and how the idea of a university is in its turn subordinated to a larger idea of culture.

The theme is first broached in a recollected conversation, probably with a factual basis, in chapter 6, "Discipline and Influence." The section suggests that Newman is thinking his way through to the Irish university project by a different and more historical path. He sketches a visit to a friend in the London suburbs and anticipates the criticism that he has been laying too much stress on the role of persons in education, not enough on the role of institutions. "I cannot help thinking," his friend says, "that your [*Dublin University*] *Gazette* makes more of *persons* than is just, and does not lay stress upon order, system, and rule, in conducting a University" (*RPU* 70). He appeals to the Church and to constitutional states as evidence of how little such centers of authority depend on individuals. In his response, "Newman" rejects the criticism: Influence and Law are "the two moving powers which carry on the world, and ... in the supernatural order they are absolutely united in the Source of all perfection. I should observe that the Supreme Being is both,—a living, individual Agent, as sovereign as if an Eternal Law were not; and a Rule of right and wrong, and an Order fixed and irreversible, as if He had no will, or supremacy, or characteristics of personality" (72). The opposing principles should be mutually dependent, but too often they encroach as rivals on each other's province. An individual can dispense with institutional system, but the reverse cannot obtain; the institution always requires persons as its agents. The theological analogue is that only the Supreme Being can combine agency and rules in His multiple functions, whereas in real life, and certainly in university life, we must deal with the tension between them.

To break intellectual as well as geographical ground for an Irish university invites an analogy with the Schools of Athens (Personality) as opposed to Rome (Rule). For Newman, the Irish project reenacts a historical moment long past, akin to the arrival of the first missionaries on English soil. Historically, he points out, universities, like governments, "begin in influence, they end in System" (*RPU* 77). System steps in where direct Influence leaves off, but the intervention may be grounded in three principles: law, expedience, and propriety. The last of these tends to conflate the beautiful with the virtuous and thus to displace Law. In Athens this was tolerable when there was a high standard of conduct in civil life, but even then, "genius and voluptuousness ever went hand in hand," whereas "the terror of the Law" requires to be "added to the persuasive of the beautiful" (85). Yet the power of Athenian beauty has been realized in Christianity. In one packed sentence, Newman brings into a single orbit his views on education, shaped by Oxford and Oratorianism: "I have ever thought that I could trace a certain resemblance between Athens, as contrasted with Rome, and the Oratory of St. Philip, as viewed in contrast with the religious orders" (86). Athens prepares the way for St. Philip, Rome for St. Ignatius or St. Dominic, whom Newman respected but who were not his cup of tea.

In the chapters that follow, Newman embeds universities in their historical and cultural contexts: the fall of the Roman Empire, the invasions from the north, the emerging position of the papacy, the tradition of Irish schools from the early Middle Ages. That renunciation of material welfare and secular advantage, that contempt for worldly goods and adherence to ascetic practice are all evident in the early Schoolmen who created an audience through their own exertions. Thus a poor monastery in Normandy became, under Lanfranc, a renowned academy, "an instance of a commencement without support, without scholars" which attracted both—perhaps an implicit reflection of Newman's hopes for Dublin (*RPU* 168). What all such instances have in common is the enthusiasm that drives them toward a great end without dependence on the rich and powerful. While the currents of institutionalization ran variously in different centers of learning, a contrary tendency was evident in the wandering scholars who sought different sciences from different teachers. "The zeal for study and knowledge is sufficient indeed in itself for the being of a University, but . . . not sufficient for its well being, or what is technically called its *integrity*." That integrity is a gift superadded to the basic nature of a university which insures some degree of support for its ends (177).

Important to Newman's argument, as always, is the distinction between professors and tutors, the university principle and the college principle. The professorial system is necessary for the existence of a university, but not for its well-being. Professors are on the forefront of knowledge, but they cannot bring their personal influence to bear effectively upon any significant number of students, who require a more personal assistance in their intellectual cultivation. Though a professor may secure popularity in the lecture hall, his followers may become a hindrance to others and a danger to himself. Tutors are less prone to the temptations of theatrics, and must listen as well as lead. The tutorial system provides a fundamentally religious influence to counteract formal disputation and the feuds that sometimes sprung up among different nationalities attending the early universities.

Once more Newman looks back on Oxford and Oratorianism as sources for his idea of small communities of men, best insured by the college principle. In his concluding chapter, which brings the special function of seminaries into the discussion, Newman takes the argument a step further in decrying the effect of university disputation on naïve youth. "In Universities, subjects of every sort were disputed publicly; and boys, who ought to have been schooled at a Seminary in distrust of the intellect and modesty of speculation, were suffered to imbibe a critical, carping, curious spirit, most unbecoming in an ecclesiastic, on the interpretation of difficulties of Scripture, or on the deepest questions of theology" (*RPU* 243). But the university must have its own sphere of activity and be strong enough to protect colleges when required. In fact, Newman regrets that the English university has so little jurisdiction over its colleges. In evoking the idea of a university, Newman is trying to conjure up a kind of Real Presence that he had never known at Oxford.

Thus Newman gives the college principle its due without idealizing it. He recognizes that the collegiate system can become a haven for self-indulgence and inactivity. Collegiate conservatism, a virtue in the age of Peel, had also worked against the larger aims of education at an earlier date in the past, when smugness and unthinking elitism were the substance of daily college life. The proper balance between university and college is between progress and stability, brilliant scholarship and modest diligence, the international world of research and the world of the nation embodying order, stability, and loyalty. One advances learning, the other forms the character, yet all this is not simply a matter of balance but of interdependence. One mind must, after all, have both sail and ballast.

Newman's chapters glance at the political squabbles which had led to his defeat at Oxford and his recent feeling of triumph over the demise of the old Hebdomadal Board that had given him so much trouble. But what is most important about *The Rise and Progress of Universities* is that Newman finds new ways of relating the history and structure of university education to its effect on both those who teach and those who learn. Personality in this work both derives from, and reciprocally affects, institutional strength. Personality and the principle of law are the interacting components of a single living system.

"University Preaching": 1855–1857

In *The Rise and Progress of Universities*, Newman had spoken of the role of teaching as analogous to preaching. In the spread of knowledge ("Science"), he had written, "the teacher is strong, not in the patronage of great men, but in the intrinsic value and attraction of what he has to communicate; and next, he must come forward and advertise himself, before he can gain hearers." Newman compares this activity to the preaching of the Apostles and Evangelists on their lonely journeys. Confidence in the power of the "divine message" to win hearts and make friends of "strangers and outcasts" motivated their behavior (*RPU* 164–65). "Missionaries of knowledge" in medieval Christendom likewise moved forth from their own center, Rome, as the Apostles had from Jerusalem, the teachers with a thirst for knowledge, the converts a thirst for happiness. The art of preaching in a university setting, as we saw in the Oxford sermons, is doubly weighty, for it marks a point at which the desire for knowledge and the need for pastoral guidance converge.

Among the separate papers later gathered into Newman's education volumes, "University Preaching" (1855) is the final distillation of his homiletic views. Although he had spoken of the necessity of the teacher's advertising himself, self-advancement need not mean self-inflation. University preaching takes place in the context of the more learned sermon preached under university auspices rather than in a parish. Yet allowing for that difference, Newman reasserts certain basic principles he regards as critical for all preaching. The preacher's object is the spiritual good of his hearers, and this requires simplicity and spontaneity, not display that draws attention to the speaker. "Simple earnestness" in oneself "creates earnestness in others by sympathy; and the more a preacher loses and is lost to himself, the more does he gain his brethren" (*IU* 305). The speaker's ethos should tend toward the spiritual good of his hearers. For this, Jesus is the ultimate model. "Who could wish to be more eloquent, more powerful, more successful ... yet who more earnest, who more natural, who more unstudied, who more self-forgetting than he?" (306).

"University Preaching" can be read as a prolegomenon to the eight sermons preached in 1856 and 1857 in connection with the opening of the University Church, Dublin, and first published in 1857 with a dedication to Henry Manning. They are now most frequently cited as *Sermons Preached on Various Occasions*, where they are followed by two sermons added in the third edition of 1860 and another in the fourth edition of 1874. They amount to a pastoral counterpart to the educational theory set out in *The Idea of a University* and *Rise and Progress*.

Newman begins the opening sermon, preached on the Feast of St. Monica, the mother of St. Augustine, with Monica's prayers for the conversion of her proud pagan son. The text is Luke 7:12, which in Newman's version reads, "And when He came nigh to the gate of the city, behold, a dead man was carried out, the only son of his mother, and she was a widow." Monica, too, was a widow who saw her son as dead to Christianity in his "ignorance, pride, appetite, and ambition." Her loving patience finally brought about the moment in which "grace melted the proud heart, and purified the corrupt breast of Augustine, and restored and comforted his mother." Monica thus becomes a type of the Church, lamenting over lost children and rejoicing at their recovery (*SVO* 2–3).

Newman sees a Monica and an Augustine in every age: the doting mother, the wandering son, whose intellectual potential and "turbulent appetite" mark him "as educated, yet untaught," whose ardor and self-will, recklessness and inexperience, are the very qualities that may be turned to the cause of religious truth. The story of mother and son is especially appropriate for the first Sunday of worship in a new church. The building is an extension of the new university as the University is an extension of the Church, in her role as Alma Mater teaching all sciences. The Church herself has both a maternal and an intellectual function. She "confute[s] and put[s] right those who would set knowledge against itself, and would make truth contradict truth, and would persuade the world that, to be religious, you must be ignorant, and to be intellectual, you must be unbelieving" (*SVO* 5). Newman undertakes to close the gap between knowledge and belief, but his tactic is double-edged, for in addition to asserting the rights of the Church in an unbelieving world, he is also referring obliquely to those Catholics hostile to his project who would have religion put intellectual halters on its own faithful. Newman was fully aware that the pursuit, not just of holiness but of wholeness, could be thwarted by believers and unbelievers alike. The task of heresy, as he had first said in his Arian history, is always to divide and to define a partial truth; the task of genuine orthodoxy is to expand rather than contract the grounds on which belief can flower. The two selves were never meant to be rivals, but too often the human personality is like an internally divided kingdom, with warring passions separately pursuing their own goals to the exclusion of others. As Carlyle, in his essay "Characteristics," had said, "Had Adam remained in Paradise, there had been no Anatomy and no Metaphysics." Likewise, Newman argues that the very division between religion and philosophy is a consequence of the Fall. What is required of the Holy See and the Church in setting up universities is "to reunite things which were in the beginning joined together by God, and have been put asunder by man." He denies that he wants the intellect to be stunted by "ecclesiastical supervision" or that he wants both religion and science to compromise or give something on each side. Each should have freedom but "should be found in one and the same place, and exemplified in the same persons. I want to destroy that diversity of centres, which puts everything into confusion by creating a contrariety of influences.... I want the intellectual layman to be religious and the devout ecclesiastic to be intellectual" (SVO 13). He cautions those present that "no system of mere religious guardianship which neglects the Reason, will in matter of fact succeed against the School. Youths need a masculine religion, if it is to carry captive their restless imaginations, and their wild intellects, as well as to touch their susceptible hearts" (14).

While the remaining sermons strike a more conventional pose, warning against undue fondness for any merely human branch of study and against intellectual pride, the inaugural sermon, in its rebuke of the excessive influence of narrow clericalism, demarcates a terrain of future tension between Newman and the Ultramontane party. A newer generation of converts, the volume's dedicatee (Manning) among them, grasped the implications of Newman's arguments and saw it as their duty to resist them.

Reconstituting the Self

HAD NEWMAN DIED at the end of the 1850s, his influence on Victorian culture would have probably waned. Outside of religious circles, his reputation would have rested principally on his contributions to educational philosophy and practice. His morale was at a low point during much of the 1850s and early 1860s. He was far from secure in his new communion. At the end of 1859, his article in *The Rambler*, "On Consulting the Faithful in Matters of Doctrine," was delated to Rome for heresy because it appeared to give an unduly prominent voice to the laity and parish clergy in Church affairs, and Newman's journal entries at this time are so uniformly despairing that those Anglicans who had confidently predicted his early return to the Church of England might have rested their case had they been privy to those entries (*AW* 249–60). Newman did not oblige; for him the question was how to look forward, not back. On January 8, 1860, his reflections led him to a familiar passage (Luke 9:62): "No man putting his hand to the plow and looking back is fit for the kingdom of God." He commented, "I am tempted to look back. Not so, O Lord with Thy grace, not so" (*AW* 252).

Memory was both a blessing and a curse; Newman was, it might be said, cursed, not only with a good memory but also with a fascination with the operations of his own memory. How might he be profitably employed in the years remaining when his lack of success weighed so heavily on him and when he sometimes saw his Protestant years as more productive than his years as a Catholic? Yet life was not complete for Newman unless he could come to terms with the past. In the spring of 1863, his sister Jemima had asked that he send her his letters from abroad written in 1832–33. Newman's response was complicated, but clearly the appeal came at a time when he himself was wondering how best to record his own past: "It has ever been a hobby of mine ... that a man's life lies in his letters" (*L&D* 20:443). Editors were more reliable than biographers, but an autobiographer could be his own editor.

Letters, memoranda, and other scraps of evidence were to be an important part of the *Apologia*. Charles Kingsley's attack on Newman's integrity gave Newman the opening he needed, but it also recalled an earlier passage in his life: the lawsuit for libel filed against him by the defrocked Dominican priest Giacinto Achilli for an attack Newman had made on him in the fifth of the lectures later published in the *Lectures on the Present Position of Catholics in England* in the summer of 1851.[1] Frightened by the possibility of a jail term, Newman this time knew how to prepare for an attack on himself. At the beginning of 1865, the publication of the *Apologia* brought about "a most wonderful deliverance ... marvelously blest." Newman's sense of triumph had never been so strong, though it was not firmly entrenched until he was awarded the cardinalate. But with the publication of the *Apologia*, he had "regained, or rather gained" the approbation of Protestants, and his reputation within the Roman Catholic communion was far more secure. In defending himself, he was also defending the integrity of a body of men whose honesty, like his own, was impugned not only by Kingsley but by a large body of English public opinion.[2] While cathartic, the *Apologia* was also a highly controlled performance, as much in what it did not say as what it said, and it had a very public purpose.

Development Doctrine Revisited

To be his own advocate, Newman had to be his own editor. His intent was to show that the child was father to the man. But if the man is what the boy was in germ, exactly how would narrative causality work? Causality is not the same thing as organic continuity; the *Apologia* is not *The Prelude*. To understand the narrative mode of the *Apologia* requires attention both to the evidence Newman collected and pored over and to the *Essay on the Development of Christian Doctrine*. While the *Development* says little directly related to Newman's views on personality, it has a great deal to do with his self-representational strategy.[3]

In chapter 4 of the *Apologia*, Newman describes how in attempting to deal with his own resistance to the Roman Catholic view of the Blessed Virgin, he read St. Alfonso Liguori and the pamphlets sent to him by Dr. Russell of Maynooth. He believes that he discovered then that "the idea of the Blessed Virgin was as it were *magnified* in the Church of Rome, as time went on,—but so were all Christian ideas; as that of the Blessed Eucharist. The whole scene of pale, faint, distant Apostolic Christianity is seen in Rome, as through a telescope or magnifier. The harmony of the whole, however, is of course what it was. It is unfair then to take one Roman idea, that of the Blessed Virgin, out of what may be called its context" (*A* 178). At the end of 1844, he tells us, he resolved to write "an Essay on Doctrinal Development, and then, if, at the end of it, my convictions in favour of the Roman Church were not weaker, of taking the necessary steps for admission into her fold" (205). To understand doctrinal development historically was to understand himself biographically: "What still remained for my conversion, was, not further change of opinion, but to change opinion itself into the clearness and firmness of intellectual conviction" (181). He would *write* his way into his "conversion."

In the passage on the Blessed Virgin just cited, development is a feature of rhetoric, not biology. The history of Christian theology is a fuller disclosure of something previously implanted. The magnifier is not a metaphor for development but for perception, closer to the foci of seventeenth- and eighteenth-century astronomy and optics than to that of nineteenth-century biology. The object remains stable; it is uncovered, but it already was what it now is. Such anticipations of present-day doctrine as are discovered in the study of the past may be, singly, "faint" enough, but as Newman had written in the *Development*, "they are various, and are drawn from many times and countries, and thereby seem to illustrate each other and form a body of proof" (*DCD* 25). Continuity in history is analogous to continuity of personal experience. Two weeks after his reception by Rome, Newman wrote to A. J. Hamner that the test of being called to the Church is ordinarily "not any great vividness of impression, but its continuance. I have generally said to persons, Fix a time, and observe whether your conviction lasts through it, and how it stands at the end of it" (*L&D* 11:60).

In Newman's thinking, history itself provides a foundation for belief, as the dramatic encounter with the Monophysite in the mirror illustrates.

"Here, in the middle of the fifth century, I found, as it seemed to me, Christendom of the sixteenth and the nineteenth centuries reflected.... The Church of the *Via Media* was in the position of the Oriental communion, Rome was, where she now is; and the Protestants were the Eutychians" (*A* 108).[4] In the summer of 1841 at Littlemore, he remembers, the "ghost had come a second time," with more force: "In the Arian History I found the very same phenomenon, in a far bolder shape, which I had found in the Monophysite.... Wonderful that this should come upon me! ... I saw clearly, that in the history of Arianism, the pure Arians were the Protestants, the semi-Arians were the Anglicans, and that Rome now was what it was then." It was now the semi-Arian in the mirror. Like a tolling bell, we are told again, "Rome now was what it was then" (130). Historical development of orthodox doctrine can only be understood as the unfolding of a stable deposit of faith, not the transmission of traits in a line of descent which might ultimately, through mechanisms of adaptation and survival, become a new species. What is sudden and ahistorical is the momentary flash in which one understands the silent records of history.

As noted (chapter 5 above), Newman had identified seven "Notes" by which to measure the truth or falsity of a particular doctrinal development. In his discussion of the fourth Note, "logical sequence," Newman had described not "a conscious reasoning from premises to conclusion" (*DCD* 189) but a psychological process, in effect paving the way for its realization in the structure of the *Apologia*: "An idea under one or other of its aspects grows in the mind by remaining there; it becomes familiar and distinct, and is viewed in its relations; it leads to other aspects, and these again to others, subtle, recondite, original, according to the character, intellectual and moral, of the recipient, and thus a body of thought is gradually formed without his recognizing what is going on within him" (190). Again, describing "the anticipation of its own future" as the fifth Note of true doctrine, Newman wrote, "Nothing is more common ... than accounts or legends of the anticipations, which great men have given in boyhood of the bent of their minds, as afterwards displayed in their history; so much so that the popular expectation has sometimes led to the invention of them" (196). In the *Apologia*, such anticipations figure in the very earliest of Newman's memories: his boyhood belief in the substantiality of angels and the innate immateriality of physical phenomena, his practice of crossing himself in the dark, his surprise that he had come across a picture of a rosary that he drew as a boy, his habit of defining reality in terms of himself and his Creator, his belief in eternal punishment, his early leanings toward celibacy. The first chapter of the *Apologia* connects the dots that the boy had perceived singly. His life has been given over to the construction of a cartography of belief. Other ideas prove their own falsity by fading away over the years: the Calvinist doctrine of final perseverance, the belief that the Pope was the Antichrist. The dual process of assimilating the true and throwing off the false is central to the method of the *Apologia*. A disposition to accept Catholicity in its full sense as understood and embodied in the Roman system is already fully there, but Newman is only uncovering it as his consciousness expands. In 1887 Newman wrote to George T. Edwards stressing the continuity of his spiritual experience. The Roman Catholic Church, he said, "has added to the simple evangelicalism of my first teachers, but it has obscured, diluted, enfeebled, nothing of it—on the contrary, I have found a power, a resource, a comfort, a consolation in our Lord's divinity and atonement, in His Real Presence, in communion [with?] His Divine and Human Person, which all good Catholics indeed have, but which Evangelical Christians have but faintly" (*L&D* 31:189). The most striking feature of the letter, however, is how Newman's self-described trajectory goes straight from Evangelicalism to Rome, while the Tractarian period becomes a suppressed middle term.

Newman's mind does not so much reenact the development of modern Catholic doctrine as work with scattered evidences, bringing them together in a single place. His mind moves backward into antiquity, forward into the present notes that distinguish the true Church, not chronologically (though assimilation and discarding is inevitably implicated in the passage of time), but synchronously. His dialogue with history is a preface to the overthrow of history, the gradual unveiling of the principle *quod ubique, quod semper, quod ab omnibus creditum est,* which renders unnecessary any further journeying in time or space. To answer Kingsley, Newman must analyze the progress of his own opinions from the vantage point of present knowledge, and it is in the fifth chapter that he is ready to show how he has moved from "history" to "position," a summing up *sub specie aeternitatis,* the vessel now lying at rest in port.

Reconstituting the Self

Autobiographical Apologetics

Hardly anyone now accepts Henry Tristram's apparent concurrence with the view that Newman determined to refute Kingsley's charges with "a plain, unvarnished account of his religious development from his early years" (*AW* 14). Newman doubtless hoped that the resulting defense would read just that way, but the opinion has not survived the work of either his defenders or his detractors, both of whom concur in seeing an extraordinary artfulness in the result. The question of genre is more contested.[5] The *Apologia* does not, as so many Victorian autobiographies do, describe a movement in the direction of spiritual independence and personal autonomy. Rather, it charts a search for a spiritual home in which the end result is submission and assimilation rather than autonomy, allegiance rather than independence. Newman's world is sacramental in sign and symbol, and defined and preserved by a hierarchical and dogmatic Church that guards the *depositum fidei*.

Though cumbersome, the title given to this section attempts to split the difference by retaining the term "autobiography" in its adjectival form, subordinate to, but checking the dangers of an exclusive focus on, apologetics. In this, as in so much else, I have taken a cue from George Levine, who describes the work as "strictly speaking...not even autobiography but apologetic; not a disinterested pursuit of the qualities of experience but a piece of controversy. It is nonetheless supremely about Newman himself, and it allows Newman to avoid very much traffic with the outside world and to focus on the inner experience, of which he is in so many ways the master."[6] The achievement is all the more remarkable in that in the preface, Newman appears to deflect attention from his own personal stake in the combat with Kingsley by referring to himself, like the eponymous author of *The Education of Henry Adams*, in the third person. "He" has long been in the public view, "he" has many who can speak of him from public knowledge, and "he" has if anything tended to speak out too much rather than too little when he would have been wiser to remain silent. Shifting to first person as he gains momentum, Newman declares early, "I will draw out, *as far as may be*, the history of my mind" (emphasis added). By being as "personal and historical" as possible, his disclosures will be reluctant and forced from him by his dislike of being "called to my face a liar and a knave" (*A* 14). What might have been materials for an autobiography more commonly understood, a work that enables the writer to understand the relationship between his inner and outer lives and communicate that relationship to others, will be excluded where that material is not applicable to the purpose at hand.

The importance of suppression in Newman's autobiographical writings is demonstrated most dramatically in what Henry Tristram called Newman's "Autobiography in Miniature." This jotting of key events in his life on a single page of paper over a period of seventy-two years reflects an entire suppression of causality and a dual fascination with looking back and looking forward into an opaque future. The document bears quoting in full; the bracketed numbers are my addition, for ease of reference:

> [1] John Newman wrote this just before he was going up to Greek on Tuesday, June 10th, 1812, when it only wanted 3 days to his going home, thinking of the time (at home) when looking at this he shall recollect when he did it.
> [2] At school now back again.
> [3] And now at Alton where he never expected to be,[7] being lately come for the Vacation from Oxford where he dared not hope to be—how quick time passes and how ignorant are we of futurity. April 8th 1819 Thursday.
> [4] And now at Oxford but with far different feelings—let the date speak—Friday February 16th 1821—[5] And now in my rooms at Oriel College, a Tutor, a Parish Priest and Fellow, having suffered much, slowly advancing to what is good and holy, and led on by God's hand blindly, not knowing whither He is taking me. Even so, O Lord. September 7, 1829. Monday morning, 1/4 past 10.
> [6] And now a Catholic at Maryvale and expecting soon to set out for Rome. May 29, 1846.
> [7] And now a Priest and father of the Oratory, having just received the degree of Doctor from the Holy Father. September 23, 1850.
> [8] And now a Cardinal. March 2, 1884. (*AW* 5)

It is not only causality but identity that is suppressed or set at a remote distance. Entries 1 and 3 use the distancing "John Newman," "he," and "his," shading once into the impersonal "we" on April 8, 1819, a proverbial usage reminiscent of Ecclesiastes ("how quick time passes and how ignorant are we of futurity"). The longest entry is the fifth, also the only one bearing the exact time of day and the only one explicitly in the first person, but even there the first person is not in the subject position but buried in the possessive "my" and objective "me" and submerged in the titles ("a Tutor, a Parish Priest and Fellow"), which identify Newman through his roles and allude circumspectly to "having suffered much." No pronominal reference appears in the last three entries, identity again being specified only through affiliation and title ("Catholic . . . Priest and Father of the Oratory . . . Doctor . . . Cardinal"). As in the *Apologia*, Newman implies a journey, to and from school and home, home and Oxford ("where he dared not hope to be"), to Alton, journeys in space anticipating the spiritual journey hinted at in 1829 ("slowly advancing to what is good and holy") later subsumed in a physical journey ("expecting soon to set out for Rome"). The effect is to blur not only personality but human agency; he is "led by God's hand blindly, not knowing where he is taking me," and the timing of such journeys, whether in his boyhood or in 1846, is not in his hands.

For Newman, dates always spoke, as the *Apologia* was to make abundantly clear. Journals, of course, are constructed not on continuous narrative but on a series of dates, but Newman's journals tend to invest dates with an exceptional degree of importance. In a journal entry of January 6, 1822, the young Newman had recorded "a very good discourse" by "Mr. Grant" of Kentish Town Chapel. Grant had recommended, in Newman's paraphrase, "that we should mark the days or seasons of mercy, and commemorate them in succeeding years by some act of charity—Ebenezer."[8] On January 23, "determined to reduce Mr. Grant's hint . . . to practice," Newman recorded the following dates without comment (this time the numbering is his):

> 1. My birthday Febr. 21, 1801. 2. the day of my baptism, April 9, 1801. 3. the first or last days of the half year of my conversion, Aug. 1 and Decr. 21, 1816. 4. The day I was matriculated at Oxford, Decr. 14, 1816. 5. The day I got the Trinity Scholarship, May 18, 1818. 6. The day I got my Testamur & lost my class, Novr. 27,

1820. 7. The day when our prospects so changed. Novʳ 3, 1821. (*AW* 181)

Certainly, celebrations and afflictions (academic failure, the final stage of his father's bankruptcy) divide the page, but the dates, pointing as they do to formal occasions, suppress the emotions. The delation of his *Rambler* article to Rome at the beginning of the 1860s led Newman in a later memorandum to dwell, almost superstitiously, on his decennial afflictions: his failure in the Schools in 1820, his retiring from the tutorship in 1830, the attack on Tract 90 in 1841, Achilli's lawsuit, and his expectation that he would be called on the carpet by Rome.

Suppression of one kind appears in these memoranda; but suppression in the *Apologia* is now put to the service of literary artifice. The most obvious omission in this regard is Newman's almost entire silence on his family. Although he mentions his "great change of thought" in 1816, he gives very little account of it, nor does he mention the fact that it corresponded to his father's first financial collapse, an event that could easily prompt a desire for religious support. Again, the early and unspecified references to "illness" and "bereavement," the first of these Newman's breakdown at the Schools[9] and the second the death of his beloved sister Mary, are admitted here apparently because the events checked his drift toward Liberalism (*A* 26). Why they did so, we are never told. Newman avoids self-revelation by the simple art of juxtaposition. A singular instance of the technique occurs at the end of chapter 1, after his journey to Sicily.

Newman's description of this journey in the *Apologia* has nothing of the self-reproach that invested his reflections during and closer to the event.[10] Rather, as we have seen, he gives the journey a providential quality, but only through the accumulation of factual details that obscure rather than illuminate the movement of his own mind. He starts with the barest factual statement, "We set out in December, 1832," followed by a description of his work on the *Lyra Apostolica* and his sense that both internal and external changes were facing him and that he had a guardian angel. Then he picks up the narrative in the first person: "I went to various coasts of the Mediterranean; parted with my friends at Rome; went down for the second time to Sicily without companion, at the end of April; and got back to England by Palermo in the early part of July" (*A* 41). This is followed by a second sentence suggesting the utterly inward solitude the journey encouraged: "The strangeness of foreign life threw me back into myself; I found pleasure in historical sites and beautiful scenes, not in men and manners." And then, as if to assert the utterly unpredictable quality of the visit, he follows with a third: "We kept clear of Catholics throughout our tour" (41).

But, with the travelogue complete, the arc of the narrative shifts to men and manners, and the travelers do not, in fact, avoid contact with Catholics. The dean of Malta was "a most pleasant man," but their conversation was mainly about the Fathers and the library. Newman knows the Abbate Santini at Rome, "who did no more than copy for me the Gregorian tomes." Newman and Hurrell Froude make two calls on Wiseman. Roman Catholic rites are glimpsed entirely in their externalities. Desires for England ("in my thoughts solely") suggest a flight from new and potentially threatening influences, as does Newman's return home *solo* when he sees the tricolor over a French vessel in Algiers and stays indoors his full twenty-four hours in Paris to avoid contagion, whether medical or political.

But the once Evangelical Newman seems no longer to fear religious contagion. We find ourselves back in Rome with the initiation of the *Lyra Apostolica* as a joint project. This time the final parting with Wiseman (whom we now realize to be one of "my friends at Rome" in the first narrative) is invested with one brief adverb. "When we took leave of Monsignore Wiseman, he had courteously expressed a wish that we might make a second trip to Rome; I said with great gravity, 'We have a work to do in England'" (A 43). This fateful commitment (at the time as yet uncomprehended in its full range of implications) is followed by Newman's sudden illness in Sicily. "Especially when left by myself, the thought came upon me that deliverance is wrought, not by the many but by the few, not by bodies but by persons" (42). After recovering from fatigue in Lyon, Newman tells us, he "got off again, and did not stop night or day, (except a compulsory delay at Paris,) till I reached England, and my mother's house. My brother had arrived from Persia only a few hours before. This was on the Tuesday. The following Sunday, July 14th, Mr. Keble preached the Assize Sermon in the University Pulpit. It was published under the title of 'National Apostasy.' I have ever considered and kept the day, as the start of the religious movement of 1833" (43).

Newman's allusion to the spectral brother is the second of only three in the *Apologia*. Its placement suggests an inversion of the theme of providential leading. As early as 1832, Frank was in his brother's opinion an apostate because he had resigned his Balliol fellowship and joined a Plymouth Brethren mission to the Middle East. Between then and the writing of the *Apologia*, Frank had embraced that liberalism in religious matters that John had always feared as the ultimate destination of Evangelicals. Familial and national apostasy have somehow merged in this compressed passage culminating in the reference to Keble's sermon. Frank, understandably, later held bitter memories of his treatment by his brother on the occasion of their "joint return from abroad."[11]

Newman's early determination to remain celibate was complicated by the breakdown of family relations, his thwarted desire to assume the role of father to his younger siblings. A frequently quoted journal entry from March 25, 1840, at the end of the manuscript on his illness in Sicily, makes the point: "The thought keeps pressing on me, while I write this, what am I writing it for?.... I only have found one who even took that sort of affectionate interest in me as to be pleased with such details—and that is H[enry] Wilberforce and what shall I ever see of him?" In the sentence immediately following the reference to Wilberforce, whose marriage had upset Newman greatly, Newman was wondering who would be interested in his narrative, or what reader would take "the sort of interest which a wife takes and none but she—it is a woman's interest—and that interest, so be it, shall never be taken in me...... Shall I ever have in my old age spiritual children who will take an interest such as a wife does? How time is getting on! I seem to be reconciling myself to the idea of being old" (*AW* 137–38). A life barren by anticipation haunts the Mediterranean voyage in the *Apologia*. Newman was in effect defending his marriage to the Church in a public forum in which the readers were the congregation and Kingsley the witness who would, if he could, introduce a bar or impediment to the solemnization of the vows. The *Apologia* papers over the familial and religious fractures, his brother, his former Anglican friends, and his sometimes hostile or suspicious Catholic superiors in later years. Newman the elder attributes the renewed energy of Newman the younger to the Mediterranean journey that nearly killed him, an "exuberant and joyous energy ... which I never had before or since.... We knew enough to begin preaching upon, and there was no one else to preach." The physical voyage is also a spiritual one: "I felt on board a vessel, which first gets under weigh, and luggage and live stock stowed away into their proper receptacles" (A 49–50). To any Victorian contemporary versed in the literature of emigration, the analogy would be familiar, but in this case the emigration is, in fact, homeward-bound, not to the Antipodes. It is rather as if, in the Acts of the Apostles, to which in spirit this section of the *Apologia* owes so much, Paul had emphasized the work that lay nearest to home. But at the same time, the cessation of the voyage, despite Newman's avowals, involves an awareness of loss, the fear of failing to transmit an inheritance to spiritual, if not biological, offspring.

Nonetheless, the writing of the *Apologia* promised a degree of compensation. A widely held critical view is that Newman's pose as a reluctant combatant was only a rhetorical device to conceal his eagerness to take up Kingsley's challenge. In this reading, the *Apologia* recalls Thomas Henry Huxley's triumphant (if apocryphal) aside to a companion on the occasion of Samuel Wilberforce's attack on evolution: "The Lord hath delivered him into mine hands." Both interpretations of Newman's behavior—reluctant combatant, eager polemicist—probably should be held simultaneously, in mutual tension, for the text supports both readings. One side of Newman undoubtedly wanted to refer his past history to futurity, accepting for the nonce the interpretation many put on his behavior—that he had evaded and shuffled in his Anglican years—as a penalty he had "naturally and justly incurred" by changing his religion. Under such circumstances, he writes in the preface, he had been willing to leave the removal of those imputations "to a future day, when personal feelings would have died out and documents would see the light which were as yet buried in closets or scattered through the country" (A 1–2). On the other hand, he had long believed that, if formally challenged by "a person of name," it would be his duty to respond. Not only did a "person of name" (whose name was deleted from the preface) obligingly come forward, but the very nature of that challenge made Newman's response no longer merely personal but one that involved "my duty to my Brethren in the Catholic Priesthood" (A 4). Again, the motives of an entire class of men, not just those of Newman himself, had been impugned. In the concluding chapter of the *Apologia*, Newman shifts from an individual to a collective voice, in which the mere recitation of the names of the brethren of the Oratory suffices to indicate his qualifications as community spokesman.

But the chapters do not tell the whole story. The appended notes contain elements of the original exchange of pamphlets and take the quarrel further. Despite brilliant moments of dramatic juxtaposition and emotion recollected in later emotion, the *Apologia* is not a unified narrative. It is, as one might have expected after the shock of the Achilli affair a decade earlier, a gathering of documents in which the narrative plays a decisive, but on its own bottom not always a conclusive, role. The notes are as much a part of the argument of the *Apologia* as the main text, like the supporting exhibits in a trial dominated by eloquent lawyers.[12] Though Newman's idea of development provides an underlying continuity through discovery of what was waiting to be known, it does not control the *Apologia*'s every narrative moment. As a whole, the work invites the speculation that had Newman overcome his natural shyness and turned his very considerable gifts to the bar, he might have become a barrister of no little distinction.

In answering Kingsley, Newman had recourse not only to the Tractarian principles of Reserve and Economy, but also to courtroom practice. A competent attorney will advise a client or a client's witness to say only what is necessary to answer a question, a lesson Oscar Wilde learned the hard way. Newman here becomes his own attorney. He had to meet the expedient of saying as little as possible about his deepest feelings while still communicating a sense of their reality.[13] Such a maneuver calls for a complicated interaction of aggression and retreat, communicating candor while controlling the narrative.

Keeping Them in Check

The primary site of the quarrel with Kingsley is Newman's sermon "Wisdom and Innocence." What enraged Kingsley was less the sermon's suggestion that Christians would seem "affected," "artificial," or "shifty" (though such terms align nicely with his imputations of effeminacy) than that they would seem to be, in Newman's words, "wanting in openness and manliness."[14] For Kingsley, the duplicity involved in the gospel of harmlessness is closely linked to the unhealthy power Newman exhibited over those "fanatic and hotheaded young men, who hung over his every word" (*A* 363). Kingsley is irritated by what he sees as Newman's affectation of passivity, whereas in reality, he thinks, Newman should have behaved in a more manly fashion by reining in his own followers. Newman in turn denies that he was ever anything more than "a leading author of a school" and attributes the real leadership to others. The ideas of the Movement, he declares, spread through the undergraduate body without his effort, and thence to the junior clergy who were taking clerical posts after graduation. Newman claims never to have seen himself as a leader: "I had a lounging, free-and-easy way of carrying things on" (63). He knows that the defense might sound unconvincing, given his self-confessed ferocity: "I am not bound to account for it; but there have been men before me, fierce in act, yet tolerant and moderate in their reasonings; at least, so I read history." He goes so far as to describe the Tracts as "short, hasty, and some of them ineffective," with a slovenly appearance when first bound into a volume (64). It is entirely typical of Newman to understate his personal leadership, but while he dismisses his organizational activity as naturally uncongenial to him, he saw and understood his quasi-apostolic role: "We knew enough to begin preaching upon, and there was no one else to preach." Despite the first person plural, such a passage tends to occlude the role of others—though he names them—like Pusey, Keble, Church, or Copeland, who carried the burden of responsibility after Newman had abandoned it.

Newman's explanation of "Wisdom and Innocence" reiterates a theme of his early writings on the lives of saints. In Note C he recalls the disappointment of those who came to hear him preach "red-hot Tractarianism" and were rewarded instead with a "plain humdrum sermon." As a result, "they got up the charitable theory which the Writer revives. They said that there was a double purpose in these plain addresses of mine, and that my Sermons were never so artful as when they seemed common-place; that there were sentences which redeemed their apparent simplicity and quietness. So they watched during the delivery of a Sermon, which to them was too practical to be useful, for the concealed point of it, which they could at least imagine, if they could not discover" (*A* 273–74). Divine Wisdom, he continues, has framed laws which the carnal world would call foolish, but "our Lord ... has substituted meekness for haughtiness, passiveness for violence, and innocence for craft: and ... the event has shown the high wisdom of such an economy, for it has brought to light a set of natural laws, unknown before, by which the seeming paradox that weakness should be stronger than might, and simplicity than worldly policy, is readily explained" (275).

By then injecting a reference to that contrary "theory of religion, called, since the Sermon was written, 'muscular Christianity,'" Newman stakes out a claim to Christian ground against what he sees as Kingsley's perversions. Yet by using "carnal weapons" to defend himself against Kingsley, he must have known that he was compromising his own assertion that innocence was stronger than craft. Newman's craft was too strong for him to resist its exercise. As he had written twenty years before, "The political principles of Christianity, if it be right to use such words of a divine polity, are laid down for us in the Sermon on the Mount. Contrariwise to other empires, Christians conquer by yielding; they gain influence by shrinking from it; they possess the earth by renouncing it" (*DCD* 184). Here Sheridan Gilley's observation is worth noting: "His dissent from Liguori's moral opinions about the lawfulness of lying did not represent the mind of his own Church.... Newman's own utterances were sometimes equivocal and his was an equivocal position in defending the intellectual honesty of his Church, when he doubted it himself" (Gilley 333).

Newman's defense of his sermon in Note C rests on the circumstances in which it was written, when his good faith was already under attack. "Base calumnies ... were heaped upon me on all sides," he wrote. These calumnies persisted and grew "when I was all the time conscious to myself, in my degree, and after my measure, of 'sobriety, self-restraint, and control of word and feeling'" (*A* 276–77). He rebuts Kingsley's claim that as a preacher he was "utterly blind to the broad meaning and the plain practical result of a Sermon like this delivered before fanatic and hotheaded young men who hung over his every word." Newman claims that by 1841 he had "severed" himself from the younger generation of Oxonians. But one need not turn to the correspondence from that period to prove otherwise, for the testimony of the *Apologia* suggests an even more complicated emotional dynamic. It is true that in chapter 4, the narrative of his Anglican "deathbed" describes the puzzlement that the *Sermons Bearing on Subjects of the Day* caused among his friends. In Newman's words, "While my old and true friends were thus in trouble about me, I suppose they felt not only anxiety but pain, to see that I was gradually surrendering myself to the influence of others, who had not their own claims upon me, younger men, and of a cast of mind in no small degree uncongenial to my own. A new school of thought was rising, as is usual in doctrinal inquiries, and was sweeping the original party of the Movement aside, and was taking its place" (*A* 150–51). Newman does not specify the extent to which the Wards and Oakeleys were pushing him ahead. Certainly he defines his relationship to this younger party by casting himself in the role of seduced rather than seducer ("I was gradually surrendering myself"). Although Newman specifically elides his own agency (the party "rapidly formed and increased" of its own internal momentum), he does hint at something which, if not quite providential, is more than merely coincidental: the coalescence of this younger party in the very summer of 1839, as if obliquely responding to his own doubts.

Newman is at pains to point out that these younger men ended up in at least three different camps: Anglicanism, Rome, and Liberalism. He claims that he was not the man to control their subsequent movements: "Nothing was clearer concerning them, than that they needed to be kept in order; and *on me who had so much to do with the making of them*, that duty was as clearly incumbent; and it is equally clear, from what I have already said, that I was just the person, above all others, who could not undertake it" (*A* 151, emphasis added). But is it indeed so clear? In the next sentence Newman describes the inability of old friends to listen to his troubles, confessing that his theorizing had alienated them but also implying that had they stood by him, he might have been able to exert a counterpressure that would have kept the new generation in line. One suspects that the real reason for Newman's quandary lay not in the exercise of leadership but the rule of personal affection. He was moved by the fact that they had "a great love for me" and was intensely sympathetic to their objectives. The fact that old friends were falling away quickened these sentiments for the new. When he claims that "the members of this new school looked to me," he writes as the leader in spite of himself. If he did not make a party, a party collected itself around him.

Newman's account of his recruitment of "converts" is laid out in the fourth chapter of the *Apologia* in three phases. First, in the early days of the Movement, he "was very glad to make converts," and although he claimed not to have sought disciples, yet he "made advances to others in a special way." When he "fell into misgivings as to the true ground to be taken in the controversy" and gave up his "place" in the Movement, he confined himself to trying to calm those who were "unsettled in their religious views, and, as I judged, hasty in their conclusions." Once he had turned his face Romeward in 1843, he "gave up, as far as ever was possible, the thought of in any respect and in any shape acting upon others. Then I myself was simply my own concern. How could I in any sense direct others, who had to be guided in so momentous a manner myself?" (*A* 196–97). Silence in the face of others' inquiries seemed mysterious, even duplicitous, and his friends failed to understand that he was "as perplexed as they were" (197). If his behavior was ever selfish, it was a "religious selfishness" illustrative of the adage "Physician, heal thyself" (198). His thought on his Anglican "deathbed" was Pascal's "Je mourrai seul" (197). But healing was very nearly the same as death.

Strategies of Self-Presentation

Underlying the shifting narrative modes of the *Apologia*—linear narrative, self-quotation, and apologetics—is a movement from the individual voice of the first four chapters to the collective voice of the concluding meditation in chapter 5. The narrative in the first four chapters charts a journey into exile, a pursuit of truth that alienates the narrator from family, academic community, and the Church of England. He draws on his letters and previously published works to demonstrate continuities between himself as he was then and as he is now. In the apologetic sections, he pulls back to argue or reflect on the state of his opinions at a particular moment. Chapter 1 is entirely devoid of quotations from letters, as befits the description of a youthful mind, but it is rich in the mustering of personalities, most of them Newman's seniors. Whereas linear narrative occupies over 600 lines of chapter 1, it drops to about 375 in chapter 2, where Newman introduces four letters, and the apologetic element becomes more prominent, increasing from about 350 to 850 lines.[15] The number of new actors has dropped sharply, with Hugh James Rose and Pusey as the principal newcomers. Chapter 2 moves from mentorship to colleagueship; it initiates the defense of the Tractarians against the charge of being a party, but it is unable wholly to suppress the evidence of Newman's strong personality. In the third chapter, other figures in Newman's life begin to fade as Newman's conflict becomes more internal: "I had to make up my mind for myself, and others could not help me" (*A* 112).

Chapters 3 and 4 contain the peripeteia and denouement of the action: Newman's alarmed view of himself as a Monophysite, the gradual breakdown of his anti-Romanism, the *"experimentum crucis"* of Tract 90, and his retreat to Littlemore. The Jerusalem bishopric, the resignation of St. Mary's, his retraction of his "hard sayings" against Rome, his retreat into lay communion, and the writing of the essay on development, all follow. Newman falls back increasingly on his own letters to do his work for him, with about a dozen in chapter 3 rising to nearly fifty in chapter 4. Documentation itself becomes a vent for strong emotions. It serves both privacy and revelation; in becoming his own editor, the narrator avoids the artifices of which he would have been accused had he attempted confession rather than a review (however partial) of the surviving record.

An insistence on reticence is a direct rebuke to the demand that one meet one's antagonist point by point. In the opening paragraphs of chapter 4, Newman says that because a sick man "neither cares nor is able to record the stages of his malady," his own memories of a "tedious decline" are so tenuous that he must resort to a documentary record of the sort drawn from letters. In stressing both this and the haphazardness of the evidence that survives ("I have no strictly personal or continuous memoranda to consult, and have unluckily mislaid some valuable papers"), Newman signals the privacy that he is now compelled to violate, recalling that at the time, "I was not allowed to die in peace,—except so far as friends who had still a full right to come in upon me, and the public world which had not, have given a sort of history to those last four years" (*A* 137). The muting of the most important event is signaled by the letter of October 8, 1845, which Newman wrote to "a number of friends": "I am this night expecting Father Dominic, the Passionist.... He is a simple, holy man; and withal gifted with remarkable powers. He does not know of my intention, but I mean to ask of him admission into the One Fold of Christ" (211). After the quoted postscript ("This will not go til all is over. Of course it requires no answer"), the narrator continues, "For a while after my reception, I proposed to betake myself to some secular calling" (212). The culminating event of Newman's reception exists everywhere except in the moment at which it takes place; the letter anticipates it but is withheld until after.

As the "Autobiography in Miniature" shows, knowing that one is on a pilgrimage, but not knowing whither, is a key ingredient in Newman's defense against Kingsley's charges of deliberate duplicity. It is also a dramatically vivid form of narration in itself. Far from plotting his course with devious "Jesuitical" logic, the Newman of chapters 3 and 4 more nearly resembles an animal at bay surrounded by hunters, forced into the thickets by anxious friends, eager Catholics, and hostile Anglicans. In one of the most famous passages, simultaneously anguished and bitter, passive and aggressive by turns, Newman's shift from past to present tense, quite unlike the moments of suppression in the *Apologia*, deliberately forces the reader into what was his state of mind at that time: "But they persisted: 'What was I doing at Littlemore?' Doing there! have I not retreated from you? have I not given up my position and my place? am I alone, of Englishmen, not to have the privilege to go where I will, no questions asked? am I alone to be followed by jealous prying eyes, which take note whether I go in at a back door or at the front, and who the men are who happen to call on me in the afternoon?" The change in tense accomplishes Newman's transition from the reenacted past to the memorializing present with what is the climactic metaphor of the passage: "Wounded brutes creep into some hole to die in, and no one grudges it them. Let me alone, I shall not trouble you long. This was the keen feeling which pierced me, and, I think, these are the very words in which I expressed it to myself" (*A* 158). Newman's reticence is increased by apparently unguarded moments such as these. He opens the door far enough to dramatize what, in Virgilian terms, he had called "a cruel operation, the ripping-up of old griefs, and the venturing again upon the '*infandum dolorem*' of years, in which the stars of this lower heaven were one by one going out." When, in the same passage, Newman states that "these are the very words in which I expressed it to myself," the force of the remark is emphasized if one juxtaposes it to the opening of chapter 3: "And who can recollect, at the distance of twenty-five years, all that he once knew about his thoughts and his deeds?" (*A* 90). That Newman is willing to engage in this virtual act of self-mutilation, on his terms, not Kingsley's, itself serves as a testimonial of his good faith as a narrator.

Newman seems to insist that only he, in the present, has the right to abandon the privacy he should have had at Littlemore. Yet his self-dramatization requires a reader to exercise skepticism and empathy simultaneously—a difficult if not impossible task. He could hardly have expected that he was entitled to the same privacy that someone much less influential and visible might have had a right to expect. In the *Apologia*, he quotes his own letter to Bishop Bagot from April 14, 1842, in which he denied his intention of reviving monastic orders in the Church of England and plaintively asked, "For what have I done that I am to be called to account by the world for my private actions, in a way in which no one else is called?" (*A* 160). Yet he had written two years earlier to S. F. Wood in that he had in mind "a real Monastery here" and though he may have made a subtle distinction between a monastic house and the revival of monastic orders, it is a distinction likely to elude even a discriminating reader and blurred further by the fact that he intended something like a monastic *discipline*. If Newman meant what he said, then he could hardly view his retreat to Littlemore as a purely private act. The Church of England has long since made its peace with the revival of monastic orders, but the early Victorian Church had not. It had every right to worry about just what was happening to young clergymen at Littlemore.[16] When Newman couched his role there as one of pastoral care to troubled young clergymen or prospective ordinands, he apparently saw Littlemore as an outlying defensive trench for Anglicanism rather than a halfway house to Rome. It might have been well had he left it at that.

Chapter 4 contains the heart of Newman's defense against the charge that he had become "a concealed Romanist," that he had gone over to the enemy well before the end of 1845. By far the longest of the four chapters, it is also a record of his cutting of ties, his retreat into solitude, comforted only by the fact that "from a boy I had been led to consider that my Maker and I, His creature, were the two beings, luminously such, *in rerum natura*" (*A* 177). Obstacles to joining Rome fall away as do friends and relations. Newman's famous metaphor of the Anglican deathbed perhaps also incorporates a reference to the death of his closest friend after Hurrell Froude at Oxford, John William Bowden, in 1844, only a year before Newman's reception into the Roman Catholic Church, though Bowden's name is suppressed, suggesting that death is indeed the most private of events between a man and his maker, as well as between intimate friends. But Newman is explicit about his feelings: "I never told him the state of my mind. Why should I unsettle that sweet calm tranquility, when I had nothing to offer him instead? I could not say 'Go to Rome'; else I should have shown him the way" (*A* 203). He could not respond to Bowden's obvious curiosity about the state of his mind. That he could not share his intimate feelings with his most intimate surviving friend, who on his deathbed would surely have understood all, must have jolted Newman's awareness of how loose his remaining ties were.

Coming into Port: From Memory to Dream

In the powerful eternal present of chapter 5, the governing metaphor is the vessel's coming into harbor. Conscious of no "change, intellectual or moral, wrought in my mind," Newman recurs implicitly to the *Development of Christian Doctrine*; his "conversion" is more Augustinian than Pauline; but rather than a "turning" to a new faith, it describes a new comprehensiveness bringing to light what has been there all along. The result is a homecoming, though it is to a home never fully known before.

The termination of the narrative in 1845, and the sense of exile enforced by the ending of chapter 4, was all that was necessary to meet Kingsley's challenge. That challenge required a tone of unshakeable confidence; Newman was under no obligation to describe the tensions he had (or to anticipate those he was to continue to have) with the Roman hierarchy, all of which would have been grist not only for Kingsley's mill but that of some former fellow Anglicans. The opening sentence of chapter 5, "From the time that I became a Catholic, of course I have no further history of my religious opinions to narrate," is true if one understands him to mean the basic intellectual framework with which he entered the Catholic Church. But the statement that he has not had any "anxiety of heart whatever" and has rested in "perfect peace and contentment," passes over eighteen years of cares and frustrations. Although the *Apologia* established him on a new footing among many Protestants and Roman Catholics alike, it did not end his well-recorded tensions with the hierarchy.

Newman had identified himself with the whole body of the Church and made his personal apologia a collective one. But this temporary merging of self with a larger collectivity seems to collapse when he is now required to look at the world as it is, and the effect is to invert the terms of his opening chapter where he has affirmed "two and two only absolutely self-sufficient beings, myself and my Creator." Each term is confirmed by the other, and to fail to locate that Other in the mirror is to have erased oneself. "If I looked into a mirror, and did not see my face, I should have the sort of feeling which actually comes upon me, when I look into this living busy world, and see no reflexion of its Creator" (*A* 216).[17] The only answer can be that if there is a God, "the living society of men is in a true sense discarded from his presence." Newman here employs the illustration of "a boy of good make and mind, with the tokens on him of a refined nature, cast upon the world without provision, unable to say whence he came, his birthplace, or his family connexion," whose presence can only be accounted for by parental shame.

That boy is unmistakably Newman himself, now severed from his birthplace, his parents, and, most of all, his surviving siblings. Failing to perceive himself in the mirror, he must re-create himself. The imagined disappearance of his face from the mirror requires a bulwark, which the collective witness of the Church offers, against "the aggressive, capricious, untrustworthy intellect," thereby enabling Newman's own self-refiguration. The community thus provides a site for the reconstruction of personality. According to the Church, Newman writes, "each individual man must be in his own person one whole and perfect temple of God, while he is also one of the living stones which build up a visible religious community" (*A* 222).

Such a self-refiguration, or renovation, is possible when one submits to the Church's claims as Newman describes them in chapter 5. He has, indeed, moved beyond the world of mere opinion, for he no longer has to engage in the ultimately self-canceling act of picking and choosing among opinions. The doctrine brought to light through the process of development, whether that of the Immaculate Conception or the role of the Virgin, is what gives the Church a shape and figuration of her own. In this the whole mind of the Church performs a constitutive act. Thus, "there is no burden at all in holding that the Blessed Virgin was conceived without original sin; indeed, it is a simple fact to say, that Catholics have not come to believe it because it is defined, but that it was defined because they believed it" (*A* 228).

Newman's belief that "new" dogmas are merely the coming together of many individual minds, and his dramatic view of how truths emerge through the collision of infallibility and reason, authority and private judgment, partakes of the same mid-Victorian atmosphere that produced John Stuart Mill's paean to the value of allowing the conflict and competition of opinions. The chief difference between *On Liberty* and the *Apologia* is that for Newman, the collision of ideas takes place within divinely ordered boundaries in which Authority, once it has taken the measure of the competing decisions, is the final arbiter. Newman's view is dynamic, but it does not allow for the play of historical contingency and circumstance which underwrites the disputative processes described in *On Liberty*. In another passage metaphorically redolent of an industrializing age, Newman argues that through such divine dispensation, "human beings with willful intellects and wild passions" are "brought together into one by the beauty and the Majesty of a Superhuman Power,—into what may be called a large reformatory or training school ... some moral factory, for the melting, refining, and moulding, by an incessant, noisy process, of the raw material of human nature, so excellent, so dangerous, so capable of divine purposes" (*A* 226). For Mill, history is what individuals make for themselves. For Carlyle, it may be guided from above but it also wells up from below. For Newman, the end of history is foreordained by this same Superhuman Power. But though neither Carlyle nor Mill accepted the claims of the Church, they would have agreed that truths lodge themselves in public acceptance when society has reached a state of receptivity that admits them. Newman's challenge to his contemporaries was to admit the possibility that a Catholic need not sacrifice his intellectual integrity to be a loyal member of the Church.

Newman concedes that the hierarchy may on occasion be wrong, and that truth does not always advance steadily through the actions of official bodies of the Church. But for him the Church is not an ossified bureaucracy, but a living and breathing Power, promulgating truths whatever their source. Hence his insistence, suspicious and even threatening though it was to some of his fellow Catholics, that "it is individuals, and not the Holy See, that have taken the initiative, and given the lead to the Catholic mind, in theological inquiry." Bishops "have been guided in their decisions by the commanding genius of individuals, sometimes young and of inferior rank. Not that uninspired intellect overruled the superhuman gift ... committed to the Council ... but in that process of inquiry and deliberation which ended in an infallible enunciation, individual reason was paramount" (*A* 237–38). Quietly but firmly, Newman holds fast to the position he had taken in the *Rambler* article: the laity and working parochial clergy had a right to be consulted.

Newman's dynamic yet strangely serene view of how the Church settles differences of opinion seems contradictory to his own recent experience.

But under the polemical restraints that had impelled him to write the *Apologia*, he could hardly dwell on his own negative experiences, much less the failure of the Church of his own day to live up to the idealized model of adjudicated controversy that he put forward in chapter 5. His sense of being misrepresented or perhaps even willfully misunderstood by those whom he professed to be eager to serve comes out strongly in a letter to Emily Bowles barely a year before the *Apologia* was published:

> This age of the Church is peculiar—in former times, primitive and medieval, there was not the extreme centralization which now is in use. If a private theologian said any thing free, another answered him. If the controversy grew, then it went to a Bishop, a theological faculty, or to some foreign University. The Holy See was but the court of ultimate appeal. *Now*, if I, as a private priest, put any thing into print, *Propaganda* answers me at once. How can I fight with such a chain on my arm? It is like the Persians driven on to fight *under the lash*. There was true private judgment in the primitive and medieval schools—there are *no* schools now, no private judgment (in the *religious* senses of the phrase), no freedom, that is, of opinion. That is, no exercise of the intellect.... This is a way of things which, in God's own time, will work its own cure, of necessity. (*L&D* 20:447)

The *Apologia* declares that the Church in its ideal state has always evolved through the collision of ideas, and that longer view becomes an expression of the Church, not as she has always acted, but as she works in her best moments. In chapter 5, Newman submerges the frustration he had voiced to Emily Bowles, presenting the Church as he wished his contemporaries to see it and as he thought at its best and truest it could be.

In the concluding section of the chapter, Newman moves from the defense of the Church (including its laity) to the defense of its priesthood and the character of individual priests. Ending as it does with a roll call of the names of those "who have been so faithful to me," Newman has attracted criticism for placing so much emphasis on service to him. That may be, but in the structure of the *Apologia*, so firmly rooted in the idea of personality, divine and human, the roll call itself restores the early emphasis on individual persons in his life, now, however, persons who have acted as members of one community. From that collectivity Newman can issue his prayer for the ingathering of all his friends, past and present, "into One Fold, and under One Shepherd."

The *Apologia* had required unraveling the past and thereby tracing, sometimes painfully, the process of self-reconstruction from the vantage point of an imagined harbor. Becalmed for a week in the Straits of Bonifacio on the homeward leg of his youthful Mediterranean journey (*A* 43), Newman this time was free to disembark. But the process which had engaged his attention in the writing of the work, itself a voyage to a new port, continued to fascinate him. It accounts in part, I think, for the motives that led him to write another kind of "autobiography in miniature" a few months later in January 1865, *The Dream of Gerontius*. To allegorize his own experience on his Anglican deathbed, Newman explored in dramatic form the same theme of the unweaving and reweaving of personality, the losing oneself to save oneself. The continuing preoccupation that the *Dream* represents had been evident in the fourth of the *Discourses addressed to Mixed Congregations* ("Purity and Love"), some fifteen years earlier, in which, in the peroration, Newman had imagined how the soul, once separated from its body, faces judgment: "It knows how great a debt of punishment remains upon it, though it has for many years been reconciled to Him; it knows that purgatory lies before it, and that the best it can reasonably hope for is to be sent there. But to see His Face, though for a moment! to hear His Voice, to hear Him speak, though it be to punish! O Saviour of men, it says, I come to Thee, though it be in order to be at once remanded from Thee" (*DMC* 81).

In part 1, Gerontius, on his deathbed surrounded (unlike Newman) by his friends, expresses a fear of extinction, feeling that "my very being had given way, / As though I was no more a substance now, / And could fall back on nought to be my stay" (lines 18–20). The fear of becoming immaterial is at one with the fear of absorption into the cold, "that shapeless, scopeless, black abyss, / That utter nothingness, of which I came" (lines 24–25) and the loss of personality along with corporeality. Hence "that sense of ruin which is worse than pain, / That masterful negation and collapse / Of all that makes me man" (lines 109–11).[18] A fear of the capacity of self-will is compounded by a desire not to relinquish the distant hope of acquiring a future voice.

In part 2, the Soul of Gerontius has entered a new realm of feeling. Rather like the sensations of an amputee, his limbs seem to tell him that his body is still intact. But he also senses that he is held within a mysterious "ample palm," pressed equally on all sides, no longer in control of his own motion. Receiving angelic comfort, he is assured that, contrary to his sensations, he is only just now "disembodied," and that it is the persistence of consciousness of self, his "very energy of thought," that keeps him from God (lines 363–64). Despite the Soul's belief that he still has his senses, the Angel assures him that he has passed beyond touch, taste, and hearing, to "a world of signs and types, / The presentations of most holy truths, / Living and strong" (lines 526–28). He no longer has any extension or sense of power over his own limbs (lines 546–48).

This unmaking of the self, the necessity of total surrender, including surrender of what in the *Apologia* Newman had called "the aggressive, capricious, untrustworthy intellect," is necessary if the Soul, as it desires, is to glimpse God. The moment requires passing beyond even the semblance of sensation and the pang of the conflict between "longing for Him, when thou seest Him not" and "the shame of self at the thought of seeing Him" which is his "veriest, sharpest purgatory" (lines 735–37). Granted one brief sight of God, the Soul is "scorch'd, and shrivell'd" (line 844) and welcomes the reminder of the purgatorial experience when, "Lone, not forlorn," it will sing its "sad perpetual strain / Until the morn" (lines 853–55). The Angel, in a second baptism, dips the Soul into the lake, where it sinks into the flood of "penal waters" bearing the promise of ultimate renewal. Self-forgetfulness and trust in the wisdom of the ultimate Divine Judgment, whatever its outcome, constitute the ideal state of the believer's mind. Newman provides an orthodox Christian response to Tennyson's anxiety about a future state in which once-separate personalities should "fall, / Remerging in the general Soul," a "faith as vague as all unsweet" (*In Memoriam*, Section 47). Newman agrees but offers an alternative to Tennyson's somber vision.

In calling the poem a "Dream," Newman opens the window on an ambiguous reality. Is the poem Gerontius's dream of what is to come, a dream from which he will awake to find himself still a sentient human being, fated to spend more years without the directly realized presence of God? Or is it the poet's dream *about* Gerontius, the self-reflexive dream of an alter ego through whom he could project both his recent "real life" purgatory that had required the subdual of a proud and powerful self to another kind of authority, and some future purgatory that would bring blissful oblivion? Whatever the answer—and various possibilities may be allowed to coexist peacefully—the words "lone but not lorn" take us back to an early episode of Newman's life when, on one of his youthful solitary walks around the grounds of Oriel, he had encountered Hawkins's predecessor as provost, Edward Copleston. "He turned around, and with the kind courteousness which sat so well on him, made me a bow and said, 'Numquam minus solus, quam cum solus'"—one is never less alone than when alone (A 27). The psychic energies which the strategy of evasion had short-circuited in the *Apologia* at last find their voice in Newman's greatest poem. Gerontius no longer needs to look in his mirror. He has been vouchsafed a glimpse of God's face directly.

Oppositions and Resolutions

THE DECADE FOLLOWING the publication of the *Apologia* is marked by one major publication, the *Essay in Aid of a Grammar of Assent* (1870), and several lesser works—Newman's review of J. R. Seeley's *Ecce Homo* (1866), his response to Pusey's *Eirenicon*, published in the same year, and his *Letter to the Duke of Norfolk* (1874)—that represent the consolidation of his particular views on Catholics, Catholicism, and the role of a nonestablished church in a secularizing society. This period also marks some of Newman's most serious difficulties with the hierarchy, which the *Apologia*, though it had brought him a measure of support among Catholics and Protestants alike, did not resolve and—as we shall see presently—may indeed have heightened. Freed from the confines of Oxford, Newman entered the stage as a Victorian intellectual, a writer whose claim to attention transcended the boundaries of a particular religious affiliation and aligned him more nearly with the main intellectual currents of the age. Not just Christians of whatever stripe, but secular humanists, scientists, and unbelievers had to come to terms with Newman as a representative man—representative, that is, of one current of thought that was not of merely confessional or sectarian interest—who spoke to the larger community of earnest seekers. The central question of the *Essay in Aid of a Grammar of Assent*—how does one arrive at belief?—was a living, vivid, and personal reality for many Victorians of whatever religious or irreligious stripe.

Newman may have found a safe port, but even ports can be buffeted by high winds, and he realized that to discover certainty in a particular haven did not insulate him from bad weather. A defining event of the decade for him was the Vatican Council of 1870, which declared the doctrine of papal infallibility. Newman awaited the declaration, which he sensed was almost inevitable, with apprehension, but struggled to come to terms with it once it had been promulgated. It was the culminating chapter in his dislike of the Ultramontane party and his long-standing, if simmering, distrust of Henry Manning, but it must have also brought to his mind his struggles with another hierarchy. That earlier period of insubordination and final departure was a consequence of Newman's attempt to arouse an apparently somnolent Church of England to truths it had lost sight of; his Catholic period was marked by an often reluctant obedience and sometimes covert resistance as he attempted to fence off a space for freedom of inquiry for believers as well as theologians. The experience made Newman a more charitable person than he had been as an Anglican reformer, partly because of the natural mellowing process of time, but partly also because he was no longer in a position to wield much influence.

Newman was now less reliant on individuals. In a much-quoted letter to Sir Frederic Rogers written early in 1868, Newman lamented, "I have found in the Catholic Church abundance of courtesy, but very little sympathy, among persons in high places, except a few—but there is a depth and a power in the Catholic religion, a fulness of satisfaction in its creed, its theology, its rites, its sacraments, its discipline, a freedom yet a support also, before which the neglect or the misapprehension about oneself, on the part of individual living persons, however exalted, is as so much dust, when weighed in the balance" (*L&D* 24:25). Thus Newman reiterated the final "position of my mind" that he had set forth at the end of the *Apologia*. Personal slights, he reminded himself, were as nothing in light of the totality of the Catholic faith. Perhaps the most accurate way of describing his "submission" is to say that it took the form, not of overt submission to the authorities, but submission of his always strong self-will to the idea of a greater Church than that represented by its present leaders. The Church was vindicated by its entire history, not condemned by the passing errors of individuals who purported to speak for it. In *The Dream of Gerontius*, he had dramatized a movement from an earthly to a heavenly community to which the Church was a gateway. This spiritual ideology kept Newman afloat during the years of his unhappiness with the Roman hierarchy.

Not surprisingly, then, Newman's personalism—his fascination with how individuals, including himself, were molded, his continuing references to human personality as rooted in divine Personality, and his employment of human analogies to express the relationship of persons to Persons—remained constant in his writing. But his review of J. R. Seeley's *Ecce Homo*, a Straussian essay on the humanity of Jesus, displays a Newman capable of sympathizing with a book from which he would have recoiled as an Anglican zealot.

Irenic Gestures

Seeley's title is taken from Pilate's words in John 19:5 and reflects his intention of offering a "survey" of Jesus's "life and work" before he was known as the Christ "but was simply, as St. Luke describes him, a young man of promise, popular with those who knew him and appearing to enjoy the Divine favor." Following in the footsteps of Renan and Strauss, though he nowhere mentions them, Seeley promises to "trace his biography from point to point, and accept those conclusions about him, not which church doctors or even apostles have sealed with their authority, but which the facts themselves, critically weighed, appear to warrant" (Seeley 3). At the outset of his review of Seeley, republished in *Discussions and Arguments on Various Subjects* (1872) as "An Internal Argument for Christianity," Newman states that such a purpose was coeval with the origins of Christianity, and simply retraces the character of Jesus from the records of the Evangelists, dispensing with extrinsic proof and authentically witnessing to the faith and devotion of all those reading it. Newman does rebuke Seeley for selective misreading of some biblical texts, a tendency to read the Gospels as if they were novels, instances of spurious logic, and a naiveté reflected in moments of wayward imagination. But nearly half of Newman's review is given over to an essentially favorable and supportive view of Seeley's enterprise.

Seeley, like Newman, places personality at the heart of his inquiry. Newman agrees that "without an intimate apprehension of the personal character of our Saviour, what professes to be faith is little more than an act of ratiocination. If faith is to live, it must love; it must lovingly live in the Author of faith as a true and living Being" (*D&A* 367). Newman probably subscribed to Seeley's own statement of the question: "It was neither for his miracles nor for the beauty of his doctrines that Christ was worshipped.

Oppositions and Resolutions

Nor was it for his winning personal character, nor for the persecutions he endured, nor for his martyrdom. It was for the inimitable unity which all these things made when taken together" (Seeley 56–57). The method of Jesus, for Seeley, is personal authority, exercised less through "preaching and catechizing" than through personal influence acting either by example or by impassioned exhortation. "When Christ would kindle it in his disciples he *breathed* on them and said, 'Receive the Holy Spirit,' intimating by this great symbolical act that life passes into the soul of a man, as it were by contagion from another living soul" (232).

Unthreatened by Seeley's emphasis on the humanity of Jesus, Newman is more critical of Seeley's view of the Church. He challenges Seeley on essentially empirical grounds: if there are those who believe merely because of their fear of damnation, they would be barred from "Catholic communion." Protestants may well embrace faith at the ground of probability rather than settled convictions on all points at dispute, and that position is better than nothing; but unless they can go further, they cannot become Catholics. No good Catholic would give countenance, says Newman, to a man's forcing of his own conscience.

Newman's larger point is that while Seeley's book may bring consolation to doubting Protestants, it is entirely gratuitous from a Catholic point of view. In dispensing with theology, Seeley has ignored the Catholic awareness of a reality that transcends theology, and in the process has implied that the Church has not known how to preach Him to believers. Seeley, according to Newman, fails to follow through on his own principles. He affirms the need for a "visible organized Church" as a "main part" of Christ's plan; he acknowledges the primacy of Jesus's personal authority; yet what is all this, Newman asks, but a shortcut in its own right, "believe and be saved"? Seeley cannot both accept Revelation and pick and choose parts of it.

But Newman remained a generous opponent. When the Evangelical Lord Shaftesbury held Seeley's work up to excoriation as "the most pestilential book ever vomited from the jaws of hell," Newman wrote to Sir Frederic Rogers in puzzled good humor, "What on earth, or rather below the earth, can Lord Shaftesbury really intend by his Exeter Hall judgment upon the book?" If Seeley's book might be of use in awakening consciences toward Catholic truths, "I should feel great interest in him—As it is, I do not go further than to welcome him heartily, though he 'followeth not us,' and to look with great hope on the effect of his work on the religious world" (May 15, 1866; *L&D* 22:233). By 1866 Newman was more open to the possibility that aids to belief might come from very divergent, even unexpected quarters.

Newman's calm acceptance of Seeley's views contrasts with his sense of alienation from fellow Catholics as well as the Anglo-Catholic party within the Church of England. At times during this period, Newman writes as though he has been homeless in two communions. The papal party suspected the depth of his commitment because he never manifested the zeal of his fellow converts Ward and Manning. Some Anglo-Catholics suspected he might have designs to make converts at Oxford. Both misapprehensions came together in a singular way.

At the beginning of August 1864, Newman had been approached by an elderly Catholic offering him a five-acre plot of ground in Oxford as the site of a Catholic college. Newman saw this as a possible location for an oratory, could he find the money. Armed, as he thought, with the support of Bishop Ullathorne, Newman was caught off-guard by the bishop's not unnatural assumption that Newman would want to live there himself. Nothing was further from Newman's mind. He feared that returning to Oxford as a Catholic would strain his relationship with Pusey and the Anglo-Catholic party that had gathered around him, and, besides, too many such projects had failed in the past. In the meantime it was clear that Ullathorne's consent had been premised on an Oxford Oratory being countenanced only for the sake of a mission. Here Newman ran up against the opposition of Manning and Ward to the attendance of Catholics at the two leading English universities. Newman had no objection to Catholics attending the universities, and when the hierarchy formally opposed it, in a declaration of December 1865, he counseled Sir John and Lady Simeon, heads of an Old Catholic family, who had sought his advice on allowing their son to attend Oxford, to follow their own consciences in reaching a decision.[1]

It was in this atmosphere of mutual suspicion that Pusey published his *Eirenicon*, an attempt to proffer terms of peace between England and Rome. Newman read it and felt that Pusey's attacks on Manning and his inadequate understanding of the role of the Virgin Mary would worsen rather than improve relationships. He thought the book intellectually slovenly, particularly in its attempt to summarize Marian doctrine, and decided to respond to Pusey in print. This was a difficult maneuver, because this time Newman was fully conscious of two different audiences, Catholic and Anglican, alike suspicious of himself. His most telling observation on Pusey appears in a private letter to T. W. Allies (February 1866): "From that radical peculiarity of mind which interferes with his being a Catholic, [Pusey] goes by books, not by persons." He had no colleagues to counteract his impulses. "He goes into print with the same heedless readiness and decisiveness with which he would say words in conversation" (L&D 22:158). In affirming his personalism this way, Newman showed how far he had moved from the Hampden controversy and Tract 90. It was Pusey, not he himself, who had remained hopelessly academic.

The resulting *Letter to Pusey on the Occasion of His Eirenicon of 1864* (to shorten its cumbersome title) was dated by Newman from the Birmingham Oratory on December 7, 1865. It provides an interesting if neglected complement to the *Apologia*. Here Newman, reiterating his offices of personal friendship, had to write an *Eirenicon* of his own. He does not linger over Pusey's doctrinal missteps, but rather focuses on the tangibility of concrete devotions that prove the intellectual seriousness and spiritual commitment of his Roman Catholic brethren.

Newman faults Pusey for being anything but irenic himself. Has not "my dear Friend" made too much of differences between Catholics and Anglicans? "It is the object of an Irenicon to smooth difficulties; I shall be pleased if I succeed in removing some of yours" (CD 2:77). After defending the evolving role of Mary in Church tradition, Newman reminds his former coworker, echoing a passage in his *Development of Christian Doctrine* twenty years before, "Life in this world is motion, and involves a continual process of change." We cannot bypass, though we may help shape, the process by which "living things grow into their perfection" and subsequently decline and die. Newman claims that he wants to be "first generous and then just; to grant full liberty of thought; and to call it to account when abused" (79). Thus Newman manages to address both his Anglican friends and that element in the Roman communion which would have imposed limits on liberty of thought in matters not definitively settled by ecclesiastical edict.

In responding to Pusey's criticism of superstitious Roman devotions, Newman once more upholds the good intentions of the humble believer whose worship may be vulgar but is also heartfelt. Throughout every page of his reply runs the most familiar of his themes, that Christianity is "eminently an objective religion," and he cites to this effect St. Athanasius's declaration "that Man is God and God is Man, that in Mary they meet, and that in this sense Mary is the centre of all things" (CD 2:86). By focusing on the tangible and objective, Newman replays his role as plainspoken Englishman, advising his friend to draw on sound rather than inconsistent sources. More in sorrow than in anger, he criticizes Pusey's lack of charity and appeals to what he believes is, at the core, Pusey's true view of the Virgin. He concludes with a prayer: "May the sacred influence of this tide [the Feast of the Immaculate Conception and Christmas] bring us all together in unity! May it destroy all bitterness on your side and ours!" (118). But those of Newman's fellow Roman Catholics who read his pamphlet could doubtless see that the prayer was addressed to them as well.

The Hierarchy

Dealing with Pusey was one thing; dealing with the Roman hierarchy quite another. In a letter of 1864, Newman had written to Emily Bowles despondently that "we are sinking into a sort of Novatianism, the heresy which the early Popes so strenuously resisted. Instead of aiming at being a world-wide power, we are shrinking into ourselves, narrowing the lines of communion, trembling at freedom of thought, and using the language of dismay and despair at the prospect before us, instead of, with the high spirit of the warrior, going out conquering and to conquer" (L&D 22:314–15). Whatever spirit as a warrior Newman had manifested in the past, he was ill equipped to take on the hierarchy directly, and he reacted awkwardly even to friendly gestures. When in 1868 he was invited to attend the Vatican Council and consult with one of the commissions preparing the agenda, Newman pleaded an array of excuses—health, the pressure of other duties, even his poor Italian—but reserved what was probably his real reason for a private memorandum (October 14, 1868): "I have never ever got on intimately with ecclesiastical superiors. It arises from my shyness, and a sort of nervous continual recollection that I am bound to obey them, which keeps me from being easy with them.... I never could make my presence felt" (L&D 24:162). He undoubtedly also recognized that in such a role he could not be candid about his dislike for the already-apparent direction of the Council. "God forbid," he wrote in his journals, " I should liken them [certain of the hierarchy] to the 'Scribes and the Pharisees'—but still I obey them, as Scribes & Pharisees were to be obeyed, as God's representatives, not from devotion to *them*" (*AW* 263).

Newman had every reason to congratulate himself for having stayed away from Rome. As the time drew near, it was increasingly evident that the Vatican Council was to provide a platform for declaring papal infallibility. A long and careful letter of November 1869 to Mrs. William Froude spelled out his objections. Newman's resistance was less to the doctrine itself, which he claimed always to have held in principle, than to the Ultramontanists' haste to articulate it. He felt that the Church was oblivious to its own history and traditions, and inattentive to the potential impact of the promulgation on the laity and prospective converts. The doctrine of infallibility was not aimed at any heresy that needed to be put down. Furthermore, as he saw it, such a promulgation would open a long controversy that would alter the Church's rudimentary polity, substituting the Pope *solo* for the Pope in council. The retroactivity of the doctrine would open the actions of previous Popes to question. Even though "the doctrine must be inwardly received as true, its definition may still be most unseasonable and unwise." The Ultramontanes, being unwilling to accept freedom of inquiry, would play into the hands of skeptics (*L&D* 24:378). In his Anglican career, Newman had put his emphasis on individual initiative over bodies of safe, sound, sensible men. He now found himself defending the conciliar principle as a safeguard against the unchecked will of an individual.

Newman's reaction is of a piece with his preference for the "living mind" over abstract definitions, especially when the doctrine was part of a political gambit by a party within the Church. It was not a question of the character of a Pope *in propria persona,* but a question of the living mind of the Church itself. The speed with which the doctrine was proceeding toward enactment violated the right of clergy and laity to be consulted. In the *Rambler* article he had written, "I think certainly that the *Ecclesia docens* is more happy when she has such enthusiastic partisans about her ... than when she cuts off the faithful from the study of her divine doctrines and the sympathies of her divine contemplations, and requires from them a *fides implicita* in her word, which in the educated classes will terminate in indifference, and in the poorer in superstition" (*OCF* 230).² The Church, he told Robert Whitty, a Jesuit priest, in April 1870, was not a "mere philosophy" but "a communion ... bound to consult for charity, as well as for faith. You must prepare men's minds for the doctrine, and you must not flout and insult the existing tradition of countries" (*L&D* 25:93). It was a bitter irony that Newman must now labor, as he had labored within the Church of England, to persuade the Roman Church that the acts of Councils and the intentions of the Church Fathers as well as the deeds of earlier Popes must be weighed in order to achieve doctrinal clarity. Corporate personality was needed as a counterweight to what might be no more than personal whim.

Newman saw clearly that certain political consequences flowed from the fact that "a grave dogmatic question seemed to be treated merely as a move in ecclesiastical politics." In England the danger was great, because it would undo the work of Gladstone's pro-Catholic ministry and his desire to help the Irish Catholic University; it would lend credibility to the ludicrous efforts of the select committee convened under the chairmanship of the Conservative MP Charles Newdegate to inquire into the property of conventual establishments (Arnstein), and it would feed anti-Catholic agitation. His reasoning evinces more than a hint of the residual Anglicanism that made Manning and the Italians uneasy. Newman's resistance to an imposed Roman uniformity had its roots not only in his respect for persons but in his adherence, dating back to his Anglican years, to the principle of decentralized decision making. His guarded hope for the forthcoming Council, he told J. R. Bloxam in February 1870, was that each part of the Church would know the minds of co-religionists in other parts of the world, and learn sympathy and mutual reliance; Rome herself would have a more accurate view of the lay of the land (*L&D* 25:37).

Such was not to be the case, and the correspondence of the ensuing months shows Newman scrambling to make his (outward) peace with the doctrine of infallibility while retaining his private dismay at the way in which it had been promulgated. He was an accurate reader of the English domestic scene, and the consequences of the declaration led ultimately to his open *Letter to the Duke of Norfolk on Occasion of Mr. Gladstone's Recent Expostulations* (December 27, 1874) in which, through the agency of a third party, he addressed his concerns to the prime minister himself. The letter responded to the charge that under the new order in Rome, Catholics could not be counted upon to be loyal British subjects. Here Newman's rhetorical task was even more complicated than in his response to Pusey, and much more hung on the result. He had to address Gladstone and the Protestants, Manning and the Ultras, and Döllinger and the liberal Catholic adherents on the Continent who still looked to Newman as a potential ally. He was likely to be found unpersuasive by the first group, unresponsive by the second, and unsupportive by the third.

Newman's vexed relationship with Henry Manning was not the least of the products of his Catholic years. Over the last century, Manning, on the whole (and with the exceptions of such balanced scholars as David Newsome and James Pereiro) has had a bad press. He was doubtless much that he has been accused of being—ambitious, devious, and politically motivated—and he has earned a reputation for equivocation, particularly in interpreting Newman's actions to the hierarchy. Certainly temperament had much to do with their differences. Manning was a well-informed man and no mean theologian. But he was a man of the world, not a cloistered university don, and his practical experience as an archdeacon in the Church of England had shown his capacity to manage men. He was an accomplished bureaucrat who moved naturally in the complexities of Vatican politics; Newman was not. Both men craved power, but Manning through authority, Newman through influence. Yet Manning was no stranger to the joys and sorrows of the human condition. The loss of his wife in the years before his own reception into the Roman Catholic Church was a source of continuing sorrow throughout his life, though he did not make a public display of his bereavements, and his intervention in the London Dock Strike (1889) demonstrated a political pragmatism quite beyond Newman's ken.

To Newman's principle of personality, Manning posed the antagonist principle of bureaucracy as a way of containing gifted but excitable individuals who might disrupt ecclesiastical due process. Manning had small sympathy for theories of development, and even less interest in the role of the laity, whom he famously dismissed as fit for hunting and fishing but not for theological disputation. He was decisive where Newman was hesitant, but a virtue of his limitations as well as a consequence of his power was that he found it easier to eschew grudges. As John Page has noted, Newman's intellectual response to the papal claims was indirect, veering and tacking, in short (to take a term from Ian Ker) *unscholastic*, because his personality was "careful, tolerant, and given to second thoughts" (Page 421), while his historical method elevated inference over logic. His argument in counseling troubled Catholics was that confession did not demand adherence to a specific definition *de fide* as long as they had made an active avowal of faith in the Church's teaching. This would have struck Manning as worse than hairsplitting; it was a failure of loyalty and indeed of nerve.

More deeply, the two men held different beliefs on how one comes to religious faith. Newman's *Grammar of Assent*, discussed in the next section, was the product of a patient mind disentangling, over many years, the intricate processes by which individuals come to belief: how the reason cooperates, through the accumulation of probabilities, in the task of finding certitude. Manning's idea of certainty (not the same as Newman's "certitude") amounted to a rejection of the Butlerian theory of probability that Newman had embraced years before, and Manning's interpretation of the Catholic position was that right reason "leads us to the fact of a Divine Teacher; but thenceforward His voice, and not our balancing of probabilities, will be the formal motive of the faith." The Church's witness was not only "human and historical" but "supernatural and divine." Thus, "My faith terminates no longer in a cumulus of probabilities, gathered from the past, but upon the veracity of a Divine Power guiding me with His presence" (Manning 75–76). This standard, enunciated three years before the appearance of the *Grammar of Assent*, was surely behind Manning's belief that Newman had never really left off being an Anglican at heart. He had written to Cardinal Talbot on February 25, 1866, that Newman

> has become the centre of those who hold low views about the Holy See, are anti-Roman, cold and silent, to say no more, about the Temporal Power, national, English, critical of Catholic devotions, and always on the lower side.... It is the old Anglican, patristic, literary, Oxford tone transplanted into the Church ... deprecating exaggeration, foreign devotions, Ultramontanism, anti-national sympathies. In one word, it is worldly Catholicism, and it will have the worldly on its side, and will deceive many. (qtd. in Newsome, *Convert Cardinals* 257)[3]

"What is clear," Pereiro observes, "is that Manning thought Newman's views about the infallibility of the Pope were minimalist, and that they obscured the permanent action of the Holy Spirit in the Church" (234).

Additionally, the two men differed on the nature of the Church itself. Sheridan Gilley has suggested that Newman brought the concept of the Via Media into his new communion, steering a course between the priestly and prophetic functions of the Church, and refusing the "regal offices" that predominated in it. Rather, Newman saw these different functions as standing "in a judicious constitutional relationship to one another, respecting their separate provinces and maintaining an orderly balance and tension in which the one completes and supplies what the others lack." For Gilley, Newman's belief in the virtues of fruitful conflict is "a strange innovation on traditional Christian ecclesiology, in which conflict had usually been regarded as sin" (389).

In Manning's ecclesiology, the true Church was marked by the indwelling Holy Spirit. It was the true personification of the body of Christ, analogous to the hypostatic union of God and man in Jesus. Manning's devotion to principles over persons and his ecclesiology of the Holy Spirit help explain the assurance of his belief in papal infallibility and his refusal to be deterred by those persons in the Church whom he regarded as holding aberrant views. For him, Newman's appeal to antiquity was sheer rationalism because it amounted to a skeptical handling of the sources of faith. Antiquity for Manning was as unsafe a guide as bibliocentrism was for Newman. To be useful as a guide, Antiquity required the subsequent corroboration of the whole magisterium as the interpreter of the Church's faith, not the research of scholars into what the Primitive Church said. In fact, for Manning the issue was not really personal papal infallibility at all but rather the Pope's speaking with a supernatural grace or charism from that magisterium. And the rationale for the Ultramontane position "was particularly necessary for those countries where Catholics and non-Catholics lived side-by-side" (Pereiro, *Manning* 289).

What was anathema to Manning was Newman's concept of the Church as a "*conspiratio* of priests and laity" in which infallibility rested with the entire body of the faithful. For Newman, individual conscience was fulfilled in the communal conscience of the Church in its entirety (Coulson, *Common Tradition* 121–22). Newman shared Manning's view of the Church as the site of the Holy Spirit but saw the activity of the Spirit in a different light. In the words of Ian Ker, "Schematic, tidy blueprints find no place in Newman's ecclesiology because the Church is a living community made up of living people, with various gifts and talents and roles to play" (*Healing the Wound* 83). Collectively that community embodied a Divine Personality in which these human roles were subsumed. Newman's *Certain Difficulties* has been cited as evidence that for Newman "the sacramental character of the Church obliges it to function as a person and to manifest the unity of its divine personality." The connection between bishops and people must be restored if the Church is to speak for "the whole people of God" (Coulson, *Common Tradition* 71–72). In later years, "Newman expressed his idea of the Church and the conception of doctrinal development it involved less in terms of *ideas* and increasingly in terms of persons and communities, and of their functions" (81). Manning, placing trust in the corporate personality of the Church in a state of grace, was not obsessed by speculations about the motives of others. The practical consequence, reinforced by his position of power, was his refusal to take personally the strictures of those others.

Newman had expressed his doubts about Manning's trustworthiness not only to friends but, it must be said in his favor, directly to Manning himself.[4] Because of his position as well as his thick skin, it may have been easier for Manning to show generosity, but this does not mean that his efforts at conciliation should be dismissed as insincere. Along with Bishop Ullathorne, he intervened with the Vatican before an anti-Newman movement got up its steam over the *Letter to the Duke of Norfolk*. To be sure, it was no mere altruism but recognition of the perils to the Church itself that led Manning to write a strong remonstrance to Cardinal Franchi in 1875, in which he defended "the heart of Father Newman . . . as straight and Catholic as it ever was. His pamphlet has a most powerful influence over the non-Catholics of this country." Newman, he continues, "has never, up to the present, so openly defended the prerogatives and infallible authority of the Roman Pontiff, though he has always believed and preached this truth."[5] This was more than Manning needed to say, and may very well have involved the expenditure of some political capital of his own.

Oppositions and Resolutions

The Living Mind: *An Essay in Aid of a Grammar of Assent*

No work of Newman's was as long in the making as the *Grammar of Assent*. In 1876 Newman observed in a journal entry that the *Grammar* was very nearly the only exception to the rule that almost everything he had published was a response to a person or occasion. "As to the 'Assent,' I had felt it on my conscience for years, that it would not do to quit the world without doing it" (*AW* 273). The development of his ideas can be traced in his posthumously published *Theological Papers* from the early 1850s and in the *Philosophical Notebook*, comprising papers from the end of the decade, and supplemented by his correspondence with William Froude, an engineer and, like James Anthony, a younger brother of Hurrell.

The *Theological Papers . . . on Faith and Certainty* show very early Newman's interest in the limitations of reason and the way in which one's whole being breaks through those limitations to belief.[6] As early as April 1853, he was discriminating four levels by which we apprehend truth or fact, real or alleged: *opinion, doubt, certainty,* and *persuasion* (7). Truth, he wrote toward the end of that year, may be arrived at in three ways: through the accumulation of intellectual evidence, through the operations of "grace and spiritual earnestness," or through the passage of time, the "arbiter between truth and falsehood." If, finally, the contemplated truth turns out to be a delusion, time will make that clear. The workings of time, he observes, are "the common case with intellectual concerns" (30). It is the last two of these ingredients that move one past intellectual stalemate.

Another theme that can be detected early in the *Theological Papers* is the relationship between the individual mind and the larger community of which it is a part. Newman was aware that in matters of faith, the challenge was somehow to connect the personality of the individual believer to the community as a whole. In or about 1860 he distinguished intuition from what, in a neologism of his own, he called *contuition*. Intuition involves a simple and absolute assent to truth, an insight into "things as they are." Contuition, by contrast, is a complex assent in which a second truth is embedded, as in inferences of God's mode of action stemming from the fact that God *is* God. Such statements as "That God is God, He must be omniscient" or "The Creator has power over His own works" are the consequences of contuition. If intuition is private (albeit one person's intuition may correspond to another's), contuition is shared and therefore "evidently objective" (*TP* 64–65). One may apprehend God through intuition, but agreement on what the properties of God are is a matter of shared belief. Religious conviction is individual, but it cannot be disjoined from a larger communal logic and shared "body of evidence," both moral and scientific (that is, pertaining to all formal knowledge, including theology and metaphysics among the sciences). The Creeds are affirmative, doctrinal, objective, and based on a logical demonstration of each of the clauses drawn from philosophy, theology, and history. They are part of the Church's public teaching, whereas "the faith and reason, of which I speak, are subjective, private, personal, and unscientific, the mental acts of every Christian whatever, except when they are merely hereditary and mechanical" (84).

The force of religious conviction, Newman hypothesizes in his 1860 entries, can be identified by four tests: Is it rooted in our natural constitution? Is it "obvious and not abstract," intelligible to all and capable of working on all? Is it "portable," that is, capable of standing apart from books or education, accessible to all much as the stores of rhetoric are available to the orator? And finally, is it durable, capable of protecting the mind from temptations to unbelief? (*TP* 87). The important point is that God has given us "short cuts to certainty," and "individuals need not be able to analyze, understand, and explain their own grounds" (89–90). By indirection, Newman here defends the purchase of all the faithful, not just hierarchs or professional theologians, on some aspect of the divine truth. Although ultimately his focus in the *Grammar* will come to rest on the consciousness (and thereby conscience) of the individual believer, shared knowledge is possible. For even self-consciousness is based not only on personal experience but the witness of other people's experience. In 1863 he wrote, "A friend makes a remark to me; I take it up at once, and say that it had never struck me before but that it is incontrovertible. It comes to me as proved already assimilated in my mind, and as if it belonged to me of rights. This is one of the causes of those sudden sympathies which one man has for another, for the intimacies formed at first sight, and of the powerful effect of sermons on individual hearers" (1:108).

Newman's correspondence with William Froude in 1860 also allowed him to rehearse some of his ideas with a mind very unlike his own. The exchange exhibits a certain poignancy. Newman's contacts with the family always brought back the memory of Hurrell; on his side, William, an engineer and naval architect who had been responsible for forwarding his brother's literary remains, found Roman Catholic claims unpersuasive even as his wife and children were in the process of converting to Catholicism.

Froude's position briefly was "that though any probability, however faint, may in its place make it a duty to *act as if* the conclusion to which it points were absolutely certain, yet that even the highest attainable probability does not justify the mind in discarding the residuum of doubt"—doubt that he surely wished were playing a larger role in developments within his own family. William Froude, as a scientist and secularist, stood aside from the religious tergiversations of his family (*L&D* 19:270). To Froude's claim that a greater weight should be given to the role of doubt, Newman responded by referring to Froude's own son, Hurrell the younger, who had sought his counsel: "Much lies in the meaning of the words certainty and doubt— much again our duties to a *person* as e.g. a friend—Religion is not merely a *science*, but a *devotion*; but though I have much MS upon the subject, I have written nothing which so satisfied me as to make me think of publication. I don't think it practically bears upon Hurrell's case.... I am relying on no profession or promises of perseverance which he has made to me. I think he would persevere, because I think he really at present *believes* that God speaks to him through the Church" (*L&D* 19:273). A few days later, Newman added, "I think there is a sophism in considering the certainty of secular science so far superior to the certainty or persuasion, as you would call it, of the personal evidence for Christianity." A more global remark in his posthumously published *Philosophical Notebook* reflects an expansion of his views on the limitations of scientific thinking that Froude represented. "Scientific men open their eyes with wonder at hearing angels spoken of, *because* they begin from the other end of being, & never get so far as that subject. They have not the idea of God. If they have, they w^d see how *natural* it is to think of classes of being between Him & man. They only know those things which give the idea of evolution, growth, & progress" (*PN* 2:161). In such a way of thinking, doubt is apt to triumph over probability because too often scientists did not think analogically; they saw gradation in nature but not in the world of the spirit.

Newman's *Philosophical Notebook* for this period (circa 1859–67) shows him still engaged with these issues. The *Notebook* is a quarry for both the

Apologia and the *Grammar*. For the *Apologia*, it considers the role of consciousness as it functions in the act of remembering, operating with conscience to test the authenticity of a change in religious opinions. It prepares the ground for the *Grammar* insofar as it develops the idea of conscience as enforced by the sense of Divine Presence and as corroborated in relationships with other human beings. Without rejecting the scientist's way of seeing, it attempts to chart a position for the mind in a realm in which factuality as scientists understand it is necessary but insufficient as a guide to moral reasoning.

In 1859 Newman was engaged in a study of Mill's *Logic*, which he admired for its close reasoning but criticized on other grounds. In a letter to Richard Holt Hutton in 1872, he deplored Mill's failure to distinguish between the operations of the living mind on the one hand and those of abstract reasoning on the other. "Mr. Mill aims at showing that there can be no real freedom of the will, but he does so on a mere logical analysis of the antecedents of its action" (*L&D* 26:41). The appeal for Newman is always to direct experience. In 1859 he wrote that consciousness, as an experience of ourselves, "does nothing more than bear testimony to facts—and must be true. At the same time its testimony is not always so immediate and prompt as to preclude all necessity of cross examination & revision." Here Newman reverted to his favorite mirror analogy: "I may be puzzled *what* my present feeling is—just as you may look into a smeared & dustcovered mirror, and not be able to make out your features, & be aware you cannot" (*PN* 2:79). But in 1867 he seems to rethink the matter: certitude is possible if we can appeal from the dusty mirror to an original portrait. "The picture of our Lord in the gospels," strange though it may be to those who have not taken it fully into their imaginations, is familiar to the Christian who "has a reflexion of it in his own mind to help him, and a Catholic is familiar with multiplied and recent copies of it in the Lives of the Saints" (171). The recuperative powers of a rereading of the past, as Newman had undertaken it in the *Apologia*, might lead to a greater trust in one's own perceptions.

Newman's personalism was implicit in the ruminations leading up to the *Grammar* for nearly two decades. Although the term "certitude" appears only from 1865 on, the distinctions between scientific reasoning and personal practice are there throughout, and personal practice is never disjoined from conscience. Morality (assent to a thing as right) or certitude (assent to a thing as true) are matters of "public property," not just an individual affair. Personal consciousness proceeds not through stages of logical proof but by "practice and personal tact and skill." This "habit of mind which acts *pro re nata*," he wrote in 1865, is a function, then, of the believer's ethos, his determining character (*TP* 120–21).

Newman was never anti-rational, but he came to have a profound sense of the inadequacy of the reason that the *Grammar* defends. In a letter to Louisa Simeon in 1869, he pointed out that any question has "an inherent, irradicable [sic] difficulty in it." Whether one declares he will not believe in anything that he doubts, that there is no truth in anything, that there is no God, that there is a God but that He has not revealed Himself except through nature—all these, albeit negative, are statements of faith. "The question is, whether on the whole our reason does not tell us that it is a duty to accept the arguments commonly urged for its truth as sufficient, and a duty in consequence to believe heartily in Scripture and the Church" (*L&D* 24:274–75). Here Newman is pressing reason itself into a service that the scientific mind not only does not require of it but would reject. The living mind, as a consequence of the total intelligence behind it, is more than just that portion of the intelligence that operates through logic. In 1872, after the publication of the *Grammar*, he told Hutton that one must believe in the trustworthiness of a conclusion if it is commended by the "living intelligence of the prudent man." However logical one's mind, one cannot express how much and what evidence in logical form suffices for the purpose; "he only sees that logically a certain modicum of evidence would be too little, and another modicum superfluously much, and that in this particular case it is his duty to himself to receive it as true on that particular evidence which he has" (*L&D* 26:40–41).

What the *Development* did for history, what the *Apologia* did for memory, the *Grammar* now does for conscience. It places the idea of Personality at the heart of a logical method suited to religious inquiry. To operate meaningfully on us, however, Personality, or human personalities, must be vividly and really present. That is why, when approached for advice through the mail by people he did not know, Newman declined to open himself up fully. "Glad as I should be to be of service to you in your present distress of mind," he wrote one unidentified correspondent in 1867, "I have no confidence in letters, as doing more than suggesting thoughts which the reader may follow up and gradually profit by." Just as a physician will not make a judgment on someone's physical condition solely on the basis of a previous case report, so a spiritual director does not undertake the task of guidance without knowing the correspondent personally (*L&D* 23:260). Each individual is motivated by some sort of guiding purpose likely to move him or her from one religious principle to another, but choices of religious affiliation depend on starting premises, a very individual matter. Newman thought that his best testimony was his own case. The *Apologia* had dramatized certain starting premises, but more deeply than this, certain habits of mind; a mental bias led Newman to add certain elements to his creed and reject others. Over time, the balance of opinions gave way to certitudes. His mind worked most hospitably with continuities, not radical disruptions or changes of direction. Unlike Carlyle, he mostly kept apocalypse at a distance.

As the *Apologia* had dramatically charted a movement from alienation to assimilation into a more expansive faith, so does the *Grammar* bridge that same gap, not through narrative but through logic, by asking how we reach certitude in matters of faith. It is Butlerian in tenor, for Bishop Butler's triad of presumption, opinion, and full conviction provided Newman with a scaffolding by which he could analyze how the human mind ascends to that state of conviction Newman calls certitude. Butler's belief that "the apprehension that religion may be true does as really lay men under obligation as a full conviction that it is true." For "doubting necessarily implies some degree of evidence for that of which we doubt" (*Analogy* 196, 198). Personality is not the ostensible subject of the *Grammar*, but it is thematically interwoven with Newman's focus on the workings of the individual conscience and his categorization of kinds of assent.[7] In a typical passage, Newman cites Locke in the course of arguing that that the standard of certitude in specific cases rises above the merely syllogistic, for "a proof, except in abstract demonstration, has always in it, more or less, an element of the personal" (*GA* 205). Certitude, as the "active recognition of propositions as true," is the property of individual minds, the "personal action of the ratiocinative faculty," whose highest form is the "Illative Sense" (223).

In Newman's logic, the Illative Sense plays a role somewhat analogous to that of the Primary Imagination in Coleridge's poetics. The Illative Sense engages in a complex process of reasoning in which "the personality ... of the parties reasoning is an important element in proving propositions in concrete matter[s]" (207). The Illative Sense, in perhaps the best-known passage describing it, is that "reasoning faculty, as exercised by gifted, or by educated or otherwise well-prepared minds," functioning as "a rule in itself and appeal[ing] to no judgment beyond its own." It "attends upon the whole course of thought from antecedents to consequents, with a minute diligence and unwearied presence, which is impossible to a cumbrous apparatus of verbal reasoning" (233).[8]

What Newman calls variously the "living mind" or "the living intellect" is the site of the operations of the Illative Sense, the faculty which, as a function of individual character, is the power of judging and concluding, leaping beyond formal logic. Thinking, perhaps, of the questions raised in his earlier correspondence with William Froude, Newman writes, "Science, working by itself, teaches truth in the abstract, and probability in the concrete, but what we aim at is truth in the concrete."[9] Not only is this true in the way an engineer or navigator applies mathematical science to make certain practical judgments, but also in the convergence of nonmathematical inferences which "come to no definite conclusions about matters of fact, except as they are made effectual for their purpose by the living intelligence which uses them" (181). Logic's "most elaborate exhibitions fail to represent adequately the sum-total of considerations by which an individual mind is determined in its judgment of things" (185). In describing the *Grammar* as an essay rather than a "treatise," Newman conveys the flexibility and tentativeness that the term "living mind" preserves. While the *Grammar* is sometimes described as Newman's only piece of systematic theology, one can reply that if so, it amounts to a systematic defense of the unsystematic.

The Grammar of Assent could be read as one of the most radical charters for individualism in the mid-Victorian era. Many contemporary reviewers charged that the Illative Sense was too personal to take the place of a common standard for establishing truth (Ferreira, *Doubt and Religious Commitment* 44–45). Newman even seems to undercut theology itself, for if no two men seem to be anything more than themselves as individuals, each with his own "identity," "incommunicability," and "personality" (GA 184), how are they to reach agreement on fundamental religious premises? This might open the door to untrammeled private judgment (for which the Illative Sense might be only a fancy name), inasmuch as Newman locates his "authoritative oracle" not in the "jejune generalizations" of "treatises" but "in the mind of the individual, who is thus his own law, his own teacher, and his own judge in those special cases of duty which are personal to him" (228). The Illative Sense "supplies no common measure between mind and mind, as being nothing else than a personal gift or acquisition" (233). If indeed the living action of the mind overrides syllogistic reasoning, where beyond that mind can one look for a standard?

Deferring for the moment our attention to the larger context in which such statements are embedded, one might reasonably respond that first of all, Newman never denies the proper exercise of private judgment in its appropriate sphere within the Catholic faith, nor does he ignore the possibility that the Illative Sense might be wrongly exercised. What he is defending is the inevitability of starting the process of inquiry with oneself: "I am what I am, or I am nothing. I cannot think, reflect, or judge about my being, without starting from the very point which I aim at concluding" (224). Unlike approaches that begin with theoretical hypotheses, Newman accepts the facts of the world as they are, and one's own self is the starting point for understanding those facts. "I am suspicious," he writes, "of scientific demonstration in a question of concrete fact, in a discussion between fallible men.... For me, it is more congenial to my own judgment to attempt to prove Christianity in the same informal way in which I can prove for certain that I have been born into this world, and that I shall die out of it" (264). Newman appeals empirically to shared human experience as the groundwork for religious faith; one discovers oneself but one also discovers others like oneself. It is human experience that rejects both the solipsism and the fatalism which might otherwise attend the sense of pervasive "incommunicability."

Newman's argument is based on the premise that a reality exists outside the self beyond our "individual identities," and that one belongs to, "a system with parts and a whole, a universe carried out by laws" (117). The fact that not all men and women are initially privy to objective truth is no denial of that truth's objective reality. What is required to rescue one from imprisonment in the self is a sense of community in "the interposition of a Power, greater than human teaching and human argument, to make our beliefs true and our minds one" (242). From the existence of one's own mind, one infers the existence of a great Mind to which ours is to be referred as well as other human minds capable of a similar action. Real as opposed to Notional

Assent involves the embrace of that reality. Newman here articulates the foundation of his developed ecclesiology: a common standard does in fact emerge, over time, through the convergence of individual minds, just as the convergence of probabilities leads to personal belief. In ecclesial terms, this convergence of beliefs is the *consensus fidelium,* the answer to the solipsism of a Pater or to the uncertainty of some of Newman's Anglican sermons like "The Individuality of the Soul." The idea of duty is implanted in us universally; it implies a duty to God.[10] As he wrote to Louisa Simeon in 1869, "I will not assume it is a personal God, or that it is more than a law (though of course I hold that it is the Living Seeing God) but still the idea of duty, and the terrible anguish of conscience, and the irrepressible distress and confusion of face which the transgression of what we believe to be our duty, cause us, all this is ... a clear evidence, that there is something nearer to religion than intellect" (*L&D* 24:275). The operations of conscience involve assent to a living Being, not an inanimate rule. So in prayer, those who "begin all their works with the thought of God, acting for His sake, and to fulfill His will" will be "brought into His presence as that of a Living Person, and are able to hold convene with Him, and that with a directness and simplicity, with a confidence and intimacy, *mutatis mutandis,* which we use towards an earthly superior" (*GA* 81). In prayer, we are like the child "who assents to his mother's veracity" because of his experience of her love for him (18). The image of One all-knowing and good can be grasped in a unified act of Real Assent even by a child, at least "one who is safe from influences destructive of his religious instincts" (78).

Dogma, if really and truly held as itself a living truth, comes from our common awareness of such a relationship. Assent to that truth requires imagination and affection, not merely a religion of rule which is notional and sentimental. A proposition commonly held, if it is also activated by the affections, becomes the basis for a truth held both theologically and religiously, theologically because it involves notional apprehension, religiously because it involves the imaginative faculties that lead to the devotional life. But while theology can exist without religion, true religion must include theology so that "devotion falls back upon dogma" (83). Once the Personal Image is held in the imagination, the operations of logic also "fall back" to their appropriate supporting place.

Oppositions and Resolutions

What distinguishes us from the rest of the animal kingdom, according to Newman, is that inasmuch as we all have a sense of conscience, however developed, we also have the power to create our "own sufficiency, to be emphatically Self-made" (225). But this is not Emersonian self-reliance, because our self-making is limited by the nature of our individual gifts as well as by Original Sin, to which the distance between ourselves and our Creator attests. If one's intellect does not develop a rule sufficient for one's needs, then one must have "some other living, present authority, to supply it for him," an "immediate guide in matters of a personal, social, or political character" (229). The starting point of religious inquiry is the self, but the self is not our final resting place, nor can it purport to speak for the experience of others. The limits of what we can do are shaped, but not finally determined, by our own experiences, which are indeed not only primary but authoritative, if not final. To the work of our own minds is superadded the voice of humankind and the course of the world as we observe it. Our conscience is dispositive, but our religion is social; we work and sacrifice for each other, gaining by our sufferings and those of others, "for man never stands alone here, though he will stand by himself one day hereafter; but here he is a social being, and goes forward to his long home as one of a large company" (261).

Hence, too, the role of other individual human exemplars. Real assents "form the mind out of which they grow, and impart to it a seriousness and manliness which inspires in other minds a confidence in its views, and is one secret of persuasiveness and influence in the public stage of the world." Real assent underpins Newman's educational theory and his idea of *ethos*. In one of his most Carlylean moments, he declares that such assents are the property of those who become great visionaries or reformers or saints, "men of one idea, of immense energy, of adamantine will, of revolutionary power. They kindle sympathies between man and man, and knit together the innumerable units which constitute a race and a nation" (63). Affections are kindled into action. "Thus the life and writings of Cicero or Dr. Johnson, of St. Jerome or St. Chrysostom, leave upon us certain impressions of the intellectual and moral character of each of them, *sui generis*, and unmistakable." We know a good person as more than "a mere impression on our senses, but a real being, we know by instinct; that he is such and such, we know by the matter or quality of that impression" (72). The inner life of such persons is manifest in deeds. But decency and sobriety do not stir the emotions, whereas the good and holy have the capacity to inspire devotion.

In all the prominent events of the world—wars, the rise and fall of nations, natural catastrophes, the advances of the intellect—"the spontaneous piety of the human mind discerns a Divine Supervision" (GA 259). Unity in faith combines with the individual conscience to provide a common sense of direction to many separate beings who confirm each other in belief. Newman is back on the ground of Augustine's *securus judicat orbis terrarum*. The collective sense of purpose balances the potential excesses of private judgment. Some consciences, like probabilities in Newman's logic, converge in a spontaneous unity of purpose from below, rather than being imposed upon from on high. Newman is at odds with both Manning's ecclesiology as well as the less democratic implications of Carlyle's politics.

Newman's distrust of "paper logic" should not be confused with the Carlylean sense of the potentially chaotic rule of the irrational, and Newman's admiration of good men whom we can trust differs sharply from Carlyle's idea of great men whom we must obey. The right working of the Illative Sense represents the healthy action of our reasoning powers, in which a common sense of duty and intellectual conscientiousness converge. To fall short of the pure demonstrations of conscience does not mean that the reason has been thrown overboard, but only that it knows its limits. In mathematics we may withhold—in fact, we are obligated to withhold—assent from a conclusion not justified by logical demonstration. Conscience, by contrast, holds us to the search for truth and certainty "by modes of proof, which, when reduced to the shape of formal propositions, fail to satisfy the severe requisitions of science" (GA 265). But a meeting of minds does require common principles of "a personal character"; hence conversion is neither the work of logic nor the product of brute force (266). In the case of Christianity, the evidences required for shared premises "presuppose a belief and perception of the Divine Presence, a recognition of His attributes and an admiration of His Person viewed under them; a conviction of the worth of the soul and of the reality and momentousness of the unseen world" (268). To the extent that we imitate the divine attributes, "we are dear to Him"; to the extent that we fail, we see more clearly "our guilt and misery" and experience "an eager hope of reconciliation to Him" (269). Furthermore, the moral sense, the testimony of religious rites, and the character and conduct of religious persons are our teachers, not logical demonstration.

The *Grammar of Assent* is the culmination of decades of effort to articulate the processes of Newman's own mind and experience as well as to distinguish the standard of proof required for religious belief from that required by the sciences—that is to say, any kind of secular knowledge. But it also grows out of his pastoral experience in counseling religious seekers. His audience, Newman makes clear, is not those who need to be convinced, but the committed who need to understand their ground for trusting their own beliefs. It is the task of the spiritual director to put others in touch with themselves as individuals who both inquire and reason. Christianity addresses us through both the mind and the imagination, leading to a personal certitude. "Nor need reason come first and faith second (though this is the logical order), but one and the same teaching is in different aspects both object and proof, and elicits one complex act both of inference and of assent." Each of us receives that teaching personally "as the counterpart... of ourselves, and is as real as we are real" (316). We will indeed stand individually before the judgment seat, but we are all part of one visionary company diversely and at different times journeying to that end point. As Stephen Prickett has pointed out, alluding to Keble's idiosyncratic modification of Wordsworth, "Real assent... is *both* so deeply personal as to be almost incommunicable *and* simultaneously the product not just of an individual but of a linguistic and symbolic community. To the theologian the paradox may seem an odd one, but to the poet it is immediately familiar. We recall Keble's idea of the poet as a man speaking to men, but *necessarily* under tension, and by disguise, hiding his own feelings even as he arouses them in others" (*Words and the Word* 219).

In a multitude of ways, the *Grammar* brings together the full development of Newman's ideas on the centrality of personal agency, with its source in God, as mediated by the saints and martyrs, and as reflected in the daily lives of ordinary Christians who seek God both privately and in community. To reiterate an earlier point, Newman's ecclesiology broadly comports with Manning's view of the Church as a site of the indwelling Spirit, but Newman is less committed to the belief that this Spirit guarantees infallibility, since it is possible to be given spiritual gifts that one does not use rightly. The Church remains a human institution, sufficiently moved indeed by the

Holy Spirit as the source of truth, but expressing the Spirit's movement as an intermediary between human beings and God that allows individual seekers to find their own way while aiding them in their quest. The work is also yet another personal testament in itself to the centrality of personality in Newman's thought. Having previously charted the development of belief historically in the *Development of Christian Doctrine* and personally in the *Apologia*, Newman now completes his unintended trilogy with an analysis of how belief is processed in the mind of the believer and made cooperant with that of other believers (Loesberg, chap. 6). At bottom, then, the *Grammar of Assent* is as surely motivated by the dynamics of self-scrutiny as are its two predecessors.[11]

Afterword

By the time of his death, Newman's secession from the Church of England was no longer a serious obstacle to his appreciation by scores of Churchmen and other Protestants as well as his standing as one of the most eminent of Victorians, a respected exponent of his own faith, an intellectual whose spiritual pilgrimage had become a matter of public record and was admired even among those whose reconstruction of faith had taken quite a different path from his. The two most significant events of his later years came from quite different quarters: the award of the first honorary fellowship ever offered by his undergraduate college, Trinity, in 1877, and the award of the cardinalate by Pope Leo XIII in 1879; the two events, taken together, attest to his ecumenical standing.

Such honors may also have served to stress Newman's "past-ness." Valedictories are two-edged—honorific but also a way of politely relegating someone to irrelevance. Newman's place in the canon of English literature is secure but does not occupy a great deal of space. The years following the publication of the *Letter to the Duke of Norfolk* are hardly more than a coda to his literary career. The letters that made up "The Tamworth Reading Room," the fifth and sixth of the Dublin University lectures, and a few high moments from the *Apologia* just about mark the horizons of the nonspecialist, including even Victorian scholars whose primary interests have lain elsewhere.

The effects of the Movement, as the work of Geoffrey Rowell and John Shelton Reed shows, were lasting. Nevertheless, Newman's disproportionate place in the historiography of the English Church is in large part a triumph of his own rhetoric, whether as a compelling preacher or as a nimble antagonist. His powers of self-dramatization in the *Apologia* have raised the suspicion that he was commodifying his career, but it is in the hands of others that it has proved to be a marketing tool. Newman's narrative of himself has become the master text of the Oxford Movement, and that Movement in turn has become the dominant narrative in the history of the Victorian Church. But the secessions that followed cannot all be laid at his door, and they seem less numerous to us than they did to a panicked generation of Victorian clerics. If one looks at Church history from the bottom up, it becomes clear that the high drama of the Movement was less than urgent to many a working clergyman. One such case was that of Francis Massingberd, a graduate of Magdalen and a vicar in Lincolnshire. Somewhat unsettled by Newman's secession, Massingberd had arrived at his own views by the time he learned of Manning's secession five and a half years later. He noted in his diary that "the deep affliction of others did not seem to touch me." This might be the product, he felt, of "a more hopeful spirit or indifference, or a mind too much set on the world," but he seems to have attributed it primarily to his "blessing of a more abiding love of the Church of England" (Knight 149).

Two and a half generations later, other Anglicans were quietly repositioning Newman in their own scale of importance. Evelyn Underhill (a spiritual directee of Baron von Hügel, and therefore a spiritual granddaughter of the Cardinal himself) wrote with crisp confidence to one correspondent, "If all the Tractarians had imitated Newman's spiritual selfishness, English religion to-day (unless God had raised up other reformers) would be as dead as mutton!" (*Letters* 210). Presumably Underhill was speaking of Newman's decision to leave the English Church, but her discovery of Pusey a decade earlier in 1924 had given her an alternative allegiance. She was probably thinking of Newman when she wrote to her friend Lucy Menzies that "contemplation which is exclusively of the *à deux* type certainly does run a grave risk of falling into spiritual selfishness. But a true contemplative vocation (whether lived in or out of the world) is surely not this at all. It involves (in the end—gradually—never with violence) the development of a spiritual force by which you exercise not only adoration, but also mediatorship—a sort of redemptive and clarifying power working on other souls—a tiny co-operation in the work of Christ" (323). Did Newman succeed in exercising the spirit of devotion and mediatorship, or was he so self-obsessed and driven by party spirit that he could not offer "a redemptive and clarifying power... on other souls"? Though such a power in Newman has been attested by a number of contemporaries, a negative critique has persisted, and it involves both philosophical and personal themes in the study of Newman.

Of these interrelated concerns, one strand is Newman's skeptical temper, an object of criticism in James Martineau's mid-century summing-up and now more likely to be congenial to those for whom the details of Newman's specific religious projects are not only history but a peculiarly dead history. The other is the question of Newman's fascination with himself, variously interpreted as egocentricity or, in Henri Bremond's somewhat less loaded term, "autocentrism." Perhaps there is an element here of spiritual selfishness, but the question also opens up the way for a reconsideration of Newman's orthodoxy.

Newman himself was well aware of his capacity to skirt the edge of unbelief. He wrote to Frank Scott Haydon in 1858, "If it is not impertinent then to refer to myself personally, I will say, that this sense of God's presence is the only protection which I have had (though an abundantly sufficient one) to keep me from unlimited scepticism" (*L&D* 31: Suppl. 66*). His last public controversy grew out of just this issue. In the *Contemporary Review* for May 1885, A. M. Fairbairn, a Scottish Congregational theologian, published an article, "Catholicism and Religious Thought," in which Newman was given special attention.[1] The gravamen of Fairbairn's critique was that Newman's line of argument led to skepticism because, in erecting so many protections against the functioning of reason, Newman had thrown would-be believers back on a highly personal and subjective form of argument that gave them no rational basis for arriving at the same conclusions he did. Surveying the new "Catholic apologetic" represented by Joseph de Maistre and his followers on the Continent, Fairbairn argued that to base religion on infallible authority "is the most fatal of all skepticisms. The arguments that prove it" suggest "an ineradicable atheism of nature" (CR 47:659).

Fairbairn was not the first to grasp the extent to which Newman's mind worked autobiographically, beginning with his supreme consciousness of two beings, God and himself. It was the very force of his individualism that made him a Catholic, Fairbairn rather paradoxically argued, for only in an organization like the Church could Newman find a safe haven from atheism. "The position, a Catholic because a theist, really means, when translated out of its purely individualistic form, a Catholic in order that he may continue a theist" (CR 663). Furthermore, in his claim that there was no middle ground between atheism and Catholicity, Newman (Fairbairn believed) had divided human nature into reason and conscience in a way that made proofs impossible. If conscience became the sole authority and reason was seen as skeptical and infidel when divorced from conscience, then indeed there was no possibility of a middle ground. The result was a theism that could not satisfy "the whole nature of man" and led inevitably to an individualism in which "the deliverance of his conscience" worked for himself but for no one else; "it has interest as a fact of practical testimony, but has no value as a ground of belief" (669). Newman's idea of reason was "so inimical to Theism that if he had not become a Catholic, he must have become an atheist" (669–70).

In short, according to Fairbairn, Newman's argument about there being no middle ground was perfectly true as it regarded himself only. The fact that history attests to former Catholics becoming atheists showed that "in a curious sense, submission to Catholicism is the victory of unbelief; the man who accepts authority lest it lead him into Atheism, is vanquished by the Atheism he fears. He unconsciously subscribes to the impious principle, that the God he believes has given him so godless a reason that were he to follow it, it would lead him to a faith without God." Fairbairn drives his point home in the last sentence of his first article: "He who places the rational nature of man on the side of Atheism, that he may better defend a church, saves the church at the expense of religion and God" (672). If Newman had conceived of reason and conscience as organically interrelated, his work would not be subject to the same objections, but if reason, to the contrary, plays no part in the proofs for God, then our very idea of God is itself impoverished—an opinion that, at the very opposite end of the denominational spectrum, Henry Manning would have approved.

Fairbairn had drawn a connection between skepticism and untrammeled individualism, but at bottom his critique has at various times been widely aired by Protestants: that one flees to Roman Catholicism out of weakness. In his reply to Fairbairn, Newman denied that he was "a hidden sceptic." He pointed to the numerous occasions on which he had *praised* the powers of reason. He invoked his entire life as a contradiction of Fairbairn's argument, asserting his "thankful recognition that for a long seventy years, amid mental trials sharp and heavy, I can, in my place and in my measure, adopt the words of St. Polycarp before his martyrdom: 'For fourscore years and six I have served my Lord and He never did me harm, but much good, and can I leave Him now?" (CR 48:487). Reason had an appropriate use within its own province, but where faith was absent, reason could indeed be put to "corrosive" uses and lead a man from Catholicity to atheism, the very progression whose inevitability Fairbairn had denied. Despite the versatility of reason, its great drawback was that the success of its exercise depended on "the assumption of prior acts similar to that which it has itself involved, and therefore is reliable only conditionally." Reason proceeds from an antecedent to a consequent, and the issue of that process is involved in its origins. In the province of religion it is under the happy guidance of the moral sense, but "in the hands of enemies" it will start from false premises with disastrous results. He had denied the omnipotence of Reason in the discovery of religious truth; if that made him a skeptic, Newman declared, he was in good company. Reason was "a mere instrument, an inferential instrument" from which nothing great could come. It was dependent for its full realization on other faculties. To all this, Fairbairn replied that Newman had succeeded in expressing precisely the views that he had attributed to him.

It is difficult to avoid the conclusion that the two men were talking past each other. Newman, no close student of scholastic theology, had denied the power of the very reason that St. Thomas had painstakingly built into the edifice of faith. Obsessed with the dangers of the Enlightenment spirit of free inquiry, Newman, in Fairbairn's view, had retreated into a kind of obscurantism rather than welcoming the challenge posed by that spirit. Newman, for his part, felt that certitude involved much more than the exercise of reason; the *Grammar of Assent* had set forth a communitarian rather than a purely individual model of inquiry, though all such inquiries began, as it must, with the individual on his or her own agency.

Fairbairn's point was taken up by another critic, the Anglican dean W. R. Inge, after Newman's death. When Inge reviewed Wilfrid Ward's biography of Newman (1912), he prepared his case on ethical grounds: "Newman's influence was disturbing and subtly disintegrating in every cause in which he laboured. His startling candour often seemed like treachery. He could not work with others, and broke with nearly all his friends, retaining only his disciples." Rome may have judged rightly in not making fuller use of his very real talents (Inge 187). Newman's suspicion of the adequacy of logical proof led Inge to conclude that "we can imagine nothing more calculated to drive a young and ingenious mind into flippant skepticism than a course of Newman's sermons. The *reductio ad absurdum* of his arguments is not left to the reader to make; it is innocently provided by the preacher" (188). Newman's "extreme disparagement of the intellect seems to preclude what he calls 'real assent' to the creeds and dogmas of Catholicism; for these clearly consist of 'notional' propositions" (189–90). Newman, Inge conceded, might have replied that the Church was a concrete fact to which real assent could be given, but "since reason is put out of court as a witness to truth, on what faculty, or on what evidence, does Newman rely?" In sum, Inge argued, Newman had relied on the "verdicts of the personality," which he not infrequently identified with conscience rather than objective fact.

Inge pointed out that early in the nineteenth century, the liberal Anglican and Coleridgean Julius Hare had expounded a "personalism" that allowed for factors other than the purely personal in arriving at judgments, a personalism not inconsistent with a "robust faith." But when personalism is put to the service of a Lockean sensationalism in which first principles are extracted from facts rather than a priori truths, "it naturally suggests that every man may and should live by the creed which bests [sic] suits his idiosyncrasies" (180–90). Inge's judgment was that Newman was "only half a Catholic" because he believed the authority of the Church and all it taught but denied the role that scholastic philosophy assigned to reason. As an organizing principle of personality, reason could bring us "into real contact with the higher world of Spirit" (192). Newman had in fact ignored Locke's caution that a man knows whether he is a lover of truth by whether he clings to any assurance greater than what the proofs warrant. True personalism "protects against any philosophy which makes life irrational or base, or incurably evil." It requires the activities of the intellectual, aesthetic, and moral faculties. "But it is absurd to suppose that our personality, acting as an individual whole, can decide whether the institutional Church, or one branch of it, is the Body of Christ and the receptacle of infallible revelation" (199).

Inge concluded that in a world riven with religious divisions, you cannot echo the Augustinian formula that the whole world judges aright when the Roman Church itself has lost credibility with large sections of European thought. Rome is where she is, not because of her truth of doctrine, but because of the political roles she assumed during the Middle Ages. Thus, the non-Catholic half of Newman "was based on principles which, when logically drawn out, must lead away from Catholicism in the direction of an individualistic religion of experience, and a substitution of history for dogma which makes all truth relative and all values fluid" (202). Stripped of these theological confusions, as Inge sees them, Newman's main importance for the new century lay in his skills as a rhetorician—an emphasis reflected in the subsequent work, at least through the 1960s and 1970s, of literary scholars for whom the *Apologia* was Newman's *chef d'oeuvre*.

In sum, for both Fairbairn and Inge, Newman exemplified the private judgment he claimed to abhor; in this judgment they had indeed been anticipated by more than one of Newman's Catholic contemporaries, and the target, explicitly or not, was the individualism of the *Grammar of Assent*. Modern scholarship has provided a more nuanced view. In *Skepticism and Reasonable Doubt*, M. Jamie Ferreira sees Newman as exercising a "constructive skepticism," constructive in that it gives us sufficient certainty for daily living, but skeptical because it denies that dogmatism is the only alternative to skepticism. Ferreira distinguishes Newman's attitude from the "skeptical fideism" that undermines the pretensions of reason to legitimate beliefs against or beyond reason. Newman, like Reid before him, refuses to "denigrate reason in the interests of religious faith" (224–25). To Ferreira's argument it might be added that Newman did have something in common with skeptical fideism as the British philosopher John Gray has defined it, a view "which sees asking unanswerable questions as essential if we are to learn the limitation of human understanding."[2] For Newman, Reason in matters of religious faith eventually comes up short against Mystery. But Mystery is not a mere escape hatch. Newman would have agreed with Gerard Manley Hopkins when the latter wrote to Robert Bridges, "You do not mean by a mystery what a Catholic does. You mean an interesting uncertainty: the uncertainty ceasing[,] interest ceases also.... But a Catholic by a mystery means an incomprehensible certainty.... The clearer the formulation, the greater the interest."[3]

My own argument throughout this study has been that there is a constant interplay between Newman's sense of human potentiality and that of the Divine Persons. His personalism is rooted ultimately in creedal orthodoxy, not merely the wayward imaginings of the self, even though in his personal behavior Newman did not always make the distinction between self and other clearly. He admitted this and appealed, tacitly or explicitly, to the fact that human beings are, on the one hand, very imperfect registers of the divine, but that, on the other, they can be brought together in a discursive community that provides a shared context for diverse understandings of divine truth and different roads toward it.

We have already dealt briefly with the charges of egocentrism that have attached themselves in particular to the two mirror passages in the *Apologia*. Jonathan Loesberg has argued that Newman "never moves away from being self-regarding," and that his need for an institutional church derived from the terms of his self-awareness as, along with God, one of only two "luminously self-evident beings" (153). It is, however, a long way from Loesberg's careful choice of the term "self-regarding" to the claim that in such passages Newman "reaffirms the primacy of the self, while God almost drops out of the picture" (Henderson 61).[4]

Louis Bouyer has affirmed the essential catholicity of Newman's emphasis on self and Creator by arguing that the phrase "does not mean any kind of pious egotism. It simply means that the root of the human problem, as it has to be solved solitarily by each one of us, is in setting up a relation with the God who has made us after His own image. All depends upon this; any real good we can do for our fellow beings and, just as much, any good they can do for us" (*Newman's Vision of Faith* 34). We should add that in Newman's thought, the human personality is the mirror, the divine Personality the Object mirrored in the consciousness of the believer. They are not interchangeable in the sense of being coequal, but they are part of a metaphorical exchange in which each is validated by the other.

For Newman, the analogy of human personality made an approach to one's Creator possible. Though Newman was careful always to note the limitations of such analogies, the reality of the person is grounded in the reality of God. In the vexed passages in the *Apologia*, it is useful to employ John Macquarrie's distinction between ontological and existential understandings of the Personality of God. The conduct of human beings can exile them from God's presence, just as God has the power to withdraw Himself. In such a case, the mirror into which one looks gives back no intimation of His presence. But the erasure equally constitutes self-erasure, since the believer's existential identity must be grounded on His ontological Being. It is no depreciation of the ultimate power of God to say that existentially, the relationship of divine to human image is a reciprocal self-disclosure. Newman lends that moment its weight and drama by comparing the disappearance of God to the vampire-like vacuity at the heart of human alienation from the Creator, which cannot register any presence in the mirror. God does not require our existence to certify His reality, Newman believed, but we know our reality only through His. To proclaim where knowledge begins, "to rest in the thought of two and two only absolute and luminously self-evident beings, myself and my Creator," is not to assert that all knowledge terminates there, nor does it confine Newman to a sort of paradoxically theocentric solipsism that can then be employed to prove that he lacked sympathy for the sufferings of others. Newman's only point is that one starts with what one knows best, and that if the Creator has ontological priority, neither self nor Creator has existential dimensions without the other.

The point is, again, perfectly orthodox. Catherine of Siena had written that God's nature reflects man's as man's reflects God's. The soul knows God's goodness "in herself, the sweet mirror of God." But the soul also "knows her own indignity.... Wherefore, as a man more readily sees spots on his face when he looks in a mirror, so the soul who with true knowledge of self, rises with desire and gazes with the eye of the intellect on herself in the sweet mirror of God."[5] Other people in their turn seek God in their own way. Newman does not deny to other human beings the same privilege of uniqueness he himself enjoys; he merely, in a characteristically reticent gesture, denies himself the right to speculate on it. "*Secretum est mihi*" is a motto that guarantees the same privacy for others that he claims for himself.

For Newman, such terms as *person* and *personality*, when not capitalized as doctrinal postulates, are in some respects not very far from their meaning in common parlance today. They exceed the Latin sense of either appearance or legal status, and draw closer to our modern usage, although (again) still antedating the findings of modern psychology. Newman was fully aware that the terms in their origin did not carry the range of implications already attributed to them in his own century. In this he might be said to have romanticized orthodoxy, not in the colloquial sense of idealizing or sentimentalizing it, but in the sense of spiritualizing it. Personality implicitly involves self-consciousness, not only understood materially but in the fullness of mental and physical being, as these are canvassed by a human consciousness that can probe and brood on its own reality. A central challenge of the *Apologia* for today's reader is to understand Newman's idea of agency, to ask how much has lain within the capacity of the narrator either to shape himself or to control events through the exertion of his own will, and how much falls (as Newman would argue) within the province of divine grace.

Despite the concerns of Thomas Mozley cited at the outset of this study, no easy substitute for "personality" is readily available as a term of reference. And the radical uniqueness of each human being in Newman's thought means that a resulting loneliness can only be mitigated, not banished, by a sense of one's uniqueness in the eyes of God, mediated by the Church in history. In Newman's world, radical aloneness on the psychological level can only be endured by clinging to the presumptions that others are similarly situated. Ian Ker, like Bouyer, rebuts the charge of egotism in these terms: "The individual Christian's relation to God is inseparable from the communion of other Christians. Not only that, but it is a characteristically Newmanian theme that our charity towards others is formed and influenced by our own particular personal friendships" (*Healing the Wound* 101).

Nonetheless it must be conceded that Newman, if not an egotist in the pervasively negative sense of the term, nonetheless manifested a form of egocentrism. Given his human personality, how could he not? His reliance on others, notably the unswervingly loyal Ambrose St. John, at times had an obsessive quality that in practical affairs could make him insensitive to their needs. But this problem was not rooted in selfishness. Quite the contrary: it lay in a recurring despondency about his own prospects. He sought out the company of those who sympathized with him, not with those who posed a challenge to his most deeply held convictions. The idea of a friendship that might be strengthened by the vigorous exchange of contrary ideas never seems to have ranked very highly in Newman's mind or habits. Because of this curious astigmatism, he could not will himself into a state of mind allowing for the possibility that a Dissenter or a theologically experimental Broad Churchman might have as acute a sense of Divine Personality as he. Wrong opinions trumped right feelings, disrupting even familial bonds.

As his relationship with Faber shows, Newman could be unforgiving, and such behavior tends to freeze old animosities in place. Much of his autobiographical writing, particularly that which was unpublished until after his death, witnesses to his inability to forget old slights, whether from Hawkins in his Anglican years or Archbishop Cullen in his Irish university years. Newman seems to have been haunted by what Richard Sennett, in *The Fall of Public Man*, has described as "the tyranny of intimacy." Not surprisingly, he seems often to have felt closer to those of his friends who had died than to those still living, precisely because those tyrannies were at an end. It may seem chilling to admit the possibility that such losses spur spiritual development, but Newman realized that grief and loneliness are prerequisites for spiritual growth. He also believed that total self-disclosure was impossible even to one's self, much more so to the closest of friends, that only God took full measure of our human personalities; it is just as likely that this recognition, as much as if not more than a sublimated sexuality, led to his decision to remain celibate. And yet to the extent that human relationships were imitations, however pale, of a relationship with the divine, he sought more than friendship could provide. Marvin O'Connell has shrewdly observed that "it is not too much to say that the more affection Newman felt for an individual, the more eager he was to make that individual over" (227). It is true that Wilfred Ward said of him, as had Newman's younger colleague J. D. Dalgairns many years before, that Newman "seemed able to love each friend with a peculiarly close sympathy for his mind and character and thoughtfulness for the circumstances of his life" (2:348). But in such cases Newman had made up his mind in the friend's favor.

Of course, solitude can heighten egotism of a different sort. Yngve Brilioth stressed that Newman's contemporaries testified to the "magic powers" of an "irresistible personality" and his capacity to inspire, which, at its most extreme, exerted the opposite effect, one of alienation and oppression. Newman's self-centeredness, the indictment runs, was a defining trait and accounted for "an inability to give himself away in love to a fellow man, which is in strong contrast to the excess of love and admiration which other men lavished on him" (106). For Brilioth, Newman's lifelong dedication to Thomas Scott's urgings, "Holiness rather than peace" and "Growth the only evidence of life," amounted to a persistent Calvinist undercurrent to which could be attributed "the dark shadow which always rested on Newman's preaching, and made many a visitor to the old spiritual adviser at the Birmingham Oratory come away depressed" (33–34). Baron von Hügel observed that the love of God, "where uninhibited and full, brings Joy—it seeks God, Joy; and it finds Joy, God. I used to wonder, in my intercourse with John Henry Newman, how one so good, and who had made so many sacrifices to God, could be so depressing." Comparing him to the Abbé Huvelin, he continued, "I came to feel that Newman had never succeeded in surmounting his deep predestinarian, Puritan, training; whilst Huvelin had nourished his soul, from boyhood upward, on the Catholic spirituality as it flowered in St. Francis" (*Essays and Addresses* 242).[6] We have no record that Newman ever succumbed to despair of God's grace, but the letters and journals reveal that, at moments, he seems to have lacked the assurance that he was loved by God. This failure of nerve, if so it may be called, was at the heart of all too many of his fractured friendships. If God's love cannot be relied on, how much more anxious may one be about the loyalty of one's friends, and as a result place an intolerable weight on the relationship?

But that is not the last word on Newman. In the "Biglietto" speech in which he accepted the cardinalate from Pope Leo, Newman confessed that he had made many mistakes in his lifetime and had "nothing of that high perfection which belongs to the writings of Saints, viz. that error cannot be found in them." But he defended the honesty and disinterestedness of his intentions and alluded to his struggle against liberalism in religion, "the doctrine that there is no positive truth in religion" ("Biglietto" 171). And then he made an important qualification. A "liberalistic theory" that was "good and true" did not try to "supersede" religion, but to inculcate the principles of "justice, truthfulness, sobriety, self-command, [and] benevolence" within a fideistic framework (173–74). In the end it was the enlarged idea of Christian (not merely decorative) gentlemanliness that came to the fore.[7] It was that enlargement of vision that did, in fact, make Newman a consoler of many perplexed Catholics, and a defender of their rights.

Newman's confidence came after many years of personal struggle within two different communions. But come it did. No less certain of his honest intentions than his illusions, we must take him for what he was: a formidable spiritual presence, a fallible human being.

Notes

INTRODUCTION

1. Simon Skinner, "History vs. Hagiography: The Reception of Turner's *Newman*," *Journal of Ecclesiastical History* 61 (2010): 764–81; Eamon Duffy, "The Reception of Turner's *Newman*: A Reply to Simon Skinner," *Journal of Ecclesiastical History* 63 (2012): 524–38; Skinner, "A Response to Eamon Duffy," *Journal of Ecclesiastical History* 63 (2012): 540–47. The thirteen contributors to the Cambridge *Companion* are all professional theologians. Newman readers of whatever stripe will be grateful, as I have consistently been, for their expertise; but the entire exclusion of literary scholars and historians, and the minimization of questions they might in turn wish to raise about Newman from the vantage points of their own disciplines, suggest less an onward march of hagiography than a clericalization of Newman studies.

2. "Liberalism" is a slippery term in the context of this subject; Newman himself defined it as "the anti-dogmatic principle and its development" (*A* 84) and more expansively in Note A at the end of the *Apologia* (254–62). In an earlier letter to Charles Marriott (1834 or 1835), he uses "liberalism" interchangeably with "latitudinarianism," whether in Church doctrine or discipline (*L&D* 32:11–12). In an important article on Newman and theological liberalism, Terence Merrigan has shown how both liberals and conservatives have missed the nuances of Newman's argument. "The key to Newman's complexity is his ability to hold in tensile unity apparently opposite tendencies and concerns" (621). See chapter 3, n. 12, for further discussion.

3. As Newman explains (*A* 44), this form of reference is intended to distinguish Palmer from William Palmer at Magdalen College, who subsequently became a Roman Catholic. All references in this book are to the first William Palmer, who did not convert and later became a critic of Newman.

4. The study that most explicitly anticipates mine in its stated topic is Sister M. Therese Waldmann's 1967 Fordham University dissertation, written under the direction of Vincent F. Blehl, SJ: "Personal Influence according to John Henry Newman: Idea and Reality." Our interests are obviously closely contiguous at a number of junctures, but the second half of her study is largely an examination of Newman the letter writer; she also confines herself to the early Anglican writings.

5. Mill, "Thoughts on Poetry and Its Varieties," *Collected Works* 1:343–65; on poetry and eloquence in particular, see 344–49. Bremond (144–69), comparing Newman's

homiletic style with the more formal oratory of the French pulpit, makes much the same point.

1. Self and Others

1. The Monophysite heresy was that Christ had two natures, partly divine and partly human, whereas according to the formula of the hypostatic union set forth in the Athanasian creed, and developed by the Council of Chalcedon in CE 451, in Him both natures existed and were each present in their fullness.

2. On the distinction between "personality" and "personhood," the first being "accidental and variable," the second (which Newman shared with St. Athanasius) being "the real foundation of all human life," see Myers 3–17, 90.

3. See Evelyn Underhill's comment on the Lord's Prayer: "The personalist note, never far from a fully operative religion, is struck at the start, and all else that is declared or asked is brought within the aura of this relationship" (*Abba* 131). Sheridan Gilley points out that in Catholic theology, human personality is grounded in divine Personality, and the power of personal presence has been represented once and for all in God's gift of his Son, "that complete revelation given in the person of Christ of the personality of God" (84).

4. For a general discussion, see Landow 154–88.

5. On the place of the *Ethics* in Newman's education, see Culler, in particular 16–18, 75–79.

6. For more on this point, see Kelly; also Myers 77–82.

7. There appears to have been a deliberate impulse toward colorlessness in some Tractarian preaching, a consequence of the wish to direct the attention of the worshipper to the Eucharist rather than the pulpit. Sara Coleridge wrote of listening to Pusey: "It is wrong to talk of *style* in respect of a preacher whose very merit consists in his striving for no style at all." Pusey "is as still as a statue all the time he is [preaching], looks as white as a sheet, and is as monotonous in delivery as is possible" (332–33). For one of Newman's fullest critiques of vehemence in preaching, as leading either to self-congratulation or self-satisfaction of the speaker, see the 1836 sermon "True Gospel Preaching" (S 4:244–51). On the severity of his own preaching, see Ker, *Achievement* 74–93, and Strange, "Newman at Oxford"; on the sermons as a means of preaching his Christology, see the more recent essay by Denis Robinson in *Cambridge Companion*.

8. Ker (*John Henry Newman* 98–99) comments on a Carlylean passage in the *Parochial and Plain Sermons* in which Newman ranks action over words. David Goslee writes that Newman's view of action as "self-authenticating" reiterates "those responses to a chaotic universe proposed by Goethe and preached in England by Carlyle" (138; compare 149).

9. By a somewhat ironic coincidence, Shadwell was to be named provost of Oriel, the same post that Newman's nemesis, Edward Hawkins, had held earlier.

10. The Ignatius Press edition (1997) of *Parochial and Plain Sermons*, the basis of quotation here, collects within a single volume W. J. Copeland's 1868 reissue of the sermons in eight volumes (1868). The Ignatius edition preserves the original volume divisions and order of the sermons within each volume but employs consecutive pagination. To facilitate cross-reference to the 1868 printing and its reissues, I have provided the volume and sermon number. Thus PPS 4.6.785 refers to volume 4, sermon 6, page 785 in the 1997 edition.

11. What became the controversial conclusion to *The Renaissance* was lifted from the ending of an article on William Morris that Pater had published five years earlier: "Poems by William Morris," *Westminster Review*, October 1868.

12. For background see DeLaura, "Newman and the Theology of Marius" (*Hebrew and Hellene* 314–28) and Downes's opening chapter.

13. Monsman points out that despite the lapse of thirty years, "Newman's rather public religious struggle was an important intellectual stimulus for [Pater's] novel"; he traces several verbal echoes of Newman that "create a Newmanesque atmosphere" (65, n. 1).

14. For an expert summary of Pater's own religious position, see Monsman 159–61. His reading of *Marius* should be paired with Knoepflmacher's (*Religious Humanism* 149–223).

15. The Ecclesiastical Titles Act was a response by the government of Lord John Russell to the Vatican's revival of the diocesan system in existence before the Reformation; since that time, the old hierarchy had been replaced by a system of missionary bishops *in partibus infidelium*. Though the system was for purposes of internal administration only, its reception was complicated by an unnecessarily triumphalist note struck by Nicholas Wiseman, and some of the more excitable anti-papal party in England reacted rather as if the Papal Guard had been dispatched across the Channel to seize Lambeth Palace. Newman, always fearing the Vatican's misgauging of English opinion, was initially uneasy but attempted to assuage Protestant concerns while stoutly defending Rome against Russell's accusations of superstitious "mummery."

2. The Journey from Evangelicalism

1. The point has been frequently made: see, for example, Brilioth 32–43; Chadwick, *Spirit* 18–19, see also 223; Schlossberg, *Silent Revolution* 82–83, 292–97; Nockles, *Oxford Movement* 221–23; Reed 178–80.

2. Stanley 1:33. "When Arthur Stanley left Rugby for Oxford, he went to hear Newman preach and found himself reminded of none other than Arnold" (Schlossberg, *Silent Revolution* 297). For additional background, see J. C. D. Clark 293–300; Newsome, "Evangelical Sources"; Lossky, "Oxford Movement"; Pereiro, *Ethos* 65–71. Toon (210) offers a guide to what might be involved in a change from Evangelical to Tractarian views.

3. "Inward Witness to the Truth of the Gospel" (1825), *PPS* 8.8.1630–31. Compare "Holiness Necessary for Future Blessedness" (1826[?]) in which holiness is described not merely as "the doing a certain number of good actions" but as "an inward character which follows, under God's grace, from doing them" (*PPS* 1.1.10).

4. See J C. D. Clark and Robert Hole for background on the national scene; for an Oxford context, see W. G. Ward, *Victorian Oxford*, and M. C. Brock, "The Oxford of Peel and Gladstone."

5. On the controversy in detail, see the discussion by Culler, chapter 3, which remains one of the best summaries. David Newsome attributes Hawkins's subsequent objections to "fear of favouritism," a preference on the tutors' part for the "reading men" over the "gentleman commoners" (*Parting of Friends* 93–94). Brock allows for Hawkins's "excessive rigidity" but adds that he "did not want influential parents to suspect that their sons were being exposed to religious influences which they might regard as excessive or unsuitable" ("Oxford" 61). Nonetheless, Brock concludes that the damage done to Oriel by the dismissal of the three tutors was considerable.

6. Jay, *Oxford and Evangelical Movements* 38–42. In his early preaching days, Newman experimented with Simeon's method but ultimately abandoned it. For a brief but useful account of Newman's change of method, see McGrath and Murray, *S* 3:xix–xxii.

7. Brad Faught explains, "The ineffability of baptismal regeneration was attractive to Newman because . . . it stood beyond the reach of private judgment, outside the critical, subjective spirit that seemed to characterize the evangelical approach to salvation (66; compare Sheridan 134). For some of Newman's preaching on the subject, see "Infant Baptism" (1828), the first of a series of three, *PPS* 7.16.1543–49; "Regenerating Baptism" and "Infant Baptism" (1835), *PPS* 3.19–20.655–73; and a sermon of 1841, *S* 3:269–76.

8. I do not, of course, intend to argue that Newman had never previously understood or accepted the doctrine of the Incarnation, only that he was becoming gradually aware of its power to focus his thoughts on personality, human and divine. For a mature statement (1837) on the relationship of the Atonement to the Incarnation, see his sermon on the Cross of Christ: "as the doctrine of the Incarnation comprehends most in its meaning, so the doctrine of the Atonement implies most in its consequences" (*S* 4:259).

9. In the first edition of 1833, following the words "principally to the affections," Newman had written "and though definite according to the criterion of practical influence, vague and incomplete in the judgment of the intellect" (161).

10. Toon 25–34, 64–65. Toon's *Evangelical Theology* is a salutary corrective to the one-sided view of the Evangelicals as theologically unsophisticated, a view encouraged by the Tractarians themselves. On the range of Evangelical views on such issues as baptismal regeneration and the Eucharist, see Toon 188–210.

3. Polarities

1. *L&D* 4:49, n. 2. The query is the editors'; the emphasis, the writer's.

2. In contrast to both Newman and Keble (who, despite his reputation for saintliness, was known to have crossed the street to avoid those whose opinions he found distasteful), militancy was not Pusey's mode. On January 22, 1836, he wrote to Newman, "I am weary of reading in order to censure; it is a hurtful office, and my study of Zwingli, &c in the summer was more than enough for some time" (Liddon 1:367).

3. See also "Rebuking Sin" (1831), the sermon placed immediately after "Tolerance of Religious Error," *PPS* 2.23.412–17, where Newman does, however, take pains to differentiate appropriate from inappropriate occasions for rebuke.

4. Meriol Trevor observes correctly that Newman "said he hated rows, but in fact he enjoyed a straight fight" (*Newman* 1:535; compare 558). Some of his opponents, however, questioned whether the fights were quite so "straight."

5. Newman declared in the *Apologia* that he could not remember saying the words ascribed to him, "How are we to know that Dr. A. is a Christian?," but went on to tell Anthony Grant, the intermediary between them, that "there were statements in one of Dr. Arnold's works, which implied in the judgment of many men a most painful irreverence towards that Sacred Record [the Hebrew scriptures], its Divine Author, and His servants revealed in it" (16 November 1833, *L&D* 4:106). This denial of a rumor, followed by an admission that the rumor did in fact convey what he might have said, is of a piece with the young Newman's inability to leave well enough alone. He employed the same tactic to Whately when the latter reported a rumor that on the occasion of one of his visits to Oxford after leaving for Dublin, Newman had avoided attending a communion service at which Whately had been present.

6. Somewhat to the discomfiture of his allies, Hampden refused to recuse himself from the Hebdomadal Board vote that secured his future at Oxford—en route, as it turned out, to the see of Hereford.

7. Brendon shrewdly observes that Newman "wanted to erect a permanent monument to his friend, impervious to the obliteration of time ... to forge a distinctive iconography for the movement" (182).

8. Newman told John Taylor Coleridge that the preface to the first series of the *Remains* (vol. 1) was Keble's, excepting the portion on "Romanism" (ix–xv); the preface to the second series was all Keble's "except a few formal lines at the end, which I think are mine" (7 February 1869, *L&D* 31: Suppl. 87*). [Vol. 31 of the *Letters and Diaries* (*L&D*) contains a "supplement" in which earlier letters, not heretofore included in the edition, are added. The editors affix asterisks to the page numbers in the supplement to set them off from those already published chronologically.]

9. Newman's position here is squarely aligned with the Anglican formularies, specifically Article 26, "Of the Unworthiness of Ministers, which hinders not the effect of

the Sacrament." For an excellent discussion of Tractarian views of the pastorate, see Skinner, *Tractarians and the Church of England* 139–87; the earlier work of G. Kitson Clark still merits attention.

10. See Selby; also G. B. Tennyson, *Victorian Devotional Poetry* 138–72.

11. See also Newman's notes for his sermon "On the Objects and Effects of Preaching," immediately following (*S* 1:23–31).

12. I have previously commented (n. 2 in the introduction) on the slipperiness of this term; see also J. C. D. Clark 5–8, and Perry Butler, who describes the term "liberal" as "secular, utilitarian, committed to the 'march of mind'" (*Gladstone, Church, State* 151). Thomas Norris provides a sustained discussion of the term in Newman's contrast of scientific logic and the experiential certitude not capable of strict logical demonstration (Norris 85ff., especially 101–3). W. R. McKelvy has recently expanded the implications of the term in connection with Newman's reaction to Broughamite ideas of education (see "The Tamworth Reading Room") as an aspect of his fear of the undisciplined reader (McKelvy 135). In another recent study, though he says little about Newman's use of the term, Schlossberg (*Conflict and Crisis*) has much to say about its currency in the wider Victorian-Edwardian religious debate. In fact, the trajectory of Schlossberg's argument seems to be described in what he perceives as the paradoxically self-defeating triumph of religious liberalism. But see also the afterword to this book for a significant course correction Newman made on the occasion of accepting the cardinalate.

13. "Apostolical Tradition," *ECH* 1:111. See Stephen Thomas's excellent discussion of Tract 73, *On the Introduction of Rationalist Principles into Revealed Religion* (*Newman and Heresy* 108–38), for an elaboration of how Evangelical emotionalism tended to reduce the content of revelation to a purely utilitarian standard. In the letter already cited to Lord Lifford, Newman painted his case with very broad strokes: "That [Evangelical] system has become rationalistic in Germany, Socinian in Geneva—Socinian among English Presbyterians and Arian among Irish—Latitudinarian in Holland—it tends to Socinianism among our own the [sic] Evangelical party" (*L&D* 6:133).

14. For a similar argument that appeared after my earlier draft on this point, see Conn 69–73, 82–85.

4. Notes of the Church

1. *Holy Scripture in Relation to the Catholic Creed*, delivered in 1835 and published in 1836 as Tract 85, pt. 1.

2. Reprinted in *D&A* 1–43 as "How to Accomplish It."

3. See, for example, the letter to Thomas Kirkpatrick, 6 March 1842: "Catholicism is . . . *in the air*. . . . It is being breathed. A wonderful power is abroad" (*L&D* 8:478).

4. "Dr. Wiseman's Lectures on the Catholic Church," *British Critic* (October 1836): 364.

5. Toon (13–45) writes that the *Lectures*, in addressing the doctrine of baptismal

regeneration, drove a wedge into whatever little may have remained by way of an Evangelical-Tractarian rapprochement in the wake of the Hampden affair. Gilley (166–70) expertly disentangles Protestant and Catholic threads in Newman's argument.

6. See, for example, "Transgressions and Infirmities" (1838), *PPS* 5.14.1083–91.

7. The Donatists were fourth- and early fifth-century Christians in Africa who claimed to be the only true Church and declared the baptisms and ordinations of the orthodox wing to be invalid. They caused considerable dissension and even violence within Christendom, but were effectively answered by Augustine, who argued on grounds of doctrine and church unity that they had no claims to speak for the wider Church. Newman's reference to Augustine ("Austin") reflects the Augustinian formula *securus judicat orbis terrarium* ("the entire world judges correctly") in cases where a sect separates itself from the rest of the world. For further elucidation, see Svaglic's note in his edition of the *Apologia*, 543–44.

8. Newman's defenders included William Palmer, R. W. Church (with reservations), and, more unexpectedly but logically, the liberal A. P. Stanley, who grasped that if Newman could stretch the meaning of the Articles in a Catholic direction, so might they be pressed into Latitudinarian service. Somewhat mischievously, Lytton Strachey later observed that Newman was merely "taking the Church at its word" and initiating what had since become a common practice in the Church of England (Strachey 32). The most recent study of substance is by Nockles, "Oxford, Tract 90, and the Bishops."

9. Palmer is here referring to Pusey's patience when forbidden the pulpit for two years after the condemnation of his sermon on the Real Presence by the authorities. See chapter 5 below.

10. The Jerusalem Bishopric was proposed by Baron Bunsen, the Prussian ambassador to England, who suggested that the Prussian and British governments alternately name a bishop of Jerusalem to serve the Continental Protestants and Church of England communicants there, and also (some thought) to convert the Jews in that area, who were few in number. An odd mixture of Evangelicals and Liberals supported the move, the first as a setback for the Tractarians, the second on behalf of pan-Protestantism, and political considerations (an English as well as Protestant presence in the near East) also weighed in the proposal, while some High Churchmen seem to have been placated by the promise of episcopal oversight. Ian Ker offers a concise summary in *John Henry Newman* (234–35). For Newman, the whole scheme smacked of consorting with heretics and even the possible appointment of a heretical bishop. His view of the matter, rehearsed at the end of chapter 3 of the *Apologia*, was regarded at the time even by some of his own friends as overheated.

11. "The Nature of Faith in Relation to Reason," *OUS* 144 (13 January 1839), and "Private Judgment," published in July of 1841, in which Newman speaks of how Lydia's heart, being opened by hearing Paul preach, was "drawn on to accept the Gospel by a moral persuasion" (*ECH* 2:344).

12. "Love the Safeguard of Faith against Superstition," sermon for Whit-Tuesday, 21 May 1839 (*OUS* 163); see also the sermon for the same church day in 1841, "Wisdom as Contrasted with Faith and with Bigotry": "The sheep could not tell how they knew the Good Shepherd; they had not analyzed their own impressions or cleared the grounds of their knowledge, yet doubtless grounds there were: they, however, acted spontaneously on a loving Faith" (*OUS* 191).

5. Anglican Deathbeds

1. O'Connell 385; full description at 384–89. On the multiple ironies of the affair, see Nockles, "'Lost Causes'" 248–53.

2. "The Eucharistic Presence" (1838), *PPS* 6.11.1272–81. Härdelin's *The Tractarian Understanding of the Eucharist*, though maddeningly diffuse, is the most thorough study of its subject. For Pusey, material change in the elements amounted to an overthrow of the sacramental principle (Hardelin 195–98).

3. Lockhart's long and apologetic letter to Newman (22 August 1843) is now available in *L&D* 9:471–72.

4. Letter to John Keble, 1 September 1843, *L&D* 9:495. Newman's letter to Hope on 5 September is more explicit: "He was quite overcome by the fascination of Dr. Gentili . . . and is going forthwith to enter the order of Charity (Rosminians)" (*L&D* 9:503). The language suggests that Newman, reverting to the view that some Protestants took of him, saw Gentili as a kind of seducer.

5. O'Connell (375) observes that though Littlemore was regarded as a house of prayer insulated from the respectable self-indulgence of Oxford dons, "there was a lack of intellectual quality among the men at Littlemore, and even the brightest of them, Dalgairns, was too romantic and immature to allow his considerable mental powers full scope."

6. White had gone to Dublin as tutor for the Whately children, a position to which Newman at one time had aspired before his break with the future archbishop. Whately had been one of Newman's earliest mentors at Oriel, but Newman had later opposed his policy in Ireland and there was a bitter falling-out, to which I have alluded indirectly (chapter 3, n. 5). Some personal resentment may still linger in Newman's recollections of White.

7. Francis McGrath, one of the volume's editors, cites "To F. W. N. A Birthday Greeting" as the source of these lines.

8. Newman himself had been attracted to some features of the Protestant Episcopal Church in the United States, especially its independence of state support, but deplored the role given to the laity in ecclesiastical matters, especially the election of bishops. See the little-noted article "The Anglo-American Church," which appeared in the *British Critic* in 1839 (*ECH* 1.309–79).

9. For further discussion of Sermon 15, see Earnest and Tracey, eds., *OUS* xcix–cxi.

Nicholas Lash (64) points to the limits, even in Newman's own terms, of an analogy between an individual's history and that of the Church. Still, Newman's persistent use of personification to describe the churches themselves strongly suggests his attraction to the analogy. As Gilley points out (229–35), Newman's treatise is a preliminary step towards his later ecclesiology, in which the Church is the gathered company of all believers—a view in turn anticipating Newman's defense of the role of the laity within the Church and particularly against the Ultramontane party. Valuable additional (Oxford) background has been provided by Prickett in *Modernity and the Reinvention of Tradition*; see especially chapter 8, "Keble and the Anglican Tradition," and chapter 9, "Newman and the Development of Tradition."

10. Suzy Anger (28–48) aptly shows how the techniques of biblical hermeneutics spilled out into the larger cultural atmosphere; in this sense, Newman's *Development of Christian Doctrine* and Darwin's *Origin of Species* can be said to have a common progenitor.

11. I agree in principle here with Owen Chadwick that Newman's theory had nothing in common with "evolutionary, immanentist, progressive German liberal theories" (*From Bossuet to Newman* 97). Jonathan Loesberg (104) adds that for Newman, development is to be seen in the context of "a stable truth whose changing forms are necessitated by the limitations of human understanding." George Levine distinguishes innovation from Newman's "spelling out for fallen man in the visible world of what is already given in Revelation, of what is permanent and unchangeable" (187).

6. "A Deliverance from the Nightmare"

1. For a treatment of related religious texts at mid-century, see Dawson, *Victorian Noon* 105–22. Prickett compares the theories of development held by Newman and his leading critic of the day, F. D. Maurice (*Romanticism and Religion* 152–73). For the historical context, in particular the "papal aggression" panic, see the works by Robert Klaus and Denis Paz.

2. "The Duty of Hoping against Hope," preached on the occasion of the opening of a new parish church and school at Harrow Weald, 1 July 1846 (*Sermons Academical and Occasional*, especially 329–30).

3. The case in question was *Ditcher v. Denison* (1856), in which the archbishop of Canterbury had ruled that the doctrine of the Real Presence was not in keeping with Anglican doctrine. In Keble's judgment, this was a repetition of the earlier Gorham Judgment (1851), in which the Privy Council, acting as the ultimate court of appeal, overruled the attempt by Henry Phillpotts, the bishop of Exeter, to bar a clergyman (C. G. Gorham) from taking up canonical residence in his diocese because of Gorham's perceived unsoundness on the doctrine of Baptismal Regeneration. Both decisions antagonized the Catholic-leaning party within the Establishment, and the earlier of the two (*Gorham*) was the precipitating event in Henry Manning's secession to Rome.

See Chadwick on Gorham (*Victorian Church* 1:250–71) and Ditcher (1:491–95); Bowen (96–111) also discusses Gorham.

4. Though in the first bankruptcy Newman's father repaid all his debts in the wake of the failure of his bank, in the second the family's goods were distrained and sold on the street.

5. William Robbins makes essentially the same point about Frank's later writings in the 1870s, when he "struggled to rationalize his intuition of God, to retain the element of personality without the concept of Persons" (Robbins 154; see also 178–79).

7. Building Community

1. Of these three works, I omit the *Lectures on the Present Position of Catholics in England* as least relevant to the chapter. Written after the Ecclesiastical Titles Act, the lectures set forth preliminary considerations on Catholics as English citizens, a subject to which Newman reverted years later in his response to Gladstone, *Letter to the Duke of Norfolk*.

2. Undated notes, ca. 1848, in Wilfrid Ward 1:207.

3. When the sees of Nottingham and Liverpool were briefly and mysteriously dangled over his head at the time of the planning for the Irish university project, Newman disclaimed any ability to rule men or to promote doctrine (as a bishop must do). Rather, he preferred to deal gently with individual consciences. See, for example, his letters to Archbishop Cullen, 2 March 1853 (*L&D* 15:316–17); to David Moriarty, bishop of Kerry, 25 November 1856 (*L&D* 17:460–61); and to William Fraser, 9 December 1864 (*L&D* 21:336–38).

4. For a characteristically balanced treatment, see Newsome, *Convert Cardinals* 187–88.

5. The asterisk denotes separate pagination for the *L&D* "supplement." See full explanation in chapter 3, n. 8, above.

6. See the helpful discussion by James Tolhurst in his introduction to *SN* (xxxviii–xlii). Since Tolhurst wrote, the publication of the latest (and final) volume of the *Sermons 1824–1843* has made available a sermon on "the faith of Mary" that Newman preached as early as February 1826 at St. Clement's (*S* 5:385–91), when for all practical purposes he would have still classified himself as an Evangelical. Newman enumerates Mary's numerous virtues—her devotion, humility, "spiritual instinct"—but grants her no theological significance. "Let us not suppose that she is different from ourselves in any other way than that she is better.... If we do not surpass her, it will be entirely through our own fault, our own slothful and carnal hearts" (391).

7. Newman says that were he to search for signs of Catholic heroism like that of St. Martin, St. Francis, Tertullian, or Ignatius among Protestants, he would look to the Methodists before the Anglicans. The point was not new. In an article on Selina, Countess of Huntingdon, the patroness of George Whitfield, in the *British Critic* some

years before, he had written, "The history of Methodism is, we do not scruple to say, the history of a heresy; but never surely was a heresy so mixed up with what was good and true, with high feeling and honest exertion" (*ECH* 1:387). Newman preferred Wesley to Luther or Calvin, and he rebuked the Establishment for its inadequate response to the phenomenon Wesley represented. He seems to be revisiting his own Evangelical past and finding a closer approximation to the Primitive Church among such movements than he could find in mainstream Anglicanism.

8. See, for example, Barr, *Paul Cullen* 3. In a more recent study, however ("Catholic Fact"), Barr has also pointed out that Cullen had envisioned Newman's retaining his role at the Oratory during his rectorship (231–32). Cullen may have underestimated the complexities of Newman's position; he may also, however, have felt it convenient that Newman's influence be more circumscribed than it would have been had he been resident full time in Dublin. More central to Barr's essay is its fine-tuning of what Newman meant by a Catholic education and in what respects he thought that both the curriculum and the faculty should indeed be Catholic.

9. "What Adam de Brome had conceived when he established the college in the fourteenth century was a body in which there were no tutors for the simple reason that there were no students. Or rather, all were students and tutors together, all learning from each other and all using their learning in the service of God" (Culler 89).

8. Reconstituting the Self

1. For a summary of the Achilli affair, see Ker, *John Henry Newman* 372–75, 397–99. More documentation is made available in the most recent volume of *L&D* (32:60ff.), which collects letters from Newman's entire career not previously incorporated in earlier volumes. Newman had relied secondhand on remarks Wiseman had made about Achilli's reputed scandalous behavior in the June 1850 *Dublin Review*. Documentation from Wiseman that might have spared Newman the proceeding was not forthcoming, for Wiseman had mislaid his own papers and was dilatory in procuring alternative documents from Italy. The long and the short of it was that Newman ultimately got off with a fine of £300 (promptly covered, along with considerably higher legal costs, by his Catholic friends) and a scolding from the bench by Justice John Taylor Coleridge.

2. See MacDougall (90–94) for an explanation of the Newman-Acton relationship in connection with his defense of his fellow clergy. The real question lies deeper still, since the *Apologia* also defends the Church as an organic unity; to attack any of its members, for Newman, was to attack its integrity as a whole.

3. For an overview of the interconnections between tradition, development, and the self-disclosure of God, see Biemer, especially 112–49. According to Biemer, "The act of tradition may be described as the functioning of the conscience of the Church" (147). Thomas (281) has pithily observed that Newman employed "an idea of development about himself to show that he had always believed the idea of development." Schmidt,

however, finds the relationship between the *Development* and the *Apologia* somewhat problematic: "Beneath his conscious avowals of ontological faith in the *Apologia*, there is ... always the underlying sense of separation from his early self" (128). On the connection between development and reserve, see Selby 67–75.

4. According to the online Catholic Encyclopedia (www.newadvent.org), "Eutychianism and Monophysitism are usually identified as a single heresy," the only difference being that the former flourished in Armenia. Eutyches has no real claim to the invention of a new heresy.

5. Those who, on the whole, treat the *Apologia* as an autobiography include Houghton, DeLaura, Peterson, Fleishman, Loesberg, Turner, and Gagnier. Those of a different persuasion, or who accept the classification only with broad reservations, include Deen, Svaglic, and Ker. Particularly revealing on the question of voice, that is, the voice one "hears" in Newman's narrative, is Vargish (172–88) and Shaw (228, 234–50).

6. Levine 237. Levine compares the *Apologia* to Carlyle's *Sartor Resartus* in that "both books imply that the beginning is different from the end only in that what was initially implicit is by the end spelled out" (243).

7. Newman never expected to be at Alton because, after the failure of the bank, his father unexpectedly moved to the management of a brewery there. The clause conceals the pain of having to leave Norwood.

8. The stone that Samuel names in commemoration of God's help in recovering Israelite territory (1 Samuel 7:2–12).

9. Newman's preparation for the final examinations and his breakdown when called in for the oral examination (November 1820) is described by Culler (15–20).

10. My discussion here owes much to Levine's suggestive remarks (246–51) on this supercharged passage.

11. F. Newman, *Contributions* 62–63. In this passage he shared his wounded feelings at his brother's sentiment insensitively made public in the *Apologia*: "You cause division; therefore I must avoid you." A few pages later, Frank tried to best his brother by accusing him of being "almost factious and seditious" in his conduct toward Church and State, "which was just *what Paul meant by* 'Heretical'" (65).

12. My discussion of the forensic nature of the *Apologia* has been suggested by a remark by Conn (76).

13. See Colby's mythopoeic reading of the work as a classically allusive blend of epic and drama. Colby argues (456–57) that "Newman's literary problem [is] the representation of a series of contemplative religious states with the vigor and concreteness possible to the epic and dramatic poet."

14. For extended commentary on this and related matters, particularly in Notes F and G, see Griffiths, who sees Newman as aligned with Jerome, Cassian, and Chrysostom on the subject of the defensible lie (*Lying* 199–200). Griffiths suggests

that given his preference for "material" lying over equivocation, Newman's ethic of the English gentleman trumps that of the Christian. This may be an instance of Newman's deliberately choosing to engage Kingsley on the most superficial ground, a characteristic rhetorical maneuver in Newman's controversial writings.

15. I take these figures from a rough count of the numbered lines in the Svaglic edition.

16. The documentation is complex, but Newman's drift was plain. See, for example, the letters to Wood, quoted above, 17 March 1840 (*L&D* 7:267); to Pusey the same day (264–65); to Charles Marriott, 22 and 27 March (275, 279–80); to J. R. Bloxam, 29 March (282); to Tom Mozley, 10 June (342–43); and to his sister Jemima [Mrs. John Mozley], 28 May (334).

17. For good commentaries on this passage, see Rupp, Schmidt (132–35), and the more extended treatment by Loesberg (148–72).

18. See the acute if somewhat hostile article by Elisabeth Jay, who sees Gerontius at the end as a "disembodied soul" who gradually relinquishes his "last vestiges of individuality" ("Newman's Mid-Victorian Dream" 224). See also Sharrock.

9. Oppositions and Resolutions

1. See Newman's letter to Lady Simeon, 19 November 1867, *L&D* 23:365–67, and to Sir John, 19 December (380–82). For a fuller description of the ensuing imbroglio over an Oxford mission, see Ker, *John Henry Newman* 561–69.

2. Mary Katherine Tillman points out that for Newman the "cognitive method" varies from one individual to another, and that "when he shifts from the individual seat of judgment to that of the ecclesial community, the illative sense [see below] becomes the sense of the faithful, and conscience is translated into the principle of tradition in the Church" ("Economies of Reason" 50).

3. On the reaction of both Manning and Talbot to Newman's published response to Pusey, see Newsome, *Convert Cardinals* 254–58.

4. Newman to Ullathorne, 8 January 1867 (*L&D* 23:17); see the exchange between Manning and Newman in November 1869 (*L&D* 24:362–63); Newman to Lady Simeon, 18 November 1870 (*L&D* 25:230.)

5. Quoted in Newsome, *Convert Cardinals* 284.

6. The editors apply the subsection title "Papers in Preparation for *A Grammar of Assent*" to the period 1865–69, but almost the entirety of the published entries in the first volume show Newman's thought processes leading to that work.

7. Of particular value for my discussion here are Ian Ker's introduction and notes to his edition of *A Grammar of Assent*, and the studies by Moleski and Norris. See also Coulson's contrast of Coleridge's idea of the Church with Newman's "personation" of it (*Common Tradition* 180; the key term is Newman's). Vargish offers a valuable

companion-piece to the *Grammar*. See also Ferreira, "Grammar of the Heart"; Magill; and Edward Norman for his discussion of the *Grammar*'s connection with works of a more political and social character.

8. "The Illative Sense makes use of that Christian self-consciousness so important to Newman's Evangelical period. But, based as it is upon concrete experience, and judging principally of the truth of things outside the self, it avoids the dangers of self-contemplation to the exclusion of the objects of faith" (Vargish 68–69).

9. *GA* 181. For an interesting attempt to draw parallels between Newman's method and that of Michael Polanyi, see Moleski, who develops a connection first noted by Avery Cardinal Dulles (45). Colin Gunton has also noted the resemblance of the two writers' views on personal knowledge ("Newman's Dialectic." 311).

10. On conscience and personality, see Dessain and the more specialized inquiry by Gave.

11. For various views on the role played by individualism in this work, see Reardon 98–105; Nicholls; and Coulson, *Common Tradition* 132–47.

Afterword

1. See Fairbairn, "Catholicism and Religious Thought," *Contemporary Review* (May 1885); Newman's response, "The Development of Religious Error," in the same journal for October; Fairbairn, "Reason and Religion: A Reply to Cardinal Newman," in December. Newman considered a further rejoinder; but not wanting to prolong the controversy in public, he added several paragraphs to his original reply and published the whole privately, sending it to Fairbairn. That fuller reply is now available as "Revelation in Its Relation to Faith," printed in *TP* 1:140–57. A good albeit brief critique of the controversy has been provided by Rupp (201–2).

2. "A Rescue of Religion," review of Leszek Kolakowski's *Why Is There Something Rather Than Nothing?*, *New York Review of Books* 55, no. 15 (9 October 2008): 45.

3. Letter of 24 October 1883, in Hopkins 187. See Shaw generally for an overview of "mystery" as a Victorian concept.

4. Further commentary is offered by Thomas (151). Loesberg's analysis reminds us that the metaphor suggests the absence of God, but not (as an incautious reader might infer) His nonexistence.

5. "A Treatise of Direction," in *Christian Ethereal Library*, http://www.ccel.org/ccel/Catherine/dialog.

6. A similar view of Newman's "dark side" has been developed at greater length by Hilda Graef.

7. Terence Merrigan's study of Newman's encounter with theological liberalism provides a much-needed background for understanding the position he had arrived at by the time of the "Biglietto" speech.

Bibliography

Adams, James Eli. *Dandies and Desert Saints: Styles of Victorian Masculinity.* Ithaca, NY: Cornell University Press, 1995.
Anger, Suzy. *Victorian Interpretation.* Ithaca, NY: Cornell University Press, 2005.
Aristotle. *The Nicomachean Ethics.* Translated by Christopher Rowe. Oxford: Oxford University Press, 2002.
Arnold, Matthew. *The Complete Poems of Matthew Arnold.* Edited by Miriam Allott. 2nd ed. New York: Longmans, 1979.
——— *The Complete Prose Works of Matthew Arnold.* Edited by R. H. Super. 11 vols. Ann Arbor: University of Michigan Press, 1960–77.
Arnold, Thomas. "The Oxford Malignants and Dr. Hampden." *Edinburgh Review* 63 (April 1836): 225–39.
Arnstein, Walter L. *Catholic versus Protestant in Mid-Victorian England: Mr. Newdegate and the Nuns.* Columbia: University of Missouri Press, 1982.
Augustine. *Concerning the City of God against the Pagans.* Translated by Henry Bettenson. London: Penguin, 2003.
Barr, Colin. "Newman, Catholic Fact, and Higher Education." In *Newman and Truth*, edited by Terence Merrigan and Ian Ker, 227–50. Leuven, Belgium: Peeters, 2008.
———. *Paul Cullen, John Henry Newman, and the Catholic University of Ireland, 1845–1865.* Notre Dame, IN: University of Notre Dame Press, 2004.
Biemer, Gunter. *Newman on Tradition.* Translated and edited by Kevin Smyth. London: Burns and Oates, 1967.
Bouyer, Louis. *Newman: His Life and Spirituality.* Translated by J. Lewis May. 1958. Reprint, New York: Meridian Books, 1961. Originally published as *Newman: Sa vie, sa spiritualité* (Paris: Lers Editions du Cerf, 1952).
———. *Newman's Vision of Faith: A Theology for Times of General Apostasy.* San Francisco: Ignatius Press, 1986.
Bowden, John Edward. *The Life and Letters of Frederick William Faber, D.D., Priest of the Oratory of St. Philip Neri.* London: Thomas Richardson and Sons, 1866.
Bowen, Desmond. *The Idea of the Victorian Church: A Study of the Church of England, 1853–1889.* Montreal: McGill University Press, 1968.
Brady, Ciaran. *James Anthony Froude: An Intellectual Biography of a Victorian Prophet.* Oxford: Oxford University Press, 2013.

Bibliography

Bremond, Henri. *The Mystery of Newman.* Translated by H. C. Corrance, with an introduction by the Rev. George Tyrrell. London: Williams and Moorgate, 1907. Originally published as *Newman: Essai de biographie psychologique* (Paris: Librairie Bloud, 1906).

Brendon, Piers. *Hurrell Froude and the Oxford Movement.* London: Paul Elek, 1974.

Brilioth, Yngve. *The Anglican Revival: Studies in the Oxford Movement.* London: Longmans, Green, 1925.

Brock, M. G. "The Oxford of Peel and Gladstone, 1800–1873." In Brock and Curthoys, 7–71.

Brock, M. G., and M. C. Curthoys, eds. *Nineteenth Century Oxford.* Pt. 1. Vol. 6 of *The History of the University of Oxford*, general editor, T. H. Ashton. Oxford: Clarendon Press, 1997.

Browning, Robert. *Poetical Works, 1833–1864.* Edited by Ian Jack. London: Oxford University Press, 1970.

Buckley, J. H. "Newman's Autobiography." In Ker and Hill, 93–110.

———. *The Turning Key: Autobiography and the Subjective Impulse since 1800.* Cambridge, MA: Harvard University Press, 1984.

Butler, Joseph. *The Analogy of Religion.* Edited by Ernest C. Mossner. New York: Frederick Ungar, 1961.

Butler, Perry. *Gladstone, Church, State, and Tractarianism: A Study of His Religious Ideas and Attitudes, 1809–1859.* Oxford: Clarendon Press, 1982.

Carlyle, Thomas. *Works.* Edited by H. D. Traill. Edinburgh Edition. 30 vols. New York: Scribner, 1903–4.

Carter, Grayson. *Anglican Evangelicals: Protestant Secessions from the* Via Media. Oxford: Oxford University Press, 2001.

Chadwick, Owen. *From Bossuet to Newman.* 2nd ed. Cambridge: Cambridge University Press, 1987.

———. *The Spirit of the Oxford Movement: Tractarian Essays.* Cambridge: Cambridge University Press, 1990.

———. *The Victorian Church.* Pt. 1. London: Adam and Charles Black, 1966.

———. *The Victorian Church.* Pt. 2. London: Adam and Charles Black, 1970.

Church, R. W. *The Oxford Movement: Twelve Years, 1833–1845.* 3rd ed. London: Macmillan, 1892. Reprint, Hamden, CT: Archon Books, 1968.

Clark, G. Kitson. *Churchmen and the Condition of England, 1832–1885: A Study in the Development of Social Ideas and Practice from the Old Regime to the Modern State.* London: Methuen, 1975.

Clark, J. C. D. *English Society, 1660–1832: Ideology and Politics during the Ancien Regime.* 2nd ed. Cambridge: Cambridge University Press, 2000.

Colby, Robert A. "The Poetical Structure of Newman's *Apologia pro Vita Sua.*" *Journal of Religion* 33 (1953): 47–57.

Bibliography

Coleridge, John Taylor. *A Memoir of the Rev. John Keble, M.A., Late Vicar of Hursley.* Oxford: James Parker, 1869.

Coleridge, Sara. *Memoir and Letters.* London: Henry S. King, 1873.

Conn, Walter L. *Conscience and Conversion in Newman: A Developmental Study of Self in John Henry Newman.* Milwaukee, WI: Marquette University Press, 2010.

Cornwell, John. *Newman's Unquiet Grave: The Reluctant Saint.* London: Continuum, 2010.

Coulson, John. *Newman and the Common Tradition: A Study in Church and Society.* Oxford: Clarendon Press, 1970.

Coulson, John, and A. M. Allchin, eds. *The Rediscovery of Newman: An Oxford Symposium.* London: SPCK, 1967.

Culler, A. Dwight. *The Imperial Intellect: A Study of Newman's Educational Ideal.* New Haven, CT: Yale University Press, 1955.

Davies, Horton. *Worship and Theology in England.* Vol. 2, *From Watts and Wesley to Maurice, 1690–1850.* 1961. Reprint, Grand Rapids, MI: William B. Eerdmans, 1996.

Dawson, Carl. *Victorian Noon: English Literature in 1850.* Baltimore, MD: Johns Hopkins University Press, 1979.

Deen, Leonard. "The Rhetoric of Newman's *Apologia.*" *ELH* 29 (1962): 224–38.

DeLaura, David J. *Hebrew and Hellene in Victorian England: Newman, Arnold, and Pater.* Austin: University of Texas Press, 1969.

———. "'O Unforgotten Voice': The Memory of Newman in the Nineteenth Century." In *The Use of Nineteenth Century Literary Documents: Essays in Honor of C. L. Cline,* 23–55. Austin: Department of English and Humanities Research Center, University of Texas, 1975.

Dessain, C. S. *John Henry Newman.* London: Nelson, 1968.

Downes, David Anthony. *The Temper of Victorian Belief: Studies in the Religious Novels of Pater, Kingsley, and Newman.* New York: Twayne, 1972.

Dulles, Avery Cardinal, SJ. *Newman.* London: Continuum, 2002.

Dunn, Waldo Hilary. *James Anthony Froude: A Biography.* 2 vols. Oxford: Clarendon Press, 1961, 1968.

Faber, Geoffrey. *Oxford Apostles: A Character Study of the Oxford Movement.* 1933. Reprint, AMS Press, 1976.

Fairbairn, Andrew. "Catholicism and Religious Thought." *Contemporary Review* 47 (May 1885): 652–74.

———. "Reason and Religion: A Reply to Cardinal Newman." *Contemporary Review* 48 (December 1885): 842–61.

Faught, C. Brad. *The Oxford Movement: A Thematic History of the Tractarians and Their Times.* University Park: Pennsylvania State University Press, 2003.

Ferreira, M. Jamie. *Doubt and Religious Commitment: The Role of the Will in Newman's Religious Thought.* Oxford: Clarendon Press, 1980.

———. "The Grammar of the Heart: Newman on Faith and Imagination." In Magill, *Discourse and Context* 129–41.

———. *Skepticism and Reasonable Doubt: The British Naturalist Tradition in Wilkins, Hume, Reid, and Newman*. Oxford: Oxford University Press, 1986.

Fleishman, Avrom. *Figures of Autobiography: The Language of Self-Writing in Victorian and Modern England*. Berkeley and Los Angeles: University of California Press, 1983.

Froude, James Anthony. "The Oxford Counter-Reformation." In *Short Studies in Great Subjects*, 4th ser., 151–235. New York: Charles Scribner and Sons, 1886.

———. "Reminiscences." In Dunn, vol. 1.

Froude, Richard Hurrell. *Remains of the Late Rev. Richard Hurrell Froude*. [Edited by John Henry Newman and John Keble.] 2 pts. in 2 vols. London: J. G. and F. Rivington, 1838–39.

Gagnier, Reginia. *Subjectivities: A History of Self-Representation in England, 1832–1920*. Oxford: Oxford University Press, 1991.

Gave, S. A. *Conscience in Newman's Thought*. Oxford: Clarendon Press, 1980.

Gilley, Sheridan. *Newman and His Age*. Westminster, MD: Christian Classics, 1991.

Goslee, David. *Romanticism and the Anglican Newman*. Athens: Ohio University Press, 1996.

Graef, Hilda. *God and Myself: The Spirituality of John Henry Newman*. New York: Hawthorn Books, 1967.

Griffis, James F. *The Anglican Vision*. Cambridge, MA: Cowley, 1997.

Griffiths, Paul J. *Lying: An Augustinian Theology of Duplicity*. Grand Rapids, MI: Brazos Press, 2004.

Gunton, Colin. "Newman's Dialectic: Dogma and Reason in the Seventy-Third *Tract for the Times*." In Ker and Hill, 309–22.

Härdelin, Alf. *The Tractarian Understanding of the Eucharist*. Uppsala, Sweden: Acta Universitatis Uppsaliensis, 1965.

Harrold, Charles Frederick. *John Henry Newman: An Expository and Critical Study of His Mind, Thought, and Art*. 1945. Reprint, Hamden, CT: Archon Books, 1966.

Henderson, Heather. *The Victorian Self: Autobiography and Biblical Narrative*. Ithaca, NY: Cornell University Press, 1980.

Hole, Robert. *Pulpits, Politics, and Public Order in England, 1760–1832*. Cambridge: Cambridge University Press, 1989.

Holland, Henry Scott. "Newman." In *A Bundle of Memories*, 112–20. London: Wells Gardiner, Darnton, 1915.

Holloway, John. *The Victorian Sage: Studies in Argument*. 1953. Reprint, New York: W. W. Norton, 1965.

Hopkins, Gerard Manley. *The Letters of Gerard Manley Hopkins to Robert Bridges*. Edited by Claude Colleer Abbott. 2nd ed. Oxford: Geoffrey Cumberlege, 1955.

Bibliography

Houghton, Walter E. *The Art of Newman's* Apologia. New Haven, CT: Yale University Press, 1945.

Hügel, Friedrich von, Baron. *Essays and Addresses on the Philosophy of Religion.* 2nd ser. 1926. Reprint, New York: E. P. Dutton, 1963.

———. *Letters from Baron Friedrich von Hügel to a Niece.* Edited by Gwendolen Greene, with preface by John E. Sheridan, CSP. Chicago: Henry Regnery, 1955.

Hutton, R, H. *Cardinal Newman.* 2nd ed. London: Methuen, 1891.

Inge, W. R. "Cardinal Newman." In *Outspoken Essays,* 172–203. London: Longmans, Green, 1921.

Jay, Elisabeth. "Newman's Mid-Victorian Dream." In Nicholls and Kerr, 214–32.

———, ed. *The Oxford and Evangelical Movements.* Cambridge: Cambridge University Press, 1983.

Jones, O. W. *Isaac Williams and His Circle.* London: SPCK, 1971.

Keble, John. *The Christian Year: Thoughts in Verse for the Sundays and Holydays throughout the Year.* 1897. Reprint, Detroit: Gale, 1975.

———. *On Eucharistical Adoration.* Oxford: John Henry and James Parker, 1857.

———. *Sermons Academical and Occasional.* Oxford: John Henry Parker, 1847.

Kelly, Edward J. "Identity and Discourse: A Study in Newman's Individualism." In Magill, *Discourse and Context* 15–32.

Ker, Ian. *The Achievement of John Henry Newman.* Notre Dame, IN: University of Notre Dame Press, 1990.

———. *Healing the Wound of Humanity: The Spirituality of John Henry Newman.* London: Darton, Longman and Todd, 1993.

———. *John Henry Newman: A Biography.* Oxford: Oxford University Press, 1988.

———, and Alan G. Hill, eds. *Newman after a Hundred Years.* Oxford: Clarendon Press, 1990.

Klaus, Robert J. *The Pope, the Protestants, and the Irish: Papal Aggression and Anti-Catholicism in Mid-Nineteenth Century England.* New York: Garland, 1987.

Knight, Frances. *The Nineteenth-Century Church and English Society.* Cambridge: Cambridge University Press, 1995.

Knoepflmacher, U. C. *Religious Humanism and the Victorian Novel: George Eliot, Walter Pater, and Samuel Butler.* Princeton, NJ: Princeton University Press, 1965.

———. Introduction to F. Newman, *Phases of Faith.*

Landow, George. *Elegant Jeremiahs: The Sage from Carlyle to Mailer.* Ithaca, NY: Cornell University Press, 1986.

Lash, Nicholas. *Newman on Development: The Search for an Explanation in History.* London: Sheed and Ward, 1975.

Levine, George. *The Boundaries of Fiction: Carlyle, Macaulay, Newman.* Princeton, NJ: Princeton University Press, 1968.

Liddon, Henry Parry. *Life of Edward Bouverie Pusey.* 4th ed. 4 vols. London: Longmans, Green, 1884–88.

Loesberg, Jonathan. *Fictions of Consciousness: Mill, Newman, and the Reading of Victorian Prose.* New Brunswick, NJ: Rutgers University Press, 1986.

Lossky, Nicolas. "The Oxford Movement and the Revival of Patristic Theology." In Vaiss 76–82.

MacDougall, Hugh. *The Acton-Newman Relations: The Dilemma of Christian Liberalism.* New York: Fordham University Press, 1962.

Macquarrie, John. *Principles of Christian Theology.* 2nd ed. New York: Charles Scribner and Sons, 1977.

Magill, Gerard. "The Living Mind: Newman on Assent and Dissent." In *Discourse and Context: An Interdisciplinary Study of John Henry Newman,* edited by Gerard Magill, 144–64. Carbondale: Southern Illinois University Press, 1993.

Manning, Henry Edward. *England and Christendom.* London: Longmans, Green, 1867.

Martineau, James. "Personal Influence in Present Theology: J. H. Newman, S. T. Coleridge, T. Carlyle." *National Review* 3 (October 1856): 448–94. Reprinted in *Essays, Reviews, and Addresses,* 2 vols. Vol. 1, *Personal and Political* 219–82. London: Longmans, Green, 1891.

McKelvy, William R. *The English Cult of Literature: Devoted Readers, 1774–1880.* Charlottesville: University of Virginia Press, 2007.

Merrigan, Terence. "Newman and Theological Liberalism." *Theological Studies* 66 (December 2005): 605–21.

Mill, John Stuart. *Collected Works.* Edited by J. M. Robson et al. 33 vols. Toronto: University of Toronto Press, 1963-.

Milner, Joseph. *Works of the Late Rev. Joseph Milner in Eight Volumes.* London: Lane, Cadell, and W. Davies, 1810.

Moleski, Martin S., SJ. *Personal Catholicism: The Theological Epistemologies of John Henry Newman and Michael Polanyi.* Washington, DC: Catholic University of America Press, 2000.

Monsman, Gerald. *Pater's Portraits: Mythic Patterns in the Fictions of Walter Pater.* Baltimore, MD: Johns Hopkins University Press, 1967.

Mozley, Thomas. *Reminiscences, Chiefly of Oriel College and the Oxford Movement.* 2nd ed. 2 vols. London: Longmans, Green, 1882.

Myers, William. *The Presence of Persons: Essays on Literature, Science, and Philosophy in the Nineteenth Century.* Ashgate: Aldershot and Brookfield, 1998.

Newman, Francis. *Contributions, Chiefly to the Early History of the Late Cardinal Newman, with Comments.* 2nd ed. London: Kegan, Paul, Trench, Trubner, 1891.

———. *Phases of Faith.* Edited by U. C. Knoepflmacher. Reprinted in The Victorian Library. New York: Humanities Press, 1970.

Bibliography

———. *The Soul: Her Sorrows and Her Aspirations: An Essay towards the Natural History of the Soul, as the True Basis of Theology.* London: John Chapman, 1849.

Newman, John Henry. *Apologia pro Vita Sua, Being a History of His Religious Opinions.* Edited by Martin J. Svaglic. Oxford: Clarendon Press, 1967.

———. *The Arians of the Fourth Century.* Edited by Rowan Williams. Notre Dame, IN: University of Notre Dame Press, 2001. [Vol. 4 of the Millennium Edition].

———. *Autobiographical Writings.* Edited by Henry Tristram. London: Sheed and Ward, 1956.

———. *Callista: A Tale of the Third Century.* 1856. Reprint, New York: Garland, 1973.

———. *Certain Difficulties Felt by Anglicans in Catholic Teaching Considered.* Vol. 1: *In Twelve Lectures Addressed in 1850 to the Party of the Religious Movement of 1833.* London: Longmans, Green, 1900–1901.

———. *Certain Difficulties Felt by Anglicans in Catholic Teaching Considered.* Vol. 2: *In a Letter Addressed to the Rev. E. B. Pusey on the Occasion of His Eirenicon of 1864 and in a Letter Addressed to the Duke of Norfolk on Occasion of Mr. Gladstone's Expostulation.* London: Longmans, Green, 1900–1901.

———. *The Correspondence of John Henry Newman with John Keble and Others,* edited at the Birmingham Oratory. London: Longmans, Green, 1917.

———. "The Development of Religious Error." *Contemporary Review* 48 (October 1885): 457–69.

———. *Discourses Addressed to Mixed Congregations.* Edited by James Tolhurst. Notre Dame, IN: University of Notre Dame Press, 2002. [Vol. 6 of the Millennium Edition].

———. *Discussions and Arguments on Various Subjects.* Edited by Gerard Tracey and James Tolhurst. Notre Dame, IN: University of Notre Dame Press, 2004. [Vol. 7 of the Millennium Edition].

———. *The Dream of Gerontius and Other Poems.* Oxford: Oxford University Press, 1914.

———. *An Essay in Aid of a Grammar of Assent.* Edited by Ian Ker. Oxford: Clarendon Press, 1985.

———. *An Essay on the Development of Christian Doctrine.* Edited by Ian Ker. Notre Dame, IN: University of Notre Dame Press, 1989.

———. *Essays Critical and Historical.* 2 vols. London: Longmans, Green, 1901;

———. *Fifteen Sermons Preached before the University of Oxford between A.D. 1826 and 1843.* Edited by James David Earnest and Gerard Tracey. Oxford: Oxford University Press, 2006.

———. *The Idea of a University.* Edited by Martin J. Svaglic. Notre Dame, IN: University of Notre Dame Press, 1982.

———. "John Henry Newman's *Biglietto* Speech." Edited by Ian Ker. *Logos: A Journal of Catholic Thought and Culture* 6 (Fall 2003): 164–74.

———. *Lectures on the Doctrine of Justification.* London: Longmans, Green, 1900. [Original 1838 title, *Lectures on Justification*, employed in text].

———. *Lectures on the Present Position of Catholics in England.* Edited by Andrew Nash. Notre Dame, IN: University of Notre Dame Press, 2000. [Vol. 1 of the Millenium Edition].

———. *Lectures on the Prophetical Office of the Church* (1837). Republished as *The Via Media of the Anglican Church* (1877) and newly edited by H. D. Weidner. Oxford: Clarendon Press, 1990.

———. *A Letter Addressed to His Grace the Duke of Norfolk on Occasion of Mr. Gladstone's Recent Expostulations.* London: BM. Pickering, 1875. Reprinted in *Newman and Gladstone: The Vatican Decrees*, edited by Alvin S. Ryan. Notre Dame, IN: University of Notre Dame Press, 1962.

———. *The Letters and Diaries of John Henry Newman.* Edited by Stephen Dessain et al. 32 vols. Oxford: Clarendon Press, 1961–2008.

———. *Loss and Gain: The Story of a Convert.* Edited by Alan G. Hill. New York: Oxford University Press, 1968.

———. *Newman the Oratorian: The Unpublished Oratory Papers.* Edited by Placid Murray, OSB. Dublin: Gill and Macmillan, 1969.

———. "On Consulting the Faithful in Matters of Doctrine." Originally published in *The Rambler*, July 1860. Reprinted in *Modern History Sourcebook*, edited by Paul Halsall, October 1998, http:www.fordham.edu/halsall/mod/newman-faithful.html.

———. *Parochial and Plain Sermons.* Introduction by Louis Bouyer. San Francisco: Ignatius Press, 1997.

———. *The Philosophical Notebook of John Henry Newman.* Edited by Edward J. Sillem. 2 vols. Louvain, Belgium: Nauwelaerts, 1969–70.

———. "Revelation in Its Relation to Faith." In J. H. Newman, *Theological Papers* 1:140–57.

———. *The Rise and Progress of Universities* and *Benedictine Essays.* Edited by Mary Katherine Tillman. Notre Dame, IN: University of Notre Dame Press, 2001. [Vol. 3 of the Millennium Edition].

———. *Sermons, 1824–1843.* Vol. 1: *Sermons on the Liturgy and Sacraments and on Christ the Mediator*, edited by Placid Murray, OSB. Oxford: Oxford University Press, 1991.

———. *Sermons, 1824–1843.* Vol. 2: *Sermons on Biblical History, Sin and Justification, the Christian Life, and Biblical Theology*, edited by Vincent Ferrer Blehl, SJ. Oxford: Oxford University Press, 1993.

———. *Sermons, 1824–1843.* Vol. 3: *Sermons and Lectures for Saints' Days and Holy Days and General Theology*, edied by Francis J. McGrath, FMS, and Placid Murray, OSB. Oxford: Oxford University Press, 2010.

———. *Sermons, 1824–1843.* Vol. 4: *The Church, and Miscellaneous Sermons at St.*

Mary's and Littlemore, 1828–1842, edited by Francis J. McGrath, FMS. Oxford: Oxford University Press, 2011.

———. *Sermons, 1824–1843*. Vol. 5: *Sermons Preached at St. Clement's, Oxford, 1824–1826, and Two Charity Sermons*, edited by Francis J. McGrath, FMS. Oxford: Oxford University Press, 2012.

———. *Sermon Notes of John Henry Cardinal Newman, 1849–1878*. Edited by James Tolhurst. Notre Dame, IN: University of Notre Dame Press, 2000. [Vol. 2 of the Millennium Edition].

———. *Sermons Bearing on Subjects of the Day*. London: Longmans, Green, 1902.

———. *Sermons Preached on Various Occasions*. Edited by James Tolhurst. Notre Dame, IN: University of Notre Dame Press, 2007. [Vol. 9 of the Millennium Edition].

———. *The Theological Papers of John Henry Newman: On Faith and Certainty*. Edited by J. Derek Holmes, with Hugo M. de Achaval, SJ, and introduction by Charles Stephen Dessain. Oxford: Clarendon Press, 1976.

Newsome, David. *The Convert Cardinals: John Henry Newman and Henry Edward Manning*. London: John Murray, 1993.

———. "The Evangelical Sources of Newman's Power." In Coulson and Allchin, 11–30.

———. *The Parting of Friends: The Wilberforces and Henry Manning*. London: John Murray, 1966.

Nicholls, David. "Individualism and the Appeal to Authority." In Nicholls and Kerr, 194–213.

———, and Fergua Kerr, eds. *John Henry Newman, Reason, Rhetoric and Romanticism*. Carbondale: Southern Illinois University Press, 1991.

Nockles, Peter. "'Lost Causes and . . . Impossible Loyalties': The Oxford Movement and the University." In Brock and Curthoys, 195–267.

———. *The Oxford Movement in Context: Anglican High Churchmanship, 1760–1857*. Cambridge: Cambridge University Press, 1994.

———. "Oxford, Tract 90 and the Bishops." In Nicholls and Kerr, 28–87.

Norman, Edward. "Newman's Social and Political Thinking." In Ker and Hill, 153–73.

Norris, Thomas. *Newman and His Theological Method: A Guide for the Theologian Today*. London: E. J. Brill, 1979.

Oakeley, Frederick. *Historical Notes on the Tractarian Movement (1834–1845)*. Edited by E. Jones. 2006. http://anglicanhistory.org/England/Oakeley/Tractarian. First published 1865 by Longman, Green and Roberts.

O'Connell, Marvin R. *The Oxford Conspirators: A History of the Oxford Movement, 1833–45*. New York: Macmillan, 1969.

O'Leary, Joseph S. "Impeded Witness: Newman against Luther on Justification." In Nicholls and Kerr, 153–93.

Page, John R. *What Will Dr. Newman Do? John Henry Newman and Papal Infallibility: 1865–1875*. Collegeville, MN: Liturgical Press, 1994.

Bibliography

Paley, William A. *A View of the Evidences of Christianity, in Three Parts.* 2 vols. London: R. Faulder, 1796. Reprint, Farnborough, Hants.: Gregg International Publishers, 1970.

Palmer, William. *A Narrative of Events Connected with the Publication of the "Tracts for the Times" with an Introduction and Supplement Extending to the Present Time.* 1843. London: Rivington, 1883.

Pater, Walter. *Marius the Epicurean.* 2 vols. London: Macmillan, 1910.

———. *Miscellaneous Studies: A Series of Essays.* Edited by Charles L. Shadwell. New York: Macmillan, 1895.

———. *The Renaissance: Studies in Art and Poetry: The 1893 Text.* Edited by Donald L. Hill. Berkeley and Los Angeles: University of California Press, 1980.

Pattison, Mark. *Memoirs.* London: Macmillan, 1885.

Pattison, Robert. *The Great Dissent: John Henry Newman and the Liberal Heresy.* Oxford: Oxford University Press, 1991.

Paz, Denis. *Popular Anti-Catholicism in Mid-Victorian Britain.* Stanford, CA: Stanford University Press, 1992.

Pereiro, James. *Cardinal Manning: An Intellectual Biography.* Oxford: Clarendon Press, 1998.

———. *The Ethos of the Oxford Movement: At the Heart of Tractarianism.* Oxford: Oxford University Press, 2008.

Peterson, Linda. *Victorian Autobiography: The Tradition of Self-Interpretation.* New Haven, CT: Yale University Press, 1985.

Prickett, Stephen. *Modernity and the Reinvention of Tradition: Backing into the Future.* Cambridge: Cambridge University Press, 2009.

———. *Romanticism and Religion: The Tradition of Coleridge and Wordsworth in the Victorian Church.* Cambridge: Cambridge University Press, 1976.

———. *Words and the Word: Language, Poetics, and Biblical Interpretation.* Cambridge: Cambridge University Press, 1986.

Reardon, Bernard M. G. *Religious Thought in the Victorian Age: A Survey from Coleridge to Gore.* 2nd ed. London: Longman, 1995.

Reed, John Shelton. *Glorious Battle: The Cultural Politics of Victorian Anglo-Catholicism.* Nashville, TN: Vanderbilt University Press, 1996.

Robbins, William. *The Newman Brothers: An Essay in Comparative Intellectual Biography.* Cambridge, MA: Harvard University Press, 1966.

Robinson, Denis. "Preaching." In *The Cambridge Companion to John Henry Newman,* edited by Ian Ker and Terence Merrigan, 241–54. Cambridge: Cambridge University Press, 2009.

Rowell, Geoffrey. *The Vision Glorious: Issues and Personalities of the Catholic Revival in Anglicanism.* Oxford: Oxford University Press, 1983.

Rupp, Gordon. "Newman through Nonconformist Eyes." In Coulson and Allchin, 195–212.

Bibliography

Schlossberg, Herbert. *Conflict and Conscience in the Religious Life of Late Victorian England*. New Brunswick, NJ: Transaction Publishers, 2009.

———. *The Silent Revolution and the Making of Victorian England*. Columbus: Ohio State University Press, 2000.

Schmidt, Paul H. "The Struggle for Continuity of Being in Newman's *Apologia pro Vita Sua*." In *Critical Essays on John Henry Newman*, edited by Ed Block Jr., 121–38. English Literary Studies, monograph no. 55. Victoria, BC: University of Victoria, 1992.

Scott, John. *The Life of the Rev. Thomas Scott, D.D., Rector of Aston Sandford, Bucks. Including a Narrative Drawn Up by Himself, and Copious Extracts of His Letters*. New York: White, Gallagher, and White, 1828.

Scott, Thomas. *The Force of Truth: An Authentic Narrative*. 3rd ed. Philadelphia: William Young, 1793.

Seeley, J. R. *Ecce Homo: A Survey of the Life and Work of Jesus Christ*. Boston: Little, Brown, 1907.

Selby, Robin C. *The Principle of Reserve in the Writings of John Henry Cardinal Newman*. Oxford: Oxford University Press, 1975.

Sharrock, Roger. "Newman's Poetry." In Ker and Hill, 43–61.

Shaw, W. David. *Victorians and Mystery: Crises of Representation*. Ithaca, NY: Cornell University Press, 1990.

Sheridan, Thomas J. *Newman on Justification: A Theological Biography*. Staten Island, NY: Alloa House, 1967.

Short, Edward. *Newman and His Contemporaries*. New York: T&T Clark International, 2011.

Skinner, S. A. *Tractarians and the Church of England: The Social and Political Thought of the Oxford Movement*. Oxford: Clarendon Press, 2004.

Stanley, Arthur Penrhyn. *The Life and Correspondence of Thomas Arnold, D.D.* 2 vols. 1845. Reprint, New York: AMS, 1976.

Stephen, Leslie. "Newman's Theory of Belief." In *An Agnostic's Apology and Other Essays*, 168–241. New York: G. P. Putnam, 1893.

Strachey, Lytton. *Eminent Victorians*. Reprint, Garden City, NY: Garden City Publications, n.d.

Strange, Roderick. *Newman and the Gospel of Christ*. Oxford: Oxford University Press, 1981.

———. "Newman at Oxford: Preaching a Living Faith." In Vaiss 223–37.

Sumner, John Bird. *Apostolical Preaching Considered, in an Examination of St. Paul's Epistles*. 4th ed. London: J. Hatcherd and Sons, 1824.

Svaglic, Martin. "John Henry Newman: Man and Humanist." In *Victorian Prose: A Guide to Research*, edited by David J. DeLaura, 115–65. New York: Modern Language Association of America, 1973.

Tennyson, Alfred, Lord. *The Poems of Tennyson*. Edited by Christopher Ricks. London: Longmans and Norton, 1964.
Tennyson, G. B., ed. *A Carlyle Reader*. Cambridge: Cambridge University Press, 1984.
———. *Victorian Devotional Poetry: The Tractarian Mode*. Cambridge, MA: Harvard University Press, 1981.
Thomas, Stephen. *Newman and Heresy: The Anglican Years*. Cambridge: Cambridge University Press, 1991.
Tillman, Mary Katherine. "Economies of Reason: Newman and the *Phronesis* Tradition." In Magill, *Discourse and Context* 45–53.
Toon, Peter. *Evangelical Theology, 1838–1856: A Response to Tractarianism*. London: Marshall, Morgan, and Scott, 1979.
Tracts for the Times, by Members of the University of Oxford. 1833–41. Reprint, New York: AMS Press, 1969.
Trevor, Meriol. *Newman*. Vol. 1: *The Pillar of the Cloud*. London: Macmillan, 1962.
———. *Newman*. Vol. 2: *The Light in Winter*. London: Macmillan, 1962.
Turner, Frank M. *John Henry Newman: The Challenge to Evangelical Religion*. New Haven, CT: Yale University Press, 2002.
Underhill, Evelyn. *Abba: Meditations Based on the Lord's Prayer*. 1940. Reprint, Cincinnati: Forward Movement Publications, 1982.
———. *The Letters of Evelyn Underhill*. Edited by Charles Williams. London: Longmans, Green, 1943.
Vaiss, Paul, ed. *From Oxford to the People: Reconsidering Newman and the Oxford Movement*. Leominster, MA: Placewing, 1996.
Vargish, Thomas. *Newman: The Contemplation of Mind*. Oxford: Clarendon Press, 1970.
Viswanathan, Gauri. *Beyond the Fold: Conversion, Modernity, and Belief*. Princeton, NJ: Princeton University Press, 1998.
Ward, W. G. *Victorian Oxford*. London: Frank Case, 1965.
Ward, Wilfrid. *The Life of John Henry Cardinal Newman, Based on His Private Journals and Correspondence*. 2 vols. London: Longmans, Green, 1912.
Watts, Isaac. *The Improvement of the Mind, Containing a Variety of Remarks and Rules for the Attainment and Communication of Useful Knowledge in Religion, the Sciences, and in Common Life*. Washington, DC: William Cooper, 1813.
White, Joseph Blanco. *The Life of the Rev. Joseph Blanco White, Written by Himself, with Portions of the Correspondence*. Edited by John Hamilton Thom. 3 vols. London: John Chapman, 1845.
Williams, Isaac. *The Autobiography of Isaac Williams, Tutor of Trinity College, Oxford, ed. by his brother-in-law, the Ven. Sir George Prevost, as Throwing Light on the History of the Oxford Movement*. London: Longmans, Green, 1892.

Index

Abelard, Peter, 175
Achilli, Giacinto, 183, 190, 257n1
Adams, Henry, 187
Adams, James Eli, 50
Allies, T. W., 214
Ambrose, St., 63, 161
Anger, Suzy, 131–32, 255n10
Apostolic Succession, 3, 50, 66; Keble on, 82
Aquinas, St. Thomas, 239
Arian heresy, Newman's treatment of, 53–57
Aristotle, 16, 21–22, 248n5
Arnold, Matthew, 5, 9, 29, 67, 173; "The Buried Life," 22–23; on Newman's preaching, 26–28; "Preface to Poems, 1853," 116
Arnold, Thomas, 27, 40, 58; "The Oxford Malignants," 73–75, 249n2, 251n5
Arnold, Thomas, Jr., 27
Articles of Religion (Thirty-Nine Articles, Church of England, 1571), 57, 251n9; in Newman's Tract 90, 103–6
Assisi, St. Francis of, 246, 256n7
Athanasian Creed, 248n1
Athanasius, St., 53, 63, 144, 215, 248n2
Atonement, doctrine of the, 39–40, 49, 88; Newman on, 11, 49–50, 250n8
Augustine, St., 40, 101, 142, 179–80, 202, 232, 240, 253n7; *The City of God*, 72; *Confessions*, 35

Bagot, Richard, 104–5, 113, 114, 118, 120, 201
Baptism, sacrament of, 49; Newman on, 98–99, 250n7; and Baptismal Regeneration, as opposed to Evangelical conversion experience, 49–50; in Gorham v. Bishop of Exeter, 255n3. *See also* sacraments
Barberi, Dominic, 136, 142, 199

Barr, Colin, 170, 257n8
Basil, St., 63, 69, 101
Beethoven, Ludwig van, 28
Bellasis, Edward, 25–26
Biemer, Gunther, 257n3
Blair, Tony, 137
Blehl, Vincent F., 247n4
Bloxam, J. R., 116, 217, 259n16
Bowden, John William, 65–66, 76, 98, 101, 159, 201–2; authorship of Tract 29, *Christian Liberty*, 78–79
Bowden, Mrs. J. W., 161
Bowles, Emily, 205, 215
Bowles, John, 85
Bouyer, Louis, 241, 244
Brady, Ciaran, 30
Bremond, Henri, 1, 237, 247–48n5
Brendon, Piers, 77, 251n7
Bridges, Robert, 241
Brilioth, Yngve, 98, 245
British Critic and *British Magazine*, Newman's work for, 91–95
Brock, M. G., 250n5
Brown, David, 88
Browning, Robert, 17, 30, 137
Buckland, William, 4
Buckle, Henry, 140
Bulteel, Henry, 129
Butler, Joseph, 42–43, 219, 227
Butler, Perry, 252n12
Butler, Samuel, 90

Calvin, John, 40–42, 123, 156, 245–46, 257n7
Capes, J. M., 19–20
Carlyle, Thomas, 4, 5, 12, 17, 18, 21, 29–31, 36, 62, 63, 67, 87, 155–56, 204, 227, 231, 232, 248n8; "Characteristics," 180; *The French*

273

Index

Carlyle, Thomas (*continued*)
  Revolution, 29–30; *Sartor Resartus*, 31, 55, 258n6
Carter, Grayson, 129
Cassian, John, 258n14
Catherine of Siena, St., 243
Catholic Emancipation (1829), 3, 8, 44
Chadwick, Owen, 255n11
Chalcedon, Council of (451 C.E.), 248n1
Chambers, Robert, 132
Channing, William Ellery, 125
Chrysostom, St. John, 231, 258n14
Church, R. W., 57–58, 121, 140, 195, 253n8
Clark, G. Kitson, 252n9
Clark, J. C. D., 3, 252n12
Clark, John Alonzo, 27
Clement, St., 69
Colby, Robert A., 258n13
Coleridge, John Taylor, 44–45, 144, 251n8, 257n1
Coleridge, Samuel Taylor, 153–54, 155–56, 227, 240, 259n7
Coleridge, Sara, 248n7
Conn, Walter L., 252n14, 258n12
Copeland, W. J., 33, 140, 195, 249n10
Copleston, Edward, 208
Cotton, R. L., 66
Coulson, John, 23–24, 164, 220–21, 259–60n7, 260n11
Council of 1870. *See* First Vatican Council (1869–70)
Cox, George William, 9
Cranmer, Thomas, 77
Cromwell, Oliver, 31
Cullen, Paul, 164, 170–71, 245, 256n3 (chap. 7), 257n8
Culler, A. Dwight, 171, 248n5, 250n3, 257n9, 258n9

Dalgairns, J. D., 25–26, 159, 163–64, 245, 254n5
Dante Alighieri, 31–32, 71–72
Darby, John Nelson, 129, 154
Darwin, Charles, 4, 131, 134, 255n10
Davies, Horton, 39–40
Dawson, Carl, 255n1

de Brome, Adam, 91, 257n9
DeLaura, David J., 27, 29, 249n2
Dessain, C. S., 145, 260n10
Dionysius, St., 69
disciplina arcane, 55. *See also* Economy; Reserve
Disraeli, Benjamin, 8
Dissenters, 2, 129, 167
Ditcher v. Denison (1856), 255n3. *See also* Eucharist, sacrament of the
Dodsworth, William, 118
Döllinger, Ignaz von, 218
Dominic, Fr., 136, 142, 199
Dominic, St., 176
Donatist heresy, 101, 109; defined, 253n7
Downes, David Anthony, 37, 249n12
Duffy, Eamon, 1
Dulles, Avery Cardinal, 260n9
Dunne, D. B., 170

Earnest, James David, 131, 254n9
Ecclesiastical Titles Act (1851), 37, 249n15, 256n1
ecclesiology, High Church and Evangelical, 18, 23–24, 50, 61–62, 78, 98; Newman and Manning compared, 220–21; Newman on, 12, 18, 99, 168
Economy, in communicating doctrine, 53, 55, 80. *See also disciplina arcane*; Reserve
Edwards, George T., 196
Eliot, George, 30, 90
Emerson, Ralph Waldo, 26, 231
Erastianism, 63, 66, 97, 104
ethos, Tractarian concept of, 12, 16, 22
Eucharist, sacrament of the, 16, 40, 42, 49, 84–85, 118; *Ditcher v. Denison*, 255n3; Real Presence in, in Keble, 143–44; in sermons by Newman and Pusey, 118, 253n9, 254n2. *See also* sacraments
Eutychian heresy, 185; defined, 258n4
Evangelicalism: Newman's early, 10–11, 39–42; and Liberalism, 85–87; and Tractarianism, 39–40, 61, 99, 252n5

Faber, Frederick William, 158, 161, 162–65, 214
Faber, Geoffrey, 58

274

Index

Fairbairn, A. M., 237–39, 241, 260n1
Faught, C. Brad, 250n7
Fénelon, Francois, 58
Ferreira, M. Jamie, 228, 241
First Vatican Council (1869–70), 37, 210, 215–17
Franchi, Alessandro, 221
Francis, St., 246, 256n7
Fraser, William, 256n3 (chap. 7)
Froude, Hurrell, 28, 39, 45–46, 191, 222, 224; "The Duty of Following the Guidance of the Church," 82; *Remains*, 16, 64, 72, 76–78, 251n8
Froude, Hurrell, Jr. (son of William Froude), 224
Froude, James Anthony (brother of Hurrell), 12, 28–30, 58, 103–4, 162, 222; *The Nemesis of Faith*, 156
Froude, Robert Hurrell (father, Archdeacon of Totnes), 39
Froude, William (brother of Hurrell), 222–24, 228
Froude, Mrs. William, 109, 216

Gave, S. A., 260n10
Gentili, Luigi, 119, 254n4
gentleman, Newman's idea of, 160–61, 169, 172–74
Giberne, Maria, 140
Gilley, Sheridan, 196, 220, 248n3, 253n5, 255n3
Gladstone, W. E., 27, 127, 138
Goethe, Johann Wolfgang von, 248n8
Golightly, C. P., 77
Gorham v. the Bishop of Exeter (Gorham Judgment), 143, 255n3. See also Baptismal Regeneration
Goslee, David, 25, 248n8
Graef, Hilda, 260n6
Grant, Anthony, 74, 251n5
Grant, Mr., of Kentish Town Chapel, 189
Gray, John, 241
Gregory the Great, St., 63
Gregory Nazianzen, St., 69
Griffiss, James F., 7
Griffiths, Paul J., 258–59n12
Gunton, Colin, 260n9

Hamner, J. A., 184
Hampden, Renn Dickson, 64, 73–75, 103, 118, 126, 148, 214, 251n6, 253n5
Härdelin, Alf, 254n2
Hare, Julius, 240
Hawkins, Edward, 44–46, 49, 65, 73, 162, 245, 248n9, 250n5
Haydon, Frank Scott, 237
Hildebrand, St., 63
Hill, Alan G., 146
Holland, Henry Scott, 25
Holloway, John, 13
Hook, Walter Farquahar, 85–86
Hooker, Richard, 81
Hope-Scott, James (James Hope), 23, 159, 254n4
Hopkins, Gerard Manley, 30, 241
Hügel, Baron Friedrich von, 58, 236, 245–46
Hutton, Richard Holt, 5, 56–57, 116, 225
Huvelin, Abbé Henri, 246
Huxley, Thomas Henry, 193

Ignatius of Antioch, St., 112, 256n7
Illative Sense, 227–29, 232, 259n2, 260n8
Incarnation, doctrine of the, 6, 7, 9, 11, 39, 49, 88; Newman's evolving view of, 49–52, 59–60, 61, 97, 250n8
Inge, W. R., 239–41
Inglis, Sir Robert, 44, 46

James, St., 84
Jay, Elisabeth, 47, 259n18
Jeffrey, Francis, 73
Jerome, St., 236, 258n14
Jerusalem Bishopric, 109, 199, 253n10
Johnson, Manuel, 140
Jones, O. W., 141
Julian the Apostate, 222
Justification, doctrine of, 98–99; *Lectures on Justification* (Newman), 80–81, 91, 98–101, 252–53n5

Keble, John, 42–45, 114, 117, 119–22, 130, 137, 141, 146, 148, 150, 160, 195, 233, 251n2, 251n8, 254n4, 255n3; Assize Sermon ("National Apostasy"), 65, 181; *The Christian Year*,

Index

Keble, John (continued)
43, 51; collaboration with Newman on publication of Froude's *Remains*, 72, 76–78, 251n8; *On Eucharistical Adoration*, 143–44; *Sermons Academical and Occasional*, 142–43, 255n2
Kelly, Edward J., 248n6
Ker, Ian, 218, 221, 244, 248nn7–8, 253n10, 257n1, 259n1
Kingsley, Charles, 2, 9–10, 20, 42, 84, 115, 154, 183, 186–87, 192, 193–96, 199–200, 202, 259n14; *Alton Locke*, 90
Kirkpatrick, Thomas, 252n3
Klaus, Robert J., 255n1
Knoepflmacher, U. C., 153, 249n14
Knox, John, 31

Lash, Nicholas, 255n9
Latimer, Hugh, 77
Lenin, Vladimir, 4
Leo XIII (pope), 235, 246
Levine, George, 29–30, 187, 255n11, 258n6, 258n10
Liberalism: Newman on, 3, 93, 190, 197, 247n2, 252n12; and Evangelicalism, in Newman's thought, 85–87
Liguori, St. Alfonso, 184, 196
Lockhart, William, 27, 119–20, 254n3
Loesberg, Jonathan, 241, 255n11, 259n17, 260n4
London Dock Strike (1889), 218
Lossky, Nicolas, 161
Loyola, Ignatius, 159, 176
Luther, Martin, 257n7
Lyell, Charles, 132

Macaulay, T. B., 146
MacDougall, Hugh, 131, 257n2
Macquarrie, John, 18–19, 242
Manning, Henry, 8, 37, 120–21, 138, 164, 181, 210, 213, 217, 218–19, 232, 238, 255n3, 259nn3–4; ecclesiology and compared to Newman's, 220–21
Marriott, Charles, 247n2, 259n16
Martineau, James, 12, 125, 138, 237; "Personal Influence in Present Theology," 155–56

Marx, Karl, 4
Massingberd, Francis, 236
Maurice, F. D., 85–86, 155, 255n1
Mayers, Walter, 40
McGrath, Francis J., 130, 250n6, 254n7
McKelvy, W. R., 252n12
Menzies, Lucy, 236
Merrigan, Terence, 247n2, 260n7
Metaphysical Society (London), 5
Methodists, 256–57n7
Mill, John Stuart, 2, 6, 10, 17, 125; *Autobiography*, 2; *On Liberty*, 203–4; *Logic*, 225; "Thoughts on Poetry and Its Varieties," 10, 247n5
Milman, Henry Hart, 9, 110
Milner, Joseph, 41, 44, 63, 85
Moleski, Martin S., 259n7, 260n9
Monica, St., 179–80
Monophysite heresy, 15, 258n4; defined, 248n1
Monsman, Gerald, 249nn13–14
Morris, William, 249n11
Mozley, Thomas, 18–19, 244, 259n16
Murray, Placid, 49, 250n6
Myers, William, 248n2, 248n6

Neri. *See* Philip of Neri, St.
Newdegate, Charles, 217
Newman, Charles (brother), 141
Newman, Elizabeth (aunt), 124
Newman, Francis (Frank, brother), 12, 73, 128–29, 147, 152–55, 191–92, 256n5 (chap. 6); *Contributions, Chiefly to the Early History of the Late Cardinal Newman*, 25, 258n11; and John Nelson Darby, 129, 192; *Phases of Faith*, 138, 152–55; *The Soul*, 138, 152–53
Newman, Harriett (sister, m. Thomas Mozley), 18, 64–65
Newman, Jemima (sister, m. John Mozley), 30, 73, 75, 102, 130, 182, 259n16
Newman, Jemima Foudrinier (mother), 42
Newman, John (father), 28, 42, 256n4 (chap. 6), 258n7
Newman, John Henry: on the Atonement, 11,

Index

39, 49–50, 250n8; on Baptism and Baptismal Regeneration, 98–99, 250n7; and the Dublin University project, 170–71; early Evangelicalism of, 10–11, 39–42, 85–87, 252n13; ecclesiology of, 12, 18, 99, 168, 220–21; on Eucharist, 84–85, 118, 253n9, 254n2; F. W. Faber, quarrel with, 162–65, 244–45; Froude's *Remains*, controversy over, 76–78; in Hampden affair, 73–75; gentleman, idea of, 160–61, 169, 172–74; hierarchy, tensions with, 182, 210, 215–17, 218–21; Illative Sense, in *Grammar of Assent*, 227–29, 232, 259n2, 260n8; Incarnation, evolving view of, 49–52, 59–60, 61, 97, 250n8; Lockhart's secession and, 119–20; on Liberalism, 3, 85–87, 93, 190, 197, 247n2, 252n12; on Notes of the Church, 93–94, 95, 106–10, 134–35, 185; Oriel tutorships controversy, 44–49, 65; on personality, contrasted with *discipline, rule,* or *system*, 44–46, 169–74, 175–78; as preacher and lector, 26–28, 57–58, 80–85, 252n11; on Real and Notional Assent, 229–31; secession to Rome, reaction of Keble and Pusey to, 142–44; on scripture, 46, 54–55, 57, 86, 88–89, 134, 252n1; Tract 90 controversy, 103–6, 119–20; Trinity, personification of, 19, 53–55, 57; Via Media, in thought of, 2, 5, 24, 93, 96–97, 146, 185, 220; Virgin Mary, evolving view of, 11, 166, 184, 203, 213–14, 215, 256n6; Joseph Blanco White, effect of memoir on, 124–28. *See also* Personality

—, major works excepting sermons: *Apologia pro Vita Sua*, 5, 9–10, 12–13, 15–16, 22, 24, 40, 56, 65, 67, 73, 92, 95–96, 102, 114, 130–31, 133, 136, 139–42, 145, 152, 158, 166, 182–206, 209, 210, 225–26, 234, 235–36, 241, 244, 247n2, 251n5, 253n7, 253n10, 257n2, 257–58n3, 258n6, 258nn10–12; *The Arians of the Fourth Century*, 11, 53–57, 63, 66, 185; *An Essay in Aid of a Grammar of Assent*, 13, 43, 130, 131, 209, 219, 222–34, 239, 241, 259n6, 259–60n7; *An Essay on the Development of Christian Doctrine*, 12, 13, 114, 130–36, 137–39, 183–85, 202, 214, 234, 255nn10–11, 257–58n3; *The Idea of a University*, 160, 168–74, 179, 235; *Lectures on Justification*, 80–81, 91, 98–101, 252–53n5; *The Prophetical Office of the Church*, 75, 91, 96–97, 110, 131; *The Rise and Progress of Universities*, 174–78, 179

—, sermons: "The Apostolical Christian," 110; "Christ Hidden from the World," 83; "Christ, the Son of God Made Man," 60–61; "The Christian Church a Continuation of the Jewish," 111; "Christian Zeal," 70–72; "Connection between Personal and Public Improvement," 111; "Contest between Truth and Falsehood in the Church," 71; *Discourses Addressed to Mixed Congregations*, 158, 160, 163, 166–67, 206; "The Duty of Self-Denial," 73; "Elijah the Prophet of the Latter Days," 111; "Equanimity," 35; "The Eucharistic Presence," 254n2; "Faith and Doubt," 163; *Fifteen Sermons Preached at the University of Oxford*, 20–21, 47, 51, 131, 139; "God's Will the End of Life," 160; "The Gospel Witnesses," 59, 84; "The Greatness and Littleness of Human Life," 33; "Grounds for Steadfastness in Our Religious Profession," 108; "Guilelessness," 84; "Holiness Necessary for Future Blessedness," 250n3; "The Humiliation of the Eternal Son," 59–60; "The Incarnation," 59; "The Individuality of the Soul," 32, 230; "Infant Baptism" (1828 and 1835), 250n7; "The Influence of Natural and Revealed Religion Respectively," 51–52; "Invisible Presence of Christ," 107; "Inward Witness to the Truth of the Gospel," 250n3; "Jereboam," 90; "Jewish Zeal, a Pattern to the Christian," 70–72; "Knowledge of God's Will without Obedience," 82–83; "Love the Safeguard of Faith against Superstition," 254n12; "Moral Consequences of Single Sins," 139; "Nature and Grace," 160; "The Nature of Faith in Relation to Reason," 253n11; "Obedience without Love, as Instanced in the Character of Balaam," 71; "On the Objects and Effects of Preach-

Newman, John Henry (*continued*)
—sermons (*continued*)
ing," 252n11; "Outward and Inward Notes of the Church," 107; *Parochial and Plain Sermons*, 33, 35, 50, 57–59, 70–73, 76, 79, 82, 84, 87–90, 139, 147, 172; "The Parting of Friends," 112–13; "Personal Influence, the Means of Propagating the Truth," 20, 46–47; "Profession without Hypocrisy," 82–83; "Profession without Obedience," 82–83; "Purity and Love," 206; "Rebuking Sin," 251n3; "Regenerating Baptism," 250n7; "The Religion of the Day," 72; "Religious Joy," 50; "Religious Worship a Remedy for Excitements," 76; "Reverence a Belief in God's Presence," 89; "Saving Knowledge," 87, 89; "Self-Contemplation," 79, 87–88, 89; *Sermons Bearing on Subjects of the Day*, 106–13, 114, 121, 124, 196; *Sermons Preached on Various Occasions*, 179–81; "Tears of Christ at the Grave of Lazarus," 19, 60; "The Theory of Development in Religious Doctrine," 21, 139; "The Thought of God the Stay of the Soul," 33; "Tolerance of Religious Error," 71–72, 251n3; "Transgressions and Infirmities," 253n6; "True Gospel Preaching," 248n7; "University Preaching," 179; "The Visible Church for the Sake of the Elect," 83; "Wisdom and Innocence," 84, 115–16, 194–96; "Wisdom as Contrasted with Faith and with Bigotry," 254n12; "The World's Benefactors," 147

—, other writings: "The Anglo-American Church," 254n8; "Apostolical Tradition," 86, 252n13; "Autobiography in Miniature," 188–89, 199; "Biglietto" speech, 246, 260n7; *Callista*, 11, 34–35, 175; "The Catholicity of the English Church," 93, 102, 112; *Certain Difficulties Felt by Anglicans in Catholic Teaching Considered*, 86, 158, 166–68; *The Church of the Fathers*, 63; "On Consulting the Faithful in Matters of Doctrine," 182, 190, 204, 216–17; "The Development of Religious Error," 260n1; *The Dream of Gerontius*, 206–208; "Dr. Wiseman's Lectures on the Catholic Church," 252n4; *Elucidations of Dr. Hampden's Theological Statements*, 73; "Home Thoughts from Abroad," 92, 96; "An Internal Argument for Christianity" (review of J. R. Seeley, *Ecce Homo*), 209, 211–13; *Lectures on the Present Position of Catholics in England*, 158, 183, 256n1; *Letter Addressed to His Grace the Duke of Norfolk on Occasion of Mr. Gladstone's Recent Expostulations on the Vatican Decrees*, 112, 209, 217–18, 221, 235, 256n1; *Letter to Dr. Pusey on the Occasion of His Eirenicon of 1864*, 209, 213–15; *Loss and Gain*, 8, 12, 138, 140, 144–52, 162, 163; *Lyra Apostolica*, contributions to, 190–91; "Milman's *History of Christianity*," 110; "Palmer's *Treatise on the Church of Christ*," 92–93; poems, shorter, 43–44, 69–70; "Poetry, with Reference to Aristotle's *Poetics*," 22; *The Philosophical Notebook*, 173, 222, 224–25; preface (with John Keble) to Hurrell Froude's *Remains*, 72, 76–77, 251n8; "Private Judgment," 101, 253n11; "Revelation in Its Relation to Faith," 260n1; "Selina, Countess of Huntingdon," 256–57n7; "The State of Religious Parties," 93; "The Tamworth Reading Room," 21, 30, 235, 252n12; *Theological Papers on Faith and Certainty*, 222–23, 226, 259n6; Tract 73, *On the Introduction of Rationalistic Principles into Revealed Religion*, 153, 252n13; Tract 85, *Holy Scripture in Relation to the Catholic Creed*, 134, 252n1; Tract 90, *Remarks on Certain Passages in the Thirty-Nine Articles*, 68, 92, 103–106, 190, 199, 214

Newman, Mary (sister), 147, 190
Newsome, David, 218, 250n5, 256n4 (chap. 7), 259n3
Nicaea, Council of (325 C.E.), 53
Nicholls, David, 260n11
Nockles, Peter, 75, 76, 85, 253n8, 254n1
Norman, Edward, 260n7
Norris, Thomas, 252n12, 259n7
Notes of the Church, Newman on, 93–94, 95, 106–10, 134–35, 185

Oakeley, Frederick, 24, 27, 103, 146, 197
O'Connell, Marvin, 245, 254n5

Index

Ogle, James, 140
O'Leary, Joseph S., 100–101
Oratorian Brotherhood, 145, 158–66. *See also* Philip of Neri, St.
Origen, 69

Page, John R., 218–19
Paley, William A., 79–80
Palmer, William, of Magdalen College, 247n3
Palmer, William, of Worcester and Dublin, 6, 67–68, 105–6, 137–39, 150, 247n3, 253nn8–9; *Treatise on the Church of Christ*, reviewed by Newman, 91–93
Pascal, Blaise, 198
Pater, Walter, 12, 17, 29, 31–38, 220; "Diaphaneitè," 31–32; *Marius the Epicurean*, 33–36; *Studies in the History of the Renaissance*, 32–33, 249n11
Pattison, Mark, 12, 28, 140, 156–57
Pattison, Robert, 4
Paul, St., 16, 19, 71, 75, 82, 84, 107, 110, 112, 142, 151, 173, 193, 202, 253n4, 258n11
Paz, Denis, 255n1
Peel, Sir Robert, 44, 46, 178
Perceval, A. P., 67, 109
Pereiro, James, 22, 218–19
Personality, defined in theological and human terms, 6, 13, 16–21, 52, 211, 241–44; and conscience, 260n10; contrasted with *discipline, rule,* or *system,* in Oriel tutorship debate, 44–46; in *The Idea of a University*, 169, 174; in Manning's view of church authority, 218; Thomas Mozley on, 18–19; Francis Newman on, 152–53; as a note of the Church, 18, 23–24; in *The Rise and Progress of Universities*, 175–78. *See also* Trinity, doctrine of
personhood, in Tractarian and Evangelical thought, 61
Peter, St., 20, 70
Peterson, Linda, 40
Philip of Neri, St., 158, 160, 162, 163, 165, 172, 174, 176. *See also* Oratorian Brotherhood
Phillpotts, Henry, 255n3
Pius IX (pope), 171

Plymouth Brethren. *See* Darby, John Nelson; Newman, Francis
Polanyi, Michael, 260n9
Polycarp, St., 239
Pope, S. L., 76
preaching: Newman as preacher and lector, 26–28, 57–58, 80–81; Newman's sermon on, 252n11; Pusey as preacher, 248n7; Tractarian and Evangelical views of preaching compared, 78, 80–85
Prickett, Stephen, 112, 233, 255n9 (chap. 5), 255n1 (chap. 6)
Protestant Episcopal Church (U.S.), 254n8
Pusey, Edward Bouverie, 5, 28, 46, 66, 75, 77, 98, 105, 114, 117, 121, 124, 126, 137, 140, 143, 144, 146, 195, 198, 218, 248n7, 251n2, 253n9, 254n2, 259n16 (chap. 8), 259n3 (chap. 9); sermon on Eucharist and suspension from pulpit, 118; *Eirenicon*, 213–15

Real and Notional Assent, 229–31
Real Presence. *See* Eucharist, sacrament of the
Reardon, Bernard M. G., 260n11
Reed, John Shelton, 235
Reform Act, First (1832), 3
Reid, Thomas, 241
Renan, Ernest, 211
Reserve, in communication of religious knowledge, 53, 79–80. *See also disciplina arcane*; Economy; Williams, Isaac
Rickards, Samuel, 68–69, 116
Ridley, Nicholas, 77
Robbins, William, 256n5 (chap. 6)
Robinson, Denis, 248n7
Rogers, Sir Frederic, 210, 212
Rose, Hugh James, 19, 24, 48, 52, 53, 198
Rowell, Geoffrey, 235
Rupp, Gordon, 259n17, 260n1
Russell, Lord John, 249n15
Ryder, Henry Dudley, 75

sacraments: materiality of, 49; reception of, 82. *See also* Baptism, sacrament of; Eucharist, sacrament of the
Santini, Abbate Fortunato, 191
Savonarola, Girolamo, 163

Schlossberg, Herbert F., 249n2, 252n12
Schmidt, Paul H., 257–58n3, 259n17
Scott, Sir George Gilbert, 77
Scott, James (James Hope-Scott), 23, 159, 254n4
Scott, John (son of Thomas), 41
Scott, Thomas, of Aston Sandford, 40–41, 76, 85, 245
scripture, Newman on, 46, 54–55, 57, 86, 88–89, 134, 252n1
Seeley, J. R., 209, 211–13
Selby, Robin C., 258n3
Sennett, Richard, 245
Shadwell, Charles, 31, 248n9
Shaftesbury, Lord, 212
Shairp, J. C., 27
Shaw, W. David, 258n5, 260n3
Shelley, Percy Bysshe, 4
Sheridan, Thomas J., 99, 250n7
Simeon, Charles, 40, 47–48, 129, 250n6
Simeon, Louisa, 226, 230
Simeon, Sir John and Lady Catherine, 213, 259n1, 259n4
Skinner, Simon, 1, 252n9
Southey, Robert, 4
Stanley, Arthur Penrhyn, 75, 249n2, 253n8
Stanton, Richard, 165
Stephen, James, 81, 83, 85
Stephen, Leslie, 12
St. John, Ambrose, 140, 244
Strachey, Lytton, 2, 253n8
Strange, Roderick, 7, 248n7
Strauss, David, 211
Sumner, John Byrd, 47, 49, 80–82, 90
Svaglic, Martin, 1, 253n7

Talbot, George, 219, 259n3
Tennyson, Alfred, Lord, 2, 4–5; *In Memoriam*, 207
Tertullian, 135, 256n7
Test and Corporation Acts, repeal of (1828), 44
Thirty-Nine Articles. *See* Articles of Religion
Thom, John Hamilton, 124
Thomas Aquinas, St., 239

Thomas, Stephen, 53, 252n13, 257n3, 260n4
Tillman, Mary Katherine, 175, 259n2
Tollhurst, James, 256n6
Toon, Peter, 249n2, 250n10, 252–53n5
Tracey, Gerard, 131, 254n9
tradition, role of, in Anglican theology, 57, 61–62
Trevor, Meriol, 46, 251n4
Trinity, doctrine of, 6, 17, 52, 54–57, 61–62; Newman's personification of, 19; in relation to Newman's idea of Personality, 53–55; scriptural warrant for, 57
Tristram, Henry, 186–87
Trollope, Anthony, 2–3
Turner, Frank M., 1, 86–87, 98, 129, 141

Ullathorne, W. R., 161, 164, 213, 221, 259n4
Underhill, Evelyn, 236, 248n3

Vargish, Thomas, 173, 258n5, 259–60nn7–8
Via Media, 2, 5, 24, 93–94, 96–97
Virgil, *Aeneid*, 200
Virgin Mary, Newman's evolving view of, 11, 166, 184, 203, 213–14, 215, 256n6
Viswanathan, Gauri, 8–9

Waldman, M. Therese, 247n4
Ward, Mary Arnold, 2
Ward, Wilfrid, 239, 245
Ward, William G., of Balliol, 24, 26, 103, 146, 197, 213
Watts, Isaac, 40, 44
Weedall, Dr. Henry, 23
Weidner, H. G., 97
Wesley, John, 3, 257n7
Whately, Richard, 44, 125, 251n5, 254n6
White, Joseph Blanco, 16, 32, 114, 124–28, 254n6
Whitfield, George, 256n7
Whitty, Robert, 217
Wilberforce, Henry, 120–21, 125–27, 192
Wilberforce, Robert, 45, 146
Wilberforce, Samuel, 12, 81, 114, 146, 193
Wilde, Oscar, 194
Williams, Isaac, 26, 64, 141–42; authorship of

Tracts 80 and 87, *On Reserve in Communicating Religious Knowledge*, 80
Williams, Rowan, 137
Wilson, R. F., 66, 79
Wiseman, Nicholas, 96, 101, 109, 112, 159, 161, 162, 170, 191, 249n15, 257n1

Wood, S. F., 119, 201, 259n16
Wordsworth, William, 233; *The Excursion*, 148; *The Prelude*, 183

Zwingli, Ulrich, 251n2

Recent Books in the
VICTORIAN LITERATURE AND CULTURE SERIES

Constance W. Hassett
    Christina Rossetti: The Patience of Style

Brenda Assael
    The Circus and Victorian Society

Judith Wilt
    Behind Her Times: Transition England in the Novels of Mary Arnold Ward

Daniel Hack
    The Material Interests of the Victorian Novel

Frankie Morris
    Artist of Wonderland: The Life, Political Cartoons, and Illustrations of Tenniel

William R. McKelvy
    The English Cult of Literature: Devoted Readers, 1774–1880

Linda M. Austin
    Nostalgia in Transition, 1780–1917

James Buzard, Joseph W. Childers, and Eileen Gillooly, Editors
    Victorian Prism: Refractions of the Crystal Palace

Michael Field
    The Fowl and the Pussycat: Love Letters of Michael Field, 1876–1909 Edited by Sharon Bickle

Dallas Liddle
    The Dynamics of Genre: Journalism and the Practice of Literature in Mid-Victorian Britain

Christine L. Krueger
    Reading for the Law: British Literary History and Gender Advocacy

Marjorie Wheeler-Barclay
    The Science of Religion in Britain, 1860–1915

Carolyn Betensky
> *Feeling for the Poor: Bourgeois Compassion, Social Action, and the Victorian Novel*

John O. Jordan
> *Supposing "Bleak House"*

Edward Adams
> *Liberal Epic: The Victorian Practice of History from Gibbon to Churchill*

Charles LaPorte
> *Victorian Poets and the Changing Bible*

W. David Shaw
> *The Ghost behind the Masks: The Victorian Poets and Shakespeare*

Emily Harrington
> *Second Person Singular: Late Victorian Women Poets and the Bonds of Verse*

Aeron Hunt
> *Personal Business: Character and Commerce in Victorian Literature and Culture*

Lawrence Poston
> *The Antagonist Principle: John Henry Newman and the Paradox of Personality*